S0-BRR-293

Publications

OF THE

University of Pennsylvania

SERIES IN

HISTORY

No. 2

THE SUFFRAGE FRANCHISE IN THE THIRTEEN ENGLISH COLONIES IN AMERICA

BY

ALBERT EDWARD MCKINLEY

Sometime Honorary Fellow in American History in the University of Pennsylvania

Published for the University

PHILADELPHIA

1905

GINN & Co., Selling Agents, 29 Beacon Street, Boston, Mass.

Copyright, 1905, by
ALBERT EDWARD MCKINLEY

Printing Statement:

Due to the very old age and scarcity of this book, many of the pages may be hard to read due to the blurring of the original text, possible missing pages, missing text, dark backgrounds and other issues beyond our control.

Because this is such an important and rare work, we believe it is best to reproduce this book regardless of its original condition.

Thank you for your understanding.

PREFACE

THIS historical sketch of the colonial suffrage is the outgrowth of studies begun several years ago in the Department of Philosophy of the University of Pennsylvania. The purpose of the writer has been to present the dynamic or developmental aspect of the subject rather than the analytic; he has not been content with a mere summary of the suffrage qualifications in the several colonies, but has endeavored to trace the growth of colonial ideals and practices respecting the elective franchise. A comparative or analytic treatment might have been of value to the student of colonial institutions, but there were sufficient reasons for putting this method aside. In the first place, the excellent analysis to be found in Bishop's *History of Elections in the American Colonies* could scarcely be improved upon; and, secondly, the comparative arrangement would give but slight opportunity for the narrative element. Consequently, the subject has been treated locally; and, wherever the existing records have rendered such treatment possible, sufficient details have been given to lead to a comprehension of the motives of colonial legislators in their policy of suffrage restrictions. The disadvantages of repetition have been braved rather than sacrifice the consecutive narrative in any colony.

To a complete knowledge of the suffrage franchise, an acquaintance with the representative systems, the methods of voting and the whole elective machinery is necessary; and frequent references have been made to these subjects. The author has, however, had in mind the fact that detailed studies of some of these features have already been made, and he has governed himself largely in the inclusion or rejection of such material, by the extent to which it has hitherto been used. Thus in the New England colonies, the systems of which have been carefully studied, he has limited himself narrowly to the suffrage qualifications; in other cases, as in

iii

the Carolinas and New York, more attention has been given to these circumstances under which the suffrage was exercised.

The material for the study has been gathered almost exclusively from the printed records of the several colonies, and from the various editions of colonial laws. For the latter, continuous use has been made, during the preparation of the work, of the valuable Charlemagne Tower Collection of Colonial Laws in the library of the Historical Society of Pennsylvania. The writer regrets that the two volumes of Professor H. L. Osgood, which have done so much to classify the facts and clarify our ideas of colonial administration in the seventeenth century, were not in print during the preparation of this volume. The absence of an extended bibliography is to be accounted for by the copious use of foot-notes.

In conclusion, the author wishes to extend his thanks for the encouragement and advice given so generously by the members of the Department of History of the University of Pennsylvania, and particularly to express his appreciation of the interest in the work shown by Professor John Bach McMaster and Professor Herman V. Ames. At a time when it seemed that the work must remain unfinished, their interest led to its completion. Acknowledgment is gratefully made also of the uniform courtesy shown to the author by the librarian of the Historical Society of Pennsylvania, Mr. John W. Jordan, and by his assistants, during many months of almost continuous use of the Society's collections.

ALBERT E. McKINLEY.

PHILADELPHIA, January, 1905.

CONTENTS

THE SUFFRAGE FRANCHISE IN THE ENGLISH COLONIES

❧❧

CHAPTER I.

PARLIAMENTARY SUFFRAGE IN ENGLAND.

The thirteen American colonies were communities whose thoughts and habits as well as language were English. Groups of settlers from other nations might be found along the Atlantic seaboard in the seventeenth and eighteenth centuries, but their numbers were, proportionately, small, and their influence upon American institutions slight. But while the colonies were distinctively English, they were also American. Frequent reference will be made in the following pages to the purely arbitrary English suffrage qualification of an annual income of forty shillings from freehold land, which at one time or another the strength of English precedent forced upon the voters of more than half of the colonies. On the other hand, the only reason for making this study has been to show the adaptation of English political ideals and practices to American conditions; had the new environment or conscious endeavor forced no change in the English customs, this story would have been but a short one.

The body of this work will, therefore, be devoted to an account of the attempt in each colony to administer the English theories of election and representation under widely different conditions from those which held good in the England of colonial days. We shall trace the influence of cheap land, of religious zeal, or of frontier ideals of equality upon the English aristocratic political system; and we shall notice the ever-continuing effort of the English authorities to duplicate in the diverse American settlements the political franchise of England. In the final chapter the features of divergence from the English system will be summarized and the points of similarity collated. The present chapter will be devoted to a short account of the parliamentary suffrage in England.

In the seventeenth century, the age of greatest American colonization, the English House of Commons was still representative, as it had been for over three hundred years, of two quite distinct constituencies. There were, first, the county representatives, two of whom were elected for each county of England, and one for each Welsh county; and secondly, the corporation members, two of whom usually, but in a few cases only one, came from the cities,[1] certain designated towns or boroughs, the Cinque ports and the two universities. Previous to 1677 frequent changes in the number of members of the house were made; but after that date, until the reform act of 1832, there were 513 representatives of England and Wales. Of this number, 92 came from the counties, and the remainder, 421, represented the various corporations.[2]

The electors of these county and corporation members were required to possess definite qualifications, certain of which were imposed upon all electors of members of parliament, while others were required only of narrow groups of electors. The ancient age restriction of twenty-one years was required of all electors,[3] and the immemorial exclusion of women from political life was always adhered to in the letter, although perhaps broken in the spirit in the elections

---

[1] London alone sent four representatives.

[2] Porritt, *The Unreformed House of Commons,* I, 15–17.

[3] Originally there were several ages at which men of different classes of society reached a legal station (Pollock and Maitland, *History of English Law,* II, 436); but at the time of the colonization of America the age of twenty-one years required for those who held by knight's service had been extended from the gentry and had become the lawful age for all classes (*ibid.;* Coke, *Inst.,* I, 78 b, 171 b, 245 b; Blackstone, I, 173).

of a few boroughs.[1]   The actual presence of the elector, a requirement which made proxy voting illegal,[2] was found throughout the English elective system, and led to an opposition in England to the establishment of balloting methods in America.[3]   The voter in all cases must be either a native-born English citizen, or a naturalized foreigner.[4]

Besides these time-honored qualifications, there were more temporary ones which for a greater or less length of time were imposed upon all electors.   These were commonly some form of oath or attachment to the established government. Thus under Cromwell, the Instrument of Government of 1653 excluded Catholics from all elections for members of parliament, and disfranchised all who had " aided, advised, assisted or abetted" the war against Parliament, "unless they have been since in the service of the Parliament, and given signal testimony of their good affection thereunto." [5] After the Restoration there was no such intervention with the suffrage.   The legislation of the Cavalier Parliament was directed against the holding of office by dissenters in the national government or in the municipalities, but it did not

---

[1] In the boroughs where the right of suffrage was dependent upon the holding of certain ancient lands or lots, called therefore burgage-boroughs, women who held such land were permitted to transfer the right to vote in virtue thereof to their husbands, sons, sons-in-law, or their nephews (Porritt, I, 40, 223) ; and in freeman boroughs, where the freemanship was conferred by marriage with a freeman's daughter, such marriageable females were much in demand (*ibid.*, 78–80).   See also *History of Richmond in County of York* (anon., 1814), 138.

[2] 5 *Day's Reports*, 333, quoted by Baldwin, *New Haven Hist. Soc. Papers*, V, 196.   Except in the case of peers, who were privileged to select proxies to vote for them in the House of Lords (Blackstone, I, 168).   At a very early period proxies may have been permitted (Cox, *Antient Parliamentary Elections*, 109).

[3] See *post*, 131, 156, 157.

[4] As the foreigner possessed few civil rights even in England at common law, so he could exercise no political rights while out of allegiance to the king.   Even naturalized persons could not serve as members of the House of Commons until 1870 (33 and 34 Vict., chap. 13).

[5] *Instrument of Government*, sects. xiv–xviii.

extend to a general restriction upon the suffrage.[1]   The
Revolution of 1688, however, brought a more general and
more permanent qualification upon electors.   By a statute
of 1696[2] the sheriffs or officers of election for members of
Parliament were required, upon the request of any candidate, to administer certain oaths to electors, and no person
refusing to take the oaths could vote " for the Election of
any Knight of the Shire Citizen Burgesse or Baron of the
Cinque Ports to serve in Parliament." The enforcement of
this provision,[3] later amended [4] and extended to parliamentary elections in Scotland,[5] while not excluding Catholics
by name, must necessarily have cut out many of them from
parliamentary elections, especially those who had Jacobite
sympathies.[6]

These qualifications,—age, sex, attendance upon election,

[1] The " Five-Mile Act," 17 Chas. II, ch. 2, practically excluded all
dissenting *preachers* from voting for members of Parliament in boroughs; but it did not extend to all dissenters, nor, presumably, did it
even exclude these preachers from voting in the counties.

[2] 7 and 8 Wm. III, ch. 27, sect. xviii.

[3] The oaths are as follows:

" I A B doe sincerely Promise and Sweare That I will be
Faithfull and beare true Allegiance to Their Majestyes King
William and Queene Mary.   Soe helpe me God &c.

" I A B doe Sweare That I doe from my Heart Abhor
Detest and Abjure as Impious and Hereticall that Damnable
Doctrine and Position That Princes Excommunicated or Deprived by the Pope or any Authoritie of the See of Rome
may be Deposed or Murthered by their Subjects or any other
whatsoever.

" And I doe Declare That noe Forreigne Prince Person
Prelate State or Potentate hath or ought to have any Jurisdiction Power Superiority Preeminence or Authoritie Ecclesiasticall or Spirituall within this Realme.   Soe helpe me
God &c."   (1 Wm. and M., ch. 8).

[4] 6 Ann., ch. 23.

[5] 1 Geo. I, St. 2, ch. 13, sect. 4.

[6] Catholics were, of course, excluded in a more definite way from
serving in the House of Commons by reason of the denial of belief in
transubstantiation taken by all members of the House.   It is probable
that Catholics during the eighteenth century abstained from political
activities (Amherst, *History of Catholic Emancipation*, I, 78–80).

native or naturalized citizenship, and the taking of certain oaths,—were the general restrictions imposed upon all electors in England during the colonial epoch. In addition to these, however, there were numerous local or special qualifications which made the suffrage in England a most unsystematic political practice. These can best be appreciated by separating the uniform suffrage for county members from the heterogeneous qualifications required of electors in the boroughs.

A. THE COUNTY FRANCHISE.

During the first two hundred years of the history of parliamentary representation, it seems probable that the knights of the shires were elected by all the *free men* of the respective counties.[1] Not freeholders alone, but persons of lower standing took part in the elections during the thirteenth, fourteenth, and early part of the fifteenth centuries. In 1430, however, Parliament restricted this wide franchise.[2] The reasons for so doing are set forth in the preamble of the statute:

"Whereas the Elections of Knights of Shires to come to the Parliament of our Lord the King in many Counties of the Realm of England have now of late been made by very great outrageous and excessive Number of People dwelling within the same Counties of the Realm of England, of the which most Part was of People of small Substance and of no Value whereof every of them pretended a Voice equivalent as to such Elections to be made, with the most worthy Knights and Esquires dwelling within the same Counties, whereby Manslaughters Riots Batteries and Divisions among the Gentlemen and other People of the same Counties, shall very likely rise and be, unless some convenient and due Remedy be provided in this Behalf."

Whereupon it was enacted,

"That the Knights of the Shires to be chosen within the same Realm of England, to come to the Parliaments of our Lord the King, hereafter to be holden, shall be chosen in every County of the Realm of England by People dwelling and resident in the same Counties, whereof every one of them shall have free Land or Tenement to the Value of Forty Shillings by the Year at the least above all Charges."

[1] H. Cox, *Antient Parliamentary Elections*, 64–86 *passim;* 103–108, 124; Grego, *History of Parliamentary Elections*, 7.
[2] 8 Hen. VI, ch. 7.

The persons having the greatest number of such " choosers" in their favor were to be the knights for the county; and sheriffs were impowered " to examine upon the Evangelists" every chooser to determine if he possessed the required qualification.

In spite of the great changes in the value of the shilling; in spite of the growth of the copyhold and other tenures than the freehold; in spite of the difficulty of determining the value of a freehold under the law, and in spite of the indefinite meaning of the word freehold itself; despite all these facts, English conservatism retained the forty shilling freehold as the exclusive qualification of county voters for over four hundred years, and as an alternative to other qualifications it is still a part of the English elective system.

It will be noticed from the above excerpt that the voter was required to reside within the county. A similar provision had been enacted some years before the property requirement was adopted;[1] and it was continued in subsequent statutes.[2] In spite of the statutory provision, however, by the time of American colonization, the opposite practice had been adopted; the freeholder was no longer required to be a resident of the county where his freehold lay and where he voted; but he could vote in several counties if he possessed the necessary freehold in each. The process by which this change had come about is not very clear, but the right of non-residents to vote was well-established in the seventeenth century;[3] and, in 1774, when the early residence acts had been found " by long usage to be unnecessary" and obsolete, they were formally repealed.[4] A poll in Northampton County in 1730 showing a proportion of about seven per cent. of " outvoters," or non-residents,[5] gives an

[1] 1 Henry V, ch. 1.

[2] A convenient work upon elections is *A Collection of the Statutes Now in Force Relative to Elections down to the Present Time*, R. Troward, London, 1790.

[3] Porritt, *House of Commons*, I, 24; A. Kelly, *An Essay on the Elective Franchise*, 25.

[4] 14 Geo. III, ch. 58.

[5] See *Copies of the Polls taken at the Several Elections for Members to Represent the County of Northampton in Parliament in the Years*

idea of the extent to which non-residents voted in the county elections.

Throughout the eighteenth century, while no change was made in the forty-shilling freehold, yet there was abundant parliamentary legislation relating to the conduct of elections. Some of these acts, particularly those of 1696,[1] and 1711,[2] exercised a wide influence upon the machinery of elections in the colonies, and their provisions were sometimes copied verbatim into the colonial election laws. For convenience of comparison with the American legislation, a few of the terms of these acts may be mentioned in this connection. In 1696, to prevent "charge and expense" in elections, various forms of bribery were forbidden.[3] In the same year a comprehensive election act was passed to abolish the evil practices which had " greatly injured and abused" the right of election.[4] The method of issuing and returning election writs and precepts was fixed; the place of election was to be the most public and usual place of meeting of the county court for the last forty years; in case the election could not be determined "upon the View with the Consent of the Freeholders there present," a poll was to be taken by the sheriff and clerks, who were sworn to "truely and indifferently" take down the names of each freeholder, the place of his freehold, and the persons for whom he voted. Voters could be required to swear or affirm that they possessed a freehold of the yearly value of forty shillings; and the poll should be continued from day to day until all the freeholders had been polled. Trustees and mortgagees were not to be

1702, 1705, 1730, 1745, and 1806, Northampton, 1832, p. *79–185 passim.* At the election of June 8, 9, 10, 1730, there were at least 288 outvoters out of 4171 electors.

[1] 7 and 8 Wm. III, chs. 7 and 25.

[2] 10 Ann., ch. 31 (so numbered in *Statutes of the Realm,* IX, 698–700, but in previous editions of the *Statutes at Large* it was ch. 23).

[3] 7 and 8 Wm. III, ch. 7. No candidate shall "directly or indirectly give, present or allow, to any person or persons having voice or vote in such election, any money, meat, drink, entertainment, or provision, or make any present, gift, reward, or entertainment, or shall at any time hereafter, make any promise, agreement, obligation or engagement to give or allow any money, meat" etc. Elections so obtained were to be void. [4] 7 and 8 Wm. III, ch. 25.

permitted to vote by virtue of their trusts or mortgages, unless they were in actual possession or in receipt of the rents and profits of the estates.[1]   Conveyances to multiply votes, or to split and divide the interest in freeholds in order to qualify several persons for the suffrage were to be void.[2] Another clause provided that *"noe more than one single Voice shall be admitted to one and the same House or Tenement."*

By the preamble of the act of 1711,[3] it is stated that " many fraudulent and scandalous Practices have been used of late, to create and multiply Votes at the Election of Knights of the Shires;" and it is enacted that all such conveyances, instead of being void as was provided in the former act, were to be good and valid against the persons making them, while all bonds given to defeat the purpose of the present act were to be void.   Further, both the person making such a transfer and the one voting by virtue of it were to be liable to a fine of forty pounds apiece.   Two other provisions were in the nature of direct additions to the old forty-shilling qualification.   The first of these provided that no person could vote by virtue of lands or tenements " which have not been charged or assessed to the publick Taxes, Church Rates, and Parish Duties, in such Proportion as other Lands or Tenements of Forty Shillings per Annum;" [4] thus virtually re-

---

[1] " Noe Person or Persons shall be allowed to have any Vote in Election of Members to serve in Parliament for or by reason of any Trust Estate or Mortgage unless such Trustee or Mortgagee be in actual possession or receipt of the Rents and Proffits of the same Estate, but that the Mortgager or *Cestui que trust* in possession shall and may vote for the same Estate notwithstanding such Mortgage or Trust."

[2] " And that all Conveyances of any Mesuages Lands Tenements or Hereditaments in any County, City, Borough, Towne Corporate, Port or Place in order to multiply Voices or to splitt and divide the Interest in any Houses or Lands among severall Persons to enable them to vote att Elections of Members to serve in Parliament are hereby declared to bee void and of none Effect."

[3] 10 Ann., ch. 31 (23).

[4] By 12 Ann., ch. 5, it was explained that this ought not to exclude persons from voting who were in possession of the required amount of freehold land, which legally was not taxed—such as church lands.

quiring the elector to be a taxpayer as well as a freeholder.[1]
The second provision required the elector to be in receipt of
the rents and profits of the freehold, or entitled to receive
them for one year before an election " unless such Lands or
Tenements came to such Person within the Time aforesaid
by Descent, Marriage, Marriage Settlement, Devise or Presentation to some Benefice in the Church or by Promotion to
some Office, unto which such Freehold is affixed."

By later legislation annuities and rent-charges must have
been registered with the clerk of the peace twelve months
before the date of the election;[2] and in 1757 it was provided that no person could be qualified to vote for knights
of the shires by virtue of a copyhold estate.[3]

In concluding the subject of the county suffrage it may
be mentioned that the franchise under the forty-shilling freehold provision was extended in two ways. The first of these
was by means of the splitting up of estates into parcels just
large enough to qualify a person as an elector. Such voters
were called " faggot" voters, and, as has been noticed, parliament attempted by statute to prevent their multiplication.
There is no question, however, that as the value of money
declined, the forty shilling qualification became easier of
attainment, and thus led to a wider franchise. The same
result was reached in a second way by a broader interpretation of the word freehold as an estate for life or greater
dignity. What had originally been attached to real estate
alone, now came to be applied to annuities or to rent-
charges, or any other form of income continuing during the
life of the holder. It was even extended to positions in the
church or the judicial service where the tenure and income
were for life. Thus, clergymen of the Church of England,
the holders of lectureships, judicial officers and clerks of the
peace, schoolmasters, and even choristers in the cathedrals [4]
voted in respect of their offices. By the increase in the num-

---

[1] The statute only required the freehold to have been assessed for
the taxes, they need not have been paid; but in the majority of cases
at least tax-assessing and tax-paying would be equivalent terms.

[2] Blackstone, I, 173.

[3] 31 Geo. II, ch. 14.

[4] Porritt, *Unreformed House of Commons*, I, 22, 23.

ber of freeholds, and by the extension of the term freehold the suffrage under the act of 1430 was thus gradually expanded.[1]

B. THE BOROUGH AND CORPORATION FRANCHISE.

While the suffrage in the counties was based upon a single and uniform legal requirement, there existed in the seventeenth and eighteenth centuries a bewildering variety of qualifications for the borough and corporation suffrage franchise. There was no law imposing a general qualification upon the electors in these places, but their franchise was fixed by local custom, by royal charters, or by the " last determination" of the House of Commons.[2] The right of suffrage might extend to all the householding inhabitants of the borough, or it might be limited solely to the score of officers of the corporation; it might include hundreds of resident and non-resident freemen, or pertain only to the holders of a dozen or fifty ancient land-tenures; in some places it included the forty-shilling freeholders, in others the occupants of certain original houses, often little more than dilapidated hovels, in others still every potwalloper, or man boiling his own pot, had the right to vote. For the sake of clearness a short statement will be made of the suffrage under each of the following heads: (1) The inhabitant, and inhabitant-householder suffrage; (2) the potwalloper suffrage; (3) the burgage tenure suffrage; (4) the freeman suffrage; (5) the corporation suffrage; and (6) the university franchise.[3]

1. *The Inhabitant and Inhabitant-Householder Franchise.* This was the broadest borough suffrage, the most natural

[1] After the Reform Act of 1832 had added several new optional qualifications, it could be said that there were eighty-five avenues to the suffrage, most of which led to the county franchise through various interpretations of the term freehold (*ibid.*).

[2] 7 and 8 Wm. III, ch. 7; 2 Geo. II, ch. 24.

[3] This analysis is nearly identical with that used by Porritt, *Unreformed House of Commons,* I, chap. III. I cheerfully acknowledge my indebtedness to this writer for many of the following illustrations concerning the borough suffrage.

one, and that which conformed most closely to the early English custom. In the earliest days of borough representation, it is probable that the suffrage included all the legal burgesses, and these are believed to be the householding inhabitants who bore a part in the taxes and other burdens of the community,—in other words, paid scot and lot.[1] This early suffrage continued to be exercised in many boroughs throughout the period of English history we have under consideration. During the eighteenth century there were over fifty boroughs in which the inhabitants, or inhabitant-householders, exercised the suffrage, either alone or in conjunction with other classes of voters.[2] In some cases the ancient scot and lot provision appears to have been lost,[3] while, on the other hand, in most of these boroughs, an inhabitant receiving alms could not act as an elector.[4] There was no general residence requirement in these places during the period we are studying, and not until after the American Revolution was there a compulsory six months' residence before the election.[5]

2. *The Potwalloper Franchise.* This was similar to the inhabitant-householder franchise, except that it extended the right to vote to those who, not owning or renting an entire house, yet had a separate fireplace, or boiled the pot for themselves and their families.[6] Potwallers or potwallopers, as determined in one contested case, were " persons furnishing their own diet, whether householders or only lodgers." [7] In such cases usually the elector must, as in the inhabitant-householder boroughs, be assessed for the local taxes (pay scot and lot) ;[8] and, generally also, those receiving alms

---

[1] Cox, *Antient Parliamentary Elections,* 165–181.

[2] Kelly, *Essay on the Elective Franchise,* 27–41 *passim.*

[3] *Ibid.*

[4] Oldfield, *History of Boroughs* (ed. 1794), *passim;* Grego, *History of Parliamentary Elections,* 5.

[5] 26 Geo. III, ch. 100.

[6] Wallop = *ebullire, infervescere;* walling = boiling (Cox, *Antient Parliamentary Elections,* 191, note).

[7] Kelly, *Elective Franchise,* 33.

[8] But even this was not required in Honiton; Porritt, I, 31.

were excluded.   As in the inhabitant boroughs there was no general residence qualification.[1]

3. *The Burgage Tenure Franchise.*   A burgage tenure has been defined as land or tenements lying in a borough and paying to the king or other lord a certain annual rental.[2] These tenures dated back hundreds of years from the seventeenth century, and often formed but a small part of the land of a populous community.   Yet to them and them alone in many towns was the privilege of electing members of Parliament attached.

In no group of boroughs did the suffrage vary more than it did in the burgage boroughs, and local custom here seems to have done its best to bring confusion into the elective system.   In some cases the right to vote was given to the freeholders only of the original burgages, as in Petersfield, where the electors were " the freeholders of lands, or ancient dwelling-houses or shambles built on ancient foundations;" [3] in other boroughs the franchise was vested in the inhabitants of the ancient tenures, as in Weobley, where it rested upon the " inhabitants of certain ancient vote-houses of twenty shillings per annum and upwards, residing in the houses forty days before the election and paying scot and lot, and also in the owners of such houses paying scot and lot and resident in the houses at time of election." [4]   Again it might be the leaseholders for a certain term of years, or even, in two cases, the copyholders [5] of the estates, who possessed the right to vote.   There was a similar diversity within the thirty-nine burgage boroughs respecting the residence of voters.   In Cricklade [6] and Weobley [7] a residence of forty

---

[1] In only three boroughs, apparently, did the potwalloper suffrage rest upon parliamentary determination (Tregony, Honiton, and Taunton; see Oldfield, *Hist. of Boroughs*, I, 92, 171; II, 53) ; probably it existed in other places under local interpretations of the words inhabitants or housekeepers.

[2] Coke, *Inst.*, I, 108 b, 109 a.

[3] Oldfield, *Boroughs*, I, 297.   [4] *Ibid.*, 308.

[5] In the two boroughs of Westbury and Cricklade occur the only instances known of the suffrage based upon copyholds (Oldfield, *Boroughs*, II, 216, 223).

[6] Porritt, I, 34.   [7] Oldfield, *Boroughs*, I, 308.

days was required of the voter; while in other places the vote-houses were occupied only a few days before the election;[1] and in others still no residence at all was required, or indeed could be where, as at Droitwich, one of the burgage-holds was in the middle of a water course.[2]

The attachment of the suffrage to these ancient land-tenures led to the greatest anomalies of the English representative system. The case of Old Sarum has become famous; in Westbury the twenty-four tenures comprised one long stone wall;[3] in Calne the electors were of the same number, all possessing a right of common in a certain field;[4] in Droitwich the members of the corporation, who were the sole electors, must each " be seized in fee of a small quantity of salt water arising out of a pit."[5] The number of the burgage-holds was rarely over two hundred;[6] it often was under fifty;[7] and in Old Sarum there were nominally seven voters for the two members of Parliament.[8]

4. *The Freeman Suffrage.* In the common sense in which the word freeman was used in England during our colonial period, it meant that the person so called was accepted into some commercial or municipal corporation and therefore was free to exercise all the privileges and franchises of the corporation. In this sense the freemen or burgesses of sixty-two boroughs[9] possessed either the exclusive right to elect members of Parliament, or exercised that right in conjunction with other groups of electors.[10]

There were many ways in which a man could become a freeman of the English boroughs. He might be admitted

---

[1] Porritt, I, 35. [2] *Ibid.*, 37.

[3] Oldfield, II, 216.

[4] *Ibid.*, 218. The same requirement of participation in a common field is found in Richmond (*ibid.*, II, 276).

[5] *Ibid.*, 261; Porritt, I, 36.

[6] There were 330 in Pomfret (*ibid.*, 285), 270 in Richmond (*ibid.*, 276).

[7] *Ibid.*, 147, 160, 166, 192, 215, 216, 218, 281.

[8] *Ibid.*, 236.

[9] Porritt, I, 30.

[10] The former was the more common custom, but for instances of the latter feature see Oldfield, *Boroughs*, I, 5, 106, 148, 253, 319, 350, etc.

by the gift and direct vote of those who were already free-men,[1] or he might purchase the freedom;[2] he could gain it by serving an apprenticeship, usually of seven years, to a free-man in the borough,[3] or by serving to a freeman of the borough anywhere;[4] he could obtain it because he was the son of a freeman,[5] or the heir of a freeman;[6] or because he was the eldest son,[7] or the youngest son,[8] or a son born after his father had obtained the freedom;[9] or because he had married a freeman's daughter,[10] or widow.[11]

In over half of the freeman boroughs a local attachment of some form was maintained, either by the relationship of birth, servitude and marriage, or by the more definite one of residence.   But in more than a third of the bor-oughs, where the freedom could be obtained by gift of the corporation or by purchase, even residence was not re-quired.[12]   In these cases the freemen could dwell in any part of the country, and simply journey to the town whose freedom they possessed at the time of the election.[13]   The

[1] Porritt, I, 58–66 *passim;* Brooke, *Liverpool during last Quarter of Eighteenth Century,* 208.

[2] *E.g.,* St. Albans; Oldfield, *Boroughs,* I, 314; Zacke, *Memorials of Exeter,* 38, 39.

[3] *Ibid.;* Creighton, *Carlisle,* 194; in Coventry, see Oldfield, *Boroughs,* II, 173.

[4] When the apprentice was also the younger son of a freeman; in Nottingham (Oldfield, *Boroughs,* II, 2).

[5] *Ibid.,* I, 120, 314, 359; II, 45, 312, 338.

[6] In Exeter, Zacke, *Memorials of Exeter,* 39, 74.

[7] In East Retford, Hastings, Rye, Richmond, etc.; Oldfield, *Bor-oughs,* II, 8, 301–304, 333; *Hist. of Richmond* (anon.), 120.

[8] In Durham; Oldfield, *Boroughs,* I, 244.

[9] In Newcastle-on-Tyne, London, Sudbury, etc.; *ibid.,* I, 418, 380; II, 122.

[10] In Ludlow, Bristol, Wells (*ibid.,* II, 39, 45, 50), Dover (Kelly, *Elective Franchise,* 57), etc.

[11] In Sandwich (Kelly, *Elective Franchise,* 66).

[12] The short pamphlet on the *Elective Franchise* by Arthur Kelly is a study of the residence and non-residence conditions in the English boroughs; see *passim,* especially 70, 71.

[13] So many freemen of various boroughs dwelt in London that some-times parliamentary candidates called meetings in London of the free-men of the respective constituencies (Porritt, I, 63).

freeman must pay the local taxes of scot and lot [1] in some boroughs, while in others the freemanship admitted to the suffrage such irresponsible persons as could be brought from jails or work-houses.[2] In the non-resident freeman boroughs the greatest election evils existed. The travelling expenses of non-residents were often paid by the candidates, who also felt themselves under the necessity of furnishing refreshments to the electors; and often wholesale admissions to the freemanship were made upon the eve of an election.[3]

5. *The Restricted Corporation Franchise.* The election evils in the freeman boroughs usually arose by reason of the extension of the franchise to those who possessed no interest in the locality; but in a number of boroughs the right of electing members of Parliament had taken a different, but equally vicious form,—an election by a group of corporation officers. This right, like the status of freemen, had developed from the earlier inhabitant-householder franchise of the boroughs; [4] and in this case it was often strengthened not only by local custom but by the actual grant of such powers in royal charters of incorporation. The municipal officers, also, in many places became self-perpetuating bodies, thus bringing them still farther away from the early liberal suffrage. To the features of exclusive control of elections and of self-perpetuation there was often added the equally vicious principle of non-residence, which permitted a person to hold office, even the office of mayor, in a select municipal corporation without entering the borough once a year.[5] Over forty boroughs elected their members of Parliament in this manner, and the number of officers or select burgesses actually participating might be as low as two.[6] Usually, however, the number was about twenty-five,[7] and in a few cases

---

[1] Oldfield, *Boroughs*, I, 43, 112, 234, 312, 342; II, 104, 117, 173, etc.
[2] Porritt, I, 69, 70.
[3] *Ibid.*, 58-84 *passim.*
[4] Cox, *Antient Parliamentary Elections*, 186–190.
[5] Porritt, *Unreformed House of Commons*, I, 53, 54.
[6] In Castle Rising; Oldfield, *Boroughs*, I, 409.
[7] *Ibid.*, I, 25, 137, 293; II, 24, 49, 126, 264, 274.

it might rise to almost fifty.   In the town of Bath, at the close of the eighteenth century, twenty-two municipal officers elected the two members to represent themselves and the other thirty thousand inhabitants of the borough.

6. *The University Suffrage.*   The charters of James I (1603) conferred the right of election of members of parliament upon the chancellor, masters and scholars of each university.[1]   Under the terms of these charters, the elections became limited to the " senates" of the two universities,—that is, to those who were masters of arts, or doctors in one of the three faculties of divinity, civil law, or physic, and who retained a connection by residence or otherwise with some college of the university.[2]

The suffrage for university members is interesting because it furnishes the only instance, so far as the writer knows, of the use of the ballot in parliamentary elections before the nineteenth century.   The written ballot or " scrutiny" appears to have been used at an early date in the elections for university officers;[3] later it was applied to the elections of members of Parliament; and in 1780, it was even held up as a grievance[4] by a group of reformers at Cambridge.   In the university elections no other qualifications were required other than those set by the statutes of the university respecting membership in the university senate.

---

[1] The words of the charter of Cambridge are " Praedicti Cancellarius Magistri et Scholares Universitatis Cantebrigiæ, et Successores sui, Virtute Praecepti, Mandâti, seu Processus super Breve nostri, Hæredum et Successorum nostrorum in ea Parte debitè directi, habeant et habeunt Potestatem, Auctoritatem, et Facultatem eligendi et nominandi duos de discretioribus et magis sufficientibus viris de prædicta Universitate pro tempore existentibus fore Burgenses Parliamenti" (Dyer, *Privileges of Cambridge,* 135, 136).

[2] For further details see the calendars of the universities.

[3] Mullinger, *op. cit.,* 112; *Present State of the Universities* (London, 1744), I, *Oxford,* 284, 288, 419. The ballots were burnt after the result was determined (*ibid.;* Cox, *Recollections of Oxford,* 66). The term scrutiny in canon law meant a written ballot.

[4] Porritt, I, 102.

CHAPTER II.

THE SUFFRAGE IN VIRGINIA.

The first twelve years of Virginia's history present few facts on the American side of the Atlantic for the student of political institutions. The early life of the colonists was an intense physical struggle for existence in which no general political consciousness is apparent. The terrible contests with the fevers of the river valley, the struggle against the ever-impending famine, the horrors of Indian warfare, and the animosities of domestic quarrels together left scant opportunity for political action; while the arbitrary powers granted by the English authorities to the governors and councillors repressed any movement towards popular government which might have arisen. The personal and epic interests are aroused by the facts of this period, but there is practically no institutional development.

For this development of institutions the student must look at the Virginia Company of London and the royal charters of 1606, 1609, 1612. The first charter left the control of the colony largely in the hands of the king or his appointees; the second charter shifted the responsibility upon the council of the company; and the third one gave large powers to the democratic general court of the Virginia Company. Under the last charter quarterly meetings of all the stockholders could be held for the consideration of company affairs, the election of officers, the making of laws for the colony, the hearing of complaints from the colony, and the admission of new members. When it is remembered that there were six hundred and fifty-four stockholders in 1609, and that others were added from time to time, it will be seen that these meetings of the Virginia Company were truthfully spoken of as a " seminary to a seditious parliament." [1]

A large party in the newly organized company of 1612

---

[1] Cooke, *Virginia*, 114.

was composed of Puritans, and this faction gradually increased in power in the succeeding years.   They introduced the democratic ballot-box in place of *viva-voce* voting in their company;[1] and at last they elected as chief officer of the company ("treasurer"), Sir Edwin Sandys, who, although an attendant of the established church, was the firm friend of the Puritans.   The election of Sandys was the culmination of a struggle between the faction favoring arbitrary control and those of the company who desired a more popular form of government in the colony.   Sandys himself was known to favor the erection "of a free state in Virginia;"[2] and while he held the office of assistant treasurer, a "great charter of privileges" was ratified at a quarter court of the company and dispatched to the colony for the guidance of the governor and council in Virginia.[3]   In this charter there is found the origin of the first representative government in America.

While these changes had been accomplished in the organization of the London Company, affairs in the colony had become more settled and its permanence was now assured. (The improved economic condition of the colony in 1619 made the new popular policy of the Puritan stockholders of London almost a necessity, and contributed largely to its success.) The instructions of 1606 to the first councillors of the colony gave authority to the councillors and president to "govern, rule, and command all the captains and soldiers, and all other of his Majesty's subjects of his colony," according to the terms of the king's instructions.[4]   For three years after the landing in May, 1607, the colony did not possess even a definite code of laws, but was governed by the councillors, or the strongest one among them.   One of these councillors apparently intended to call a "parliament" of the colonists, but was prevented from doing so by the arrival of new instructions.[5]   This is the period of

[1] Neill, *Virginia Company of London*, 189, 204. Brown, *First Republic in America*, 305, 307.
[2] Brown, *First Republic*, 251.
[3] November 28, 1618, Brown, *First Republic*, 293.
[4] Neill, *Virginia Company of London*, 4-8.
[5] According to Wingfield, in Brown, *First Republic*, 55.

quarrels among the councillors and the final election of John Smith, or,—shall we say,—his assumption of control. After the lifting of Smith's strong hand, more quarrels of the councillors took place; until at last the arrival of Governor Delaware with his broad personal powers in government [1] put an end to the council jealousies.

(The colony now entered upon the second stage of its political history. The first had been the troublous times under a plural executive) the new era saw the governor a petty despot in the colony, bringing order out of confusion, repressing factions by retaining the government in his own hands, but yet ruling according to known laws. Up to 1610 the colony had possessed no legal code, even of a criminal nature, except the occasional instructions given to the councillors. For three years the colonists had been compelled to conform to the whim or will of the councillors. From 1610 to 1619 the governors and the councils appointed by them had arbitrary power, but this was used, in general, according to published regulations.[2] Within this period of nine years the colony prospered, increased in population, and at last the colonists solved the economic problem of making the vast natural resources of Virginia meet the needs of Europeans.

At this point, when the economic life was broadening, and when it would soon have come into conflict with the arbitrary powers of the governor, the colony received from London the instructions for the holding of a representative assembly. The Virginia Company of London held one of its quarterly courts or meetings on November 28, 1618, and agreed upon the following measures:

"I. The great charter of privileges, orders, and Laws, which had been previously drafted, and considered, was ratified, signed, and directed to the Governor and the Council of Estate in Virginia."

[1] See Lord De la Warr's commission in Brown, *Genesis of United States,* I, 375 ff.
[2] See Laws of Gates, Delaware, and Dale in Force's *Tracts,* III, No. 2. There are twenty-four capital crimes according to these laws, some religious rules, and some sanitary measures; but no constitutional provisions whatever.

"II. The commission for establishing the Council of Estate and the general Assembly (two Burgesses out of every Plantation), wherein their duties were described to the life."

"III. Sundry instructions" for governor, council, and colony.

Thus through the action of the radical members of the Virginia Company the foundation was laid for popular government in the colony.

It is generally believed that the privileges and orders of 1618 were similar to those given to Governor Wyatt in 1621.[1] The latter document is called "An Ordinance and Constitution of the Treasurer, Council, and Company in England, for a Council of State and General Assembly,"[2] and in it the Company authorities expressed their intention of establishing a form of government in the colony which would be of the "greatest benefit and comfort" to the people, and would keep "off as much as possible" all "injustice, grievances, and oppression." It provided also for a general assembly composed of the council of state and "two burgesses out of every town, hundred, or other particular plantation, to be respectively chosen by the inhabitants."

Governor Yeardley, with the instructions for an assembly, arrived in the colony early in 1619, and shortly afterwards issued a proclamation announcing that the services due to the company would be remitted to all persons who had come before April, 1616, that the former cruel laws had been abrogated, and that a share in government was to be given to the colonists.[3] He said,

"And that they might have a hand in the governing of themselves, it was granted that a General Assembly should be held yearly once, whereat were to be present the Governor and Counsell, with two Burgesses from each Plantation freely to be elected by the inhabitants thereof; this Assembly to have power to make and ordaine whatsoever laws and orders should by them be thought good and proffittable for our subsistence."

[1] Brown, *First Republic,* 293. Brown even thinks that similar instructions were given to Governor Delaware.

[2] Hening, *Statutes at Large of Virginia,* I, 110–113.

[3] Brown, *First Republic,* 312.

In accordance with the terms of this proclamation the famous first representative assembly met in the church at Jamestown. The facts concerning this assembly have been told so frequently and so well that it would be presumption to repeat them here. We are, however, interested in the suffrage for this assembly, and can but regret that the details concerning the election are so meagre. The governor's proclamation had declared all "inhabitants" to be electors, but there is no certainty of meaning attaching to the word. Brown in one place makes inhabitants synonymous with "planters," while in another case he says that suffrage "was general." [1] Another writer holds that "all the settlers had a voice in public affairs, first in the daily matters of the hundreds, and after 1619 in electing burgesses." [2] I have found no contemporary description of the voting class other than the word inhabitants, or the still more vague statement that burgesses were elected "by the major part of voices;" [3] but from later legislation it seems apparent that all free men not bound to service had the right to vote. For, when the assembly in 1646 levied a fine upon freemen who did not vote, they thought it necessary to state that this fine should not be collected from freemen who were covenanted servants, thus extending *compulsory* voting throughout the whole class of free laborers and planters. [4] Another later act was based upon the principle of the union of taxpaying and political rights; [5] but it is unlikely that such a definite theory was held in the time of the first assembly. It seems true that all men not bound to service were privileged to vote in the first and subsequent early elections.

As we are in doubt concerning the persons who held the

[1] Brown, *First Republic,* 616, 315.

[2] Cooke, *Virginia,* 223.

[3] This phrase was applied to the election of 1624, Brown, *First Republic,* 570. Rolfe in his account merely said that burgesses were "chosen in all places;" and the journal of the assembly said "two Burgesses elected out of each Incorporation and Plantation;" *N. Y. Hist. Soc. Coll.,* Second Series, III, 332, 335.

[4] Chapter XX, 1646, Hening, I, 333-4.

[5] Ch. XVI of March, 1655-6, Hening, I, 403. Discussed more fully in the following pages.

franchise in these early days, so the manner of voting is by no means clear. Brown quotes the Virginia Company records as requiring the " principall officers in Va. To be chosen by balloting box;" [1] but it is not believed that this formal method was used. *Viva voce* voting is implied in the phrase " major part of voices," used in 1624, and by the writs requiring personal attendance at the elections.[2] On the other hand, it is plain that some form of proxies, or " subscribing of hands," was used, and sometimes this was so general that " it happeneth that few or none doe appeare personally according to the summons." [3] In what form this " handwriting" was produced is not stated. It might have been gained by candidates or their friends as signatures to papers; it may have been in the form of proxies, as in the neighboring colony of Maryland; the names may have been taken by the sheriff as he went from settlement to settlement giving the legal warning of the election at each house; or the votes may have been in the form of individual ballots. The custom, in whatever form, probably was furthered by the act of 1639–40, which said, " No sheriff to compell any man to go off the plantation where he lives to choose burgisses;" [4] for, since several plantations made up a county,[5] the sheriff would be obliged to adopt some proxy system or other method of collecting the votes from the different plantations.

After the first assembly, almost ten years passed before the representative system was permanently adopted. Governor Wyatt, who succeeded Yeardley, kept up the assembly system; at first issuing regular writs according to the company's instructions, and later, after the Virginia Company's

---

[1] *First Republic*, 315. It is more likely that this requirement related to the election of colony officers by the Company in its London meetings.

[2] Hening, I, 333.

[3] *Ibid.*

[4] *Ibid.*, 227.

[5] Counties were erected and became the formal unit of representation in 1634. But the burgesses from a county may have continued to be elected by the plantations within the county instead of by the county at large. There can be no doubt this was true of some parishes; Hening, I, 154, 250, 277.

charter had been forfeited, he discussed public affairs in meetings of " The Governor, Council, and Colony of Virginia assembled together." [1] In spite of petitions from the people praying that no military government be established over them,[2] and in spite of Governor Yeardley's request that he be allowed to call an assembly and have officers elected by the people,[3] neither King James in 1624, nor Charles in his first commission for the government of Virginia, granted any popular political features.[4] But the colonists petitioned against the tobacco monopoly Charles had granted, and in the fall of 1627 Charles sent out instructions for the election of assemblymen in the colony. In accordance with this permission the first assembly under royal authority was held in March, 1627–8,[5] and thereafter the representative system was to continue with slight interruptions until the revolution of 1776.

The next interesting fact concerning the suffrage is the attempt of the people to extend the elective principle from the choice of the legislature to the choice of their executive officer. It was not an unusual thing in the colonies for a small settlement of Englishmen to choose a governor.[6] Such action is seen quite frequently in the New England settlements; in West Jersey there is a succession of elected executives; on Long Island occurred the short and strange career of President John Scott; in Maryland and the Carolinas other instances can be found; while in Virginia itself the assumption of power by John Smith in 1608 was, in fact, a popular choice of the most powerful of the councillors. In 1635 this popular choice is seen, when the people " thrust out" an obnoxious English governor, John Harvey, and put

[1] Brown, *First Republic,* 647. For these early assemblies, see Hening, I, 119–136; Neill, *Virginia Company,* 274–5; Brown, *First Republic,* 458, 647, 648; Neill, *Virginia Carolorum,* 55.

[2] *Ibid.,* 573.

[3] Neill, *Va. Carolorum,* 27.

[4] See the Commissions in Hazard, *Historical Collections,* I, 183–205, 230–234.

[5] Neill, *Va. Carolorum,* 55; Brown, *First Republic,* 648; Hening, I, 134–136.

in his place one Captain John West. West, in explaining his election to the English government, said,

" The counsell with one consent were so pleased as to fasten their votes on mee to wch the peoples suffrages as willingly condiscended;"[1]

It is not likely that the election of West was a formal matter on the part of the people. Previous meetings of discontented persons had been held,[2] and it is probable that after the council had selected Captain West the choice was submitted to the burgesses and the people present for ratification. It is scarcely necessary to say that Charles I. would suffer no such assumption of " regal power," as he termed the action of the colonists; Harvey must be sent back, if only for a day, to maintain the royal authority.[3] While there was no choice for the Virginians but to accept the governor, yet, fortunately for them his new administration lasted only a short time.

During the first twenty years there was no permanent unit of representation. Up to 1634 the country was divided into plantations,[4] and each of these was originally entitled to send two representatives; but later some of the plantations were grouped into hundreds, and from one to four burgesses came from each hundred or plantation or " corporation."[5] In 1634 the colony was divided into eight

[1] Neill, *Virginia Carolorum*, 129; see also, *ibid.*, 116-133; Hening, I, 223; *Va. Mag. of History*, III, 21-34; VIII, 147 ff, 398 ff.

[2] Neill, *Va. Carolorum*, 119. De Vries, who stopped in Virginia in May, 1635, said a new governor had been made by the council and people.

[3] Neill, *Virginia Carolorum*, 126.

[4] A plantation was generally a settlement made by servants or free laborers under the direction of some one person who had received a large land grant. Under such circumstances the elections must have been in the control of the local proprietor; and in the first assembly the burgesses from one plantation were called Mr. Martin's burgesses (*N. Y. Hist. Soc. Coll.*, 2d Ser., III, 338, 344).

[5] The list of burgesses to the assembly of February, 1632-3, shows this irregularity; Hening, I, 202-3. See also Chandler, *Representation in Virginia*, *J. H. U. Studies*, XIV, Nos. 6-7, 6-14.

counties,[1] which were made the new units of representation;
yet for many years after this time the burgesses are spoken
of as coming from the several plantations.[2]   No definite
number was at first given to each county, but the actual
representation varied from one to eight burgesses for a
county; and the total number of burgesses in the assemblies meeting between the years 1634 to 1662 varied from
eighteen to forty-four, the number of counties meanwhile
growing from eight to eighteen.   Later legislation fixed the
number of burgesses for each county at four,[3] and still later
it was reduced to two.[4]

It is not believed that the early county burgesses were
always elected at large, but that in some counties they continued for a time to be elected by the plantations or parishes.   The act of 1639–40 forbidding sheriffs to compel
any man to go off his plantation to choose burgesses has
already been quoted, but the exact meaning of the act is
obscure.[5]   As early as February, 1631–2, parishes are mentioned as a representative unit;[6] and later, when some of
the counties were divided into parishes, each parish was
permitted to choose a burgess or burgesses within its own
limits.[7]   Until 1662 it was permissible for any parish to
send its own burgesses if it desired to do so, although after
1656 the wages of such " parochial" burgesses were to be

[1] Hening, I, 224; Brown, *English Politics in Early Virginia History*,
100.

[2] Hening, I, 239, 282, 298, 373, 379, 527.

[3] Hening, I, 299–300, act of Nov., 1645. James City County was permitted to elect five burgesses for the county and one for the city.

[4] Hening, II, 20, 106; acts of 1660–1, 1661–2. See also act of 1669
making the sending of two burgesses compulsory; and that of 1670
laying a fine of 10,000 pounds of tobacco upon counties refusing to
elect (Hening, II, 272, 282).

[5] Hening, I, 227. Hening found only abstracts of the laws of this
session.

[6] Hening, I, 153, 179.

[7] Hening, I, 249, 250, 251, 277. I have not found the original act giving
general power to all parishes to choose burgesses; but the preamble
of an act of 1656 says that " by a former act of Assembly priviledge
was granted to any parish to send one or two Burgesses." Hening,
I, 421.

paid by the parishes electing them.[1]   The vestry of the parish had the power of determining if parochial burgesses should be elected, and, when requested, the sheriff of the county was compelled by law to attend such parish elections.[2]   While parish burgesses were thus permitted,—and no doubt in many cases were elected,—they were chosen for the " particular occasion" of the parish,[3] and the county paid only for the usual number of burgesses as formerly.[4] It may be that the distinction between parish and county burgesses is only another expression for our modern ideas of election by general ticket and by districts.   James City (Jamestown) received the right to send one burgess in 1645,[5] and continued to exercise this privilege until the Revolution.   The promise was also made in 1662 that every county which would lay out a town of one hundred acres and people it with one hundred tithable persons should have the right to another representative.[6]

Returning now to our main topic of the suffrage, it is noteworthy that a quarter of a century elapsed after the assembly of 1619 before a single important act was passed bearing upon the suffrage.   The subject came up in 1646, owing to the inconveniences which were occasioned " by disorderly and illegal election of Burgesses, by subscribing of hands contrary to the warrant."[7]   The act then forbade the use of handwriting, and imposed a fine upon those who did not appear to vote.   It was ordered

"That noe election shall be made of any Burgesse or Burgesses but by a plurality of voices and that no hand writing shall be admitted: Be it alsoe further inacted, That what freeman soever haveing lawful sumons of the time and place for election of Burgesses that shall not make repaire accordingly, Such person or persons vnless there be lawfull cause for the absenting himselfe shall forfeit 100 lb. of tob'o. for his non-appearance ffreemen being covennt. servants being exempted

[1] Hening, I, 421.
[2] Hening, I, 520, 545.
[3] Hening, I, 421.
[4] *Ibid.*
[5] *Ibid.,* 300.
[6] Hening, II, 106.
[7] Hening, I, 333–4.

from the said fine to be levyed by distresse in case of refusall and is to be disposed of towards the defraying of the Burgesses charges in the county."

Thus, under a penalty of a fine of one hundred pounds of tobacco, compulsory *viva voce* voting was imposed upon all freemen who were not covenanted servants. •The act shows clearly that manhood suffrage was the rule in early Virginia as it was in early Maryland.

The next suffrage question arises out of the civil war in England. Berkeley and the Virginians had shown their loyalty to the Stuart family, and in September, 1651, the English Council of State appointed four commissioners to reduce the plantations along Chesapeake Bay.[1] The instructions of the commissioners directed them to offer a general pardon, and to permit the election of burgesses by " those taking the oath to be true and faithful to the Commonwealth of England, without a King or House of Lords." [2] On March 12, 1651–2, the governor, council, and assembly surrendered the government on favorable terms to the commissioners.[3] The inhabitants were offered the new oath to Parliament, and a few weeks after the surrender elections were held for assemblymen.[4] The oath was widely taken; in Northumberland County alone one hundred and seventy-five persons subscribing to it, and the first assembly under the commonwealth was, with one exception, the largest which had met since 1632. •For the next nine years the assembly of the colony was practically supreme, not only performing acts of legislation, but electing the governors and other general and county officers.[5] They exercised the powers of the Long Parliament of England without the monarchical restraint of a Cromwell.

During the Commonwealth period an attempt was made to change the existing broad basis of the suffrage. An act

---

[1] McMahon, *Hist. of Maryland*, 204.

[2] Neill, *Virginia Carolorum*, 218. For exact words of oath, see *ibid.*, 221, note 2. The same form of oath was administered in Maryland.

[3] Hening, I, 363–368; Neill, *Virginia Carolorum*, 221–224.

[4] *Neill, Virginia Carolorum*, 224.

[5] Hening, I, 358–9, note; 369, note; 371–2.

of March, 1654–5, limited the suffrage to housekeepers, and allowed no more than one voter in each family.[1]   It provided

" That all housekeepers whether freeholders, lease holders, or otherwise tenants, shall onely be capeable to elect Burgesses, and none hereby made vncapable shall give his subscription to elect a Burgesse vpon the pennalty of four hundred pounds of tobacco and cask to be disposed of by the court of each county where such contempt shall be vsed: Provided that this word housekeepers repeated in this act extend no further then to one person in a family."

Perhaps growing out of the experience of the last few years [2] the burgesses were now required to be " persons of knowne integrity and of good conversation, and of the age of one & twenty years." [3]   It was made the sheriff's duty, by himself or deputy, to go from house to house and warn all persons interested in elections of the time and place of choosing burgesses; and the *viva voce* provision of the act of 1646, whereby the burgesses were elected by the " plurality of voices," was now changed to an election " by subscription and of the major part of the hands of the electors."

The limitation of the suffrage to housekeepers did not long continue.   The next legislature, adopting to the full the English ideas of taxation and representation, in March, 1655–6, declared that " we conceive it something hard and vnagreeable to reason that any persons shall pay equall taxes and yet have no votes in election." [4]   They therefore repealed that part of the earlier act which " excludes freemen from voters," but they required the voters to " fairly give

[1] Hening, I, 411–412.

[2] In 1652 two persons were ejected from the house, one for scandalous libel, and the other for mutinous declarations.   A minister was also excluded from the assembly in the following year, and the subscribers to a certain mutinous paper were forbidden to hold office.   Hening, I, 374, 378, 380.

[3] This clause is drawn literally from Article XVII of the English Instrument of Government of 1653.

[4] Hening, I, 403.   In 1659 tithables were all white male servants of any age imported into the colony, all imported negroes, male or female, all Indian servants over sixteen years of age, and all Christian (white) males over sixteen.

their votes by subscription and not in a tumultuous way."
The policy of manhood suffrage was expressed still more
definitely by the assembly in March, 1657–8, when they permitted " all persons inhabitting in this collonie that are freemen to have their votes in the election of Burgesses."[1] It
need scarcely be remarked that the word freemen as used
here means free man, and has no connotation of membership
in corporations such as it contains in the northern colonies.
This was manhood suffrage extending to all adult males
who were not slaves or indentured servants; and all the
voters, too, were taxpayers, for the poll-tax was levied upon
all males over sixteen years of age.

By the speedy repeal of the limiting act the commonwealth
government in Virginia showed its regard for universal
suffrage. During these years the government of Virginia
was practically a republic, with the legislature exercising
supreme power. Yet after electing three governors, the
assembly took the strange step of electing a council of state
for life, and providing for the election of the governor from
among the life councillors;[2] but, fortunately, the council
refused to accept the honor, and the next assembly passed an
act " for the annihilation of councillors."[3] At the same
time they declared that the " supreme power of the government" was resident in the assembly, and in their second act
elected Sir William Berkeley as governor.[4]

After the restoration of Charles II. there was no immediate change in the government. Berkeley was accepted as
royal governor and was directed by his instructions to call
assemblies according to the usages of the colony.[5] These
instructions were carried out to the letter, and elections and
the suffrage were practically unchanged; indeed it may be
said that popular suffrage scarcely existed until 1676, for
fifteen years passed without an election of assemblymen.

[1] Hening, I, 475.
[2] Hening, I, 517; March, 1658–9. The new organization of the council was very likely suggested by that of the English Council of State.
[3] Hening, I, 537.
[4] Hening, I, 530.
[5] Dated September 12, 1662; Hazard, *Historical Collections*, II, 607–
611; *Virginia Historical Magazine*, III, 15.

Berkeley's "long parliament" in Virginia almost equalled in duration its English namesake. Some minor changes in county representation and the abolition of the parochial burgesses made in 1661 and 1662 have already been mentioned.[1] The fear that some candidates for the assembly might promise to serve for low wages led the assembly in 1661 and 1662 to fix a regular daily allowance of one hundred and fifty pounds of tobacco for each member, in order that "diverse heart burnings" might be allayed, and interested persons might not "purchase votes by offering to undertake the place at low rates and by that means make the place both mercenary and contemptible."[2]

The subjects of taxation and the suffrage appear to have been mingled in an attempt made in 1663 to abolish the poll-tax, but the exact form of the contest is not clear. Burk[3] thinks that there was an effort to change the basis of taxation to property and at the same time limit the suffrage to freeholders. If this were the aim of a party in the assembly, it met with no immediate success.

In 1670, however, a decided change from universal suffrage was made, and the first step taken towards elections by a definite propertied class. The preamble of the act of October, 1670,[4] shows the fear universal suffrage would bring certain evils into the elective system, and that this belief had worked a change in the opinions of the assembly since the days when it was held that tax-paying and political privileges should go hand in hand. It is probable, too, that a change in the personnel of the assembly had taken place, and that the wealthier planters had more weight now than in the commonwealth period; while the emigrant cavaliers who had fled to Virginia during the Cromwellian rule were now directly influencing politics.[5] The reasons for the passage

---

[1] *Ante,* p. 25.

[2] Hening, II, 23. In the year 1663 a burgess who was charged with sympathy for the Quakers and opposition to the baptism of children was dismissed from the assembly when he refused to take the oaths of allegiance and supremacy (Hening, II, 198).

[3] Burk, *History of Va.,* II, 137.

[4] Hening, II, 280.

[5] Cooke, *Virginia,* 226–230.

of the new act were, first, that

" the usuall way of chuseing burgesses by the votes of all persons who haveing served their tyme are ffreemen of this country who haveing little interest in the country doe ofner make tumults at the election to the disturbance of his majesties peace, then [than] by their discretions in their votes provide for the conservasion thereof, by makeing choyce of persons fitly qualifyed for the discharge of soe great a trust;"

and, secondly, that

" the lawes of England grant a voyce in such election only to such as by their estates real or personall have interest enough to tye them to the endeavor of the publique good."

The law then provided

" that none but freeholders and housekeepers who only are answerable to the publique for the levies shall hereafter have a voice in the election of any burgesses in this country; and that the election be at the court-house." [1]

Thus the first limitation of the suffrage, ostensibly adopted on account of evil practices in the colony and because of the force of English custom, restricted the voters to the house-holding and freeholding classes.

In 1673, when Charles II gave away Virginia to Arling-ton and Culpepper, the colonists took measures to assert their rights; and in the correspondence concerning this grant, while no mention is made of the suffrage, yet the right of representation is most strongly asserted.[2] The colony agents in applying for a new charter for the province asked that " no manner of impositions or taxes shall be laid or imposed upon the inhabitants and proprietors there, unless by the common consent of the governor, council, and burgesses, as

---

[1] Hening, II, 280. Bishop, *Elections in American Colonies,* p. 71, calls attention to the fact that the customs of England permitted only free-holders, and not those possessing a certain amount of personal prop-erty, to have a voice in county elections.

[2] For facts and papers relating to the Culpepper grant, see Hening, II, 311, 427-428, 518-521, 578-583; Beverly (London ed. of 1722), 64-66; Burk, *Hist. of Va.,* II, 142-152, Appendix xxxiii to cxii; Neill, *Virginia Carolorum,* 381 ff.

hath been heretofore used." [1]   The right of taxation in their own assembly, they said, "contains that which we conceive to be the right of Virginians, as well as all other Englishmen, which is not to be taxed but by their consent, expressed by their representatives." [2]

While this question was exciting the colonial land-owners, a greater danger threatened the authorities in Virginia. Many reasons for discontent had arisen throughout the colony; heavy taxes had been laid and unwisely expended, the Indian wars were poorly managed, forts had fallen into decay, the usual meetings of the assembly had been costly, evils had crept into the management of county and parish affairs, and the governor had kept one assembly without dissolution since 1661. [3]   The hostility aroused by these evils in administration found its outlet in the uprising called Bacon's Rebellion.   It is not our part to enter into the causes or purposes of this popular movement.   There can be no doubt that Bacon's followers were not simply the lower and disfranchised classes, but that many of the revolutionists were well-to-do Englishmen, indignant against certain wrongs and willing to take what appeared to be a good opportunity to obtain redress of their grievances. [4]   Bacon's energy and arguments won over many usually conservative citizens, and even gained control of the assembly which met in June, 1676; while among the people his courage and rough eloquence gained the support of the poor freemen, who had recently been excluded by the Virginia Long Parliament from political power.   It appears that non-property-

[1] Burk, II, appendix, p. xl.

[2] Neill, *Virginia Carolorum,* 383.

[3] See the very interesting sets of grievances presented to the royal commissioners after the rebellion, *Va. Mag. of Hist.,* II, 166–173, 289–292, 380–392; III, 132–147. The "long parliament" convened for the first time March 23, 1660–1, and its last session began March 7, 1675–6; see W. G. and M. N. Stanard, *The Colonial Virginia Register,* p. 76.

[4] After the insurrection was suppressed, the Isle of Wight electors instructed their burgesses in assembly, "Wee desire you our Burgesses to give none of our estates away as formerly ye have done, but if ye must give such great sumes dispose of your own," *Va. Mag. of History,* II, 387.

holding freemen participated in the elections for members of the assembly of June, 1676,[1] and the assembly took pains to restore the suffrage to such persons.

One of the most significant features of " Bacon's Assembly" of 1676[2] is the broader democratic basis which was given to the state; not only was the suffrage restored to its former extent, but many offices which had been appointive were now for the first time made elective.   Chapter VII of the acts of this assembly provided that the statute of 1670,

" which forbids freemen to have votes in the election of burgesses be repealed, and that they may be admitted together with the freeholders and householders to vote as formerly in such elections." [3]

All militia officers had formerly been appointed by the governor, but now it was permitted that in certain troops " the soldiers for greater encouragement have free liberty to nominate theire owne officers," provided they were chosen from the militia officers of the respective counties.[4]   In the same manner the " long continuance of vestries" was declared a grievance;   the old self-perpetuating vestrymen were set aside for new boards elected for a term of three years by the " freeholders and freemen of every parish," and the members of the vestries were to be freeholders or substantial householders.[5]   Still another step towards democracy is seen in the provision for a representative county levy court, composed of the justices and an equal number of representatives elected by the majority of votes of freeholders, householders, and freemen in each parish of the county.[6]

Bacon's power was of short duration, and his changes in the laws did not long survive the overthrow of his authority. Royal instructions sent to Governor Berkeley in November, 1676,[7] said:

[1] Campbell, *History of Virginia*, 289; Cooke, *Virginia*, 245.
[2] For legislation of this assembly, see Hening, II, 341–365.
[3] Hening, II, 356.
[4] Hening, II, 348.
[5] Hening, II, 356.
[6] Hening, II, 357.
[7] Hening, II, 424-5.

"I. You shalbe noe more obliged to call an assembly once every yeare, but only once in two yeares, unlesse some emergent occasion shall make it necessary, the judging whereof wee leave to your discretion. Alsoe whensoever the assembly is called ffourteene dayes shalbe the time prefixed for their sitting and noe longer, unlesse you finde goode cause to continue it beyond that tyme.

"II. You shall take care that the members of the assembly be elected only by ffreeholders, as being more agreeable to the custome of England to which you are as nigh as conveniently you can to conforme yourselfe."

The king further directed Berkeley to declare all the legislation of Bacon's Assembly null and void, an instruction which was enacted into law by an assembly of February, 1676–7.[1] It is not certain that the suffrage was at once limited to freeholders, for after the repeal of the Bacon acts no new law was passed for a number of years, and it is thought probable that the freeholder and householder clause of the act of 1670 was enforced for a time.[2]

Lord Culpepper's commission as governor of Virginia gave him power to call assemblies elected by the " ffreeholders and Planters" of the colony according to the former usage of the province.[3] An assembly of 1684, however, passed a resolution which is the first formal act limiting the suffrage to land-holders. From this year, 1684, until 1830, no one but freeholders could vote in Virginia. The assembly

"Resolved, That it is the undoubted right of every person who holds lands, tenements or hereditaments for his owne life, for the life of his wife, or for the life of any other person or persons to vote in Election of Burgesses for the county where such lands, tenements, &c, doe lye."

This resolution, by a negative interpretation, might be taken as excluding from elections those who did not possess land; but it did not expressly do so, and it contained no punitive provision for irregular voting.

These errors were corrected fifteen years later in an act

[1] Hening, II, 380.

[2] Lord Culpepper's instructions of 1680 provided that voters should be freeholders and householders, Neill, *Virginia Carolorum*, 390.

[3] *Calendar of Virginia State Papers*, I, 14–16

of 1699, the purpose of which was said to be the " prevention of undue elections of Burgeses." [1] This act distinctly disqualified from voting those who were not freeholders of the respective counties and towns, and imposed a fine of five hundred pounds of tobacco upon any disfranchised person presuming to vote. An important feature of the act was the exclusion of certain freeholders who under the earlier vague phrases might have claimed a voice in elections:

" *Provided always* and it is the true intent of this act that no woman sole or covert, infants under the age of twenty-one years, or recusant convict being freeholders shall be entitled to give a vote or have a voice in the election of burgeses."

The direct exclusion of women is unusual in colonial laws, the practice of male suffrage generally being so strong that no formal exclusion was considered necessary. This clause, by excluding " recusant convicts," deprived Catholics of the right to vote, an exclusion which was continued until the Revolution; and an act of the same session rendered popish recusants convict incapable of being witnesses in any case whatever.[2] Other sections provided that if the sheriff could not determine the election " upon the view," that he should appoint clerks, who were to write down the electors' names and the persons for whom they voted; that where a person's freehold were in doubt, he might be compelled to swear or affirm to his qualification; that a candidate bribing electors should be rendered incapable of sitting in the assembly for which he had been chosen; together with a number of other administrative provisions.

An act of the same year with this election law restricted jury service also to freeholders who possessed one hundred pounds sterling real and personal estate.[3] In 1705 the details of the elective system were much more fully elaborated.[4] The forms of writs and their proclamation in the churches, the duties of sheriffs and their deputies, the manner of

[1] Hening, III, 172–175. *Cf.* English Statute, 7 and 8 Wm. III, ch. 25.
[2] Hening, III, 298.
[3] Hening, III, 175–176.
[4] Hening, III, 236–246.

making election returns, and many other features were now specified. Some slight change was made in the suffrage provisions. The new section said that,

" After publication of writs, and time and place for election of burgesses as aforesaid, every freeholder, actually resident within the county where the election is to be made, respectively shall appear accordingly, and give his vote at such election, upon penalty of forfeiting two hundred pounds of tobacco to such person or persons as will inform and sue for the same."

Thus to freeholdership inhabitancy was added, and a fine was again levied upon those neglecting to vote. The term freeholder, already limited by the resolution of 1684, received another definition in this act. It was now held to extend to " every person who hath an estate real for his own life, or the life of another, or any estate of greater dignity."

A curious provision is to be found in another law of the year 1705.[1] This act declared that negro, mulatto, and Indian slaves should be accounted real estate, and with some slight changes should descend in fee simple according to the rules for the descent of land. But if slaves were to be held as real estate, the question would arise whether a man could vote who possessed this form of real estate alone. This question the assembly answered in the negative, expressly stating that the holders of slaves and not of other real estate should not possess the privilege of a freeholder in elections.

Women, Catholics, and minors being freeholders had been expressly excluded from the suffrage by the acts of 1699 and 1705. In the latter year negroes, mulattoes, and Indians were forbidden, under penalty of heavy fines, to hold any civil, military, or ecclesiastical office in the colony.[2] A further limitation came in 1723, perhaps as a result of an attempted negro insurrection,[3] when the assembly enacted " That no free negro, mulatto, or Indian whatsoever shall

[1] Hening, III, 333.

[2] Hening, III, 251. A mulatto was defined as a child of an Indian, and the child, grandchild or great-grandchild of a negro.

[3] J. A. C. Chandler, *The History of Suffrage in Virginia, J. H. U. Studies,* XIX, Nos. 6 and 7, p. 12.

hereafter have any vote at the elections of burgesses, or any other election whatsoever." [1]   The attorney of the Board of Trade, Richard West, when commenting upon this law, gave expression to views which show the English tendency towards legal equality, but which also prove that he knew little of colonial conditions. He wrote,

"I cannot see why one freeman should be used worse than another, merely on account of his complexion. . . . It cannot be right to strip all persons of a black complexion from those rights which are so justly valuable to any freeman." [2]

His opinion was not accepted either in England or the colony, and after 1723 the voting privilege was limited to white male Protestant freeholders, twenty-one years of age, who resided in the county where they offered to vote.

Thus by successive limitations Virginia was getting away from the earlier manhood suffrage, and another restriction was soon to come. As early as 1710 we learn of election frauds and contested seats in the assembly.[3] In a letter of October 15, 1712, Governor Spotswood described the evil to the Board of Trade, as follows: [4]

"This unhappy State of her Maj't's Subjects in my Neighbourhood is ye more affecting to me because I have very little hopes of being enabled to relieve them by our Assembly, which I have called to meet next Week; for the Mob of this Country having tryed their Strength in the late Election and finding themselves able to carry whom they please, have generally chosen representatives of their own Class, who as their principal Recommendation have declared their resolution to raise no Tax on the people, let the occasion be what it will. This is owing to a defect in the Constitution, which allows to every one, tho' just out of the Condition of a Serv't, and that can but purchase half an acre of Land, an equal vote with the Man of the best Estate in the Country."

The governor here hinted at the next restriction which would be placed upon the freedom of elections, although the

---

[1] Hening, IV, 133–134.
[2] Neill, *Virginia Carolorum,* 330, note 1.
[3] *Calendar of Va. State Papers,* I, 142–3.
[4] *Letters of Governor Spotswood,* II, 1.

defect in the constitution which he mentioned was not reme-
died until almost a quarter of a century after the date of his
letter.   The English Board of Trade instructed Spotswood
to try to have a law passed for raising the qualifications of
voters, and they promised to see that something was done
in England to force the colonists to adopt such a measure.[1]
There can be no doubt that the granting of the suffrage to
all freeholders without placing any lower limit to the size
of the freehold led to many evils.   " Divers frauds" were
practised " to create and multiply votes" by the making of
" leases of small and inconsiderable parcels of land upon
feigned considerations, and by subdividing lots of ground
in towns;" all of which was declared to be " in prejudice of
the rights of the true freeholder."[2]

To remedy these conditions the act of 1736 was passed,[3]
which named a minimum amount of freehold to be held by
electors.   The limiting clause directed

"That no person or persons whatsoever shall hereafter have a right
to vote at any election of members to serve in the general assembly,
for any county, who hath not an estate of freehold, or other greater
estate, in one hundred acres of land, at least, if no settlement be made
upon it; or twenty-five acres with a house and plantation, in his possession, or in the possession of his tenant or tenants, for term of years,
in the same county where he gives such vote."

Where the freehold had come by purchase, the holder could
not vote in virtue of it until he had been in possession one
year.   In the case of joint tenants, only one vote was to be
given, unless the freehold was sufficient in quantity to give
each joint tenant the amount required for legal electors.   In
towns the qualification was different from that in the country
districts, and was based upon houses and lots rather than
acres of freehold.

"*Provided always*, that nothing in this act contained shall be con-
strued to hinder any person to vote at such elections, in respect or in
right of any houses, lands, or tenements, lying and being in any city

[1] Chandler, *The Suffrage in Va., J. H. U. Stud.*, XIX, 12.
[2] Hening, IV, 475.
[3] Hening, IV, 475–478. *Cf.* English statute, 10 Ann., ch. 31.

or town, laid out and established by act of assembly, so as such person be a freeholder, in any house or lot, or a house, and part of a lot; but where the interest in any such house and lot, or house and part of a lot, is or shall be divided among several persons, no more than one single voice shall be admitted for one and the same house or lot." [1]

A fine of forty pounds was laid upon any one making or drafting a fraudulent conveyance in order to qualify voters, and upon those voting by virtue of such estates; and all these conveyances, whether made before or after the passage of the act, were pronounced null and void. It is to be noted also, that neither this act nor the later ones of 1762 and 1769 contained the limitation imposed by the act of 1705, that voting freeholders should be inhabitants of the county. Later, plural voting was apparently permitted where freeholders held the requisite amount of land in several counties, and elections in neighboring counties were held on different days.[2]

The Virginia act of 1736 has a number of interesting features. It is remarkable for the attempt to adapt the suffrage qualifications to different classes of the inhabitants. The three alternatives,—one hundred acres of land, or twenty-five acres and a house, or a town house and lot,—

[1] A town lot by some early laws must be one-half an acre (Hening, III, 417, 423); but by the later acts it might be less but could not be greater than that amount (Hening, IV, 235; V, 193, 198). In the laws erecting towns many specifications are given concerning the size, position, and manner of building houses in the towns; and as these regulations differed in the several towns, the exact nature of the suffrage clause would be a matter of local interpretation. In Williamsburg, houses on the main street must be twenty by forty or fifty feet, and on the other streets each house must cover four or five hundred feet (Hening, III, 429); in Fredericksburg, houses were to be twenty by twenty feet with a pitch of nine feet (Hening, IV, 236); in Leeds the building rules were similar to those in Fredericksburg (Hening, V, 193); while in Suffolk the legal size of houses was sixteen by twenty feet, with a height of eight feet (Hening, V, 198).

[2] See a contested election case hinging upon plural voting, quoted by J. F. Jameson, *The Nation*, Vol. 56, 309. Also Beverly (1722), 206: " The freeholders are the only electors, and wherever they have a freehold . . . they have a vote in the election."

while all requiring a freehold, so adapted the freehold qualification to the varying circumstances of the people that in
reality the restriction upon the suffrage was not so great as
at first might appear. Later, when the act of 1762 lowered
the freehold to fifty acres, and reduced the size of town
houses, the franchise was placed upon a more liberal basis
than in many of the other colonies. Further, after 1736,
two places, Williamsburg and Norfolk, had a peculiarly
wide borough franchise. The act contains, too, the unique
feature of fractional voting.[1] Plural voting has been mentioned in this work in several places, but it is believed that no
case of fractional voting for colonial assemblymen is to be
found except in Virginia, where a number of joint-tenants
could unite to cast one vote for their freehold. Thus,
throughout this act, and the later ones of 1762 and 1769
which liberalized, rather than restricted, its provisions, there
is an evident intention to examine closely the various classes
of landholders and frame a law which would admit all the
reputable freeholders to the elective franchise.

An elaborate election law, which set the voter's qualifications and explained in detail the electing process, was
passed in 1762. The former laws had "proved defective,"
and the new law organized the electoral system so thor-
oughly that its provisions remained in force long into the
commonwealth period. The act[2] provided for the election
of "most able and fit men" as burgesses; two elected by
the freeholders of each county, one by the freeholders of
James City, and one each by the city of Williamsburg, the
borough of Norfolk, and the College of William and Mary
according to their respective charter privileges. No assembly could continue longer than seven years, and a new election must be held at least three years after a dissolution
of an assembly. The general elector's qualification was
changed in the direction of a broader suffrage by lowering
the amount of unsettled land from one hundred acres with a
fifty acres; the old provision of twenty-five acres with a
house and plantation was now rendered more explicit by

[1] Reference will be made to fractional voting on Long Island and
in New England.

[2] Chapter I of November, 1762, Hening, VII, 517–530.

requiring the house to be at least twelve feet square; and the same sized house was required of town voters,[1] except in Williamsburg and Norfolk, where the charters and former laws should govern the elections.[2]

" Every person shall have a right to vote at any election of Burgesses for any county who hath an estate of freehold for his own life, or the life of another, or other greater estate in at least fifty acres of land, if no settlement be made upon it, or twenty-five acres, with a plantation and house thereon, at least twelve feet square, in his possession, or in the possession of his tenant or tenants, for term of years at will or sufferance, in the same county where he gives such vote; . . . and every person possessed of a lot, or part of a lot, in any city or town established by act of assembly, with a house thereon at least twelve feet square, shall have a right to vote at such elections."

Joint tenancies should qualify all the joint owners only when the freehold was of sufficient quantity to furnish the legal amount to each, and where it was less than this, but one vote was to be given for the tenancy, and that only in case all the parties interested could agree. The disfranchised class remained the same as under the earlier acts, except that a convict freeholder was excluded from voting only during the time for which he had been transported. The fine of five hundred pounds of tobacco upon disqualified persons who voted illegally was retained, as also that of two hundred pounds upon qualified persons who neglected to vote. Freeholds, as previously, must be held for one year before qualifying a person to vote, unless the lands came by descent, marriage, marriage settlement, or devise. The act of 1762, while attaining a desirable end by carefully outlining the management of elections, must also have worked an extension of the suffrage, since it cut down the general land requirements from one hundred to fifty acres, and lowered the legal size of houses in the towns. The qualifica-

[1] The size twelve by twelve feet would work an extension of the suffrage in the towns also, for the legal requirement for house-building in the towns always specified a larger structure than twelve by twelve feet, the usual proportions being twenty by twenty feet.
[2] Hening, VII, 529.

tions thus established were practically unchanged down to 1830.[1]

Turning from these uniform suffrage qualifications, we must now notice three exceptions to the general election provisions,—the cases of electors in the city of Williamsburg, in the borough of Norfolk, and in the College of William and Mary.[2] The first law relating to the city of Williamsburg was passed in 1699,[3] and this was followed by a supplemental act in 1705.[4] The plot of the city was divided into half-acre lots upon which the owners were required to erect buildings within two years after purchase, and the height, size, and position of houses were determined by law and by regulations of the commissioners appointed under the law. On July 28, 1722, the city received a charter[5] which established a municipal corporation with self-perpetuating officers, and gave the city the privilege of sending one burgess to the assembly. Following the English and general colonial custom, the borough franchise was placed upon a basis differing from the county freehold qualification. The electors in the city were (1) the mayor, recorder, aldermen, and common councilmen; (2) all freeholders owning a whole lot of ground with a house built thereon according to law,[6] (3) all actual inhabitants and residents of the

---

[1] The act of 1769 (Chapter I, November, 1769, Hening, VIII, 305–317) re-enacted almost all the provisions of the law of 1762. The most important omissions were the sections requiring the dissolution of assembly at least once in seven years, and an election at least three years after the dissolution. By the new act lands need be held only six months before the election, and unanimity upon the part of joint tenants was not required.

[2] Jamestown, which was another exception to the uniform county representation, was not the recipient of any special suffrage privileges.

[3] Hening, III, 197.

[4] Hening, III, 419–432.

[5] Partially recited in Hening, V, 204.

[6] The act of 1705 had given many details concerning the building of houses; requiring those on the main street of Williamsburg to measure twenty by fifty feet, or if possessing two brick chimneys and bricked cellar, then twenty by forty feet; and houses on other streets were to cover four or five hundred square feet according as bricks did or did not enter into their construction. (Hening, III, 425, 429, 430.)

city who had a visible estate of fifty pounds current money; (4) all persons who had served five years to any trade in the city, and after the expiration of their service, were actual housekeepers and inhabitants of the city. These provisions were explained at large by an act of 1742,[1] but no change was made in them except that a residence of twelve months was required of those voting as inhabitants, and unanimity of joint tenants was required before a vote could be cast for their lot.

The charter of Norfolk, of 1736, made the voting class almost identical with that of Williamsburg.[2] As later explained by the assembly,[3] the suffrage was vested in freeholders owning at least one-half a lot of ground with a house of the size required for a whole lot, or inhabitants having resided twelve months in the town and owning fifty pounds visible estate, or tradesmen who had served five years to a trade in the town, had received a certificate from the court of hustings and were actually inhabitants and housekeepers. Indentured and covenanted servants were especially excluded from voting as inhabitants.

The elaborate act of 1705[4] for "establishing ports and towns," so notably unsuccessful, also contained a clause permitting each town, after receiving sixty families of inhabitants and becoming fully organized as a borough, to send one burgess to the assembly, who was to be elected by adult male freeholders and housekeepers of the town.[5] This provision was not carried out within the next five years, and at the end of that time the act was repealed by the governor in accordance with the Queen's instructions.

An inspection of the suffrage features of the charters of Williamsburg and Norfolk shows their close similarity to the city or borough charters in the neighboring colonies

[1] Hening, V, 204–207.

[2] See charter in Ingle, *Local Institutions in Virginia, J. H. U. Studies,* III, No. 2, 121–126. It was later confirmed by act of assembly (Hening, IV, 541).

[3] Act of 1753, Hening, VI, 261–265.

[4] Hening, III, 404–419; repealed by Governor Spotswood's proclamation in 1710.

[5] Hening, III, 414.

of North Carolina, Maryland, Delaware, and Pennsylvania. Indeed, wherever population was grouped in cities or towns in the middle or southern colonies, the colonial custom followed the English precedent of adapting the suffrage qualifications to the variant economic conditions of the townspeople. The freehold requirement, which in the country districts excluded few honest and industrious men, would be almost prohibitive among the merchant and artisan classes in the towns. The colonial legislators, undoubtedly acquainted with the English borough charters, recognized this economic difference when defining the voting class.

A third exception to the uniform election laws is to be found in the representation granted to the College of William and Mary according to the terms of its charter of 1693. Following the privileges granted to Oxford and Cambridge, the Virginia college received the right to send one burgess to the assembly, who should be elected by the president and six masters of the college from their own number, or from the board of visitors or from among the citizens of the colony.[1] This right was respected by subsequent legislation, and the elections of representatives for the college were made by the seven persons authorized to do so by the charter.[2]

[1] The charter provided:
"XVIII. and, also, of our special grace, certain knowledge and mere motion we have given and granted, and by these presents, for us and our successors, do give and grant to the said President and masters or professors of the said College, full and absolute power, liberty, and authority to nominate, elect, and constitute one discreet and able person of their own number, or of the number of the said visitors, or governors, or lastly of the better sort of inhabitants of our colony of Virginia, to be present in the house of Burgesses of the General Assembly of our colony of Virginia, and there to act and consent to such things as by the common advice of our said colony shall (God willing) happen to be enacted."

[2] At a meeting of the President and masters on January 8, 1729–30, the following action was taken:
"Upon the Governor's writt to elect a Burgess according to the Charter to serve in the Assembly, which is prorogued to the —— of february, the election fell unanimously on Dr. George Nicholas;" *William and Mary College Quarterly*, I, 134. See also Morrison, *History of William and Mary College*, 48.

We have been noting heretofore the elections for the assembly. The facts concerning local suffrage can be told in a few words, since Virginia possessed very few local elections, the most important of which were those for church officers. Church wardens were to be chosen annually under the acts of 1631–2, 1632, and 1642–3, but no description is given of the method of election.[1] In 1644–5, after vestries had been in existence for some time, the assembly directed that the vestrymen should be chosen by the " major part of the parishioners, . . . by pluralitie of voices." [2] The minister was chosen by the vestry, but in an election in 1649 it was stated that the vestry made choice of a minister, with the full and free consent of the freemen of the parish.[3] The early laws do not provide for any changes in the vestry, but in 1661–2 [4] they were empowered to fill vacancies in their own number, and with the minister to elect the two church wardens from among themselves. Bacon's Assembly in 1676 limited the term of vestries to three years, and provided for their election by the " freeholders and freemen" of every parish, thus granting manhood suffrage in their election; [5] but this, together with all the other legislation of this assembly, was of short duration. In 1708 the governor and council ordered that in an approaching vestry election, " for avoiding all tumult and confusion, which usually happens on such occasions," " every freeholder and Householder paying Seott and Lett [scot and lot] in the parish and no other have vote at the said election." [6] The rule here laid down was followed by the assembly in the later acts, when for any reason a new vestry must be elected. Thus, whenever a new parish was erected, or the vestrymen of an old parish neglected their duties or were proved to be dissenters, a new vestry was chosen by the freeholders and householders of the parish.[7] Although not regularly chosen, yet when ves-

[1] Hening, I, 155, 180, 240.
[2] Hening, I, 290.
[3] *Lower Norfolk County Virginia Antiquary*, II, 63.
[4] Hening, II, 44–5.
[5] Hening, II, 356.
[6] *Calendar of Virginia State Papers*, I, 122.
[7] See Hening, passim; *e.g.*, IV, 304 305, 443, 467; V, 80, 96, 211,

trymen were elected the suffrage was on a broader basis than in the assembly elections.

The abortive town act of 1705 contained a number of provisions for popular elections, in which the suffrage was extended to all free adult inhabitants and freeholders of the proposed towns, but these features were not put in force under this act; and under the later town charters the local government was of the close corporation type without elective features.[1]   The same absence of elective officers is seen in the county government, where the only exception is the temporary provision for local county representatives, who were joined with the county court in the levying of taxes.   These, under Bacon's laws, were to be elected in each parish by the " freeholders, householders, and freemen,"[2] but subsequently the freemen were excluded and the election limited to freeholders and householders.[3]   Only one reference has been found to elective militia officers, and this, too, was among the transitory work of Bacon's Assembly.[4]

In closing the subject of the suffrage in Virginia, reference must be made to some figures and conclusions given by Professor J. F. Jameson and President L. G. Tyler concerning the numbers of the voting class in Virginia.   Professor Jameson, in a comparison of the extent of the suffrage in Virginia with that in Massachusetts, comes to the conclusion that about six per cent. of the white population of Virginia took part in thirteen elections between 1744 and 1772, the individual cases varying from four to nine per cent.[5]   President Tyler has developed the idea, and in a series of election returns [6] has shown that the proportion of voters was even greater than that given by Professor Jameson.   These figures

254, 259, 274, 381 ; VI, 256, 276, 381 ; VII, 132, 144, 153, 301, 303 ; VIII, 432. Returns of vestry elections in 1761 will be found in *Lower Norfolk County Virginia Antiquary*, I, 18–19.

[1] See charters of Williamsburg and Norfolk already quoted.

[2] Hening, II, 357.

[3] Hening, II, 441.

[4] Hening, II, 348.

[5] *N. Y. Nation*, April 27, 1893, Vol. 56, 309–310.

[6] *Virginians Voting in the Colonial Period, William and Mary Quarterly*, VI, 7–13.

give eight per cent. of the white population voting in an election in Elizabeth City County in 1758, ten per cent. in King George County in the same year, and seven and one-half per cent. in Prince William County in 1741. In Westmoreland County for 1741, 1748, 1752 the proportions are seven and one-half, ten, and eight and one-half per cent. respectively; while in Essex County in 1761 and 1765 the voters numbered about ten per cent. of the white inhabitants. Taking the average of these poll-lists, it would appear that almost nine per cent. of the white population actually participated in these elections; or that one white person in eleven not only had a right to vote, but did perform that duty. In this respect Virginia compares favorably with the New England and the middle colonies. Taking the figures of a somewhat later period in Massachusetts,[1] or the poll-lists given for New York City,[2] it is apparent that the franchise was more widely exercised, if not more widely conferred, in Virginia than in the more northern colonies.

[1] J. F. Jameson, *New Eng. Magazine,* Jan., 1890.
[2] See p. 217.

CHAPTER III.

THE SUFFRAGE IN MARYLAND.

The suffrage in Maryland furnishes a number of peculiarities which mark off its political conditions from those in other colonies. The presence of the Catholics in a considerable number complicated the political question with the religious one, and led through an alternation of toleration and persecution to a policy of constant repression. The early primary assemblies and universal suffrage, and their development into a proxy system and a true representative organization, are most interesting for the light they throw upon the inevitable growth from pure democracy to representation. And the successive processes of suffrage limitation show the transition from an early economic and political equality to a condition of diversity in wealth and privileges.

The royal charter to Baltimore [1] enjoined upon the proprietor the necessity of admitting the inhabitants of the province to a share in the making of laws:

> He had power " to ordain, make, and enact laws . . . with the advice . . . of the free men of the said province, or of the greater part of them, or of their delegates or deputies, whom we will shall be called together for the framing of laws, when and as often as need shall require, by the aforesaid now baron of Baltimore. . . . So nevertheless that the laws aforesaid be consonant to reason, and be not repugnant or contrary, but (so far as conveniently may be) agreeable to the laws, statutes, customs, and rights of this our Kingdom of England. . . . "

While there could be no doubt that the charter required the association of the colonists with the proprietor in the making of laws, yet it did not clearly state the class among the colonists who should enjoy the suffrage. The document, written in Latin, used the phrases *liberi homines* and *liberi tenentes* in speaking of the political people, and it was at one

[1] Bozman, *History of Maryland*, II, 9 ff; Poore, *Charters and Constitutions*, I, 811–817; *Archives of Md., Proceedings of Council, 1637–1667*, 3–12.

time thought that the power thus granted devolved only on freeholders. Later interpreters, noting the practice of the assemblies, have taken the other view, that the charter granted the suffrage to all *free men.*[1]

No provision is made in the instructions to the first governor, Leonard Calvert, for a popular assembly;[2] but less than a year after the colonists arrived in the province they met in assembly and passed certain laws. The acts of this first meeting, evidently a primary assembly of the colonists, are shrouded in uncertainty.[3] Some legislation must have been passed, for the commission to Governor Calvert in 1637 directs him to express the proprietor's dissent to all laws heretofore passed.[4] But leaving this early assembly, whose work we know only by indirect reference, we may note the more important second assembly, the records of which have been quite fully preserved.

The governor's commission of April 15, 1637, directed him to call an assembly of the freemen in the following January and present to them certain laws drafted in England; and empowered him to call future assemblies of the freemen, whose acts must be submitted to the proprietor for his approval.[5] In accordance with this commission the governor issued writs summoning an assembly for January 25, 1637–8, by which the respective commanders were instructed " to endeavor to persuade fit freemen to attend in person," and to permit the rest of the freemen to attend in person, or elect their deputies.[6]

[1] See Bozman, II, 47, note; McMahon, *History of Maryland,* 443, note 1; G. W. Brown, *The Origin and Growth of Civil Liberty in Maryland,* 9.

[2] Instructions in *Calvert Papers, Md. Hist. Soc. Fund Publications,* 1889, 131–140; Hart, *History by Contemporaries,* I, 247–252.

[3] S. F. Streeter, *Papers Relating to the Early History of Md., Md. Hist. Soc. Fund Pub.,* 1876, 7; B. F. Johnson, *The Founding of Maryland and the Origin of the Act Concerning Religion, Hist. Soc. Fund Pub.,* No. 18, 1883, 34–5.

[4] *Archives of Maryland, Proceedings of Council, 1636–67,* 49.

[5] *Ibid.*

[6] " and to give free power & liberty to all the rest of the said freemen either to be p'nt at the said assembly if they so please; or otherwise to elect and nominate such and so many persons as they or the maior

4

The assembly had as diverse a character as the writ permitted. Some persons came in their own right, others were represented by proxies given to attending freemen, while Kent Island was represented by a regularly elected deputy.[1] In all perhaps ninety persons were either present or represented during the sessions of the assembly. An inspection of the economic station of the attendants shows great differences existing among the freemen; mariners, carpenters, a cooper, and a brick-mason were associated with the governor, the sheriff, three priests, and many gentlemen and planters.[2] The suffrage appears to have been upon the broadest possible basis. Two carpenters and two mariners who claimed a voice in the affairs of assembly were admitted and allowed to attend personally or appoint proxies;[3] and two persons from Kent Island, having previously voted for the representative, were permitted to participate personally in the meetings.[4] The freemen so met in assembly fined those who did not attend or give proxies, and even directed that all freemen present in the assembly, or who had given proxies, were to be free from arrest during the sessions of the assembly. The assembly by a decisive vote of 37 to 14 refused

---

part of them so assembled shall agree upon to be the deputies or burgesses for the said freemen, in their name and steed to advise and consult of such things as shalbe brought into deliberation in the said assembly." *Archives of Md., Proceedings and Acts of Assembly, 1637–64,* 1.

[1] *Archives, Assembly, 1637–64,* 2–6. The delegate was elected by the people in the presence of Governor Calvert, who had gone to Kent Island to enforce Baltimore's claims; *Calvert Papers* in *Md. Hist. Soc. Fund Pub.,* 1889, 185.

[2] Streeter, *op. cit.,* 61, gives the occupations of members as follows:

Governor	1	Ship-carpenter	1
Secretary	1	Brick-mason	1
Sheriff	1	Cooper	1
Marshal	1	Mariners	5
Priests	3	Planters	48
Gentlemen	10	Occupations not given	12
Councillors	3		—
Carpenters	2	Total	90

[3] *Archives, Assembly, 1637–64,* 4, 5, 6.

[4] *Ibid.,* 5, 8.

to accept the laws sent over by the proprietor, and then proceeded to adopt laws of their own making.[1]

For over ten years after 1638 no definite organization of the assemblies was established; on some occasions they were pure democratic meetings, with the proxy privilege; in other cases they were truly representative bodies; while sometimes, as in the first gathering, there was a combination of these two principles. Within this period, also, the separation of the councillors from the freemen and burgesses was accomplished and a bicameral system originated.[2] A few details of these early assemblies may not be out of place as showing the development from a primary to a representative assembly system.

The writs for the election of 1638-9 directed the election of burgesses in the respective hundreds, and summoned certain named persons to appear individually,[3] thus implying a representative body; but when two persons from Saint Maries claimed a voice because they did not assent to the election of burgesses, they were admitted to the assembly.[4] This indefinite organization was later permitted by a law of the same assembly, which gave the right to a seat in the legislature to councillors, to those summoned personally, or who were chosen by the freemen as burgesses, or who, as freemen, had not consented to the burgesses elected in any hundred and wished personally to attend.[5] This assembly further required all persons over eighteen years of age to swear allegiance to the king, under pain of confiscation of property and banishment from the province, thus limiting the rights of freemen to those taking the oath.[6] Another act guaranteed the liberties and free customs of English

---

[1] *Archives, Assembly, 1637-64*, 11-22.

[2] See *Ibid.*, 130, 141, 209, 272, etc., for bicameral system.

[3] *Ibid.*, 27-31.

[4] *Ibid.*, 32.

[5] *Ibid.*, 74, 81. The burgesses were to be " some one, two, or more able and sufficient men for the hundred;" and those personally summoned were to be " Gentlemen of able judgment and quality" or lords of manors when such have been erected.

[6] *Ibid.*, 40.

subjects to " all the Inhabitants of this Province being christians (Slaves excepted)." [1]

An assembly of October 12–24, 1640, apparently a representative body,[2] was continued until 1641, although the freemen in the hundreds were permitted to substitute new burgesses for the old ones if they desired.[3]   Some changes were
accordingly made, and when one of the displaced deputies
claimed a seat in his own right he was refused.[4]

Another change to the primary assembly was made in
March, 1641–2, when the writs for electing burgesses [5] were
subsequently changed by the governor for new writs summoning all the freemen of the province to attend in person
or to appoint their proxies or deputies.[6]   This assembly was
attended by the governor, five councillors, and thirty-nine
freemen personally, and proxies for twenty-two other freemen were held by those present.   In July of the same year a
representative assembly was held; [7]   and when two of the
members asked to vote for the proxies of Kent Island inhabitants they were refused, being permitted only to cast
their votes as deputies.[8]   It was at this assembly that we
notice the first tendency to distinguish between the burgesses
on one hand and the councillors and those summoned by
personal writ on the other.[9]

In September, 1642, the third assembly for that year met.

[1] *Archives, Assembly, 1637–64,* 41.

[2] *Ibid.,* 87–89, where the writs of election are given.

[3] *Ibid.,* 103–5.

[4] *Ibid.,* 105.

[5] *Ibid.,* 113.

[6] *Ibid.,* 115.   " These are to publish and proclaim to all Persons Inhabitants within this Province that I have appointed to hold a General
Assembly of all the Freemen of this Province on monday being the
one and twentieth day of this instant month and therefore to require
all freemen whatsoever to take notice hereof and either to repair personally . . . or else to appoint and depute some other for their Proxy
or deputy during the said Assembly there to consult and advise touchg
the enacting of new Laws and other important affairs of this Province."

[7] See writs for election of burgesses, *Archives, Assembly, 1637–64,*
127.

[8] *Ibid.,* 129.

[9] *Ibid.,* 131, 141.

This was a primary gathering, the writ directing "all free-men inhabiting within the Province to be at the said Assembly at the time & place aforesaid either by themselves or their Deputies or Delegates sufficiently Authorized." [1] In accordance with this order there appeared the governor and eighteen freemen personally, one hundred and five freemen were represented by proxies, fifteen were excused, and seventy-six were fined for not appearing, either by themselves or proxy. It is interesting to note that Brent, an inhabitant of Kent Island, held the proxies of seventy-three freemen of that island. At this meeting clear evidence is given of the extent of the suffrage and the application of the term free-man. The records show us a certain Weston, without land or certain dwelling, who claimed he was not a freeman, but the assembly decided he was such and must give attendance.[2] Such an interpretation as this makes the word freeman mean, not a formally admitted member of a distinct corporation, but a man who is free,—that is, not bound to service or a slave.

Proclamations for assemblies of all the freemen were again issued in December, 1642, March, 1643, and November, 1644, but no record of these assemblies has been noticed.[3] In January, 1647–8, another pure democratic assembly was held. According to the governor's writ, this was to be composed of "All and Singular the Inhabts of this Province either by their psonall appearances or by Proxey or delegate;" and by way of caution the governor advised "all such as shall not give their psonall attendance therein that they make choyse of such psons for their Delegates whose able iudgm't & ffortunes may render them more considerate to the weale publique." [4] A petition, unique in colonial history, was made to this assembly by Mrs. Margaret Brent,

[1] *Archives, Assembly, 1637–64,* 167.

[2] "Mr. Thomas Weston being called pleaded he was no freeman because he had no land nor certain dwelling here, etc., but being put to the question it was voted that he was a Freeman and as such bound to his appearance by himself or proxie, whereupon he took his place in the house." *Archives, Assembly, 1637–64,* 170.

[3] *Ibid.,* 201.

[4] *Ibid.,* 213.

who was executrix for the deceased governor, Leonard Calvert. She demanded a voice and vote in the assembly, and
when this was denied she protested against all the proceedings of the session.[1] This is the only instance found in all
the colonial records of a demand for the suffrage upon the
part of a woman.[2] It was in this assembly, also, that the
question of the freemenship of a certain person was decided
upon the basis of his not being bound to service.[3]

The assembly further introduced another variation in the
representative system. We have noted that freemen might
appear in person, or by proxy, and in some cases by deputy.
On January 20, 1647–8, the freemen in assembly went even
a step farther and selected from themselves sixteen persons,
who with the governor and council were to constitute an
assembly. A quorum of this secondary assembly was to be
composed of the governor, the clerk, and ten freemen.[4] This
delegated body later refused to permit other freemen to join
them, stating that the sixteen chosen freemen alone had a
voice in the assembly.[5] In this way a representative body
was erected which closely corresponds to the representative
boards chosen from the commonalty of New Amsterdam at
various occasions under the Dutch rule, and is somewhat
similar to the representative commissioners who were chosen
in Rhode Island at about this time. In 1649–50 the writs
permitted the election of delegates or the attendance of freemen as the counties or hundreds should determine, but forbade any one bringing the proxies of more than two other
freemen.[6]

[1] Jan. 21, 1647–8. " Came Mrs. Margaret Brent and requested to have
vote in the house for herselfe and voyce allso for that att the last Court
3rd Jan.: it was ordered that the said Mrs. Brent was to be looked
uppon and received as his Lps attorney. The Govr denyed that the sd
Mrs. Brent should have any vote in the house. And the sd Mrs. Brent
protested agst all Proceedings in this pnt Assembly, unlesse shee may
be pnt and have vote as aforesd." *Archives, Assembly, 1637–64*, 215.

[2] An instance of woman suffrage has been noted in New York; see
post, 192.

[3] *Archives, Assembly, 1637–64*, 218–220.

[4] *Ibid.*, 214.

[5] *Ibid.*, 217.

[6] *Ibid.*, 259.

The details given above include the more important references to this interesting system of primary assemblies and proxy voting. It will be noticed that the franchise was co-extensive with free manhood; that there was absolutely no property qualification, and evidently no religious or definite residence restrictions. The demand for the suffrage by a woman also shows how broad must have been the prevailing ideas upon the subject.

During the years 1638–1650, the greater number of the assemblies were supposed to be meetings of all the freemen, but it must not be imagined that any complete gathering of all the inhabitants ever took place. From the first the proxy system gave the freeman an excuse to stay at home, of which he was not slow to take advantage. In one assembly the eighteen freemen present held proxies for one hundred and five others, while one person held seventy-three proxies; in another case the thirty-nine present held proxies for twenty-two others, and in still another assembly fifteen named persons and " divers other inhabitants" held proxies for ninety-three freemen.[1] There can be no doubt that the evils of such a system early became apparent. Immediately after the assembly of 1638, protests were sent to the proprietor in England against a system by which no man could be sure of what he hath, " but he that canne git most proxis in every assembly shall dispose of any mans estate that he pleaseth." [2] It was said that the governor and his friends, by the many proxies they had obtained, had been able to do whatever they wished without any restraint; [3] and the fear was expressed that " any factious workingman," " if he would labor for it, might quickly get an over-swaying voice and carry by proxies what he will." [4] In spite of these objections to the system, or perhaps on account of them, the governors retained the proxy system for over ten years before the assembly was based upon the equal representation of geographical or corporate units.

---

[1] *Archives, Assembly, 1637–64,* 214.
[2] *Md. Hist. Soc. Fund Pub.,* 1889, *Calvert Papers,* 164.
[3] *Ibid.,* 160.
[4] *Ibid.,* 169. It must be noted that these objections all came from one of the strong Catholic settlers.

Before 1648, however, there began another movement, which was at length to limit the suffrage to Protestants and to exclude altogether from political activity those who had been instrumental in founding the colony. In 1642, when at least a majority, or perhaps three-fourths, of the population were Protestants,[1] a feeling of discontent arose in the province,[2] which was not allayed by acting Governor Brent's seizure of a parliamentary vessel in 1644. A year later the extreme Protestants rose in rebellion with Richard Ingle as their leader and drove out the Catholic priests and Governor Leonard Calvert. In the same year the Protestants of the colony wrote to England setting forth the tyrannical nature of their government under the popish recusants, who were seducing many to their religion; and the English House of Lords acted upon these petitions by suggesting the settling of the province in Protestant hands.[3] Petitions and counter-petitions from Lord Baltimore and from merchants of London were also sent to the Lords at this time.[4] Governor Calvert returned to the province in 1646, drove out Ingle, and restored the proprietary party. In the meantime the proprietor attempted to secure his position in the colony. This was done by commissioning Protestants to the principal offices, by granting amnesty, by proposing religious tolera-tion, and by requiring a stricter oath of allegiance to the proprietor. As early as 1638–9 such an oath had been re-quired of all inhabitants over eighteen years of age,[5] and now, in 1648 [6] and 1650,[7] additional clauses were added to

[1] B. F. Johnson, *Founding of Md.*, 32.
[2] *Ibid.*, 95.
[3] *Archives, Council, 1636–67*, 164, 173.
[4] *Ibid.*, 180, 181.
[5] *Archives, Assembly, 1637–64*, 40.
[6] *Archives, Council, 1636–67*, 196.
[7] *Archives, Assembly, 1637–64*, 304. This oath provided that the affiant be true and faithful to the proprietor; that he would protect and maintain his lordship's interests and privileges; that he would make known any plots or conspiracies to the proprietor; that he would accept no lands in Maryland from the Indians but subject to the use of the proprietor; and would take no lands from any one by purchase or otherwise, except where legal title came from the proprietor.

these oaths. During this period the famous act of toleration of April 21, 1649, was passed.[1]

But neither the act of toleration nor the stringent oaths could keep the province in Baltimore's control. Interests in England and the colony were working against him; and when, in September, 1651, the English Council of State appointed a commission to reduce all the plantations on Chesapeake Bay, one of the four commissioners was the William Claiborne who had already caused so much trouble to the colony.[2] After settling affairs in Virginia the commissioners turned their attention to Maryland, where on March 29, 1652, they issued a proclamation from St. Mary's calling an assembly, but limiting the suffrage in the election for burgesses to those who would promise to be faithful to the commonwealth as established in England.[3] Governor Stone and his council agreed to this declaration, but two years later, under directions from Baltimore, Stone issued writs in the proprietor's name, and, when the commissioners protested, he appealed to arms,[4] but was soon overcome by the Puritan forces. The commissioners thereupon issued commissions to ten persons to care for the peace and administration of justice in place of the proprietors, the governor, and council.[5] In this commission occurs the first formal exclusion of Catholics from political activity. The ten commissioners are instructed,

"Alsoe that they Sumon an Assembly to begin on the 20th day of October Next. For which Assembly all Such Shall be disabled to give

[1] For this act see "*The Foundation of Maryland and the Origin of the Act Concerning Religion of April 21, 1649,*" by B. F. Johnson, in *Md. Hist. Soc. Fund Pub.*, 1883, No. 18; and *Church and State in Early Maryland*, George Petrie, *Johns Hopkins Univ. Studies*, 10th Series, No. 4.

[2] McMahon, *Md.*, 204.

[3] *Archives, Council, 1636–67*, 271. The electors must subscribe the following engagement: "We whose names are Subscribed do promise and engage our selves to be true and faithful to the Commonwealth of England as it is now established without King or House of Lords."

[4] *Ibid.*, 300 ff.

[5] *Ibid.*, 311.

any Vote or to be Elected Members thereof as have borne arms in Warr against the Parliament or doe profess the Roman Catholick Religion." [1]

An assembly summoned in accordance with this provision met in October, 1654, and in its first act gave recognition to the Protector's power in Maryland, directed that no change could be made in the government except by order from the Protector, and required all persons in express terms to own their subjection to the present government.[2] Those refusing, or speaking and acting against the government, were to be considered offenders against the Protector. The repressive measures were successful and the Catholics appear to have refrained from voting.[3] The assembly showed its anti-Catholic feeling by repealing the religious liberty act of 1649 and passing another which declared Catholics without the protection of the laws, while it permitted freedom of religion to other Christians.[4]

[1] *Archives, Council, 1637–67,* 313.

[2] *Archives, Assembly, 1637–64,* 339.

[3] When two burgesses from St. Mary's refused to subscribe to the new agreement, urging their former oath to Baltimore, they were refused seats in the house. A new election resulted in the *unanimous* choice of two delegates who were ready to take the oath (*ibid.*). The unanimity in the election shows how well the policy of repression was working.

[4] " An act Concerning Religion."

   " It is Enacted and declared in the Name of his Highness the Lord Protector with the consent and by the authority of the present General Assembly. That none who profess and Exercise the Popish Religion Commonly known by the Name of the Roman Catholick Religion can be protected in this Province by the Lawes of England formerly established and yet unrepealed nor by the Government of the Commonwealth of England, Scotland, and Ireland and the Dominions thereunto belonging Published by his Highness the Lord Protector, but are to be restrained from the Exercise thereof, Therefore all and Every person or persons concerned in the Law aforesaid are required to take notice

   " Such as profess faith in God by Jesus Christ (although differing in Judgment from the Doctrine worship & Discipline publickly held forth shall not be restrained from but shall be protected in the profession of the faith) & Exercise of their

Pending a decision by Cromwell upon the rights of Baltimore, the latter commissioned a new governor for Maryland,[1] and drew up an agreement for the surrender of the province to him,[2] but instructed his governor to require an oath of allegiance and submission from all taking out land warrants.[3] These promises and instructions were discussed between Governor Fendall and the Cromwellian commissioners,[4] and the latter insisted upon a number of changes in them. As finally adopted [5] the agreement bound Baltimore to make no question concerning the acts of officials during the late years; fees and taxes arising during the period were to be paid, and the old oath of fidelity was not to be pressed, the people, however, engaging to submit to the proprietor's authority. A special provision was inserted prohibiting any political disqualifications on account of the late disorders. It was agreed

"That no person whatsoever within this Province shall (by reason of Any Act or Passage made or don in relation to the late Alteration of the Government made in the yeare one thousand Six hundred fifty-two) bee deemed or hereafter made vncapable of Electing, or to be Elected to all future Assemblies." [6]

By these provisions the Protestants and the anti-proprietary party hoped to shield themselves against any return of persecution upon themselves. All were expected to assent to

---

Religion so as they abuse not this liberty to the injury of others The disturbance of the publique peace on their part, Provided that this Liberty be not Extended to popery or prelacy nor to such as under the profession of Christ hold forth and practice Licentiousness."

See *Md. Hist. Soc. Fund Pub.*, No. 7, 91–3, for treatment of Catholics.

[1] July 10, 1656. *Archives, Council, 1636–67*, 323.

[2] Nov. 30, 1657, *ibid.*, 332. Baltimore promised that he would not question any of the recent offences, never repeal the act for liberty of conscience, but would permit those who had been in opposition to take up land in accordance with earlier conditions, and would not interfere with those desiring to leave the province within a year's time.

[3] *Archives, Council, 1636–67*, 335–39.

[4] *Ibid.*, 369.

[5] On March 24, 1657–8, *Archives, Assembly, 1637–64*, 369. [6] *Ibid.*

the new settlement, and those who refused to agree were, by the governor's proclamation, to be proceeded against as " Rebbells & traitors." [1]

It is not necessary for our purpose to enter into the details of the strange conspiracy of Baltimore's governor, Fendall, which came shortly after this settlement, except to notice that an incidental result was the disfranchisement of those interested in it.[2] This disfranchisement may have been the cause for the explicit statement of the power of the sheriff in elections, which was made in the spring of 1661. In answer to a protest from the lower house, the governor and council said that the sheriffs had the right to restrain those not legally qualified from voting or from being elected to office, and that no one having committed a crime could be elected.[3]

The period from 1649 to 1661 was one of great confusion in Maryland. The proprietary dues were onerous to the colonists, and his religion must have been obnoxious to many of them. In the contests which arose in the colony, the differences were not settled at the polls, but by physical force. Hence, in order to maintain in the elections what force had gained, it was often necessary to introduce political disfranchisement, and this is the principal characteristic of the period. The victorious party disfranchised its opponents, and then had the pleasure of witnessing unanimous elections.[4] Before restoring the colony to Baltimore, the Protestants exacted a promise that they should not be dis-

[1] *Archives, Council, 1636-67,* 352-3. Among those refusing to sign the agreement were some Quakers.

[2] For the principal facts of this period, see Browne, *Maryland, the History of a Palatinate,* 93-103. See *Archives, Council, 1636-67,* 404-418, for cases of disfranchisement. Three members of the assembly who had joined Fendall were debarred from public office for seven years, and rendered incapable of electing or being elected to any future assembly unless the governor should pardon them. Fendall and Gerrard were permitted to keep their property, but were forever disfranchised (*ibid.,* 406, 407). A later attempt was made to elect Fendall to the legislature (*Archives, Council, 1671-81,* 192).

[3] *Archives, Assembly, 1637-64,* 395-98.

[4] See the election of 1654, previously mentioned.

franchised for their late conduct. The period closes with the Fendall conspiracy and new political punishments.

The next change in the suffrage was upon a totally different basis. The religious restrictions were not revived until 1688, but the new movement was for a property qualification upon voters. It has been seen upon what a broad basis the early suffrage rested; and during all the period of civil strife no effort appears to have been made to restrict the suffrage to freeholders or those holding a certain amount of property. Writing in 1666, George Alsop could say respecting the assembly,

"These men that determine on these matters for the Republique are called Burgesses, and they commonly sit in Junto about six weeks, being for the most part good ordinary Householders of the several Counties, which do more by a plain and honest Conscience than by artificial Syllogisms drest up in gilded Orations." [1]

A conflict of interests between the freeholders and the landless freemen is first evident from the records in 1666, when the project for a general cessation of tobacco planting was under discussion. The price of tobacco had fallen so low that it was proposed to unite Maryland, Virginia, and North Carolina in a general agreement to restrict the production of their great staple. The lower house opposed this suggestion of the council upon the ground that it would have a tendency to drive out the greater part of the population, and thus deprive the province of the strong young freemen.[2] The upper house rejoined that there was no place to which the freemen could go, since Virginia also would cease tobacco production; but even if they should leave, they might thereby strengthen the position of the freeholders, and the council protested they would not keep the freemen if they must thereby ignore the welfare of the freeholders. The freeholders, the upper house continued, "are the Strength & only Strength of this Province, not the Freemen. It is their persons, purses, & Stocks must bear the Burthen of the Government, both in Peace & War & not Freemen, who can

---

[1] *A Character of the Province of Maryland*, London, 1666; reprinted in *Md. Hist. Soc. Fund Pub.*, 1880, No. 15, 47.

[2] *Archives, Assembly, 1666–76*, 44 ff.

easily abandon Us." [1]   These reasons convinced the lower house, and after " takeing them into their serious Consideration & debateing thereupon" they replied that they " doe rest sattisfyed." [2]   The proprietor, however, disapproved of this law, in spite of the assent of Virginia and North Carolina, urging that it would hurt his majesty's customs and would injure the poor settlers of the province who had so recently been sacrificed by the assembly.[3]

The assembly of 1666 had ignored the economic rights of the poor freemen, but shortly afterwards a further step against them was taken by the refusal to permit them to exercise the political privileges they had enjoyed since the founding of the colony.   The movement towards a restricted suffrage was taken up by the governor, and on December 18, 1670, a proprietary writ directed the sheriffs to admit as electors only those freemen of the counties who possessed a visible seated plantation of at least fifty acres of land, or owned a visible personal estate of forty pounds at the least. The same qualifications were imposed upon deputies.[4]

[1] *Archives, Assembly, 1666–76,* 47.
[2] *Ibid.,* 49.
[3] *Archives, Council, 1636–67,* 561.
[4] *Ibid.,* 77–8.

" These are to authorize and require you to call together this prest month of december four or more of the Commissioners of your County with the Clerk whom you are hereby required to impower to sit as a Court and during their sitting by Virtue of your Office to make or Cause to be made publick Proclamation thereby giving notice to all the freemen of your said County who [have] within the said County Visible seated Plantations of fifty Acres of Land at the least or Visible personal Estates to the Value of forty Pounds Sterling at the least requiring them to appear at the next County Court to be holden for the said County at a Certain day in the month next following after such Proclamation made for the election and choosing of Deputies and Delegates to serve for your said County in a General Assembly shortly after to be called by special writ at which time and place according to the said Proclamation the said freemen so required to appear or the Major Part of such of them as shall thereupon appear shall and may and are hereby Authorized and required to elect and

About the same time the settlement at St. Mary's was given separate representation; the mayor, recorder, aldermen, and common council having the right to elect the two delegates from the city.[1] This corporation franchise was used in Maryland by the governors in the same way as the kings used the borough elections in England. Charles Calvert, writing to his father the proprietor, on April 26, 1672, describes the manner in which the new city privileges could be taken advantage of by the proprietary party.

"Mr. Nottly is now Speaker of or Assembly, hee and Mr. John Moorecraft beinge Chossen Burgesses for the Citty of St. Maries, And by that Meanes I gott him into the Assembly, Though Doctor Wharton bee a good vnderstandinge Man yett Dr. Morecraft is much more for our purpose, being the best Lawyer in the Country, and has alwayes been (vpon other Assemblyes) A great Asserter of yor Lopps Charter and the Rights & priviledges thereof, I durst not putt itt to an Election in the Countyes Butt took this way which I Knew would Certainely doe what I desired." [2]

The limitation of political power was carried a step farther in 1674, when the assembly passed a law requiring grand jurors to be chosen from the freeholders of the respective counties.[3]

In 1675 the proprietor, Charles Calvert, came to the province, and in the spring of the next year issued writs for the election of four deputies from each county to the assembly,[4] apparently retaining the property qualifications as laid down in 1670. After the elections had been completed, the proprietor summoned only two of the four elected delegates from each county. The assembly thus constituted protested against the action of the proprietor in refusing to summon

choose four several sufficient freemen of your said County each of them having a visible seated Plantation of fifty Acres of Land at the least or a Visible personal Estate of Forty Pounds Sterling at the least within your said County."

[1] Mereness, *Maryland as a Proprietary Province*, 200.
[2] *Maryland Hist. Soc. Fund Pub., Calvert Papers*, 264.
[3] *Archives, Assembly, 1666–76*, 392.
[4] *Ibid.*, 507 ff.; *Council, 1671–81*, 127–140; *Council, 1687–93*, 102–103.

the other deputies, and petitioned him to admit to the assembly as many deputies as the writs directed should be elected in each county. The proprietor acceded to this request upon the condition that the members of assemblies should take an oath of allegiance to the proprietor before they elected their speaker.[1]

Baltimore left the province shortly after the meeting of this assembly, and in the following fall the heavy taxes and the limitations upon the suffrage were criticised in a paper which the proprietary party called a seditious document issued "under the specious pretences of the preservation of The Liberties of the ffreemen of this Province."[2] An attempt at armed rebellion by some sixty inhabitants of Calvert County on Sunday, September 3, 1676, failed, and on the following day a general pardon was proclaimed.[3] The grievances of the rebels were the heavy taxes, the poll-tax which required poor freemen to pay as much as the rich, and the terms of the proprietary writs which excluded poor freemen from the suffrage.[4]

The governor and council replied to the charges of the rebels in "a Remonstrance of the true State of the Province & of the causes & reasons of the publique Taxes."[5] They placed the necessity for the heavy taxes upon the Indian wars and the expenses for protection, and justified the equal poll-taxes by the argument that poor freemen were compelled to pay for themselves alone, while the rich were taxed for all their servants and slaves. Their answer to the charge of restricted suffrage was more elaborate, and as expressing the seventeenth century theory of representation and suffrage is worth quoting entire:

[1] *Archives, Assembly, 1666–76,* 507.

[2] *Archives, Council, 1671–81,* 127.

[3] *Ibid.,* 128. Four named persons were outlawed. This movement should be compared to the Bacon Rebellion in Virginia.

[4] *Ibid.,* 137. The ideas of the protest are not expressed in the clearest words: "the debarring of some ffreemen who have nothing to entitle them to a being in this Province, from voting in the Choice of Delegates for makeing of the Laws."

[5] *Ibid.,* 137–140.

"As to the votes of ffreemen who have neither lands nor visible personall Estate, in the Eleccon of Delegates for the Assembly wee doe say, that as the Lord Proprietary can call assemblys by his Patent whensoever & in what manner to him shall seeme most fitt & convenient, Itt is no wonder that he should chuse this as the fittest & most convenient manner, & most agreeable to the Lawe and Custome of England For what man in England can be admitted to the Election of Parliament men that hath not a visible Estate in lands or Goods? nay are there not infinite numbers concluded [sic] in Parliament without vote in the Elections, though they have great Estates both in lands & Goods? As namely all unmarryed women be their Estates in lands never so great, & all bothe men & woman living out of Corporations, haveing no Estates in land be their Personall Estates never so considerable This we say so to the point of reason & law. But if itt be thought an unkinde way of preceeding with the poore ffreeman, or that the ffreeman be dearer To the ffreeholder then himselfe his Wife children & fortune, & that they will needs Submitt themselves & all that is deare to them to be disposed of by the votes of the ffreemen that have nothing, & that can as easily carry themselves out of the reach of Lawes by themselves made, to the prejudice of the ffreeholder as change their Cloaths Wee doe promise to propound the case of the indigent ffreemen to his Lord^{pp} att his returne & to offer him such reasons & motives as may incline him to permitt the next Election to be made by the Votes of all the ffreemen indifferently. this is all that lyes in our powers to doe in this case, & this we doubt not but to Obtaine from his Lordshipp, if the quiett demeanour of the ffreemen in the interim doe but concurr with our Endeavours, to Oblige his Lordshipp to have a favorable regard of their Interests."

The view given in this proclamation is the one we have seen advanced ten years earlier and gradually gaining strength. Two years after the armed attempt to withstand this restricting tendency, the suffrage limitation was established by law. The assembly of October and November, 1678, after discussing elections and the suffrage at considerable length, passed the first general election law of the province.[1] The act remained in force but a short time, being

[1] *Archives, Assembly, 1678–83,* 24–37 *passim.* The records of this session are badly mutilated, and it is difficult to discern the respective

5

disapproved by the proprietor in 1681;[1] but its terms were
in part inserted into the proprietary writs and copied almost
verbatim in the election law of 1692.[2] For these reasons
the provisions of the act of 1678 have a value not implied
by the short duration of the act itself. Although the act
followed closely the forms prescribed in the proprietary writ
of 1670, yet it met with Baltimore's disapproval, perhaps
because it was passed in an assembly not organized according to his wishes, and because it placed the number of delegates at four from each county.[3]

In its preamble the act[4] reverts to the English custom,
and declares the "best rule for this Province to follow in
Electing such Delegates & representatives is the presidents
[precedents] of the Proceedings in Parliament in England
as neere as the Constitution of this Province will admitt."
The act provided for the election of four burgesses in each
county and two citizens from the city of St. Mary's. A
form of election writ is given in the act, and within the writ
occur the qualifications for the suffrage. The sheriff is
directed

" . . . by vertue of your office to make or Cause to be made Publick
Proclamacon thereby giveing notice to all the freemen of your said
County who have within your said County a freehold of fifty acres
of Land or a visible personall Estate of forty pounds starling att
least Requireing them to appeare att the next County Court . . . at a
Certaine day . . . for the electing and Chusing of Deputyes and delegates to serve for your County in a Generall Assembly. . . . "

The two representatives for the city of St. Mary's were to
be chosen by the mayor, recorder, aldermen, and common

---

views of the assembly and council. Apparently the council wished to
retain the qualification "seated" pertaining to the elector's freehold,
which had been included in the proprietary writ of 1670; while the
lower house opposed this. The upper house finally agreed to the
omission of the word (*ibid.*, 31).

[1] By proclamation of June 27, 1681, *Archives, Council, 1671-81*, 378.
[2] See *post.*
[3] *Archives, Council, 1671-81*, 378; *Assembly, 1684-92*, 79.
[4] "An act directing the manner of Electing and Summoning Delegates and Representatives to serve in succeeding Assemblyes." *Archives, Assembly, 1678-83*, 60 ff.

council of that city. Delegates were to possess within the county represented the qualifications required of electors. No sheriff or under-sheriff could sit in the lower house during his term of office, and no ordinary keeper could be elected or serve in the assembly while keeping an ordinary. The property qualifications of this act were later adopted by the proprietor and by subsequent legislatures, and in the form of fifty acres of freehold or forty pounds personal estate they continued with but slight change down to the Revolution.

Lord Baltimore expressed his disapproval of the election act of 1678 in a public proclamation, by which he changed the number of delegates for each county from four to two;[1] and shortly afterwards, on September 6, 1681, he fixed the electoral process by means of a proprietary ordinance.[2] In the preamble to this ordinance it was stated that the method of assembling the deputies of the freemen had, from the foundation of the province, been uncertain, and that the proprietor now desired to settle the minds of the freemen and establish a sure foundation for the future peace of the province. The ordinance gave the form of writ containing the suffrage qualifications in exactly the words used by the statute of 1678; it provided, however, for the election of but two delegates in every county or any corporation having the charter right to elect deputies, and fixed the same property qualifications for voters in the cities or towns as for those in the counties. The promulgation of this ordinance led to a long contest in the following assembly, but the upper house supported the legality and propriety of Baltimore's ordinance.[3] The assembly of 1683 also took up the matter, and three bills concerning the election of delegates were introduced, but apparently they failed to receive the proprietor's approval.[4] Thus during the period 1670–1689 proprietary ordinances or writs were the foundation, under the royal charter, for the suffrage and the representative system. The

[1] *Archives, Council, 1671–81,* 378.
[2] *Ibid., 1681–86,* 15–17; McMahon. *History of Maryland,* 443–5.
[3] *Archives, Assembly, 1678–83,* 345 360 ff.
[4] *Ibid.,* 445–604 *passim.*

terms of the original writ of 1670 were accepted by the legislature in 1678 with but slight change, and these changes
incorporated into the ordinance of 1681.

After almost thirty years of religious quiet in the colony,
the spirit of faction and religious strife again appeared in
the train of similar conditions in England. As the Puritan
movement in England sent its waves of influence into the
province of Maryland, so the Revolution of 1688 was re-
acted in miniature in America. It was unfortunate for the
peace of Maryland that in 1688 the proprietor was not present in person in the colony, and that the administration was
in the hands of the council acting under a president [1] as
deputy governors. The assembly meeting in the fall of 1688
began with factional disputes. The president asked both
houses to take the oath of allegiance to the proprietor, and
when the lower house refused to do so, he prorogued the
assembly and in the meantime exercised his legal right to
administer the oath to the deputies as individuals.[2] Assembling after the prorogation, the lower house drew up a list
of eight grievances against the proprietary government,
dealing largely with economic evils. Among these were the
proprietor's demand for quit-rents in money when he had
promised to receive them in tobacco; the failure to establish
ports; the collection of illegal fees; the meeting of the provincial court in the inconvenient winter time; and the ar-
resting persons without stating the cause of the arrest.[3]
There is no mention in these grievances of any violation of
real religious or political rights; they are mainly administrative details which proved unpopular.

The following year a stronger opposition to the government was shown. The proprietor's agents in Maryland took
no steps to proclaim the new monarchs of England, and this
delay gave strength to rumors of Catholic plots and conspiracies with the Indians.[4] An association of the discon-

[1] For the character of President ·William Joseff, see B. C. Steiner,
The Protestant Revolution in Maryland, Amer. Hist. Assn. Rept., 1897,
283–287.

[2] *Archives, Assembly, 1684–92,* 148–63.

[3] *Ibid.,* 170.

[4] Upon this period, see Browne, *Maryland, the History of a Pala-*

tented was formed called " An Association in arms for the defense of the Protestant religion, and for asserting the right of King William and queen Mary to the province of Maryland, and all the English dominions." [1] Coode, the leader of the movement, and his men marched on St. Mary's, compelled the president and council to surrender, and required the exclusion of all Catholics from office.[2] The leader then sent writs for an election by the Protestants of members to a convention, the writs being issued in the name of " the several commanders, officers, and gentlemen associated in arms for the defense of the Protestant religion." [3] The elections of deputies were carried through very irregularly; in one county it was claimed that only twenty persons participated in the election and one-half of these were not legally qualified.[4] In other cases the " better sort of the people" held aloof, those of mean and humble position alone supporting Coode, while drunken soldiers helped the cause of the revolutionists.[5] One writer said,

" They have assumed the power of calling an Assembly the Election of which was in most Countyes awed by their souldiers, one County disowned their power and would chuse noe members but in fine they have packed up an Assembly after the most irregular manner that ever was knowne. . . ." [6]

The convention thus elected held perhaps five sessions during the next two years,[7] at one of which they appointed a representative committee composed of two persons from each of ten counties to administer the government.[8]

---

tinate, 149–156; B. C. Steiner, *The Protestant Revolution in Maryland, passim;* F. E. Sparks, *Causes of the Maryland Revolution of 1689, J. H. U. Studies,* XIV.

[1] McMahon, 237; Browne, 152; Steiner, 299–306.

[2] *Archives, Council, 1687–93,* 107.

[3] McMahon, 240.

[4] *Archives, Council, 1687–93,* 154.

[5] *Ibid.,* 114–118.

[6] *Ibid.,* 124.

[7] Steiner, *op. cit.,* 345, 351.

[8] *Ibid.,* 326, 333–4.

In many of these details the movement in Maryland closely parallels that which took place at the same time in New York. There is this difference, however, that in the royal province of New York the revolution was unnecessary from the Crown's point of view, while in Maryland the uprising gave the new monarchs an opportunity to seize control of a province whose proprietor might justly be suspected of friendship for the Catholic cause of James II. William informally recognized the revolution in Maryland,[1] and later took advantage of it to establish a royal government in the colony. The overturning of the proprietor's government led to the exclusion of Catholics from all political power; they had no share in the election of the convention, which was the nominal seat of authority for over two years, and they were excluded from all military and civil offices.

It was but natural that Baltimore's political privileges should be declared forfeited[2] and a royal government appointed for the colony. Governor Copley's commission[3] directed him to call assemblies of the freemen of the province according to the usage of the province, but required the delegates to take the oaths and test enjoined by the acts of Parliament, thereby excluding Catholics from the assembly. Nothing was said, however, about restraining the Catholics from voting. The instructions to Copley in plain terms limited the suffrage to freeholders:

" You shall take care that the Members of the Assembly be elected only by Freeholders as being most agreeable to the Custome of England to which you are as near as may be to conform yourself." [4]

The first assembly under the royal government met in May and June, 1692, and at once the question of the oaths arose.[5] The election committee of the lower house had a number of cases before it [6] arising out of election irregulari-

---

[1] *Archives, Council, 1687–93,* 167.

[2] *Ibid.,* 185.

[3] June 27, 1691, *Archives, Council, 1687–93,* 263.

[4] *Archives, Council, 1687–93,* 271.

[5] *Archives, Assembly, 1684–92,* 254.

[6] *Ibid.,* 352–366.

ties and refusals to take the oaths; it reported Colonel Codd disqualified because of seditious practices, and of John Hewitt it said that, " being a man in sacred orders is thought not fitt to sitt as a member of the Lower house." [1] The assembly early took up the subject of elections, and an act regulating them was sent from the lower house and agreed to by the upper house apparently without debate.[2] This law, entitled " An Act directing the manner of Ellects and summoning Delegates and Representatives to serve in succeeding assemblyes," [3] gave definite statutory form to elections and the representative system, both of which had previously rested upon the writs and ordinances of the proprietor. The legislature reverted to the old act of 1678 in organizing the elective system; the new act was almost a literal copy of the earlier law. The preamble was the same, the property qualification was unchanged, and the number of delegates from each county was restored to four, as it had been before the proprietor's ordinance of 1681. The prohibition upon the sheriffs or under-sheriffs serving in the lower house was, however, removed, but that against ordinary keepers was retained. In agreeing to this measure with its personal property qualifications the governor acted contrary to his instructions, which we have noticed directed him to see that freeholders only should vote for assembly delegates; but he may have felt warranted in doing this owing to the twenty years of colonial practice preceding his administration. No restriction is placed upon Catholics by the act, and it is likely that they were now or shortly afterwards permitted to vote,[4] although the oaths required of officeholders would exclude them from political positions. Later acts, indeed, attempted to prevent the growth of

---

[1] *Archives, Assembly, 1684–92*, 359. Hewitt, after being informed of the action of the committee, was requested to give the house a sermon on the following day, being Sunday (364).

[2] *Ibid.*, 394.

[3] *Ibid.*, 541.

[4] See terms of act of 1718, *post*. Mereness, *Maryland*, 200, says Catholics were disfranchised from the beginning of the royal government, but I have found no evidence of this exclusion. There can be no doubt that they voted before 1718.

Catholicism by imposing a fine of fifty pounds upon popish priests who should baptize Protestant children or hold mass in the province, and sentenced such priests to banishment if they were found teaching school in the province;[1] but there was no formal exclusion of Catholics from the suffrage until a quarter of a century after the Protestant Revolution.

The act of 1692 continued in force about twelve years, and in the fall of 1704 it was displaced by a new election law. This new act made some slight changes in the electoral machinery, but it retained the qualifications for voters as they had previously existed; again the sheriffs were directed to admit to the suffrage " all the freemen of your said County who have within your said County a freehold of fifty acres of land or a visible estate of forty pounds sterl. at the least."[2] An act of 1708[3] apparently did not make any change in the suffrage requirements.

Governor Nicholson, the second of the royal governors, removed the seat of government to Annapolis, perhaps to avoid the Catholic influence at St. Mary's; and later, in 1708, the new capital was incorporated as a city, taking the place of St. Mary's.[4] The charter of Annapolis at first limited the suffrage for assembly delegates to the mayor, recorder, aldermen, and common councilmen, as had been done in St. Mary's; but the lower house of assembly objected to this, and even questioned the power of the governor to erect municipal corporations. When the lower house expelled the Annapolis members on these grounds, the governor

[1] Chap. 59 of 1704, given by title only in Bacon's *Laws*, but in full in *Acts of Assembly Passed in the Province of Maryland From 1692 to 1715, London, 1723*, 24. For the position of the Catholics from 1690 to 1718, see Shea, *Catholic Church in Colonial Days*, 344–373. An act of 1715 (Ch. XXXVI, Bacon's *Laws*), for various purposes and " to prevent the Importing too great a Number of Irish Papists into this Province," laid a duty of twenty shillings on Irish servants coming to Maryland. See also acts of 1717, Ch. 10, and 1732, Ch. 23.

[2] Chap. 35 of 1704, given by title only in Bacon's *Laws;* but writ given in Bishop, *History of Elections in American Colonies*, 251.

[3] Chap. 5 of 1708.

[4] Browne, *Maryland*, 167; Mereness, *Maryland*, 200; McMahon, 251–253.

replied by a dissolution of the assembly. But the corporation officers and inhabitants petitioned the governor to change the charter so as to extend the suffrage to the inhabitants of the city, and this request was granted.[1] An act of assembly subsequently confirmed and explained the charter granted by the governor.[2] The charter as amended gave the right to vote for the two city delegates in assembly to freeholders owning a whole lot of land with a house thereon, to all inhabitants (householders?) having a visible estate of twenty pounds, and to those who had served a five years' apprenticeship to a trade within the city, had held their freedom for three months, and were actual housekeepers and inhabitants of the city.[3] In the same year, 1708, St. Mary's lost its right to send deputies to the assembly.[4] Thus in Maryland, as in many of the other colonies, the borough suffrage was wider than that granted to inhabitants of the country districts. In this case the freehold qualification was changed from fifty acres to a town lot, the personal property test became twenty in place of forty pounds, and householders who had served an apprenticeship in the city could vote, no matter how small an amount of property they held.

In 1715 the election law was changed somewhat when the whole body of laws of the colony was revised. The act of June 3, 1715,[5] retained the fifty acres and forty pounds clauses, but required electors who voted under the personal property clause to be residents of the county. Ordinary keepers were again excluded from the assembly, and the disqualification was extended to persons who by the laws of England would not be qualified to sit in Parliament. The most interesting of all the additions made by this law [6] to the provisions of the earlier act of 1692 is one for the imposing of fines upon non-voters. All freeholders, freemen,

---

[1] Mereness, *Maryland,* 200–1, 420–22.

[2] Bacon's *Laws,* 1708, Ch. VII.

[3] McMahon, *Maryland,* 255.

[4] *Ibid.*

[5] Chap. 42, 1715. *Acts of Assembly Passed in the Province of Maryland from 1692 to 1715,* London, 1723, 121. Given by title only in Bacon's *Laws.*

[6] Not having access to the laws of 1704 and 1708, I cannot be sure that these changes were first introduced in 1715.

or other persons qualified to vote were subject to a fine of one hundred pounds of tobacco if they neglected to attend the elections, unless they gave a sufficient reason for absence to the county court. The features of this law were adopted in full in 1716,[1] when a new law directed that election writs should run in the name of the proprietor instead of the king's, and with this slight change the act of 1715 continued without alteration until after the Revolution.[2]

The year 1715 saw the restoration of the province to the proprietor after his acceptance of Protestantism.[3] The first assembly under the proprietor, in 1716, passed " An Act for the better Security of the Peace and Safety of his Lordship's Government, and the Protestant Interest within this province." [4] This act required all persons admitted to positions of trust in the province to take the oaths of allegiance, of abhorrency, of abjuration, and the disavowal of the belief in transubstantiation in the forms prescribed in the English statutes.[5] The Maryland act on this subject was closely similar to those passed in other colonies immediately following the Jacobite uprising of 1715, and hence was not peculiar. But two years later a special act directed at the Catholics was passed. This was in the form of a supplement to the election act, and again revived the disfranchisement policy which was first adopted in the days of the commonwealth. Section III of this act provided for a disfranchisement of the Catholics, which was unrepealed in 1776.

[1] Bacon's *Laws,* 1716, Ch. XI.

[2] With the exception of the act of 1718 concerning Catholic electors, there is no further legislation upon the suffrage. An act of 1732 (Bacon's *Laws,* 1732, Ch. V) for preventing bribery in elections in Annapolis was disapproved by the proprietor. Another act of 1769 (Hanson's *Laws,* 1769, Ch. X) shows how long the polls might remain open. It provided that in Baltimore County the elections for delegates should be open for not more than four days in Baltimore-town, and then to be adjourned to Bush-town, where they might remain open during four more days.

[3] Benedict Leonard, Lord Baltimore, 1714–15, had, before his succession to the title, publicly renounced Catholicism.

[4] Bacon's *Laws,* 1716, Ch. V.

[5] 1 George I, Ch. 13.

" III. And whereas notwithstanding all the Measures that have been hitherto taken for preventing the Growth of Popery within this Province, it is very obvious, that not only profest Papists still multiply and increase in Number, but that there are also too great Numbers of others that adhere to and espouse their Interest, in Opposition to the Protestant Establishment: And being under just Apprehensions (from what steps they have already taken) that if Papists should continue to be allowed their vote in electing of Delegates, they, with their Adherents, and those under their Influence, will make such a Party at the Elections of many of the counties within this Province, as well as the City of Annapolis, as to determine the Choice in some, of their great Favorites and Adherents, which if they should accomplish, how much it would tend to the Discouragement and Disturbance of his Lordship's Protestant Gov't, is not easy to imagine . . . therefore . . . be it Enacted . . . That all profest Papists whatsoever, be (and are hereby Declared) uncapable of giving their Vote in any Election of a Delegate or Delegates within this Province, either for Counties, Cities or Boroughs, unless they first qualify themselves for so doing, by taking the several Oaths appointed to be taken by an act of Assembly of this Province [1716, Ch. V] . . . and subscribe the Oath of Abjuration and Declaration therein mentioned." [1]

In order that no Catholic might elude the terms of the act, the election judges were authorized to administer the oath to " any person suspected to be a Papist or popishly inclined" whenever the judges saw fit, or when demanded by a qualified voter. A saving clause protected Quakers from suffering with the Catholics.

An act disfranchising the Catholics at as late a period as 1718 could have but scanty justification. There had indeed been some Jacobite sympathizers in Maryland who had committed indiscretions,[2] but this was not sufficient warrant for excluding all Catholics from voting. Neither were the numbers of the Catholics alarming, for in 1708 only 2974 Catholics were found by the sheriffs in a total population exceeding 40,000.[3] The words of the act itself justify its provisions upon the grounds of the recent growth of Catholicism, and the fear of discouragement and disturbance of Baltimore's

[1] Bacon's *Laws,* 1718.
[2] Browne, *Maryland,* 208.
[3] Johnson, *Founding of Maryland,* etc., *Md. Hist. Soc. Fund Pub.,* No. 18, 167.

Protestant government. But these phrases are so vague that they throw little light upon the motives of the assembly. It may be that the newly restored proprietary family desired to show the strength of their fresh Protestantism by positive acts against the Catholics,[1] or that the inhabitants of the province wished a guarantee against the return of the Catholics to political power through a future conversion of Baltimore to Catholicism. The members of the sect which was responsible for the original settlement of the province were now disfranchised, their religion was outlawed, while even the proprietor was estranged from them and now gave his assent to laws for their persecution.

There is little to be said concerning the suffrage in local elections. By far the greater number of local officials were appointed, either by the county court, by the governor, by acts of the legislature, or by self-perpetuating boards. In 1649 and 1650 acts were passed for the election of local tax assessors in the several hundreds of certain counties,[2] but this policy was not continued. In the cities of St. Mary's and Annapolis and the towns the officers in all but two instances were either self-perpetuating bodies or appointed by other officials.[3] Practically the only elective local officials were the officers of the parish,—the vestrymen and the church wardens. By the church act of 1692[4] the county courts were to call to their assistance the "most principall freeholders" of the counties and arrange the bounds of parishes. In each parish the freeholders were to elect six vestrymen, but after the first election the vestry could fill vacancies in their own number from the freeholders of the parish. Ten years later some changes were introduced. An act of 1701–2[5] provided that two of the six vestrymen should be elected annually by the inhabitants of the parish who were

---

[1] McMahon, 279–281. In note 3, p. 281, McMahon describes the social ostracism which was added to the political disfranchisement of the Catholics.

[2] *Archives, Assembly, 1637–64,* 238, 298.

[3] Mereness, *Maryland,* 419, mentions two cases of elective town officers.

[4] *Archives, Assembly, 1684–92,* 425.

[5] Bacon's *Laws,* 1701–2, Ch. I.

freeholders within the parish and contributed to the public taxes and charges of the parish. The act permitted the electors to determine which vestrymen should be retired, and provided for the election of the church wardens by the vestry and freeholders. A later act [1] provided for a regular rotation in the office of vestryman. Throughout the colonial period the vestry elections were more limited than the suffrage for the assembly; in the former elections only tax-paying freeholders could vote, while in the latter freeholders of fifty acres or owners of forty pounds personal estate were entitled to the franchise, and in Annapolis the suffrage included many, if not all, householders.

The representative system and the suffrage in Maryland are based in the first instance upon the royal charter to Baltimore. The terms of this charter were ambiguous, and in practice in the colony for almost forty years a most liberal interpretation was given to them. Manhood suffrage, without regard to residence, the payment of taxes, the holding of land, or any other qualifications, was exercised in the early years of the colony. Those that were not free, *i.e.*, slaves and servants, were the only men excluded. In these early years an interesting system of proxy voting arose, and the assembly, somewhat like that of Rhode Island at almost the same time, alternated from pure democracy to representation of local units. This early manhood suffrage gave way in 1670 to the requirement that voters should possess fifty acres of land or an estate worth at least forty pounds sterling. This qualification, although based upon the proprietary writs until 1692, was later adopted by the provincial legislature, and was the only property qualification which the province of Maryland knew throughout its entire history. For over one hundred years it was the test required of all voters except those in Annapolis. The borough franchise was extended to St. Mary's and Annapolis; in the former it was limited to the officers of the corporation, while in the latter practically all householders were privileged to vote for assemblymen. An act of 1715 imposed a fine of one hundred pounds of tobacco upon qualified freemen who did not take

[1] Bacon's *Laws*, 1730, Ch. XXIII.

part in elections, and this provision remained unchanged until the Revolution.

The most marked feature of the suffrage in Maryland is the attitude towards the sect which had founded the colony. In 1654 they were excluded from the suffrage and office; again in 1689 the revolution temporarily disfranchised them, and after the restoration of the province to Baltimore the Catholics were, in 1718, permanently excluded from political rights. There were practically no local elections in the colony other than the vestry elections, and in these the suffrage was more limited than in the assembly elections, the franchise being restricted to inhabiting freeholders who paid parish taxes.

CHAPTER IV.

THE SUFFRAGE IN NORTH CAROLINA.

North Carolina, like her southern sister, passed through the two stages of proprietary and royal control, exchanging in 1728 the doubtful blessings of wide independence under a weak government for the exasperating restraint of royal instructions and peevish or incompetent governors. The history of the colony varies from an absence of political control which encouraged personal license to a measure of arbitrary actions and attempted coercion which fostered popular rebellion. Like a spoilt child the colony expressed its satisfaction with the weak rule of its proprietor parents, and, unlike South Carolina, the transfer of the government from proprietary to royal control found its main initiative in England rather than in the colony. When the southern colony was overthrowing the proprietor's officials and protesting against the inadequacy of their government, the inhabitants of the northern country expressed their utter detestation of such revolutionary proceedings, and wrote to the proprietors that they were "intirely easy and satisfied under their Lordships Government."[1]

The extremes of liberty on the one hand and of arbitrary government on the other are noticeable not only in the quitrent and currency questions and other matters of an economic nature, but also in the constitutional subjects of the suffrage and representation. After a period of extensive local control of these questions under the proprietors, the colony found itself, during the time of the royal government, at the mercy of the king's prerogative and the royal veto, which on one occasion were so used that they would have thrown the whole colony into the greatest confusion had not the governor wisely, but in contradiction to his instructions,

[1] *Colonial Records of North Carolina*, II, 375.

withheld from the people the knowledge of the royal veto.[1]
Perhaps in no other colony was the veto power used against
such important and popular measures as here in North Carolina.   While in South Carolina there is practically no break
in institutional development by the transfer of the government to the Crown, in North Carolina the change was accompanied by many interferences with the established laws and
customs.   Thus the story of the suffrage in this colony falls
distinctly into two parts, in the first of which the proprietors
place few restrictions upon their colonists, and in the second
the elective and representative systems are controlled by the
English government and its governors in North Carolina.

I. *Under the Proprietary Government, 1663–1728.*

The basis for popular suffrage in North Carolina, as in
the other proprietary colonies except New York, is to be
found in the royal charters to the lords proprietors, the first
of which is dated March 24, 1662–3.   It was, indeed, antedated by the charters to Raleigh[2] and Sir Robert Heath,[3]
but only the latter possessed any provision for popular participation in the government, and both were abrogated by
the Carolina charters of 1663 and 1665.   So, too, a few
land grants had been made and a few settlers from Virginia
had come into the Albemarle country before the Carolina
patents were passed under the royal seals,[4] but among these
earliest settlers we have no record of political organization.
Thus the political clauses of the charters to the eight proprietors may be quoted as the basis of the suffrage in Carolina.   The charter of 1663[5] gave to the proprietors full and
absolute power

"to ordaine, make, enact, and under their seals to publish any laws
whatsoever, either appertaining to the publick state of the said province,
or to the private utility of particular persons, according to their best

[1] See *post,* for the repeal of the representation and suffrage acts in
1754, and Governor Dobbs' withholding this knowledge for a time.
[2] Poore, *Charters and Constitutions,* II, 1379–1382.
[3] *N. C. Col. Rec.,* I, 5–13.
[4] *Ibid.,* 14–17.
[5] *Ibid.,* 20–33; Poore, *Charters and Constitutions,* II, 1382–1390.

discretion, of and with the advice, assent and approbation of the freemen of the said province, or of the greater part of them, or of their
delegates or deputies whom for enacting of the said laws, when and as
often as need shall require, we will that the said . . . [eight proprie-
tors] and their heirs shall from time to time assemble in such manner
and form as to them shall seem best, and the same laws duly to
execute. . . . "

The second charter to the eight proprietors, dated June 30,
1665,[1] gave the patentees the right to erect and constitute
counties, baronies, and colonies within their province, having
distinct jurisdiction and privileges, and in each one to make
and enact laws in a manner similar to that established by the
first charter. Both charters used the word freeman in first
describing the voters, but both referred subsequently to assemblies of the freeholders, and thus here, as in Maryland,
led to a confusion in the political practice under the charters.
We shall see the later interpretation put upon the word.

The proprietors proceeded almost at once to promise to
intending settlers the various privileges in popular government which the charter had directed should be granted to
colonists. In August, 1663, some New Englanders proposed
settling in Carolina, and asked that they be given the New
England privilege of levying taxes " upon themselves by
themselves." [2] In the same month the proprietors issued
proposals to settlers,[3] in which they promised the under-
takers in England that they might name thirteen persons
from whom the proprietors should select one for governor
of the colony and six for his council, and that a similar nomination and selection should be made every three years by
the freeholders of the colony or their representatives. To
this liberal method of choosing the higher officials the proprietors joined a promise of a popular legislative body elected
by the freeholders.[4]

" We shall, as far as our charter permits us, empower the major part
of the freeholders, or their deputies or assembly-men, to be by them

---

[1] *N. C. Col. Rec.*, I, 102–114; Poore, *Charters and Constitutions*, II,
1390–1397.
[2] *Ibid.*, 38.
[3] August 25, 1663; *ibid.*, 43–6.
[4] *N. C. Col. Rec.*, I, 45.

chosen out of themselves, viz.: two out of every tribe, division, or parish, in such manner as shall be agreed on, to make their own laws, by and with the advice and consent of the Governor and council;"

provided that such laws be not repugnant to the laws of England, and that within one year they be presented to the proprietors for their ratification. Religious liberty was also promised to the settlers, and each man was given the privilege of taking up one hundred acres of land for himself, fifty acres for each fully armed man-servant, and thirty acres for each woman-servant that he brought to the colony.

These proposals were sent to certain intending settlers who had suggested that they be erected into a corporation [1] with the privilege of choosing a mayor and other officers. The proprietors speak in favor of their more democratic way of government set down in the proposals, which, they say, " we hold to be better for the people in Generall then the Corporation way that you demand, in which the members choasen to manage the Government doe continew for there lives, and are not to be removed but by there owne fellowes or the Major parte of them, whoe may be apter to wincke at the misdemeanors of there fellow Governors then the people that are to be governed by them will." [2] According to the plan of the proposals, the lords continue, it will be in the power of the people every three years " to leave out such as have misbehaved themselves" in making their nominations for new officers to the proprietors. The same readiness to grant popular government is to be seen in the paper sent by the proprietors in England to the only one of their number resident in America, in which they empower proprietor Sir William Berkeley, governor of Virginia, to appoint one or two governors of Carolina and a council of six persons for each governor. [3] These governors and councillors, " by and with the advice and consent of the freeholders or freemen or the Major parte of them, there deputyes or delligates," were empowered to make good and wholesome laws for the better government of the colony or colonies. Thus,

[1] *N. C. Col. Rec.* I, 42.
[2] *Ibid.,* 58.
[3] *Ibid.,* 48–50.

in the earliest history of their province, the lords proprietors show no reluctance to fulfil the terms of their charter requiring a representative legislature.

A considerably more pretentious scheme of government was outlined in January, 1664–5, as part of an agreement between the Carolina proprietors and some intending settlers in England, Barbadoes, and New England, headed by Major William Yeamans.[1] With the many interesting details of these " Concessions and Agreement" we are not here concerned, although it may be noted that they are in many particulars exactly the same as the concessions granted by Berkeley and Carteret, two of the Carolina proprietors, to settlers in their other province of New Jersey.[2] The new agreement again looked to the establishment of several distinct governments, or " countyes," as they are called in the document, and provided for a representative assembly in each, elected by " the inhabitants being freemen or chief agents to others of ye countyes" aforesaid.[3] Much more liberal grants of land were made by this agreement of 1665 than by the earlier one of 1663, to the end " that the planting of the Countyes aforesd may bee the more speedily promoted." [4]

Throughout all this early period the terms freeman and freeholder are used interchangeably, as has been noted in some of the other colonies. The royal charter had used the words synonymously, and the proprietors had merely retained the ambiguity of the charter when they directed in the concessions that elections should be by the freemen and, in another place in the same document, by the freeholders. There seems no question that the early suffrage was usually limited to freeholders, but later the identity of the two classes was lost, and in the period 1715–1734 the class of freemen, as in Maryland and South Carolina at an earlier date, was held to be wider than the class of freeholders.[5]

Another important feature of this early constitution-

---

[1] *N. C. Col. Rec.,* I, 75–92.
[2] See *New Jersey Colonial Archives,* I, 28–43.
[3] *N. C. Col. Rec.,* I, 81.
[4] *Ibid.,* 86.
[5] See *post,* act of 1734.

making is seen in the attempt of the proprietors to divide their province into distinct colonies.   This policy was strengthened by the difficulties of communication between the northern and southern parts of the province, and by the commercial association of the north with Virginia and the economic independence of the south.   These facts made the ultimate division of the province a probability, but the proprietors looked forward to several, perhaps eight, distinct principalities within their grant.   This is seen in their first instructions to Governor Berkeley; it is frequently mentioned in their concessions of 1665; distinct governments were formally permitted by the second royal charter of 1665, and the early policy of the proprietors continually encouraged the settlement of distinct groups of emigrants under independent governments.[1]   It was not the fault of the proprietors that their province did not contain several rather than only two governments; had the various proposed or attempted settlements succeeded, there would have been more than two Carolinas.   As it was, the policy of the proprietors accorded well with the geographical and economic separation of the two successful colonies, and made a separation that was almost inevitable come without acrimony on either side.[2]

Political organization in the Albemarle lands, already populated by settlers from Virginia, begins shortly after the granting of the royal charter.   A general assembly, in a letter written in June, 1665,[3] is referred to as having sent a petition to the proprietors.   William Drummond, the first governor of the county, promises the commissioners of Maryland and Virginia that he will call a meeting of his council and " committee" to consider the cessation of tobacco-planting;[4] and some time between July and October, 1666, this " committee," or assembly, met and passed a law restricting

---

[1] *N. C. Col. Rec.,* I, 48–50; 75–92 *passim;* 102–114 *passim;* and Prefatory Notes, xiv–xv; III, 574. Compare the division of New Jersey into two sections.

[2] Note the excitement attendant upon the separation of the Delaware Counties from the province of Pennsylvania.

[3] *Ibid.,* 101.

[4] *Ibid.,* 142.

the planting of tobacco.[1] In the same year in another colony to the southward, on the Cape Fear River, an assembly of fourteen persons sent a formal and elaborate petition to the proprietors.[2] But of these early assemblies in Albemarle and Clarendon Counties we know little. Unfortunately, we do not possess for North Carolina those personal details of politics and elections which are so interesting in the early history of South Carolina. Only by obscure references do we know that these assemblies have met; they have left no formal record either of their elections or of their acts as representative bodies.

When the proprietors commissioned a new governor for Albemarle County in October, 1667, they appear to have been contented with the outline of government and land policy given in their concessions two years earlier, for the principal features of the concessions are repeated in the instructions to the new governor, Samuel Stephens.[3] But this comparatively simple form of government was soon displaced, at least in the minds of the proprietors, by the aristocratic and elaborate features of the Fundamental Constitutions. Setting aside the details of palatines, landgraves, and cassiques, of seigniories, baronies, and colonies, and of courts baron and leet, we notice in the Constitutions for the first time a clear definition of the suffrage and office-holding qualifications. The " First Set" of the Constitutions, containing one hundred and eleven sections, dated July 21, 1669, has been published only recently.[4] It begins with the well-known statement that the Constitutions are established in order that " ye governmt. of this province may be made most agreable unto ye monarchy under wch. we live, & of wch. this province is a part, & yt we may avoid erecting a numerous democracy." Thus the provisions of the charters requiring a popular representative body were to be carefully

[1] *N. C. Col. Rec.*, I, 152.
[2] *Ibid.*, 145–149. The Cape Fear settlement was doomed to failure. See *N. C. Col. Rec.*, I, Prefatory Notes, x; 149–151, 157–159, 177–208; McCrady, *History of South Carolina under the Proprietary Government*, 79–93.
[3] *Ibid.*, 165–175.
[4] *Collections of South Carolina Historical Society*, V, 93–117.

balanced by the establishment of hereditary landed aristocracy.

The Constitutions contained, however, a number of sections dealing with elections. A parliament was to be formed out of the nobility and representatives of the freeholders, elected biennially, and the qualifications of members and electors were specified:

"There shall be a Parliamt consisting of ye proprietors or their deputyes ye landgraves and cassiques & one freeholder out of every presinct to be chosen by ye freeholders of ye sd. presinct respectively. They shall sit alltogether in one roome, & have every member one vote."

"No man shall be chosen a member of Parliamt. who hath lesse then five hundred acres of freehold within ye presinct for wch. he is chosen, nor shall any have a vote in choosing ye sd. member, yt hath lesse yn fifty acres of freehold within the said presinct."[1]

Other officers also elected by the freeholders were registers, constables and their assistants, and the common councilmen of incorporated towns. The possession of fifty acres did not have the same restrictive force in preventing a " numerous democracy" which a similar qualification would have possessed in England with its large tenant population. Any free man, in accordance with the concessions of the proprietors, could easily obtain more than sufficient to qualify him for the suffrage. There were three things required of the intending occupant of land: (1) that he acknowledge the existence of a God and that God is publicly and solemnly to be worshipped; (2) that he promise allegiance to the king, faithfulness to the proprietors, and obedience to the Fundamental Constitutions; (3) that after 1689 he pay a quit-rent of one penny an acre for all the land he occupied.[2] In the " Second Set" of constitutions, of March 1, 1669–70, the suffrage and representative features were the same as those in the first set.[3] A still later frame called the " Fifth

---

[1] *Collections of South Carolina Historical Society,* V, 110.

[2] *Ibid.,* 115–116; later changed to a half-penny an acre.

[3] *N. C. Col. Rec.,* I, 187–205; Poore, *Charters and Constitutions,* II, 1397–1408; *Statutes at Large of South Carolina,* I, 43–56.

Set," in 1698 divided the parliament into distinct houses for the nobility and the representatives of the freeholders respectively, and changed somewhat the qualifications of voters.[1] The provisions were as follows:

"6. There shall be a Parliam[t] consisting of the Proprietors or their Deputyes by themselves the Landgraves & Cassiques in y[e] Upper House, And the Freeholders out of every County to be chosen by y[e] freeholders of y[e] said Countyes respectively together with y[e] Citizens and Burgesses to be Elected by y[e] Cittys & Borroughs (which shall be hereafter Created), in y[e] lower House."

"9. Noe person shall be capable of giving his voyce for the Election of a Member to serve in Parliament that is not actually possest of   acres of land and is a Householder, & has a family and whose reall & personall Estates does not amount to   pounds."

A qualification such as the latter, it will be seen, would be equivalent to a decided limitation upon voting. Under it no bachelors could vote unless they were heads of families, and no freeholder unless his freehold was of a stated size and his whole estate of a certain value. In New Netherlands it was the custom for the governor to call together the heads of families, and in some cases in the Middle or New England Colonies the town suffrage was practically limited to such; but the usual borough requirement that the voter be an inhabitant or householder was not a direct exclusion of unmarried men. The proposition of the Carolina proprietors is an unusual one in its formal limitation of the suffrage for the colonial assembly to men who were heads of families.

Considerable uncertainty exists as to the exact legal position of the Fundamental Constitutions in North Carolina. There can be no doubt that they never were in force in South Carolina, but proof is not lacking that they were established in the northern colony. In a most interesting paper delivered by the assembly to Governor Burrington in 1732, it is stated that " in the Province of North Carolina (tho' not in South) the People received" the constitutions of 1669,[2] and it is intimated that the set of 1698 was also

[1] *N. C. Col. Rec.*, II, Appendix, 853–854.
[2] *Ibid.*, III, 452.

accepted.[1]   It is highly probable that certain features of the
constitutions, particularly those relating to popular elections
and concerning land matters, were accepted by the settlers,
while the more elaborate provisions for a landed nobility, a
house of lords, and feudal serfdom were simply ignored.
We have, indeed, an explicit statement of the assembly in a
law of 1699 that the sections relating to biennial parliaments
were received by the community,[2] and in 1725 the governor
writes that an assembly must " be chosen and meet according
to the Fundamental Constitutions of Carolina as you well
know." [3]   Thus the truth about these much disputed constitutions seems to be that they were *in toto* formally accepted by the people of North Carolina, but that in reality
only the sections which fitted the economic and political
needs of the settlement were put into execution.[4]   In North
Carolina the important question respecting the constitutions
is not whether they were adopted by the people or not, but
the extent to which their clauses were actually enforced.   It
would be an interesting task to determine, by a careful inspection of the later laws, how far the colonial constitution
and legislation were influenced by the proprietors' constitutions.   It seems to the writer that the result would show a
surprisingly large portion of the constitutions incorporated
into the provincial customs and laws.[5]

During a period of fifty years following the first assembly
of 1665 we have no record of the actual restrictions imposed
upon the suffrage; and one cannot be sure that the simple
freehold qualification of the constitutions of 1669 or the
more elaborate provisions of the set of 1698 were ever enforced.   It has been found impossible to determine whether
these suffrage clauses of the constitution were among the
chosen subjects or among those ignored by the assembly
and people.   From Governor Carteret's commission in 1670
down to that of Governor Johnson in 1702, the proprietors

---

[1] *N. C. Col. Rec.*, III, 453.
[2] *Ibid.;* also III, 574.
[3] *Ibid.*, 526.
[4] *Ibid.*, I, Prefatory Notes, xvii.
[5] See Governor Burrington's remarks on all the laws of 1715, *N. C.
Col. Rec.*, III, 180–189.

seem bent on establishing their constitutions; but they admit the lack of the requisite nobility, and they can only urge the governors " to come as nigh" as possible to the frame, or to select its "most expedient" parts for execution.[1] Unfortunately, no law respecting the suffrage previous to 1715 has been found, so that we cannot tell how near the colonial legislation approached to the terms of the constitutions.

In reality the suffrage during these fifty years must have been upon a very precarious basis. In this period five or six governors or presidents acting under proprietary authority were driven out of the country by force;[2] two formidable insurrections took place; and for years at a time it could be said that no lawful government existed in the colony. Under such circumstances it is in vain to look for regular election methods. It is not to be supposed that agitators like Culpepper or Cary looked carefully to see that their adherents possessed exactly the number of acres requisite to admit them to the franchise; and, on the other hand, the records show that the established authorities did not scruple to ignore formal qualifications for the suffrage. For instance, in 1677 we find President Miller charged with "making strange limitations for yᵉ choyce of yᵉ Parliamᵗ,"[3] and denying a "free election of an assembly."[4] And his opponents, meeting in a riotous manner, cursed king, proprietors, and landgraves, and proceeded to elect an assembly out of their number, making their drummer one of its members.[5]

From 1681 to 1708 the colony had comparative quiet. In the former year the proprietors attempted to establish a general legislature for the entire province of Carolina,[6] made up of representatives from both the northern and southern counties; but the governor exercised the discretion vested

[1] See Governor Carteret's commission, *N. C. Col. Rec.,* I, 181–183; President Harvey's instructions, *ibid.,* 235–239; Governor Wilkinson's, 333–338; Governor Archdale's, 389–390; Governor Johnson's, 554–555.
[2] *N. C. Col. Rec.,* II, Prefatory Notes, x–xi.
[3] *Ibid.,* I, 287.
[4] Carroll, *Historical Collections of South Carolina,* II, 336.
[5] *N. C. Col. Rec.,* I, 272, 297, 299, etc.
[6] Instructions to Governor Ludwell, *ibid.,* 373–380.

in him[1] to continue the legislative separation of the two
sections of the province. A court record for December 9,
1696, shows that Governor Archdale used no more exact
word than "inhabitants" when he described the electors in
the county of Bath.[2] Shortly after this, laws for biennial
assemblies were passed by the assembly,[3] but I have found
no reference to any suffrage provisions they may have contained.[4] A later governor said the terms of the election law
of 1715 were drawn from earlier proprietary constitutions,[5]
but Burrington's word is too scanty evidence to warrant
our projecting the qualifications of 1715 back to 1697. On
the other hand, an election writ issued by Governor Daniel
about 1703 grants the suffrage to all the freeholders of the
precinct,[6] but this, too, cannot be taken as conclusive evidence of the restriction of the suffrage to landholders.

[1] Additional Instructions, *N. C. Col. Rec.*, I, 380–381.

[2] *Ibid.*, 472.

> "Ordered that writs be issued out to the several precincts
> of the County of Albemarle, for electing five Burgesses for
> each Precinct to meet at the House of Thomas Nicolo, the
> eighteenth Day of January next."

> "Ordered that a writt be issued out to the Inhabitants of the
> County of Bath to make choice of two Burgesses to sit in the
> Grand Assembly to be holden at the House of Thomas Nicolo
> the eighteenth Day of January next."

[3] Acts of 1697 and 1699. These acts are only indirectly referred to
at a much later date (*N. C. Col. Rec.*, III, 453).

[4] Acts with similar titles were passed in South Carolina in the years
1692 and 1696–7, of whose provisions we have some idea. See *post.*

[5] *N. C. Col. Rec.*, III, 180.

[6] *North Carolina Historical and Genealogical Register*, III, 136.

> "By the Honble Landgrave Robt Daniell Esqr Lieutent Gen-
> erall Vice Admirall & Deputy Governor and the rest of the
> Lords Proprietors Deputies.

> "Whereas Caleb Bundy Jeremiah Symonds Augustine Scar-
> borough & John Hawkins Chosen Burgesses for this present
> Assembly for yor Precinct of Pascotank have refused to take
> the Oaths appointed by Law These are in the Name of his
> Excellency the Palatine & the rest of the true & absolute
> Lords & Proprietors to will & require you to Sumons all the
> Freeholders in yor precinct to meet at the usuall place for

The civil dissensions aroused by Colonel Cary in 1708, and lasting almost five years, brought the inevitable interference in elections. Again we are told that " boys and otherwise unqualified" persons voted in elections, that the candidates receiving a majority of votes were not recognized,[1] and that the rabble was treated to " good liquor, rum, and brandy." [2] In January, 1716–17, a missionary, himself not in the best repute,[3] wrote to England that " the fundamental constitutions were intended to be unalterable, but now as little regarded as Magna Charta in England, this Lawless people will allow of no power or authority in either Church or State save what is derived from them. A proprietor were he here would be looked on no better than a ballad singer." [4]

A few years after the Cary Rebellion had been suppressed the assembly provided for a general revisal of the laws of the province, and in this manuscript revision of 1715 is to be found the earliest extant election law. It is entitled " An Act relating to the Bienniall and Other Assemblies and Regulating Elections and Members." [5] The preamble states that the proprietors have considered the customs of England, and have sought to apply to their province those immunities which will encourage its settlement, among which " the frequent sitting of Assemblies is a principal safeguard of their peoples Priviledges." The act proceeds to empower " the freemen of the respective precincts" of the County of Albe-

---

Electing Burgesses on or before the —— day of —— next Ensuing then and there to Elect & Chuse four prudent & Substantiall men Freeholders of yor precinct to be Burgessses in theire Roome for yor precinct to meet at the House of Capt. John Hecklefield in Little River ———— next ensuing to advise & assent to such matters as for the weal Publick shall be most necessary. . . . "

[1] *N. C. Col. Rec.*, I, 696.

[2] *Ibid.*, 915. For short sketch of these troubles, see S. B. Weeks, *Religious Development in the Province of North Carolina, Johns Hopkins Univ. Stud.*, X, 290–302.

[3] He was indicted for drunkenness, *N. C. Col. Rec.*, II, 401.

[4] *Ibid.*, 271.

[5] *Ibid.*, 213–216.

marle to meet every two years and elect five freeholders to represent each precinct, and the " inhabitants and freemen" of each precinct in any other county to choose two representatives.   The act then limits the words " freemen and inhabitants" by imposing an age, a racial, and a tax-paying qualification, in the following words:

" And it is hereby further enacted by the Authority aforesaid that no person whatsoever Inhabitant of this Government born out of the Allegiance of his Majesty and not made free no Negro Mulatto or Indians shall be capable of voting for Members of Assembly and that no other person or persons shall be allowed to vote for members of Assembly in the Government unless he be of the Age of one and Twenty years and has been one full year resident in the Government and has paid one years Levy proceeding the election."

Further provisions required each voter to bring a ballot called a " List," containing the names of those he voted for, and to subscribe his own name, or cause it to be done before the election marshal, and the latter officer was empowered to administer an oath respecting their qualifications to all persons who, by the marshal or any candidate, were thought to be unqualified.   The method of returning the results of the election was fixed; penalties were to be imposed upon officers neglecting their duty or members refusing to serve; and the oaths of allegiance, supremacy, abjuration, and any others taken by members of the English Parliament, were to be administered to all members.   A quorum was to consist of not " less than one full half of the House."

The act of 1715 certainly meant to distinguish between freemen and freeholders; and while the royal charter had apparently used the two words synonymously, the legislature under the term " freemen" now admitted all those tax-payers to vote who were white male subjects of Great Britain and resident at least one year in the province.   And the tax-payer in North Carolina need not be either a land-holder or a slave-owner, as was the case in South Carolina.   While in the latter colony land and slaves were almost the sole objects of taxation, in North Carolina the poll-tax was practically the only form of taxation.   Thus every white male over sixteen years was tithable, and consequently, if he had paid his taxes and was of age, was eligible to vote.[1] In this respect the laws of North Carolina were more liberal than those of any other colony in 1715.

Since 1670 the only unit of representation in the province had been the precinct, but in 1715 provision was made for the representation of towns, a feature which was to be developed until North Carolina had a larger number of towns represented in her assembly than any other colony outside of New England. Chapter LII of the laws of 1715 gave to the town of Bath the right to elect a representative when it should have a population of sixty or more families,[2] and also extended the same privilege to any other town when it should attain the required population.[3] In time several towns obtained the right to send representatives, and it was thought best to define the franchise in these towns by formal act of the legislature. Accordingly, in 1723, a supplement [4] was passed to the election law of 1715. This act provided that the suffrage franchise in any town in the government was to be limited, first, to freeholders of " saved" lots in the towns who kept constantly in repair a house or houses; and secondly, to tenants of any houses in the towns who had paid poll-tax for the preceding year; but freeholders were expressly forbidden to vote in virtue of any house tenanted by a tax-paying voter. The burgess from such a town must be an owner of a " saved" lot therein, which he had held for eighteen months preceding and on which he maintained a habitable house. By a " saved" lot was meant one for which the owner had performed all the duties necessary for him to preserve its ownership; duties which usually included the erecting of a house of a prescribed size and height, with

---

[1] *N. C. Col. Rec.,* II, Appendix, 889. By this act of 1715, taxables were free males over sixteen years of age, or slaves, male and female, over twelve years. Subsequent laws provided that taxables should be white males over sixteen years of age, and all blacks (free or slave) over twelve years. (Davis, *Laws,* ed. of 1764, p. 202.)

[2] *Ibid.,* V., 150–151.

[3] *Ibid.,* VI, 228.

[4] Chapter II of 1723; given only by title in Davis, *Laws* (1751), 53, but in full in Bishop, *History of Elections in the American Colonies,* 275.

certain form of roof and chimneys, and maintaining of the house in habitable repair.[1]

So far as the writer knows, there was but one elective officer in North Carolina, other than the representatives in assembly, during the proprietary period. This officer was the public register of land transfers, births, burials, and marriages, who, under the Fundamental Constitutions, was to be appointed by the chief justice's court from triple nominations made by the freeholders of the precinct;[2] and this elective feature was enforced during the whole colonial period.[3] Apparently all the other officers in the colony were appointive. The vestries, under the law of 1715 and earlier acts, were close corporations, filling vacancies in their number and appointing the church-wardens;[4] the precinct courts were appointed by the governor and council,[5] and themselves in turn appointed constables,[6] overseers of highways,[7] packers of tobacco,[8] and other officers; while the towns were in the control of self-perpetuating commissioners.[9] Still other officers were appointed by the proprietors directly, by the governor and council, or by the corporations named above. Thus, excepting the local registers, the suffrage during this period was limited to the popular representatives in the assembly.

In conclusion, it may be said that the suffrage during the

[1] For these saving provisions, see Davis, *Laws* (1751), 62–65, 92–94, 99–101, 103–108, 210; *N. C. Col. Rec.*, II, 386; IV, 43. The usual size of house was sixteen or fifteen feet by twenty, and occasionally a height of eight feet, and one or two brick or stone chimneys were also required. *Cf.* Porritt, *Unreformed House of Commons*, I, 35.

[2] *Statutes at Large of S. C. Col. Rec.*, III, 185.

[3] As late as October 8, 1773, Governor Morton, writing to the Board of Trade, said the registers were annually elected by the freeholders under an old law of 1715 (*N. C. Col. Rec.*, IX, 691).

[4] *N. C. Col. Rec.*, I, 678, 680; II, 11, 207–217.

[5] *Ibid.*, II, 525–526, 540, 565, 572, etc.

[6] *Ibid.*, I, 523–5, 533, 548, 652, etc.

[7] *Ibid.*, 494–495, 523–525, 531, 550, 576, 611–612, etc.

[8] *Ibid.*, 652–653, 656.

[9] For an illustration of these commissions, see Davis, *Laws* (1751), 62–65.

proprietary period was not placed upon a firm basis until the restoration of internal quiet and the passage of the election act in 1715. The franchise begins with the confusion of words in the royal charter; it is given a more definite basis by the constitutions, but we are in doubt whether these provisions ever were actually enforced or not. It has been noted that proprietors and governors used on different occasions the words inhabitants, or freeholders, or freemen, as descriptive of the electing citizens; and a confusion thus existing in the royal charter and the governors' writs was not to be avoided among the common people. Particularly was this true in the troublous times, of which the colony had not a few, when private and property rights, as well as political privileges, were invaded by the conflicting parties. The quelling of the riots made possible the regular enforcement of such an election law as that of 1715. This act, perhaps, as Governor Burrington later remarked, drawn from earlier precedents, was remarkably liberal in its provisions, in that it made the voting privilege co-extensive with the poll-tax upon white male citizens. After 1715 elections were not yet freed from indirect control by the governor,[1] but without doubt they were more honestly managed than heretofore. The town suffrage introduced a slight variation in the laws, and the period closes with an election law in 1727 of which we have only the title.[2]

II. *Under the Royal Government,* 1728–1775.

The basis of the representative and elective systems in the royal colonies is generally said to be the commission and in-

---

[1] See some interesting letters of Burrington written in 1725, and coming to light in 1733, concerning the management of elections (*N. C. Col. Rec.,* III, 526). The journal of the lower house in 1726, perhaps as a result of the governor's management, shows a number of disputed elections (*ibid.,* II, 611).

[2] "An Act, for Regulating Towns, and Elections of Burgesses," 1727, Ch. II. Title only given in Davis, *Laws* (1751), 67. Governor Burrington said, "This Act was made for regulating the Town Elections of Burgesses there being three Towns in this Government that hath the priviledge of sending Burgesses and this Act was to adjust the manner of chuseing them;" *N. C. Col. Rec.,* III, 193.

structions of the royal governor for the colony. This was the view held by the English government and the one acted upon in most of the royal colonies. We shall see that in North Carolina the royal instructions and vetoes almost overturned the constitution as it had grown up under the proprietary government, and that the people or their representatives time and again turn away from these instructions back to the original charters and the Fundamental Constitutions, which they claimed were the true basis for the provincial government. The contest between the two began almost immediately after Governor Burrington, the first royal governor, entered upon his duties.

According to Burrington's commission, which is similar to those granted in other colonies at this time, the governor was authorized to call general assemblies of the freeholders and planters in a manner agreeable to the laws and customs of the province of North Carolina.[1] By his instructions, dated almost a year after the commission, he was directed to " take care that the Members of the Assembly be elected only by freeholders as being more agreeable to the custom of this Kingdom to which you are as near as may be to conform yourself in all particulars."[2] It is clear that this is far different from the tax-paying basis for the suffrage established by the act of 1715, and it did not take Burrington long to see the divergence.

Immediately after his arrival he issued writs for the election of representatives, and, ignoring the old law, he followed the terms of his instructions by requiring the elections to be by the freeholders in the respective towns and precincts.[3] Such a change in the election customs without any warning naturally led to popular opposition; the assembly journals show a number of disputed election cases,[4] and Burrington wrote to the Board of Trade that the new writs had "occasioned a great deal of heat among the people," which was " much heightened by those who love to raise a clamour against me."[5]

[1] *N. C. Col. Rec.*, III, 68; January 15, 1729–30.
[2] *Ibid.*, 93; dated December 14, 1730.
[3] *Ibid.*, 212.
[4] *Ibid.*, 289, 301, 558, 584.   [5] *Ibid.*, 207.

Burrington's relations with the people were from the first unhappy, and in his quarrel with their representatives he tried in two ways to change the constitution of the assembly and have a house elected favorable to himself; first, by restricting the suffrage, and, secondly, by reapportioning the representatives, or, when this failed, by erecting new precincts. Some time before September, 1731, he sent to England his opinions upon all the legislation between 1715 and 1729,[1] and said of the election act of 1715 that it "was an old Law taken from one of the Lords Proprietors Original Constitutions and hath undergone little alteration."[2] He pointed out that "all Freemen are qualifyed to vote as well as Freeholders which is contrary to my Instructions on that Head." Objection was also made to the holding of elections by virtue of the law without any writs, since it "occasions a great deal of Mobbing and tumults;" and the governor therefore advised the repeal of the law and the holding of elections by the freeholders according to writs issued by the governor.

From this time down to the close of his administration in 1734, Burrington is insistent in his letters to England that the law should be repealed. He later found other objections to it. The short term of the biennial assemblies made well-meaning(!) members timorous in their actions, through the fear that they might not be re-elected. The apportionment of representatives was unjust, for, said the governor, "a Small part of the Province have Twenty Six Representatives, all the Remainder but ten;" and he recommended that four precincts which together, under the act of 1715, had nineteen representatives, should be formed into only two districts, and each of these send two delegates. His reasons for such a radical change were that two precincts have "neither Persons fit for Magistrates nor Burgesses;" and that he is of the opinion that two representatives are just as sufficient for precincts in North Carolina as for counties in Virginia.[3] He closes with the sentence, " I cant help thinking we shall have more orderly Elections and more substan-

---

[1] *N. C. Col. Rec.*, III, 180-194.
[2] *Ibid.*, 180.
[3] *Ibid.*, 207.

tial men chosen if none but Freeholders vote." In February, 1731–2,[1] he writes again to urge the repeal of the Biennial Act, again looking forward to more orderly elections and expecting that the members will "behave more decently" if the law were not in force. In August, 1732, the Board of Trade replied to his repeated suggestions that until the law officers report upon the Biennial Act no change should be made in the constitution of the assembly.[2]

But before this letter was written, Burrington had tried another plan by which the assembly might be made more subservient to his interests. In May, 1732, a new precinct with the right of representation was erected by the governor and council; in October a second one was established, and this was followed shortly by a third.[3] It was claimed by Burrington's opponents that he had personally "earnestly promoted such Petitions (even forming and writing some of them himself)," for the erecting of the new precincts.[4] "Where is the necessity," these leaders of the assembly ask, "of these divisions? these new appointments?"[5] They pointed to the fact that one of the precincts had not over thirty families of inhabitants, and "can scarce make out a sufficient number of People for Justices and Jury;"[6] while among these thirty families there were only three freeholders, or voters. In another precinct the number of freeholders was but slightly larger. The protestants picture ironically an election in which, since the writs permit only freeholders to elect, the three freeholders would control the elections,— "two are to stand candidates and the third to elect them."[7]

In addition to the argument that there was no necessity for the erection of new precincts, the petitioners protested that the governor had no right to create new representative districts, arguing that this would make the whole legislature subservient to a part—to the governor and council; that it

---

[1] *N. C. Col. Rec.*, III, 325.
[2] *Ibid.*, 355.
[3] *Ibid.*, 417, 425, 442.
[4] *Ibid.*, 381.
[5] *Ibid.*, 452.
[6] *Ibid.*, 381.
[7] *Ibid.*, 450.

was contrary to the customs of the neighboring colonies, and even repugnant to the king's instructions.[1] But Burrington could quote colonial history as well as the assemblymen. He pointed out that only one instance [2] was known where a precinct was erected by law and not by the governor and council,[3] and he claimed that the opposition to the new precincts arose from two councillors who desired popularity with the assembly and people.

The governor continued sending election writs for elections by the freeholders only,[4] and in the spring of 1733 writs were issued to the new precincts. But in neither instance did the governor gain his point; the elections were not confined to freeholders, in spite of instructions and writs,[5] and the representatives from the new precincts were not permitted to take seats in the assembly.[6] The assembly of July, 1733, had a stormy meeting. The governor told them that assemblies would soon become the greatest grievance in the province if the "heat and partiality" continued. "Burgessing," he said, "has been for some years a source of lyes and occasion of disturbances, which has deterred good men from being Candidates or entering the lists of noise and Faction;" [7] "bodys of men cannot blush, and that's your advantage." For some reason, Burrington's next and last assembly showed a disposition to compromise with the governor, and bills were introduced to establish his new precincts by law [8] and to limit the suffrage to freeholders.[9] But in the midst of the session a new governor, Gabriel John-

---

[1] *N. C. Col. Rec.*, III, 383–385, 574–576.

[2] The governor was in error here, as three precincts had been erected by act of the legislature, in addition to the act of 1715, which had recognized the existence of all the early precincts (*ibid.*, 453–454, 575).

[3] *Ibid.*, 443–444.

[4] *Ibid.*, 536.

[5] Burrington said to the assembly, "Neither doth the King's Instructions that only Freeholders should vote find any weight in your Elections tho' always inserted in the Writts" (*ibid.*, 560).

[6] *Ibid.*, 611.

[7] *Ibid.*, 560.

[8] *Ibid.*, 640.

[9] *Ibid.*, 637.

ston, arrived in the province and the work of the assembly ceased.[1]

Governor Johnston almost immediately issued writs for an election of assemblymen by the freeholders of the respective precincts and towns.[2]   Although the election was not without irregularities,[3] yet the new assembly took up the work of the old one, and considered a bill for repealing the clause of the act of 1715 which permitted freemen to vote.[4] The result was a restriction of the suffrage to freeholders.[5] The preamble of the act of 1734–5 says that " it hath been found inconvenient for the Freemen" to vote, and that the royal instructions had directed that only freeholders should vote for members of assembly.   The qualifications of voters and assemblymen were then given as follows:

" no person hereafter shall be admitted to give his vote in any Election for Members of Assembly for the precincts in this Province, unless such person has been an Inhabitant in the precinct where he votes at least six months and has bona fide a Freehold in his own Right of at least fifty Acres of Land in the said precinct, which he shall have been possest of Three Months before he offers to give his vote.

   " And be it Enacted by the Authority aforesaid, That hereafter no person shall be deemed qualified or admitted to sit in the Assembly, unless he has been one full year an Inhabitant of this Province, and is possessed in his own Right of at least one hundred acres of Freehold Land in the precinct where he is Elected or Chosen."

Thus through the persistence of the royal governors and the force of the English instructions the suffrage was at last limited to freeholders; the ambiguity of the charters and proprietary writs which had permitted landless freemen to vote was cleared away, and their evident purpose finally accomplished.   In this case, as in practically all the royal colonies except South Carolina, the English government

[1] *N. C. Col. Rec.,* III, 643.

[2] *Ibid.,* IV, 3.

[3] Among the charges is one that some person " had stifled the writt of Election so that due notice was not given," *N. C. Col. Rec.,* IV, 117, 118, 119.

[4] *Ibid.,* 88, 89, 97, 98, 108, 125, 126.

[5] Chapter II of 1734–5; title only in Davis, *Laws* (1751), 79, but in full in Bishop, *History of Elections in the American Colonies,* 277–279.

rather than colonial opinion led to the restriction of the suffrage to freeholders. It must be remembered, however, that
the terms of this act, requiring six months' residence and
fifty acres of freehold, did not extend to the three towns,
where, under the terms of the act of 1723, tenants or the
owners of untenanted houses could vote. It is remarkable,
too, that the formal exclusion of negroes was laid aside, not
again to be taken up until far into the nineteenth century.

An act of the same assembly established two of the three
precincts which Burrington and his council had tried to
erect.[1] But Johnston was not satisfied with the suffrage
limitations and the legal establishment of precincts. Like
Burrington, he wrote repeatedly against the act of 1715[2]
urging many objections, but emphasizing particularly the
inequalities in representation which it established. At last,
on July 21, 1737, the King in Council, acting upon the
advice of the Board of Trade, " was graciously pleased to
declare his disallowance of the said act." [3] Yet the repeal
of the act of 1715 led to no immediate change in the method
of apportionment of representatives or the manner of holding
elections, for Johnston now issued writs calling upon the
freeholders " to choose Representatives" without stating any
number, and the counties continued to send the numbers
formerly apportioned to them.[4] Fifteen years after Burrington began his attack on the law of 1715, the precincts were
still represented in the way which to him appeared so unjust.[5]

In 1743[6] a comprehensive election law was passed which
contained many new features relating to the taking of the
ballot, but it did not change the qualifications of the suffrage.
The act provided that election inspectors to assist the sheriff
should be appointed either by the candidates or the sheriff;
it required the sheriff to come to the county election place

---

[1] *N. C. Col. Rec.,* IV, 155.

[2] *Ibid.,* 25, 204.

[3] *Ibid.,* 251.

[4] *Ibid.,* 1185; V, 87.

[5] The northern counties kept their unequal representation until 1746
(*ibid.,* IV, 493, 814–815), and it was restored to them by the royal instructions to Governor Dobbs in 1754 (*Records,* V, 1110).

[6] Davis, *Laws* (1751), 177–180.

" provided with a small Box, with a Lid or Cover, having a Hole in it, not exceeding Half an Inch in Diameter." The voter must bring a " Scroll of Paper, rolled up," on which were the names of the candidates for whom he voted; the sheriff was to take the ballot, and in the presence of the inspectors put it into the box; and he and the inspectors were each to keep a separate list of the voters' names. The persons having the greatest number of votes were to be declared elected, and in case of a tie the sheriff was authorized to cast a deciding vote. The polls were to be open from ten o'clock in the morning until one, and from half-past two until sunset. Upon the request of a candidate or any other freeholder, the voter might be required to take oath that he was properly qualified.

The fifty acres of freehold and six months' residence were still required of electors, who now, as in the act of 1715, were to be twenty-one years of age. A freeholder was now defined to be a person " who hath an Estate, Real, for his own Life, or the Life of another, or any Estate of greater Dignity." Fines were to be imposed upon unqualified persons voting, or upon qualified persons who voted twice; and candidates who had offered bribes or favors to electors were rendered incapable to sit in the assembly for which they were elected. The ballot features were also extended to elections in towns.

We now come to the time when the apportionment contest reached its culmination. It is impossible to enter into all the details of this interesting period, but a summary of the events may be given. Since the days of the proprietary government the precincts of the north-eastern section of the colony called Albemarle County had each sent five members to the assembly; while those of Bath County, in the south, sent only two each.[1] The political distinction between the two parts of the province in time came to be an economic one. We are told that imports came almost exclusively from

---

[1] The documents relating to the election and apportionment controversy take up a large part of Vols. IV and V of the *Colonial Records*. A good short summary is given in a representation of the Board of Trade to the king, March 14, 1754 (*Col. Rec.*, V, 84–91).

Virginia into the northern counties,[1] and by the merchants there were sent to the southern counties; and that the northern merchants were forbidden by contract to pay debts in Virginia in any bills of exchange.[2] The southern merchants, on the other hand, wanted a cheap paper currency, which would be an advantage to them in the settlement of debts within the province. Hence the northern members opposed, and the southern members favored, a colonial currency. The maintenance of the existing representation in the assembly was thus a vital necessity to the north, while the attainment of equality was the political ideal of the south. The twenty-nine representatives from the six northern counties voted solidly under strong leaders, and by their number could break a quorum or prevent the passage of any acts objectionable to their constituents.[3]

As early as 1741 Governor Johnston had taken the side of the southern counties, and by calling an assembly at Wilmington in the south he had hoped to keep away the northern members and have an assembly to his own taste,[4] but at this time he failed. He tried the same plan with somewhat better success in 1746. An intractable assembly meeting at Newbern in June, 1746, was prorogued to the following November, with Wilmington as a meeting place. Here, two

---

[1] The title precinct was changed to that of county in an act of 1738, Chap. III (Davis, *Laws* (1751), p. 90).

[2] *N. C. Col. Rec.,* IV, 1217.

[3] *Ibid.,* 863, 870, 1152–1153, 1164.

[4] *Ibid.,* 584. In writing to the Board of Trade, December 21, 1741, respecting a much desired quit-rent law, he says,

> "All imaginable precautions were taken to secure the success of this Affair.
>
> "The Assembly was called in the most Southern part of the Province on purpose to keep at home the Northern Members who are most numerous and from whom the greatest opposition was expected And some of the most troublesome leading men were prevailed upon to be absent.
>
> "By this management there were present but two Members more than was necessary to make a house. which then consisted of the most moderate and most sensible men of the Colony. . . . "

hundred miles away from the usual place of assembly meetings and of court sessions, at an inclement season of the
year, which made it dangerous to cross ferriages from seven
to ten miles broad,[1] the governor met, as he himself admitted,
" not much above a fourth part of the Members." [2]   Eight
members out of fifty-four met, admitted six or seven newly
elected members,[3] and then proceeded to shear the northern
counties of their political power.

The most important act was one " for the better ascertaining the Number of Members to be chosen for the several
Counties within this Province to sit and vote in General
Assembly; and for Establishing a more equal Representative of all his Majesty's Subjects in the House of Burgesses." [4].   The journals of the assembly show that the act
was rushed through both houses in three days.[5]   The preamble of the act stated that several of the northern counties
had " assumed to themselves the Privilege of choosing Five
Persons respectively to represent them in the General Assembly, without any Law, or Pretence of Law, to support such
Claim;" [6]   while the southern counties, which were more
populous and contributed much more largely to the public
taxes than the north, were given only two representatives;
" from which Inequality great Mischiefs and Disorders have
arisen, and the best Schemes for the Good and Welfare of
the Province, by this Means, have been utterly defeated."
It was then enacted that the inhabitants of each county
already erected, or which should be erected, should send two
persons, " and no more," to be their representatives, and the
freeholders of the four towns of Edenton, Bath-town, Newbern, and Wilmington should each send one representative
as formerly.

This act was followed by another for fixing the seat of
government at Newbern, passed with the same " management, precipitation & surprise when very few Members

---

[1] *N. C. Col. Rec.*, IV, 1158.
[2] *Ibid.*, 870.
[3] *Ibid.*, 870, 1157, 1158.
[4] Davis, *Laws* (1751), 223; *N. C. Col. Rec.*, IV, 1154–1155.
[5] *Ibid.*, 835, 840.
[6] Davis, *Laws* (1751), 223.

were present," as the Board of Trade wrote to the king; and containing such features that the governor ought not to have assented to it if it had been passed by a full house.[1]

Johnston made use of the new representation act at once, issuing writs in December, 1746, for the election of two members in each county.[2] The northern counties refused to recognize the law on which the new writs were founded, and insisted upon electing their old number of representatives.[3] But the assembly denied them admission, and ordered new elections for two members in each county.[4] After this the northern counties refused to elect members, they denied the authority of the legislature elected under the new act, they paid no taxes, and for seven years were in a state of practical rebellion against the governor.[5]

The contest was then taken to England, both sides using agents to represent them before the Board of Trade and the other English authorities.[6] There the decision was not reached until 1754, almost eight years after the contest had begun. In the meantime Governor Johnston had erected new counties by law and by proclamation in the southern district, and thus strengthened the position of that section.[7] Acts for emitting a paper currency and regulating quitrents were also passed,[8] and Johnston thought " that more had been done for the Settlement and Prosperity of this Country within this three years. . . . [1746–1749] than ever has been done before since the foundation of the Colony." [9] Governor Johnston died in July, 1752,[10] and for two more years the anarchy which he had done so much to bring about continued its evil influence in the colony.

The Lords of Trade sent a long representation to the

[1] *N. C. Col. Rec.*, V, 108.
[2] Copies of writs are given, *N. C. Col. Rec.*, IV, 1180–1183.
[3] *Ibid.*, 856–857, 1180–1183.
[4] *Ibid.*, 857.
[5] *Ibid.*, 1153; Prefatory Notes to Vol. IV, xix.
[6] *Ibid.*, 879–883, 1020, 1158.
[7] *Ibid.*, 887–889; V, 88.
[8] *Ibid.*, IV, 1217.
[9] *Ibid.*, 919.
[10] *Ibid.*, 1314.

king in March, 1754, reviewing the history of elections in
the colony of North Carolina, advising the repeal of a number of the colonial acts, and proposing certain instructions
for Arthur Dobbs, who had already been appointed governor.[1]   About a month later, the King in Council acted
upon this advice by repealing twenty-six of the most important laws of the colony.[2]   This remarkable action was
taken, first, to set aside the acts of the Wilmington Assembly
of November, 1746; and secondly, in order to clear away
the legal basis upon which the representative system had
rested since the proprietary period and found it solely upon
the royal instructions to the governor.[3]   Among the repealed acts were five laws relating principally to land
matters passed forty years earlier, in 1715; twelve passed
between 1722 and 1749, erecting counties or towns and con-
ferring the right of representation upon them; still others
were the elaborate election law of 1743, the vestry act of
1741, the reapportionment act of 1746, the seat of government act of the same year, and others of less importance.
It is safe to say that no colony in the eighteenth century
suffered such a complete demolition of the legal basis of its
representative system, election customs, church organization
and land laws as was here accomplished in North Carolina.
For six years after this wholesale repeal there was no general election law; for ten years the vestry acts met with successive repeals in England; while the royal veto came into
very frequent use from this time down to the Revolution in
connection with quit-rent and court laws.[4]

It was the intention of the English authorities that the
representative system and election custom should rest upon
the royal prerogative as expressed in the instructions to the
governors, but they wisely adopted the advice of the Crown's
law officers that it was not " advisable for the Crown to im-

[1] *N. C. Col. Rec.*, V, 81–108.
[2] *Ibid.*, 115–118.
[3] *Ibid.*, 92.
[4] For repealed acts, see *N. C. Col. Rec.*, V, 115–118; VI, 29, 139, 327–
328, 707, 723, 900; VIII, 266, 616; IX, 284, 287, 665.   In the nineteen
years between 1754 and 1773 the royal disallowance was signified to at
least fifty-one North Carolina laws.

peach rights heretofore granted & enjoyed." [1]   Thus it
happened that the new governor, Arthur Dobbs, received
directions to restore the unequal apportionment of representatives existing before the act of 1746, and in his instructions [2] an assembly of sixty members was provided for, composed of five members from each of five counties, three from
one county, two from each of fourteen counties, and one each
from four towns.   The members were to be elected by the
freeholders of the respective counties and towns, and a
quorum—a vital point with the northern members—was
fixed at only fifteen, one-quarter of the whole.   The governor was empowered to grant these rights in representation
by charters to the respective counties or towns, and in *the
southern district* he could erect new towns or counties and
confer upon them the right of electing representatives.[3]   The
subsequent control of the elective system, the qualifications
of electors and elected, and the apportionment of representatives was denied to the legislature in the following words:

" And it is Our further Will and Pleasure that you do not for the
future upon any pretence whatsoever give your assent to any law or
laws to be passed in our said Province by which the number of the
Assembly shall be enlarged or diminished the duration of it ascertained
the qualifications of the electors or elected fixed or altered or by which
any regulations shall be establish'd with respect thereto inconsistent
with these our Instructions to you or prejudicial to that right and
authority which you derive from us in virtue of our Commission and
Instruction." [4]

As soon as Dobbs reached the colony he saw how confusing the repeal of the fundamental laws would be, and
despite his instructions he delayed to announce the repeal
until after an assembly election had been held.   He feared
it would " put the Electors into confusion . . . and in the
unsettled State of the province & their present Divisions
wou'd have had a very bad Effect." [5]   Soon both assembly

[1] *N. C. Col. Rec.,* V, 91.
[2] *Ibid.,* 1110; June 17, 1754.
[3] *Ibid.,* 1111.
[4] *Ibid.*
[5] *Ibid.,* 326.

and governor were asking for a modification of the instructions,[1] and in June, 1755, the King in Council sent additional instructions to Dobbs, permitting the legislature to re-establish by law the respective towns and counties, provided no grant of the right of representation was made to them.[2] The privilege thus given was soon exercised by the assembly, and in 1756 acts were passed restoring the boundaries and internal organization of the counties and towns, without granting the right of representation, which the assembly expressly stated was the king's prerogative.[3] This right was conferred in special charters granted by the governor to the several towns and counties.[4]

The absence of a general election law after the repeal in 1754 of the act of 1743 soon led to the introduction of election bills into the assembly, although the need might not seem great when only one election was held between the years 1746 and 1760.[5] In 1757 a bill passed both houses containing a provision that voters should be given an oath "that you will not vote for no representative, but such as you think best qualified and most inclined to promote his Majties Interest and that of this County." [6] This act the governor imagined was introduced by a certain Murray " and his Junto," " that they might make me unpopular with the Assembly in rejecting their favourite Bill." [7] He refused to agree to it because contrary to his instructions.[8] In the following year the lower house appointed a committee of eleven members to bring in a bill for regulating elections,[9] but apparently this committee never reported.

---

[1] *N. C. Col. Rec.,* V, 297, 301–303, 326.

[2] *Ibid.,* 341, 352, 405–407, 415; XI, 124.

[3] Davis, *Laws* (1764), 86; *N. C. Col. Rec.,* V, 645.

[4] *N. C. Col. Rec.,* V, 767–768, 812; VI, 331–333, etc.

[5] The assembly elected under the new apportionment act of 1746 con tinued in session until Governor Dobbs's arrival in 1754; then an election was held in accordance with the law of 1743, although the act had been repealed. This assembly of 1754 was not dissolved until 1760.

[6] *N. C. Col. Rec.,* V, 879, 881, 889, 900, 903, 905–906, 913–914.

[7] *Ibid.,* 947.

[8] *Ibid.,* 889, 913–914.

[9] *Ibid.,* 1046.

Before any election law had been passed Governor Dobbs, in January, 1760, dissolved the assembly, in order, as he said, "to give the Constituents an opportunity of a new Election to pass proper Bills before new Cabals or Parties are formed to mislead the Assembly and carry Jobs for themselves." [1] The result of a dissolution under such circumstances might have been foreseen, but the confusion could have been lessened, if not altogether avoided, by the governor taking a clear and firm position on the subject of the suffrage, in accordance with the provision of his instructions for the restriction of the suffrage to freeholders.[2] Instead of doing this, his policy was careless and vacillating in the extreme.[3] He had, indeed, before this time granted charters to most of the counties giving them the privilege of sending representatives to the assembly. Only one of the charters has been printed in the *Records,* but in this to Orange County, Dobbs took it upon himself to expressly define the qualifications of voters and representatives, by limiting the suffrage to freeholders of one hundred acres or more, and the right of being elected to freeholders of two hundred acres or over.[4] No evidence has been found to show that this high qualification was incorporated into the charters of all the counties.

Instead of adhering to the terms of these charters, whatever they were, Dobbs, in drawing up the writs of election, went back to the original charters of the province, which placed the elections in the control of the freemen. He directed that writs should be issued for the *free inhabitants* of the counties to elect their delegates, but through an error

---

[1] *N. C. Col. Rec.,* VI, 216.

[2] *Ibid.,* V, 1110–1111.

[3] It must be remembered that in 1760 Dobbs was about seventy-six years of age (*N. C. Col. Rec.,* V, Prefatory Notes, v, and p. 737).

[4] *N. C. Col. Rec.,* V, 767–768, July 19, 1757. A little before this date the lower house of assembly had ordered "That no person that is or shall be exempt from paying Taxes shall vote for a Representative or Representatives in Assembly for any County or Town in this Province" (*ibid.,* 855). The subject arose, perhaps, over the poll-tax levy which was then under discussion. I do not know whether it was incorporated into the act or not.

of some clerk the writs came out empowering the *inhabitants* to take part in the elections.[1]   In at least one case as Dobbs admitted,[2] and perhaps in others, as the assembly claimed,[3] writs were even issued for elections by the freeholders instead of by the inhabitants.   Some changes were also made in the apportionment of representatives, which the assembly later said " is a manifest infringement on the rights of the subject, and tenders to endanger the Constitution." [4]

With such confusion in the governor's mind, and such looseness in his writs, it was but natural that the elections should be irregular and riotous.   The journals of the succeeding assembly give abundant evidence of this.   There were contested elections in four counties; [5] and under the governor's writs it was claimed that servants and criminals might vote,[6] while the governor himself admitted that sailors and non-freeholders had succeeded in electing a set of men different from those who would have been chosen by freeholder suffrage.[7]   The assembly so elected stood for the old constitutional rights of the assembly and people.   They seated a member from the town of Halifax, who had been elected without a writ from the governor, on the ground that under a clause in the act of 1715 incorporating the town of Bath, any town had the right to send a representative to the assembly when it numbered sixty families of inhabitants.[8] They refused to act until a majority was present, in spite of the governor's instructions which had made fifteen members a quorum; [9] and they drew up a protest against the recent acts of the governor in elections, in money matters, and in

---

[1] *N. C. Col. Rec.*, VI, 303.

[2] *Ibid.*

[3] *Ibid.;* and p. 413.

[4] *Ibid.*, 301, 412.

[5] Granville, Anson, Bertie, and Perquimans; *ibid.*, 364, 365, 366, 374.

[6] *Ibid.*, 303, 413.

[7] *Ibid.*, 303.

[8] For the action of the assembly, the governor, and the English authorities upon this Halifax case, see *N. C. Col. Rec.*, VI, 245, 365, 538–541, 598, 752–3, 983–989, 1006.   The question arose again in 1773, see *ibid.*, IX, 594–596, 600.

[9] *Ibid.*, VI., 470.

relation to fees.[1] To them it seemed " no longer a secret
that the Governor Intended to modell the Assembly for his
own particular Purposes," [2] while the governor felt compelled to ask that his hands be strengthened to oppose " a
republican spirit of Independency rising in this Colony." [3]

Yet there was common sense enough on both sides to permit the passage of a general election law. A bill for this
purpose was introduced into the lower house in November,
1760, during the second session of the assembly, and in two
weeks had passed both houses and received the governor's
approval.[4] The act of December 3, 1760,[5] restored the
qualifications for assemblymen and voters as they had been
adopted in 1743; the voter again must be twenty-one years
of age, six months a resident of the province, and a freeholder of fifty acres of land; while the representative must
be of the same age, be an inhabitant for one year and own
one hundred acres of land in the county for which he was
elected. / The only important change made by the act was
the abolition of the ballot-box, and the substitution therefor
of voting " openly," or *viva voce*. A fine was to be imposed
upon sheriffs who refused to take the poll in this manner,
thus making the new method compulsory.

The last four years of Dobbs's administration were spent
in a vain effort to protect the king's prerogative against the
encroachments of the assembly, in which he gained the ill-
will of the province and did not win support from home.[6]
His successor, William Tryon,[7] had the far greater diffi-

[1] *N. C. Col. Rec.*, VI, 410–415.

[2] *Ibid.*, 415.

[3] *Ibid.*, 279.

[4] *Ibid.*, 453, 463, 464, 469, 480, 501, 511.

[5] Davis, *Laws* (1764), 198–201.

[6] The principal subject of dispute was the old one of a quorum, the
assembly refusing to transact business without a majority, while the
governor tried to gain recognition for the quorum of fifteen mentioned
in his instructions (*N. C. Col. Rec.*, VI, 470, 538–541, 596, 983–989, 1006,
1024). See *ibid.*, 538, for severe rebuke sent to Dobbs by Board of
Trade because of " ill timed disputes amongst the different branches
of the Legislature in North Carolina, upon Questions of meer specu-
lative Polity, too trivial in almost any times to deserve consideration."

[7] Commissioned as lieutenant-governor April 26, 1764 (*N. C. Col.
Rec.*, VI, 1043).

culty of the Regulator movement to contend with. In the meantime although scarcely an election was held that did not lead to contested seats in the house,[1] yet a new election law of 1764 failed in the upper house.[2] In 1768 a movement was started for the election of assemblies triennially, and in spite of rejections in the upper house, four bills for this purpose were introduced and passed in the lower house between 1768 and 1774.[3] The assent of the upper house was gained in 1771 to a supplementary election act, but this was so "replete with objections," and "repugnant to the British Statutes,"[4] that Governor Tryon would not sign it;[5] and a second attempt in the fall of the same year was thwarted in the upper house.[6] The journals, unfortunately, are silent upon those features of the acts which led to their popularity in the lower house, and which made them repugnant to the council and governor.

The Regulator movement furnishes few facts bearing upon the suffrage, for although the Regulators developed some form of representative organization, yet very slight reference is made to the election of the representatives. As early as 1766 Orange County took steps towards a permanent representative organization;[7] and somewhat later an agreement is entered into by the Regulators to " choose more suitable men than we have heretofore done for Burgesses and Vestry men," and to settle differences among themselves by submission to " the Majority of our Body."[8] A regular organization of companies, chiefs, and representatives appears to have been in existence by April 4, 1768, for, by an agreement of that date, a Regulators' meeting decided to inspect the sheriffs' and vestries' lists of taxables and ac-

[1] See *N. C. Col. Rec.*, VI, 897, 902, 904, 919, 961, 1154b, 1259, 1278; VII, 350, 352, 357, 366, 722–725.

[2] *Ibid.*, 1112, 1122, 1174, 1186.

[3] *Ibid.*, VII, 903, 938; IX, 412, 457, 529, 530, 540, 713, 714, 744, 752, 798–799, 855, 899.

[4] *Ibid.*, VIII, 523.

[5] *Ibid.*, 362, 370, 376, 426, 428, 459, 479.

[6] *Ibid.*, IX, 110, 156, 168.

[7] *Ibid.*, VII, 249–252.

[8] *Ibid.*, 671.

counts of expenditures, and to meet on the first Monday of July, October, January, and April. These meetings were to continue until the " business be completed to satisfaction at the Meeting House near Moses Teague's to which each chief is to send one or more representatives from a private meeting of his own company." [1] Similar "conventions" were held at other times,[2] and one of the principal features in Governor Tryon's proclamation to the Orange County men was that they should desist from further meetings " either by Verbal agreement or advertisement," and cease using the titles of Regulators and Associators.[3]

Apart from these elections among themselves the Regulators were interested in the Assembly elections, and among the various reforms they requested, this was placed first— " That at all elections each suffrage be given by Ticket & Ballot." [4] They naturally influenced the elections in the western counties,[5] and to counteract their influence Tryon erected the borough of Hillsborough and gave it the privilege of sending a representative to the assembly.[6] It was the inhabitants of this western county of Orange which in 1773 gave the following interesting instruction [7] to their delegates in assembly:

" We have chosen you our Representatives at the next General Assembly and when we did so we expected and do still expect that you will speak our Sense in every case when we shall expressly declare it, or when you can by any other means discover it. In all other cases we suppose you left to your own discretion which is ever to be directed by the Good of our Country in general and of this County in particular. This is our notion of the Duty of Representatives, and the Rights of Electors."

[1] *N. C. Col. Rec.*, VII, 702–703.
[2] For the Regulators in general, see J. S. Bassett, *The Regulators of North Carolina, Report of American Historical Association for 1894* (140–212), 161–170, 172, 183–184.
[3] *N. C. Col. Rec.*, VII, 731–732, 793.
[4] *Ibid.*, VIII, 77.
[5] *Ibid.*, VII, 671, 722–726.
[6] *Ibid.*, VII, Prefatory Notes, xxiv; VIII, 216.
[7] *Ibid.*, IX, 699.

Turning from the county elections and representation, we must glance at the elections in the boroughs. In discussing the suffrage under the proprietors, a law of 1715 was mentioned, according to which any town was declared entitled to elect a representative to the assembly when its population reached sixty families. This was the famous " Bath-town Act," which occupies a large place in the colonial correspondence from 1760. It has also been noted that a subsequent act of 1723 extended the suffrage in towns to the tenants of houses of a legal size, who paid taxes or to the owners when the houses were untenanted. Under the provisions of these acts, three towns, Edenton, Bath Town and Newbern, sent representatives to the first assembly under the royal government.[1] In 1734–35 a new town was erected by order of the governor and council,[2] and in 1739 this town of Wilmington was by act of the legislature impowered to send a burgess to the assembly, who was to be elected by the tenants of houses in the town or by the owners of untenanted houses.[3]

Yet a year later, in an act relating to Edenton, and confirming its right to send a representative, the assembly stated that no person should be allowed to vote for representative unless he was the *owner* of a saved lot in the town, and had held it for six months before the election.[4]

The wholesale disallowance of laws in 1754 and the fol-

---

[1] *N. C. Col. Rec.,* V, 87.

[2] *Ibid.,* IV, 43.

[3] Davis, *Laws* (1751), 99–101. The suffrage provision is as follows: " Every Tenant of any Brick, Stone or framed habitable House of the Length of Twenty Feet, and Sixteen Feet wide, within the Bounds of the said Town, who, at the Day of Election, and for Three Months next before, inhabited such House, shall be entitled to vote in the Election for the Representative of the said Town to be sent to the Generall Assembly: And in Case there shall be no Tenant of such House in the said Town on the Day of Election, qualified to vote as aforesaid, that then and in such Case the Person seized of such House, either in Fee-Simple or Fee-Tail, or for Term of Life, shall be entitled to vote for the Representative aforesaid."

[4] *Ibid.,* 103–108. To save a lot the purchaser must, within two years after purchasing, erect " a good substantial, Brick, Stone or framed

lowing years resulted in the repeal of the acts of 1739 and 1740 respecting Wilmington and Edenton, but they left untouched the more important laws of 1715 and 1723, which granted representation to towns when they obtained a population of sixty families and regulated the elections in such towns. Wilmington, Newbern, Edenton, and Brunswick later received charters from the governor granting them the right to elect a representative,[1] but Bath never took out a new charter, as the act establishing it had not been repealed. Under the provisions of the Bath-town act of 1715 other towns claimed the right to send a representative when they obtained the necessary population; and in 1760 Halifax did not even wait for the governor's writ, but elected a burgess, who, after investigation of the claims of Halifax by the assembly, was admitted to a seat.[2] Dobbs later confirmed this right by charter,[3] and six towns thus had the right to elect burgesses. Later, three more towns, Campbelton, Hillsborough, and Salisbury, received the same right; Tarborough attempted to exercise the privilege, and the Board of Trade recommended that Beaufort be given a representative.

In spite of the frequent requests of the governors, the Board of Trade appears loath to advise the repeal of the Bath-town act of 1715. In 1762 they merely threaten to so advise the king if the assembly persist in the " undutiful & unreasonable claims" in cases like that of Halifax.[4] Later in 1773, they upheld the assembly in refusing a seat to a person elected from the lately chartered town of Tarborough, because the town did not possess the number of inhabitants required by the act of 1715;[5] and, on the other

---

habitable House, not of less Dimensions than Twenty Feet long, Fifteen Feet in Wedth, and Eight Feet in Height, between the first Floor and the Joists."

[1] *N. C. Col. Rec.,* VI, 228–229, 331, 333.

[2] *Ibid.,* 245, 365. The Board of Trade resolved that the claim of Halifax was " unconstitutional and not warranted by any authority whatever" (*ibid.,* 752).

[3] *Ibid.,* 245, 333.

[4] *Ibid.,* VI, 752.

[5] *Ibid.,* IX, 348, 746–747, 989.

hand, despite the expressed opinion of Governor Martin that the " present Bulk" of the assembly made it embarrassing, the lords directed him to grant a charter to Beaufort, which had petitioned for a burgess because its population consisted of over sixty families.[1]   The action of the English authorities appears much more reasonable than that of the governors; for the latter, forced by the necessities of colonial politics, granted charters to insignificant villages,[2] while refusing it to larger places.[3]

There appears to have been no general suffrage qualification applicable to all these towns.   The laws of 1715 and 1723 had given the franchise to householders either by lease or by freehold tenure, but this was not uniformly retained. It was extended to Brunswick by the general election law of 1760;[4] and yet a few months later the elections in another town, Newbern, were said to be by the freeholders alone,[5] and in Hillsborough, by the charter of 1770, the same restriction was made.[6]   Yet in Campbelton[7] and in Tarborough the electors are merely " the inhabitants." [8]   In Campbelton especially, certain freeholders charged that their charter of 1765 gave " power to all persons whom accident or design shall bring within two miles of the Court-house of Campbelton, on the day appointed for the Election of a Member to give their suffrages; altho' their proper place of residence be far out of the limits of the said Town, and although they have no property in that or any other place to become

[1] *N. C. Col. Rec.,* IX, 636, 640–641, 682.

[2] Both Hillsborough and Tarborough were smaller in size than the population fixed by the act of 1715.   The first retained while the latter lost its representative.

[3] Governor Tryon, in 1767, wrote, " The several towns in this province are created by act of Assembly but have no right upon their creation to send members to the Assembly, nor doth that right by law commence until there be sixty families residing in the town, at which time they may apply [to the governor], and are entitled to a writ for electing a representative in the Assembly" (*N. C. Col. Rec.,* VII, 473).

[4] Davis, *Laws* (1764), 201.

[5] *N. C. Col. Rec.,* VI, 672.

[6] *Ibid.,* VIII, 216.

[7] *Ibid.,* IX, 80.

[8] *Ibid.,* 746.   Cf. varying suffrage in English boroughs, *ante,* Ch. I.

the subject of representation." [1] Thus the elections were thrown into "the Hands of transient persons, Boatmen Waggoners and other Laborers," and taken "from their Employers, who are principally interested in securing or improving from their right of Representation, the property of the Town." Upon this representation the governor and council granted the town a new charter limiting the suffrage to freeholders.[2] There was no more uniformity in the election provisions of these charters than there was method in erecting the towns or reason for the granting of borough representation.[3] Apparently the ignorance or fancy, or political environment of the governors determined the town suffrage. The town elections, perhaps on account of the absence of uniformity in the suffrage provisions, were more turbulent than those in the counties, and the number of contested cases is proportionally greater than those arising from county elections.[4]

North Carolina had few local officers of an elective nature. Mention has already been made of the popular triple nomination of candidates for the office of county register, which, beginning in 1715 or before that year, lasted down to the Revolution.[5] Another group of elective officials were the commissioners of some of the towns. The early laws organizing towns placed the control of town matters in the hands of a board of commissioners, whose numbers were kept up either by appointments of the governor [6] or of the neighboring county court,[7] or elections by themselves.[8] Many of the

[1] *N. C. Col. Rec.,* IX, 79.

[2] *Ibid.,* 79–81, 274.

[3] A number of other towns were erected from time to time, but none of these ever obtained a population sufficient to give it a representative. See Davis, *Laws* (1751), 62–65, 92–94; (1764), 7, 11, 28, 32; (1773), 506, 530, 556.

[4] Out of thirty-six contested election cases noticed in the records between the years 1731–1774, fifteen arose in the towns and twenty-one in the counties. Throughout the whole period there were three or four times as many counties as towns (*e.g.,* 1767, eight towns and twenty-nine counties, *Col. Rec.,* VII, 473).

[5] See *ante,* p. 94.

[6] *E.g.,* Davis, *Laws* (1751), 100.

[7] *E.g., ibid.,* 62–65, 92–94.

[8] *E.g., ibid.,* 210.

later acts erected similar self-perpetuating bodies,[1] but in at least two cases provision was made for the election of the commissioners by popular vote. The first town to receive this privilege, apparently, was Wilmington, where, by an act of 1740, the electors qualified to vote for an assembly-man were impowered to elect annually five persons from whom the governor would choose three to serve as town commissioners for the ensuing year.[2] In 1745 all the five elected were to serve;[3] and the same privilege was extended to Newbern in 1748,[4] where previously a close corporation had existed. These rights were restored by the assembly in 1756, after the wholesale repeal of town and county acts two years earlier;[5] but no evidence has been found to show that any other towns were granted like privileges.

The North Carolina vestry from 1715 to 1741 was a close corporation usually appointed in the act erecting the parish,[6] and subsequently filling vacancies in their own number. But in the latter year an act was passed for the election of vestry-men every two years by the inhabiting freeholders of every parish.[7] This act was later amended to restrict the parish suffrage to those qualified to vote for representatives and to require the use of the ballot in such elections.[8] The Crown disallowed the vestry act in 1754,[9] and thereafter, until 1764 there was no permanent basis for the parish system. In 1758 an attempt was made to erect " select" vestries, or close corporations, but this was rejected by the lower house.[10] An act of 1760 was disallowed by the English government, and the church thrown into the greatest confusion.[11] At last a

---

[1] *E.g.*, Davis, *Laws* (1773), 470, 506, 530, 556.

[2] Davis, *Laws* (1751), 115.

[3] *Ibid.*, 204–208.   [4] *Ibid.*, 279.

[5] Davis, *Laws* (1764), 93–98, 98–105. Edenton had a close corporation of trustees (*ibid.*, 105–111). For later change in Wilmington, see Davis, *Laws* (1773), 507.

[6] Davis, *Laws* (1751), 50, 65, 67.

[7] *Ibid.*, 157.

[8] In 1751; Davis, *Laws* (1751), 352.

[9] *N. C. Col. Rec.*, V, 116.

[10] *Ibid.*, V, 1063, 1080.

[11] See letters of the ministers, *ibid.*, VI, 978, 990, 994, 999.

law was passed in 1764 which appears to have been satisfactory to the Bishop of London and the British government. This act [1] provided for a triennial election of vestrymen by those who had within the parish fifty acres of land or a town lot saved according to law. Votes were to " be given openly," not by ballot, and the suffrage was compulsory:

> "Every Person qualified to vote for Vestrymen in their respective Parishes (the People called Quakers excepted) is hereby required to attend, and give his Vote at the Election of Vestrymen, in Manner herein before directed, unless prevented by some bodily Infirmity or legal Disability, under the Penalty of Twenty Shillings, Proclamation Money." [2]

A fine was also to be imposed upon dissenters who refused to take the oath of vestrymen after they had been elected.[3]

Parish elections in North Carolina differed from those in South Carolina in the fact that the first colony required all freeholders possessing the requisite fifty acres both to vote and to take office if elected, or to pay relatively heavy penalties for neglect; while her southern neighbor restricted the suffrage in such elections to members of the Church of England. They differed from those in Maryland and Virginia in that the dissenting class was large in numbers, strong in influence, and was aided by a large portion of the community who did not care to pay taxes for any church. Under such circumstances we need not wonder that great irregularities took place at the parish elections. The absence of a vestry act for several years made the weak established church still weaker, and under the new law of 1764 the conditions became worse rather than better. On some occasions dissenters were purposely elected to prevent the organization of a vestry and the collection of tithes,[4] and in 1771 an act was

[1] Davis, *Laws* (1773), 304.

[2] For comment upon this act, see S. B. Weeks, *Church and State in North Carolina, J. H. U. Studies*, XI, 36-38.

[3] It is interesting to notice that the compulsory voting clause was insisted upon by the lower house after the upper house had voted to expunge it (*N. C. Col. Rec.*, VI, 1107-1109).

[4] *N. C. Col. Rec.*, VIII, 180, 202-210, 503.

passed which provided for the collection of parish taxes even if there was no vestry in the parish.[1]

The suffrage provisions in North Carolina may now be summarized. During the first fifty years no definite provision for the suffrage has been found, and owing to the unsettled political conditions the elections must often have been farcical if not actually riotous. Formal and regular elections may have been held after 1715, in which year the suffrage was granted to all white tax-paying free men over twenty-one years of age. This provision was retained during the remainder of the proprietary period. The instructions to the royal governors conflicted with this wide franchise, and the governors attempted to make the colonial practice square with their orders. Under Burrington the contest was closely associated with the effort on the part of the governor to erect new precincts; and under Johnston the assembly passed a law limiting the suffrage to freeholders of fifty acres who had resided six months in the province, but no longer excluded negroes. With the addition of an age requirement of twenty-one years, this qualification remained unchanged until the Revolution. In the meantime a wider suffrage was granted in some towns, where tenants of houses could vote. But the whole suffrage and representative system was overthrown by the repeal of such acts in 1754. The right of representation was thereafter restored by the charters of the governors, who in some cases also defined the suffrage qualifications. The act of 1760 restored the old qualifications for voters in the counties, but abolished the previous ballot voting and substituted the *viva voce* method. In the towns there appear to have been some variations in the qualifications for voters, and the borough franchise was, without doubt, used by the governors to further their own political plans. Of local elections there were those for registers, town commissioners, and vestrymen, none of which appears to have varied materially from the assembly elections. The most curious feature of the suffrage is that compelling qualified freeholders, even dissenters, to take part in the parish elections. Another remarkable provision is the early exclusion of negroes, and the subsequent

[1] Davis, *Laws* (1771), 498.

granting of the franchise to them. North Carolina is the only colony south of Maryland which did not forbid their voting at the time of the Revolution. Throughout the royal period the suffrage question is most intimately connected with the attempt of the governors to win control of the representative system and direct the legislation of the assembly. This connection is seen in 1731 in the contest over the erection of new precincts, in 1746 over the subject of the quorum, in 1754–1756 in the repeal of election acts, in 1760 in the question of a quorum and the right of town representation, and during the later years in the arbitrary erection of Hillsborough and Tarborough into towns with right of representation. The whole force of the English government is usually exerted in favor of the governors in these struggles. Until the days of the repressive and retaliatory measures just preceding the Revolution, no colony felt so heavily the hand of British authority, or saw more of its popular legislation mutilated by the English veto-power, than did the province of North Carolina.

CHAPTER V.

THE SUFFRAGE IN SOUTH CAROLINA.

The Carolina proprietors under the royal grants of 1663 and 1665 did not intend keeping their vast domain under one government. The struggling Albermarle settlement in the North was placed under the tutelage of Governor Berkeley, of Virginia, one of the eight proprietors who was empowered to appoint one or two governors for Carolina;[1] later the unsuccessful Cape Fear settlement was erected into an independent colony;[2] and the proprietors apparently entertained the idea of establishing eight distinct counties, one for each proprietor, possessing separate and almost independent governments.[3] This early policy later gave way to an attempt to organize a general provincial government under the elaborate provisions of the Fundamental Constitutions; but in the same month, July, 1669, that this frame was adopted by the proprietors, the same men were affixing their seals to documents which would create still another colony within their territory, and make a united province almost an impossibility. Thus at first as a result of conscious policy and later as the outcome of practical conditions, the Carolina lands tended to divide into distinct settlements. Several abortive attempts at independent colonies were made, and at last only two distinct parts of the province were recognized, —the Albermarle settlement, usually spoken of as "Albermarle County;" and "that parte of the Province of Carolina that lyeth southward and westward of Cape Feare."[4]

In July, 1669, when instructions were drawn up for the governor and council of the proposed colony at Port Royal (South Carolina), it was admitted that the number of peo-

[1] *N. C. Col. Records,* I, 48.

[2] *Ibid.,* 75–92.

[3] *Ibid.,* Prefatory Notes, pp. xiv–xv.

[4] This was for many years the only legal name of South Carolina, and was continually used in the enacting clauses of the laws; see *Statutes at Large of South Carolina,* II, 13, etc.

ple in Carolina was too small to put in force the " Grand Model," [1] and accordingly a modified and temporary form of government was ordained by the proprietors. The governor and five deputies had been appointed in England, and upon arriving in the colony these were to be joined by five more elected by the people.

" As soone as you arrive at Port Royall you are to summon all ye freemen that are in ye Collony, and require them to elect five persons, who being joyned to ye five deputed by ye respective Propriet[rs], are to be ye Counsell wth whose advice & consent, or at least sixe of them, all being summoned, you are to governe according to the Limitations & Instruccons following, observeing what cann at present be putt in practice of our fundamentall Constitutions & forme of Governm[t]." [2]

The ten councillors and the governor were to be assisted in the making of laws by deputies also elected by popular choice:

" you are to sumon ye freehoulders of ye Collony & require ym in our names to elect twenty persons, wch. together wth or [our] Deputys for ye present are to be yr Parliament, by & wth whose consent, or ye maior parte of them, you are to make such laws as you shall from time to time finde necessary." [3]

The instructions promised one hundred and fifty acres of land to every freeman who settled before March 25, 1670, and the same amount to the freemen for each male servant they brought out to the colony; one hundred acres for each woman-servant or male-servant under sixteen years of age; and promised one hundred acres to every servant upon the expiration of his term of service. Smaller amounts were to be given to those coming later, but all persons receiving land must take an oath of allegiance to the king, and of fidelity and submission to the proprietors and to their Fundamental Constitutions. A quit-rent of one penny an acre

[1] The suffrage provisions of the royal charters and the fundamental constitutions have been discussed under the heading of North Carolina, and will be mentioned here only incidentally.

[2] Rivers, *A Sketch of the History of South Carolina to the Close of the Proprietary Government by the Revolution of 1719*, Appendix, 347.

[3] *Ibid.*, 348.

was reserved upon all lands thus granted, to be paid annually after September 29, 1689.

The party of emigrants left England in August, 1669,[1] and at the Bermudas a blank commission for governor was filled in with the name of William Sayle, and this person took charge of the expedition during the days of settlement.[2] When the colonists arrived at Port Royal, the first election, in accordance with the instructions, was held for the selection of five councillors. According to the records, the governor " Sum'oned all the ffreemen, & there to Elect & choose five men to bee of the Councill;" and after five had been chosen, a certain William Owen " alwaies itching to be in Authority," questioned the legality of the election, but " wherevpon the s'd ffreeholdrs or the major p'te of them, mett a second tyme, & confirmed their former Election, by subscribeing of their sev'rall names." [3]

This election, the first held in South Carolina, is of interest because it was held so early in the history of the settlement; indeed, before the ships had reached Charleston harbor, and while temporarily lying in Port Royal, the men of the fleet were called together. It is to be noted also that here, as in the instructions, the words freeman and freeholder are used interchangeably. Section 1 of the instructions above quoted makes the election of councillors by the freemen; while Section 8 names freeholders as electors of members of the parliament. So in the account of this first election the voters are spoken of as " ffreemen" and as " ffreeholders." There can be no doubt that the electors, who did not number many over a score,[4] were simply the free men of the expedition, since of freeholders there were as yet none, as the place of settlement was not yet reached, and no definite assignments of land had been made. The freemen under the instructions were potential freeholders, but

---

[1] McCrady, *History of South Carolina under the Proprietary Government,* 120 (quoted hereafter as McCrady, I).

[2] *Ibid.,* I, 124.

[3] The Council writing to the Proprietors, March 21, 1670-71; *Shaftesbury Papers, Collections of South Carolina Historical Society,* V, 291; *Charleston Year-Book,* 1883, 371.

[4] *Collections S. C. Hist. Soc.,* V, 203, 292.

they were not actual landholders before the land was reached or apportioned.

After reaching Charleston and beginning the settlement, the colonists were apparently too much engrossed in their own affairs to think of political organization, and it was not until three months had passed that the governor and council determined to issue certain ordinances restraining the profane violation of the Sabbath and "other grand abuses." [1]

This determination was reached on July 4, 1670, and on that day, or shortly afterwards, the first assembly, although an irregular one, was elected. After seriously considering the abuses and the manner of redressing them, " and finding that the Number of ffreehould^{rs} in the Collony nott neere sufficient to Electe a Parliam^t; and the s'd late Gov'nor, by & wth the advice & consent of vs his Councell, did make such orders as wee did think convenient to suppress the same, vpon wch the s'd Gov'nor did Sum'ons all the People to heare the said Orders, all the s'd ffreemen consenting therevnto the s'd Gov'nor & Councell caused the s'd orderes to bee published." [2] But this method of promulgating laws was opposed by that William Owen who had objected to the election of councillors at Port Royal, and who was "willing to doe anything, though ever soe ill in itt selfe, rather then not to apeare, to bee a man of acc'on." Owen argued that no such orders could be made without the consent of a parliament elected according to the instructions. He appears at first to have impressed this opinion upon the governor, for the latter evidently permitted an election to take place.[3] Owen directed the election, and wrote with his own hand the list of twenty members of parliament, and so controlled the choice that it was said he moved "all the rest of the ffreemen," "in another spheere then their owne." [4] Owen's influence was of short duration; the council prevented the governor from recognizing the parliament, and the representatives "without any farthere notice takinge of the s'd

---

[1] *Coll. S. C. Hist. Soc.,* V, 291.
[2] *Ibid.,* 292.
[3] *Ibid.,* 176–177, 203.
[4] *Ibid.,* 292; *Charleston Year-Book,* 1883, 375.

will'm Owen, or their Elec'on into dignity (as the s'd Owen p'waded them itt would bee) lefte the s'd Owen & his Paper, & followed their own Labours, wch indeed neerely concerned them & vs to." [1]

Owen's factious opposition to the ordinances of the governor had a legal basis in the fact that no ordinance power was delegated to the governor and council by their instructions; and consequently the responsibility for the quarrels in the colony must be laid not solely at the door of William Owen, but also upon the neglect of the proprietors, and their anxiety to establish the parliament, council, and other forms of the Fundamental Constitutions.[2] The most practical method of legislation was that which the governor and council had adopted,—the submission of their ordinances to the approval of a general meeting of the freemen.

Upon the death of Governor Sayle in March, 1670-71, Joseph West was chosen governor by the council, after Sayle had designated him as successor.[3] During the year that the colonists had been in the colony their numbers had been considerably increased, and newcomers were frequently arriving. Accordingly, a few days after the election of Governor West, he called together the " Antient ffreehoulders" and " the New ffree men," and in a general meeting at the storehouse proposed certain ordinances to them.[4] Owen again demanded an election of a parliament, although he himself admits that there were only between forty and fifty freeholders.[5] According to his account, the people unanimously stood by the lords' instructions, that laws " were to be framed by 20 persons freehouldrs in the nature of a parlemt." But the governor replied that the time was " some what unseasonable," and that he intended calling a parliament when opportunity served, or the necessity for the making of laws required it. Ten days later, however, in writing to the proprietors, the governor and council say there is

---

[1] The Council to the Proprietors, *ibid.;* also West to Lord Ashley, *Coll. S. C. Hist. Soc.,* V, 203.

[2] McCrady, I, 133.

[3] *Ibid.,* 138.

[4] *Coll. S. C. Hist. Soc.,* V, 293.

[5] *Ibid.,* 302.

" noe great necessity att prsent of a Parliamt our tyme being well imployed, if wee cann imploy it well, in Planting & other necessary works that lyeth vpon vs." [1] Sir John Yeamans claimed also that West feared a parliament would question too closely his actions or the manner of his election.[2] The desired representative body was not granted, and the ordinances of the governor and council were enforced.

But the proprietors in England were desirous of getting a parliament as soon as possible, even while the numbers of the colonists were so insignificant. In May, 1671, the proprietors sent instructions to the " Governor and Council of Ashley River" directing them " within thirty days after receit hereof to summon ye Freeholders of ye Plantation, & require them in our names to elect 20 persons who, togeather with our Deputys as our Representatives, for ye present are to be your Parliamt." [3] The governor was required to call a parliament in this manner every two years, and as much oftener as the state of affairs in the plantation should require. The parliament in each case was to choose five of its members to act as councillors with the five deputies of the proprietors. These mandatory instructions could not have reached the colony before July 8, and so we must give Governor West the credit of calling for an election of parliament members upon his own volition. In March the governor had said there was no necessity for a parliament, but by July " more people being now arrived," he summoned " all the ffreemen" and required them to elect twenty persons to be members of the parliament. The election, completed three days later, was not managed altogether peaceably, and Sir John Yeamans, who soon was to become governor himself, advised the voters " in all elections to choose such as will stand at the greatest distance from the Gou'nor." [4]

The parliament so elected on July 11 was the first legal representative body in South Carolina. It proved to be

[1] *Coll. S. C. Hist. Soc.*, V, 295.

[2] *Ibid.*, 349.

[3] *Ibid.*, 322; Rivers, *Sketch*, Appendix, 366.

[4] *Ibid.*, 337–338, 354.

greatly in sympathy with Yeamans, and at once began to cast doubts upon the powers of the council and the legality of the governor's election. The details of this contest do not concern us here, but it is remarkable that the proprietors in England decided upon Yeamans for governor at almost the same time that he was strenuously opposing Governor West in Charleston.[1] Yeamans's commission and instructions did not reach him until the spring of 1672, and only on April 19 was he proclaimed governor.[2] On that day, " regard being had to the conveniency of the Freemen now assembled together in this Towne," a proclamation was issued " to dissolve all Parliaments & Parliamentary Conventions heretofore had or made in this Province" and requiring " all the freeholders in this Province to come before the Grand Councill at Charles Towne" on the following day to elect a parliament. Accordingly, on April 20, " came the Freemen &c at Charles Towne, and having then made their election," they presented the names of the twenty members of the parliament to the governor and the proprietary deputies. Immediately " the said Parliament &c then and there out of themselves did elect five persons" to be joined with the proprietors' deputies as a " Grand Councill."[3]

Thus did the proprietors, " fond of their new form of government,"[4] lay the foundations for republican government, while they had in mind only the final establishment of their aristocratic constitutions. All of these provisions for government were accounted temporary, and they should soon give place to the elaborate requirements of the " Grand Model." As early as June 21, 1672, steps were taken for the incorporation of the " nobillity" into the legislature, and the temporary laws of that date provided that " the Parliament shall consist of ye Governor, ye Deputys of the Lords Proprietors, the Nobillity and twenty chosen by the Freehoulders."[5] In spite of the efforts of the proprietors, their

[1] McCrady, I, 158.
[2] *Coll. S. C. Hist. Soc.,* V, 390.
[3] *Ibid.,* 390; Rivers, *Sketch,* Appendix, 378.
[4] *An Historical Account of the Rise and Progress of the Colonies of South Carolina and Georgia* (Alexander Hewatt), London, 1729, I, 60.
[5] *Coll. S. C. Hist. Soc.,* V, 405; Rivers, *Sketch,* Appendix, 355.

aristocracy of landgraves and caciques never occupied any place in the government, although the form was kept up of making the governor a landgrave before his appointment.[1]

One more of the early elections that may be mentioned is that which took place upon the death of Governor Yeamans and the succession of West to the vacant position. On August 16, 1674, the council " Resolved that the ffreeholders of this Settlem^t be sumoned to appear at Charles-towne upon Thursday next in the morning then and there to elect a Parliam^t." After the election of the parliament members, the latter proceeded to elect six from themselves to sit with the deputies as a council.[2]

In looking back now over the elections of these first four years of South Carolina's history, we are met with the fact that popular elections and a representative system are established from the first days of the settlement. Had there been no desire on the part of the proprietors to set their " Model" in motion, it is quite likely that occasional meetings of all the inhabitants would have served the political needs of the colony. In Maryland the pure democracy was retained for about twenty years, and in the New England colonies it was the usual type of early colonial organization. Its evident efficiency is seen in the way in which the two popular gatherings in South Carolina, of July, 1670, and March, 1671, accepted the ordinances of the governor and council. The demagogue William Owen would have had no power had he not based his arguments upon the proprietary instructions for a parliament. But the lords proprietors must needs approach as near as possible to their impracticable form of government; and thus in 1671, when the population did not greatly exceed 200, and there may have been somewhat over fifty freeholders,[3]—these freeholders were required to select twenty for a parliament in addition to the five deputies of the proprietors; thus making

---

[1] McCrady, I, 157, 218, 232, 266, etc.

[2] *Coll. S. C. Hist. Soc.,* V, 452; Hewatt, I, 74.

[3] In March, 1670–71, Owen said there were two hundred and odd inhabitants, of whom between forty and fifty were freeholders. By July "more people" arrived, but how many is not stated. *Coll. S. C. Hist. Soc.,* V, 302, 337.

nearly one-half of the freemen members of the parliament. If all those so elected actually attended the parliament meetings, it is probable that this assembly contained a larger proportion of the voters than the democratic meetings of Maryland or Massachusetts, in which the proxy system and the reluctance of freemen to travel kept the real attendance far below the number of those actually empowered to participate.

Another fact of significance in these early elections is to be found in the synonymous character of the words freeman and freeholder. The first term has here little semblance of the New England meaning, but if ever used apart from the freeholder sense, it meant *free man*. There is, however, no distinction in the current records between the two words. The same election, as an inspection of the preceding excerpts will show, is frequently said to have been performed by the freemen and by the freeholders; and from the point of view of the suffrage the two may be taken as absolutely synonymous. The very nature of the land grants, giving 150 acres or some smaller amount later to every free man, would necessarily make the terms equivalent in fact, as they are in the grammatical usage of the time. The Fundamental Constitutions had provided that electors should possess at least fifty acres of land,[1] and although the constitutions did not become effective, yet the smallest amount of land promised to freemen was seventy acres;[2] thus ensuring to any free man who could reach the colony, and to every servant after his time expired, an amount of land more than sufficient to qualify him as an elector. The ease with which land was acquired must be borne continually in mind when we consider the colonial real estate qualifications for the suffrage.

After 1674 the suffrage question does not become prominent until the French Huguenots had come into the colony in large numbers. A system of proxy voting, so natural in its development in all the colonies owing to the difficulties of transportation and the impelling necessity of the struggle for existence, arose in South Carolina. The proprietors in

[1] Section 66 of "First Set," *Coll. S. C. Hist. Soc.*, V, 110.
[2] Rivers, *Sketch*, Appendix, 348.

September, 1683, wrote to the governor that they were informed

> "that men are admitted to bring papers for others, and to put in their votes for them which is utterly illegal and contrary to the custom of parliament, and will in time, if suffered, be very mischievous. You are therefore to take care that such practices be not suffered for the future; but every man must deliver his own vote and no man be suffered to bring the vote of another." [1]

No further facts concerning this early proxy method have been found, but it illustrates again the reluctance of the early settlers to forsake their plantation work and take part in elections. In the intervening years there was dissatisfaction with the apportionment of representatives, as when in 1683 the governor was directed to have ten representatives for each of the counties of Berkeley and Colleton elected, in spite of the fact that the former was far more populous than the latter.[2] During this period the assembly refused to take the oath to the new Fundamental Constitutions of 1682;[3] and later, in the quarrel which arose inevitably over the payment of quit-rents, the people became turbulent, the assembly would not recognize Governor Colleton, and the province was in a condition of anarchy.[4]

Upon the revocation of the Edict of Nantes in 1685 the proprietors of Carolina encouraged the settlement of the Huguenot exiles in the province, and within two years 50,000 acres of land were granted to Frenchmen.[5] In all about 400 of these persons settled in Carolina at this time.[6] They, of course, continued to use their own language, and while some used a French translation of the English Prayer-Book, others maintained a non-conformist service. The Frenchmen were not at once admitted to the rights of citizens. Governor Southwell, who had practically gained his office by popular choice, caused an act to be passed in May, 1691,

[1] Rivers, *Sketch,* Appendix, 407.
[2] *Ibid.,* 406–7.
[3] McCrady, I, 210.
[4] Hewatt, I, 100–101; McCrady, I, 224–231.
[5] Rivers, *Sketch,* 174.
[6] *Ibid.,* 447; McCrady, I, 324.

for the naturalization of all French and Swiss Protestants;[1] but this act, with all the other laws of this parliament, was disallowed by the proprietors. Had the act been ratified, it might have prevented subsequent trouble, for in 1691 Governor Ludwell was instructed to grant five or six representatives to Craven County, which was populated almost exclusively by the French.[2] To refuse naturalization to the French, and then to give these aliens the right to elect almost one-third of the assembly, was more than the English inhabitants of Berkeley County could stand. This county, having a majority of the population, was given only one-third of the representation. It was but natural that the English should ask "Shall the Frenchmen, who cannot speak our language, make our laws?"[3]

At an assembly election in 1692, according to Ludwell's instructions, six Frenchmen represented Craven County.[4] This assembly passed the first South Carolina act " to Regulate the Elections of Members of Assembly." The act is not given in either Trott's Laws or the Statutes at Large, but an idea of its contents can be gained from a letter of the proprietors to Governor Ludwell.[5] From this it appears that the law permitted any person to vote for representatives who was willing to take oath that he was worth ten pounds, but it did not specify any term of residence for an elector. The act was in contravention to the provision of the constitutions of 1669 and 1682, which required a voter to possess a freehold of fifty acres, and yet the ten pounds qualification appears again in an accepted law of 1704.[6] The same assembly, in drawing up a list of grievances against Governor Southwell, protested that the number of representatives of the people was too small, and that the people did not, as the King's charter directed, fix the number of their delegates.[7]

Only three weeks after the assembly had passed its elec-

[1] Rivers, *Sketch*, 175.
[2] *N. C. Col. Rec.*, I, 373; Rivers, *Sketch*, 176.
[3] Rivers, *Sketch*, 176.
[4] McCrady, I, 239.
[5] Rivers, *Sketch*, Appendix, 437.
[6] *Statutes at Large of S. C.*, II, 249.
[7] Rivers, *Sketch*, Appendix, 434.

tion law, and of course without knowledge of it, the proprietors ordered, in November, 1692, that certain laws, among which were any relating to the election of representatives to the assembly, should not go into force until the proprietary confirmation had been given.[1] When the election act reached England, the proprietors hastened to disallow it. Since all the representatives were for the present elected in counties, the proprietors were of opinion that they should be chosen only by freeholders, thus by inference conforming to the English distinction between the borough and the county suffrage. And this act

" not mentioning how long any person worth tenn pounds must have been an Inhabitant of the County before he be admitted to vote for members of the Assembly, it is so loose that by this Act all the Pyrates that were in the Shipp that had been plundering in the Red Sea had been qualified to vote for Representatives in Carolina, which being of dangerous consequence to the Inhabitants, we have thought fitt to dissent to that act alsoe." [2]

Whether the personal property qualification of this law was a means to open the suffrage to non-freeholding citizens of Berkeley County—where Charleston was situated—in order to counterbalance the power of the French is not clear; but there can be no doubt that the opposition to the Huguenots was rapidly growing stronger. Their land titles were now questioned, their marriages were popularly held to be void, and interference was made with their religious services.[3] The English colonists attempted, moreover, to exclude them altogether from political privileges. They prepared an address to Joseph Blake, whom the council had chosen governor in 1694, " praying that the refugees might not only be denied the privilege of sitting as members of the legislative body, but also of a vote at their election, and that the assembly might be composed only of English members,

---

[1] Rivers, *Sketch,* Appendix, 435.

[2] *Ibid.,* 437. The " Red Sea Pyrates" is a reference to a vessel manned by seventy pirates, who ran away from Jamaica to Charles Towne, bringing with them a " vast" quantity of gold from the Red Sea (*Coll. S. C. Hist. Soc.,* I, 205).

[3] *Ibid.*

chosen by Englishmen." [1]   Blake did not grant the request, and this petition appears to have been the last serious opposition to the French.   Under Governor Archdale's administration, the attitude of the English towards the refugees changed rapidly within the next two years,—a change which the records do not adequately explain.[2]   As early as September, 1696, the proprietors had received word from the colony that the assembly was inclined to grant naturalization to the French, and they express their satisfaction at the news.[3]   The change in sentiment must have been noticed in the preceding spring, and this was not more than a year and a half after the petition praying for the total exclusion of the French from political rights had been presented.

But the naturalization act did not pass during Archdale's administration.   It was Joseph Blake, again acting as governor, who advised the French to take advantage of the change in popular sentiment and petition the assembly for admission to the rights of English citizenship.[4]   The assembly could now say, in the preamble to the act of March 10, 1696–97, in strong contrast to the feeling two years earlier,

"Prosecution for Religion hath forced some Aliens and Trade and the Fertility of this colony has encouraged others to resort to this Colony, all which have given Testimony of their humble Duty and Loyalty to his Majesty and the Crown of England, and of their Fidelity to the true and absolute Lords and proprietors of this Province, and of their Obedience to their Laws, and their good Affections to the Inhabitants thereof, and by their Industry, Diligence and Trade have very much enriched and advanced this Colony and Settlement thereof." [5]

The act then provided "that all Aliens, Male and Female, of what Nation soever, which now are Inhabitants of South-

[1] Hewatt, I, 128–9.

[2] *Ibid.*, 139–140, simply transcribes the preamble of the naturalization act of 1696–7 in assigning causes for the change in feeling; and McCrady, I, 289, does not throw much light on the reasons for the more kindly spirit of the English colonists.

[3] *Coll. S. C. Hist. Soc.*, I, 141; Proprietors to Archdale, September 10, 1696.

[4] Hewatt, I, 140; McCrady, I, 289.

[5] *Statutes at Large of S. C.*, II, 131; Trott's *Laws*, I, 61.

Carolina, their Wives and Children," might be admitted to all the rights and privileges of English subjects, and be adjudged as free as if they were born of English parents within the province. The petitioners were at once admitted to citizenship, and any others might be given the same privileges by petitioning the governor within the next three months. In all cases the petitioner must take an oath of allegiance to King William. " Full, free and undisturbed Liberty of their Consciences" was granted to all Christians, " Papists only excepted."

Although no provision was made for future alien settlers, and only three months were granted to the French to hand in their petitions and take the oaths,[1] yet the act was temporarily successful,[2] and the political position of aliens does not again appear upon the records for almost five years. A permanent naturalization act was not passed until 1704.[3] The political contest here between native-born English and aliens is almost unique in colonial history. It was brought on first by the absence of any general naturalization law; and, secondly, by the aim of the proprietors to admit the aliens to the suffrage, and grant the county inhabited by them a representation almost equal to the populous Berkeley County, in spite of the fact that the French were still aliens and could legally exercise no English political rights. We find popular opposition to alien voters again in the election troubles of the years 1701–1706, but little antagonism to the French as such. The earlier jealousy of the French settlers apparently arose from the unwise attempt of the proprietors to give such great political influence to unnaturalized foreigners.

The assembly which naturalized the French also passed an act for the regulating of elections of members of the assembly; but, unfortunately, the act is not given in the printed collections of laws.[4] From a private letter of 1703, it appears that this act contained the ten pounds qualifica-

---

[1] McCrady, I, 323, says 154 aliens in all sought naturalization under the act.

[2] Hewatt, I, 140.

[3] *Statutes at Large of S. C.,* II, 251; Trott's *Laws,* I, 107.

[4] *Ibid.,* 130; *Ibid.,* 60.

tion for voters to which the proprietors had objected in 1693, and which was now joined to a three-months' residence in the colony. The assembly in 1703, by a "noble vote," declared foreigners who possessed these qualifications entitled to vote; which caused Landgrave Smith in disgust to remark that he could not see how they could be happy in the colony unless election laws and some others were to be passed in England.[1] The terms of the act of 1696–97 were not strong enough, however, to prevent great abuses at elections within a few years.[2]

The years 1700–1706 comprised a period of contest for power between the dissenters and the Church party, in which the French took the side of the proprietors and Anglicans. During this time, as previously, all elections were held in Charleston, and election quarrels and frauds were frequent. The relative merits of the two parties are difficult to determine at the present time. Oldmixon and the earlier historians generally accepted the story of the dissenters, while Mr. Edward McCrady, in his scholarly work on South Carolina under the proprietors, partly exonorates the Churchmen from the criticism formerly heaped upon them. Our interest lies mainly with the influence of these quarrels upon the suffrage; but for the whole period the reader may be referred to McCrady, Carroll, Hewatt, Rivers, and the documents in the appendix to Rivers.

After Governor Blake's death in 1700, the council, in some confusion, elected James Moore as governor.[3] Moore

[1] McCrady, I, 413, quoting Dalcho, *Church History,* 56.

[2] An interesting election writ—the only one noticed in South Carolina —belongs to about this time. (Rivers, *Sketch,* Appendix, 439.) It is directed to the high sheriff of Berkeley County, and says:

"We . . . Command you to Summon all the King's Leidge subjects, the freemen Inhabitants of Berkly County to be and appear together with all the rest of the freemen as aforesaid of this part of our Province, at Charlestowne, on the 19th day of December next, then and there by a majority of their voices to agree to and ascertaine the number of their Representatives for this part of the Province, to consult and advise with us about making such laws as shall be necessary for the safety and defence of this Province."

[3] Hewatt, I, 145.

was a churchman whose not over-sensitive conscience was rendered more flexible by the financial difficulties in which he had become involved.[1] In the election of 1701 he determined to have an assembly of his " own complexion" elected, and in this he was greatly aided by the custom of electing members for all counties in the city of Charleston. The election was a " scene of riot, intemperance, and confusion," [2] according to one writer. A later protest by the members from Colleton County premising how elections should be free and indifferent, and how no alien not specially qualified may elect or be elected to serve in the assembly, proceeds to describe how the rights of Englishmen had been violated, the ancient usages and customs of the province broken, and the act for regulating elections ignored.

" For so it was, may it please your Lordships, that at the said Election, much threat'nings, many intreaties & other unjustifiable actions were made use of, & illegal and unqualify'd votes given in to the Sheriff, & by him receiv'd & returned; particularly the votes of very many unqualify'd Aliens were taken & enter'd, the votes of several Members of the Council were fil'd & receiv'd, a great number of Servants & poor & indigent persons voted promiscuously with their Masters & Creditors, as also several free Negroes were receiv'd, & taken for as good Electors as the best Freeholders in the Province. So that we leave it with Your Lordships to judge whether admitting Aliens, Strangers, Servants, Negroes, &c., as good and qualified Voters, can be thought any ways agreeable to King Charles' Patent to Your Lordships, or the English Constitution of Government." [3]

The assembly which met after these election frauds was naturally not a peaceable one. The governor, by prorogations, prevented an investigation of the last election, and then turned popular attention to an expedition to attack the Spaniards at St. Augustine.[4] At the next meeting of the assembly, the lower house took steps to prevent trouble at the next election. Accordingly, a bill was twice passed in the lower house " for the settling of Elections for the future,

[1] McCrady, I, 374.
[2] Hewatt, I, 150.
[3] Rivers, *Sketch,* Appendix, 455.
[4] *Ibid.,* 455–456.

and for granting as much freedom to the French and other Aliens as could be granted by the Assembly, or the French reasonably expect." [1] These bills, the contents of which are not known, were rejected by the governor and council without granting a conference. Perhaps it was with design that a more stringent election law was not passed, and aliens and unpropertied persons excluded from the suffrage. The dissenters claimed that the election of 1703 was accompanied with greater irregularities than occurred at the former one. Now, it was said " Jews, Strangers, Sailors, Servants, Negroes and almost every French Man in Craven & Berkly County came down to elect, & their Votes were taken, & the Persons by them voted for were returned by the Sheriff, to the manifest wrong & prejudice of other Candidates." [2]

The assembly so elected is one of the memorable legislatures of South Carolina. Whether truly representative of the population or not,—and the historians differ as to the proportions of churchmen and dissenters at this time,—it was strongly in favor of the English church, and in sympathy with the plans of the proprietors and the governor for a church establishment. [3] The coalition of High Churchmen and French Huguenots had given the former control of the assembly, and they now proceeded to turn the tables upon the dissenters who had attempted to cut out the French from political privileges, by presently passing an act which would exclude the dissenters themselves from the assembly. The act of May 6, 1704, in a lengthy title and preamble, stated its purpose to be the " more effectual preservation of the government," by requiring the members of the commons house of assembly to take certain oaths, conform to the

[1] Rivers, *Sketch,* Appendix, 457; Oldmixon, in Carroll, *Collections,* II, 425.

[2] *Ibid.,* 459. The authors of the Colleton County Representation say that the French, owing to their ignorance of the English language, were often made tools of and imposed upon. They advised legislation by an English assembly, for, they say, " we can't imagine that we do them any hurt, by making good and wholesome Laws for us & them, since we oblige them by no Laws whatsoever, or upon any account, then what we ourselves are obliged by, & live under."

[3] Hewatt, I, 149-153, 163-170; Oldmixon, in Carroll, *Collections,* II, 418, 436

Church of England, and take the Lord's Supper according to the service of that church.[1] Disavowing a desire to persecute for the sake of religion, the act stated that many contentions and animosities had been created by admitting persons of differing religious sentiments into the assembly, and that a policy of restricting membership to Churchmen had been adopted by the English House of Commons.[2] The act required all persons elected to the assembly to present evidence that they had partaken of the Lord's Supper according to the rites of the Church of England; or that, feeling themselves unworthy to partake, they regularly attended divine services according to the English form.[3]

Under the new act even a Churchman might be inconvenienced, for there were only two Anglican churches in the colony,[4] and to either of these the member must journey and receive the sacrament; and, indeed, it was claimed that most of the members who voted for the measure had been constant abstainers from the sacrament.[5] A most unjust clause provided for the seating of the candidate having the next highest number of votes, when a dissenter refused to qualify according to the act. Thus were the dissenters to taste the pains of political disqualification which they had recently been anxious to impose upon the Huguenots. In Colleton County, out of 200 electors, only fourteen were qualified to serve in the assembly; and at the election of 1705 only ten voters from this county came to the election in Charleston, where they voted for fourteen candidates and the sheriff returned the ten having the highest number of votes.[6] " Craven and Berkley Counties were so streightned by the qualifying act, that they had not 20 men to represent

---

[1] *Statutes at Large,* II, 232; Trott's *Laws,* I, 105.

[2] This was not true.

[3] The proprietors ratified this act, sometimes called the " Occasiona¹ Act," and the church act passed at the same time. The English House of Lords petitioned the Queen against the acts, but nothing came of this opposition. For full account of these events, see McCrady, I, 406–445.

[4] McCrady, I, 408.

[5] Oldmixon, in Carroll, *Collections,* II, 434.

[6] Carroll, *Collections,* II, 41.

them, unless they would choose a dissenter, or a man not fit to sit in the assembly." [1]

In 1704, while the Church party was in power, they passed two other important acts in addition to the church acts; one for the regulation of elections, and the other for the naturalization of aliens. The reason for passing the election act was said to be the many and troublesome complaints which lately had been presented to the assembly, and their consideration which consumed too much time, and interfered with " more necessary and publick business." [2] The voters' qualifications were apparently not changed from those required by the act of 1696–97, but we have the full text of the law for the first time. It is provided

> " That no person whatsoever, under the age of one and twenty years, shall have right to vote for any member of Assembly in any county or precinct whatsoever, and that no person whatsoever, which hath less than fifty acres of land in possession, or value of ten pounds, in money, goods, chattels or rents, and which doth not personally reside and dwell in the county or precinct for which he doth vote for, or pretend to choose members of Assembly, by the space of three months before the dates of the writts for election shall have right to vote for members as aforesaid."

The fifty acres and the ten pounds provision had probably been a part of the disallowed act of 1692, and of that of 1696–97; while the three months' residence had already been adopted in the latter act. [3]

Persons not residing in any county were to be permitted to vote with the next adjoining county or precinct; sheriffs were authorized to administer an oath to persons whose qualification was in doubt; and all county or precinct officers were forbidden to serve in the assembly. A positive prohibition of proxy voting, similar to such provisions in other colonies, was a part of this measure:

> " That every election for members of Assembly shall be in some open and publick place, and that no person whatsoever, here qualified to vote,

---

[1] Carroll, *Collections*, II, 441.
[2] *Statutes at Large*, II, 249–251.
[3] See p. 135.

shall, being absent from the place of election, give his voice or vote by proxy, letter, or any other way whatsoever, but shall be present in person or his voice to be taken for none." [1]

The polls were to be open from 8 to 12 in the forenoon and from 2 to 6 in the afternoon on not more than two days. After the adjournment on the first day, the sheriff was directed to " seal up in a paper bag or box all the votes given in that day in the presence of and with the seals of two or more of each contending party;" which is presumptive evidence that voting was performed by ballot. It is remarkable, indeed, that throughout the history of South Carolina, voting was uniformly by ballot; we have seen a subscribing of hands in the first election of councillors at Port Royal in 1670; some form of subscription or ballot was also probably used in the other early elections; and from 1683 onward to 1904 the ballot has been invariably used.[2]

Aliens were not formally excluded from the suffrage by this act, and only a year earlier the assembly by vote had held that aliens, if otherwise properly qualified, could vote under the law of 1696–97. But now, either to reward their late friends, or to place their right to vote beyond question, an act for the naturalization of foreigners was passed.[3] This law permitted aliens to be naturalized and admitted to all the rights of English citizens upon taking the oath of allegiance to the Queen, and the oath of abhorrency against the Pope's pretended power of deposition. But no alien could sit in the assembly; and none could vote for assembly members unless he was qualified according to the terms of the act of 1704. This was the first general naturalization

[1] Proxy voting had already been forbidden by the proprietors as early as 1683. In Barbadoes, by acts of 1709 and 1713, sheriffs, election officers, and candidates, not being able to visit several polling places when properly qualified in each, were permitted to send " Letters" to the election officers of other parishes, giving their votes therein. *Acts of Assembly Passed in the Island of Barbadoes, From 1648 to 1718* (London, 1721), pp. 271, 280.

[2] McCrady, I, 199, note, says, " There never has been an election in South Carolina except by ballot, as far as is known."

[3] Act of November 4, 1704, *Statutes at Large*, II, 251; Trott's *Laws*, I, 107.

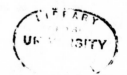

act which was enacted, since that of 1696–97 applied only to aliens then resident in the province, and gave them only three months to accept its terms. The act, although perhaps a party measure dictated by party policy, served, nevertheless, as nothing else could do, to incorporate the foreigners into the life of the community. An occasional reference is made to Frenchmen in the accounts of the succeeding election, but from that time they disappear as a distinct party from the colonial political life, and the alien question, which had troubled the country for twenty years, was now set at rest.

Even after the act regulating elections had been passed in 1704, we still hear of election evils. " Masters of ships" were sought after as voters; and " violence" still accompanied the elections.[1]   In order to protect their work, the assembly went so far as to extend their own terms of office ;[2] but the governor failed to respect this act and dissolved the legislature shortly afterwards. The objectionable religious acts of 1704 were repealed in November, 1706, and thereafter the factional animosities and election contests grew less virulent. A great excitement was, indeed, aroused at the time of the election of Robert Gibbes as governor upon the death of Governor Tynte in 1710 ;[3] but Gibbes was shortly after superseded by Charles Craven, who assumed control in 1712.[4]   Under Governor Craven the popular excitement ceased, and we are told that " The assembly in his time was not elected, as formerly, in a riotous and tumultary manner, but with the utmost harmony and regularity, and proceeded to their deliberations with great temper and mutual friendship." [5]

The following four years, apparently so peaceful for the colony, were in reality storing up wrath against the proprietors. A number of things combined about 1717 to make the proprietary government peculiarly obnoxious to the colonists, and led to the demand for the assumption of political

---

[1] Oldmixon, in Carroll, *Collections,* II, 441–443.
[2] *Statutes at Large,* II, 266.
[3] McCrady, I, 489–491.
[4] *Ibid.,* 505.
[5] Hewatt, I, 200.

control by the Crown. One of the first of these facts was the Yamassee Indian war which broke out early in 1715; and, after the perpetration of horrible atrocities by the Indians, was suppressed only by supreme exertions and great expense on the part of the colonists.[1] The weakness of the proprietary government was clearly shown in the course of this war, while its narrow policy was evidenced at the close of the war, when it forbade the provincial authorities to protect their frontier by colonizing five hundred Irish upon the deserted Indian lands.[2] Most unwisely, too, the proprietors had placed a number of the colonial offices in the hands of two unpopular men,[3] Nicholas Trott and his brother-in-law, William Rhett; who thus were enabled to exercise wide political power, and interfere with elections of members of assembly at the general elections in Charleston.[4] The proprietors gave Trott a practical veto upon all the business of the council and upon legislation by forbidding the transaction of any business unless he was present at the council meeting.[5] Quarrels also arose inevitably over the quit-rents due to the proprietors, and concerning the disposition of the profits of the Indian trade. To these causes for dissatisfaction, the proprietors added another, which at length drove the people of their province into open insurrection.

In 1716, after Governor Craven had left the colony, the assembly passed a number of important and popular measures, among which was one for the appointment of a public receiver, another for the laying of duties upon slaves and goods imported into the colony, and another for regulating elections. The last of these is the one which has most value for our purposes.

It has been noted that the assembly elections were all held in Charleston; and although members were said to be elected for one or another of the counties, yet the voters of

[1] For account of this war, see McCrady, I, 530–556; Hewatt, I, 212–230.

[2] Hewatt, I, 229–230.

[3] McCrady, I, 528–529; Hewatt, I, 231.

[4] Hewatt, I, 232.

[5] McCrady, I, 529.

all counties must assemble in Charleston on the two days of election, and there decide upon their county representatives. The burden and inconvenience of such a plan must have been felt at an early day, and for a time the proprietors favored the holding of elections in the localities. In 1683 they directed that ten assemblymen should be chosen at Charleston and ten at London in Colleton County,[1] but this method apparently did not become the custom,[2] and the proprietors " issued their commands in vain." In 1690 the proprietors write that they have received information that it is found troublesome and expensive for the inhabitants to come to Charleston, and they therefore advise that the county of Berkeley should be divided into four election precincts.[3] In 1697 the proprietors again revert to the subject, proposing the formation of districts; and adding that if the inhabitants of Charleston object, the governor may propose to erect them into a corporation with the usual privileges.[4] The last clause may give us the reason why the change was not earlier accomplished; the Charleston inhabitants would be benefited in many ways, and would gain considerably greater influence in the elections if they were held in the city, and their representatives in the assembly would doubtless oppose any district system.

But the proprietors themselves later favored these elections in Charleston, perhaps because they could be more easily influenced than a number of separate elections in distant country towns. Trott and Rhett, the proprietary workers, gained a " great Sway in the Elections." [5] which were often conducted for their purposes in a tumultuous fashion. Several grand juries had presented these Charleston elections as a public evil,[6] and at last in 1716 the assembly took

[1] Rivers, *Sketch*, Appendix, 406–7.

[2] *Collections S. C. Hist. Soc.*, I, 124.

[3] Elections in Charleston are referred to in Hewatt, I, 232, 255; Carroll, *Collections*, II, 148, 159, 162, 318, 441; McCrady, I, 198–200, 282, etc.

[4] *Collections S. C. Hist. Soc.*, I, 142.

[5] *Proceedings of the People of South Carolina*, Carroll, *Collections*, II, 149.

[6] *Statutes at Large*, II, 683.

steps to district the colony and hold the elections in the parish churches. Trott and Rhett, believing their influence would be lessened "by this new Method," endeavored in vain to prevent the passage of the bill; the assembly passed the act and sent it to England for ratification.[1] It was said that of this act, " the People were very fond; finding it gave them a greater freedom of Election, and was more to them than going out of their respective Counties to Charles Towne." [2]

The act of December 15, 1716,[3] is entitled "An Act to keep inviolate and preserve the freedom of Elections, and appoint who shall be deemed and adjudged capable of choosing or being chosen Members of the Commons House of Assembly." The preamble states that " the far greatest part of the inhabitants in their respective counties of this Province, are at a considerable distance from the stated places of election, whereby they are at great expense of time and money, besides all other hazards in comeing to choose members of the Commons House of Assembly;" and that " the several counties of this Province are divided into distinct parishes, so that in them elections for members of the Commons House of Assembly may be managed so as in a great measure to prevent the bad effects of the present manner of electing the said members." Following then the election laws of Barbadoes, as Mr. McCrady has pointed out,[4] the law provided for the use of the parishes, already established by the church acts of 1704 and 1706, as election districts; for the holding of elections in the churches or other convenient places between sunrise and sunset on not more than two successive days; and appointed the church-wardens as managers of the elections. The existence of the paper ballot is shown by the following excerpts:

"Upon the closing of the poll, at convenient hours in the time of the aforesaid election [the church wardens] shall put all the votes then

---

[1] Carroll, *Collections*, II, 149.   [2] *Ibid.*
[3] *Statutes at Large*, II, 683-691.
[4] McCrady, I, 560. See also election law of Barbadoes of 1709, *Acts of Assembly of Barbadoes* (London edition, 1721), pp. 266-274; and election law of Jamaica, 1681, *Laws of Jamaica* (London, 1684).

delivered in and rolled up by the electors, into some box, glass or paper, sealed up with the seals of any two or more of the electors that are then present, and upon the opening of the poll, shall unseal the said box, glass or paper, in order to proceed in the said election."

" . . . The names of the electors for members of the Commons House of Assembly, shall be fairly entered in a book or roll for that purpose provided by the church warden or church wardens of each parish, to prevent any persons voting twice at the same election, and that if in voting, two or more papers with persons names written thereon for members of Assembly, be (upon the scrutiny) found rolled up together, or more persons names be found written on any paper than ought to be voted for (to which paper the elector shall not be obliged to subscribe his name) all and every such paper and papers shall be invalid and of no effect. . . . "

The act went farther, however, than merely to establish the parish as the election division, for it introduced considerable changes in the qualifications of voters and members of assembly. We have seen by the act of 1704, that electors must possess fifty acres of land or ten pounds value of personal property, and they must have resided in the county at least three months before the election. The new act not only changed the existing residence and property qualifications, but also added religious and racial restrictions. Some fifteen years earlier complaints had been made that among other unqualified persons, some Jews and negroes had voted. Under the law of 1716 these classes were excluded. The act reads,

" *And whereas* it is necessary and reasonable, that none but such persons who have an interest in this Province should be capable to elect or be elected members of the Commons House of Assembly, *Be it enacted* by the authority aforesaid, That every white man, and no other, professing the Christian religion, who hath attained to the age of one-and-twenty years, and hath been in this Province for the space of six months before the date of the writs for the election that he offers to give his vote at, and upon his oath, (if required by the church warden or church wardens, or any person present qualified to vote), be proved to be worth thirty pounds current money of this Province shall be deemed a person qualified to vote for and may be capable of electing a representative or representatives to serve as a member or members of the Commons House of Assembly for the parish or precinct wherein he actually is resident."

Members of the assembly were required to own five hundred pounds current money or five hundred acres of land in the parish for which they were chosen. Persons owning lands in certain parishes, temporarily deserted on account of the Indian war, were given the strange privilege of voting for representatives for the deserted parishes and not for the parishes in which they were temporarily resident. Fines were to be imposed upon officers making fraudulent returns, and upon persons bribing or intimidating voters. Voters were to be free from civil writs in going to and coming from and while at the place of election.

From this summary of its provisions, it will be seen that the election act of 1716 established a considerably different basis for the suffrage. The franchise was now limited to white Christian male citizens over twenty-one years of age, who had been at least six months in the colony and who actually resided in the election district wherein they voted; and the fifty acres or ten pounds requirement now gave place to a uniform property qualification of thirty pounds current money. The latter phrase is not in itself intelligible unless it is understood that as early as 1702 the colony had issued paper money in the form of bills of credit. Subsequent emissions were made in 1706, 1707, 1712, 1716;[1] and the value of the currency rapidly declined. By 1714 sterling exchange was quoted at two hundred per cent,[2] and the end was not yet reached. It is safe to say that the thirty pounds currency in 1716 did not represent a greater purchasing power than that of ten pounds sterling.

Weak places in the act of 1716 were soon found, and scarcely six months after its passage, " an additional and explanatory act" was found necessary. We are told that disputes had arisen about the qualifications of voters and representatives, and that the meaning of the former act " hath been wrongfully wrested and perverted." [3] Judging from the negative provisions which were added, it would appear that apprentices or indentured servants, seafaring men, and

[1] McCrady, I, 524.
[2] Hewatt, I, 204; *Statutes at Large*, II, 713; Ramsay, *History of South Carolina*, II, 163.
[3] *Statutes at Large*, III, 2.

other transients had participated in the elections. The supplementary act of July 29, 1717,[1] made a number of minor
changes, almost all of which must have worked towards a
restriction of the suffrage. The elector was now required to
reside in the parish—not merely in the province—six months
before the election; his property qualification was changed
from thirty pounds to fifty acres of freehold, or the payment
of taxes for the support of the government upon property
worth at least fifty pounds current money; and it was especially stated that " no apprentice or other covenanted servant for term of years, whether by indenture or by custom
of the county, nor any seafaring or other transient man, who
has neither freehold nor is liable to pay tax for a stock of
fifty pounds current money" should be deemed capable of
voting for representatives. Similar changes were made in
the qualifications of a representative, who must be a free-
born subject of Great Britain or the dominions belonging
thereto, or a person naturalized by act of parliament in Great
Britain or Ireland, twenty-one years of age, a resident of the
province for twelve months, a resident of the parish which
he represents, and possessed of five hundred acres of land in
the parish or one thousand pounds value of houses, lots and
lands in other parts of the province, or the same value of
personal property.[2]

The evident purpose of this act was to approach more
closely to the ideal already expressed in the law of 1716,
" that none but such persons who have an interest in this
Province should be capable to elect or be elected." The
change in the property qualification from thirty to fifty
pounds may have been due to a renewed depreciation of the
currency after the issue of more paper money in 1716.[3] By
requiring this property to be taxable, the ordinary personal
property of uncertain value would be excluded, as the only

---

[1] *Statutes at Large*, III, 2–4.

[2] A person owning a settled plantation of five hundred acres with ten
able working negro slaves, under the care of at least one white man,
within the county where the owner resides, might be elected for the
parish where the plantation is situated, although not himself a resident
of that parish.

[3] McCrady, I, 524.

taxable property at this time consisted of land and negroes.[1] The strict residence requirements, both of voters and representatives, were also intended to include only those having " sufficient evidence of permanent common interest" [2] with the community; yet these restrictions were at variance with the usual practice in the colonies and the uniform custom of England.

But the work which the colonists had built up with such pains in the election acts of 1716 and 1717, the proprietors determined should be overthrown by a stroke of their nullifying pen. Trott and Rhett had been writing to England and urging the proprietors to disallow the election laws together with several other recent acts. Accepting their side of the question, the proprietors on July 22, 1718, placed their veto upon the election laws. They say:

> "We have likewise read and considered two Acts of Assembly . . . and finding the said two Acts tend to the entire alteration and subversion of the Constitution of the Province of South Carolina, and are contrary to the laws and customs of Parliament in Great Britain, we therefore do declare the two last mentioned Acts to be null and void, and we do hereby repeal, nullifie and make void the said two Acts, and every clause, matter or thing therein contained whatsoever." [4]

With the repeal of the election law the proprietors directed that the assembly should be dissolved, and a new one be elected in Charleston according to the old method.[3] The governor and council tried to conceal these instructions, but the substance of them became known and, joined to the disallowance of other popular laws, led to great excitement in the colony. Governor Johnson did not put himself in full accord with the popular sentiment, and, on the other hand, he received the proprietary reprimand for not carrying the orders into immediate execution.[5]

See tax act of 1721, *Statutes at Large*, III, 149–157.

[2] Virginia Bill of Rights, 1776, Section 6: the phraseology is most interestingly similar to the South Carolina act of 1716 *Statutes at Large*, II, 688.

Carroll, *Collection*, II, 149; Hewat, I, 292.

[4] *Statutes at Large*, III, 31; McCrady, I, 626–628.

Carroll, *Collection*, 150, 160 . . . .

" Thus the People were irritated and heated to a violent Degree, and the Basis of all Government being either Love, Fear or Interest, or perhaps any two, or a Mixture of all the three, but in this there was neither one nor the other." [1] The popular movement increased in strength until a general association was formed in 1719, " to stand by their Rights and Privileges, and to get rid of the Oppression and Arbitrary Dealings of the Lords Proprietors." [2] Governor Johnson was requested by the leaders to assume the government under the King, and when he refused to do so, the assembly elected by his writs denied the authority of the proprietors and the council, and called themselves " the Representatives of the People;" " a Convention, delegated by the People, to prevent the utter Ruin of this Government, if not the loss of the Province, until His Majesty's Pleasure be known." [3] To this Johnson replied:

"It is not the People's Voting for you, that makes you become their Representatives; the Leige People of this, nor any other Province have Power to convene and chuse their Representatives without being author-iz'd so to do by some Writ or Order coming from Authority lawfully impower'd." [4]

Finding Johnson firm in his intention to stand by the pro-prietary rights, the Convention elected Colonel James Moore as governor; opposed Johnson by force; and at last pro-vided for an election of councillors; " so they had now their Governor, Council, and Convention (as they call'd them-selves)." [5]   By this armed uprising of the people the pro-prietary authority in the colony was overthrown, and its place was taken by a revolutionary government which looked, not in vain, to the English government for recogni-tion.   The *de facto* subversion of the proprietors' govern-ment in the colony in 1719 was followed by a *de jure* denial of their power by the Crown's officials in England, and by

[1] Carroll, *Collections*, II, 160.
[2] *Ibid.*, 165.
[3] *Ibid.*, 168–169.
[4] *Ibid.*, 176.
[5] *Ibid.*, 180–183.

the appointment of a royal governor and a provisional government in September, 1720.[1]

Before this contest had reached its final stage still another election law had been passed.[2] This act of March 20, 1718 19 expressed in strong language the popular satisfaction with the new method of holding elections:

" The choosing members of the Commons House of Assembly for this Province, by parishes or precincts, had been found by experience to be the most easy, just and least expensive and hazardous method that can be devised and approaches nearest to the form and method of choosing or electing members in other his Majesty's dominions and plantations, and not liable to the inconveniences that attended any other method heretofore used or practised in this Province."

The act continued the suffrage requirements of the act of 1717, but it strengthened the prohibition upon servants by inserting the word *free* in the phrase describing the voting class; thereby limiting the franchise to " every free white man (and no other)," who possessed the several requirements as laid down in the former act.

The property qualifications of assemblymen were changed considerably. The representative was no longer required to be a resident of the district he represented, nor must he possess the necessary property within the district. The personal property qualification was, however, omitted, and the new requirement was the possession within the province of a settled plantation of five hundred acres with six slaves upon it, or one thousand pounds value in houses, buildings, town lots, or other lands in any part of the province. The method of balloting shows clearly that provision was made for a secret ballot:

" Each person qualified to vote as is above directed shall put into a box or sheet of paper prepared for that purpose by the said church-wardens or other persons, as is above directed, a piece of paper rolled up, wherein is written the name of the Representatives he votes for, and to which paper the elector shall not be obliged to subscribe his name."

[1] We cannot here enter into the English side of this story. For a full account, see McCrady, I, 665–673.

[2] *Statutes at Large*, III, 50–55.

A few other minor changes were made particularly in the apportionment of representatives, but with the exception of the qualifications of assemblymen, the act of 1718–19 followed closely the terms of the act of 1717. The opinions so strongly expressed in the preamble did not deter the proprietors from still further opposing public sentiment, and on July 24, 1719, they write that they "can by no means consent" to the act.[1] The controversy about the election acts then became a prominent cause of the revolution of 1719, and one of the first resolutions which the "convention" adopted was one declaring certain of the repealed acts to be still in force.[2] In February, 1719–20, when the convention had decided that they were again an assembly, they declared the election act of 1718–19 to be in force,[3] and it was so treated until formally repealed about a year and a half later.

South Carolina's overthrow of the proprietary government was thus intimately associated with the right of freedom of elections. After 1716, the assembly was engaged in passing many important economic measures, and the people of the province undoubtedly felt that these measures could not be attained without a more reasonable process of electing their representatives. The people could not be adequately represented, nor could the elections be kept free from undue influence so long as Charleston was the only polling-place. In South Carolina, as in Georgia, a true representative system could be gained only by overthrowing the personal control of proprietors or trustees, and accepting the royal form of government, in which, by this time, a definite and adequate system of representation was a fundamental fact.

The provisional royal government had been in power but a short time when still another election law was passed, and the earlier ones repealed. Governor Nicholson's instructions[4] may have tended to restrict the suffrage, for they directed him to permit freeholders only to vote for represen-

---

[1] *Statutes at Large*, III, 69.
[2] McCrady, I, 649; Hewatt, I, 259.
[3] *Statutes at Large*, III, 103; act of February 12, 1719–20.
[4] *Collections S. C. Hist. Soc.*, II, 145–147. Analyzed in McCrady, *History of South Carolina under the Royal Government*, 25–33.

tatives, while the law of 1718–19 had given the right to freeholders of fifty acres, or persons owning taxable property to the amount of fifty pounds current money. Nicholson's first assembly in September, 1721, therefore, revised the election laws, changing but slightly the machinery of election or the qualifications of representatives, but imposing new qualifications upon voters.[1]

"Every free white man, and no other person, professing the Christian religion, who has attained to the age of one and twenty years, and hath been a resident and an inhabitant in this Province for the space of one whole year before the date of the writs for the election he offers to give his vote at, and hath a freehold of at least fifty acres of land, or hath been taxed in the precedent year twenty shillings, or is taxed twenty shillings the present year, to the support of this Government, shall be deemed a person qualified to vote for, and may be capable of electing a representative or representatives to serve as a member or members of the Commons House of Assembly, for the parish or precinct wherein he actually is a resident, or in any other parish or precinct wherein he hath the like qualifications."

It will be noticed that the provisions of the acts of 1717 and 1719 requiring a voter to be a resident for six months of the parish in which he votes, are now changed to a requirement of a residence in the province for one year. The fifty acres freehold is still retained; but the fifty pounds taxable property gives place to the annual payment of twenty shillings taxes.

The tax-paying basis for the suffrage does not ostensibly conform to the governor's instructions calling for elections by the freeholders; but an inspection of the tax-laws of the time during which this act was in force (1721–1745) shows that freeholders or slaveholders were practically the only taxpayers. Thus the rates of 1721 placed a levy of five shillings upon every one hundred acres of land, and an uncertain amount upon every negro, mulatto or Indian slave.[2] A person who paid twenty shillings taxes would thus own eight times the minimum amount of land required for the

[1] *Statutes at Large,* III, 135–140.
[2] *Ibid.,* 149–157.

suffrage, or else be a slaveholder.[1] In 1724 the rates were
again five shillings on the hundred acres of land, and a definite tax of twenty shillings on each slave between the years
of seven and sixty.[2] This act shows the relative values of
land and negroes, for it practically makes one slave equivalent in value to four hundred acres of land. Down to 1734,
it may be presumed that the tax-paying qualification for the
suffrage limited that privilege to landholders and slaveholders. After 1734 a tax on mercantile stocks and cash,
and later upon all white male persons was laid;[3] but these
do not appear to have been permanent. In 1739 the taxes
are only ten shillings on slaves and ten shillings on every
one hundred acres of land.[4]

For over twenty years after 1721 the election act remained unchanged.[5] Governor Johnson's instructions of
1729 again directed that the assembly should be elected by
the freeholders;[6] but it was not until after Governor Glen's
arrival in the colony that any change was made. By a subsequent letter Glen shows his opposition to the ballot which
had been a part of South Carolina's elections from the first;
and he may have been the author or proposer of the measure
which limited the suffrage in 1745. The act of May 25, of
that year, plainly tells its purpose in the title, " An Act for
enlarging the qualifications of the Electors, as well as of
the Persons to be elected to serve as Members of the General
Assembly of this Province." [7]

Beyond the purposes given in the preamble of this act, I

[1] The act provided for the raising of £17,248 6d. by a tax of five
shillings on each one hundred acres of land; and a pro rata assessment
of the remainder upon all the negro, Indian, Mustee, and mulatto
slaves between the years of seven and sixty.

[2] Act of May 24, 1724, *Statutes at Large,* III, 238–245.

[3] *Statutes at Large,* III, 386, 438.

[4] *Ibid.,* 527.

[5] It has been said that the act of 1721 was disallowed in 1730; but if
such is the case, the disallowance was not recognized in the colony;
E. L. Whitney, *The Government of the Colony of South Carolina, J.
H. U. Studies,* XIII, 49.

[6] McCrady, II, 93.

[7] *Statutes at Large,* III, 656.

have found no reason for its passage. We are told that " it may be of evil consequence to give a right to any person or persons to vote . . . who are late residents, and are not possessed of a sufficient freehold and personal estate, and it may be of equal detriment to admit any person or persons to serve as Members of Assembly who are not amply quali- fied." The act is, therefore, passed for " the augmenting and enlarging the qualifications" of both elected and elect- ors. The " augmentation" consisted in changing the quali- fication from the holding of fifty acres of freehold or the payment of twenty shillings taxes, to the following form:

" Every free white man, and no other person, professing the Chris- tian religion, who has attained to the age of twenty-one years, and hath been a resident and inhabitant in this Province for the space of one year before the date of the writs issued for that election for which he offers to give his vote at, and hath a freehold estate in a settled planta- tion, or not less than three hundred acres of land unsettled, for which he paid tax the precedent year, or hath a freehold in houses, lands or town lots, or parts thereof, of the value of sixty pounds proclamation money, in Charleston, or any other town in this Province, for which he paid tax the precedent year, shall be deemed a person qualified to vote for and is hereby declared capable of joining in the election for a representative or representatives to serve as a member or members of the Assembly for that parish or precinct wherein he is actually a resi- dent, or in any other parish or precinct where he hath the like qualifi- cations."

The radical nature of the changes introduced by this act can be seen when it is noticed, that, for the first time since 1692, the suffrage is placed solely upon a freehold basis, a policy which the act of 1759 reversed. Again, this free- hold requisite was now considerably " augmented;" the sim- ple fifty acres being replaced by either (1) a settled plan- tation, or (2) unsettled but taxable land to the amount of three hundred acres, or (3) other forms of real estate to the value of sixty pounds *proclamation money.*[1] These pro- visions must have raised the qualifications to about five or

[1] £100 sterling was worth about £133 proclamation money; while at this time (1745) the South Carolina currency was circulating at the ratio of £700 currency to £100 sterling (Hewatt, II, 14).

six times what they had previously been. I have found no facts to show to what extent they cut down the actual number of voters, but, especially in Charleston, the act must have excluded some of the poorer electors.

The aristocratic features of the act were further increased by permitting plural voting, and giving the freeholder a vote in any parish in which he was properly qualified.[1]   The same tendency is seen in the higher qualifications of representatives, who were now required to possess a settled plantation or freehold of five hundred acres of land with twenty slaves, over and above all indebtedness, or value of one thousand pounds proclamation money in houses, lots or other lands in the province clear of all debts.   The passage of such a law is evidence of a decided increase in the economic well-being of the governing classes, for it is unlikely the assembly would pass such a law unless they expected the approval of their constituents.   It is proof, too, that the artisan and mercantile classes of the town were politically insignificant; and furnishes indirect evidence of the truth of Hewatt's statement that the merchants, artisans, and tradesmen established themselves upon plantations in the country as soon as they had accumulated sufficient capital to buy the necessary slaves and lands.[2]   The act is a result, not a cause, of the economic and political predominance of the planter in South Carolina life.

Whatever may have been Governor Glen's share in the passage of this election law, there can be no doubt that he was opposed to the democratic secret ballot of South Carolina, and wished to displace it by the English method of *viva voce* voting.   Writing to the English authorities he urges the abolition of many elective offices in both church and state; and said that the colony would be safer the closer it adhered "to the customs at home."   Elections by ballot should also be avoided because " any person who attends the

[1] It is said that large property owners took advantage of this clause to vote in several parishes; and that the practice later resulted in sectional controversy between the low country and the uplands. See W. A. Schafer, *Sectionalism and Representation in South Carolina, Amer. Hist. Assn. Report,* 1900, I, 352.

[2] See Hewatt, II, 127–130.

balloting box, may with a very little slight of hand, give the election to whom he pleases." [1] He further criticised the method of apportionment of representatives by which some places received no representation and others obtained far more than their just share. So far as we can see these propositions of Governor Glen's were without result.

Only one more election law was passed between 1745 and the Revolution. This was the act of April 7, 1759,[2] which changed the suffrage in the direction of a wider electorate. The preamble to this act was similar to that of the act of 1745, and gives no hint to the reader that the law may bring about an extension of the suffrage. The section defining the qualifications of electors is more elaborate than any heretofore adopted.

" From and after the determination of this present General Assembly, every free white man, and no other person, professing the Protestant religion, who shall have obtained the age of twenty-one years, and shall have been a resident and inhabitant in this Province for the space of one year, at any time before the date of the writ to be issued for that election at which he shall offer to give his vote, and shall have a freehold estate in a settled plantation, or not less than one hundred acres of land unsettled, for which he shall have paid tax the preceding year, or shall have a freehold estate in houses, lands or town lots or parts thereof, of the value of sixty pounds proclamation money situate in Charleston, or any other town in this Province, for which he shall have paid tax the preceding year, or shall have paid the sum of ten shillings proclamation money for his own proper tax the preceding year, shall be deemed a person qualified to vote for, and is hereby declared capable of voting at the election of, a representative or representatives, to serve as a member or members of the Assembly, for the parish or precinct where such elector shall be actually resident, or for any other parish or precinct where he shall have the like qualifications."

The most striking innovation of the act is the substitution of the word " Protestant" for " Christian" used in all the earlier laws. We are again, unfortunately, left without any reason for the change, and it seems the more remarkable that the exclusion of Catholics from the suffrage should

---

[1] *Collections of S. C. Hist. Soc.,* II, 305.
[2] *Statutes at Large,* IV, 98–101.

come at such a late time. Such treatment has been noticed
in many of the other colonies, but in them it came early in
the eighteenth century, when the restoration of the exiled
Stuarts was not yet considered an impossibility.

In South Carolina in 1759 there could be no fear of the
Stuarts, but a number of Catholics had about two years
earlier been brought into the province. It may be that the
act was directed against these French Acadians, who had
been dispersed by the English government, and over a thousand of whom arrived at the port of Charleston;[1] but of this
I have found no proof.

Important changes were also made in the property qualifications of voters. Four alternatives were now offered to
the prospective voter; he might vote by virtue of the ownership of a settled plantation as formerly; or by owning one
hundred acres of unsettled taxable lands in place of the
earlier three hundred acres; or on account of sixty pounds
value in proclamation money of houses, lots or lands in any
town in the province; or by virtue of the payment of ten
shillings (proclamation money) taxes during the preceding
year. The country franchise was thus extended by lowering the alternative qualification from three hundred to one
hundred acres of freehold; and, on the other hand, it is
likely the suffrage among the town population was extended
by permitting those paying a certain amount of taxes to vote
in the assembly elections. Looking at the tax-assessments
at about this time, it is to be noticed that the earlier restriction of taxes to slaves and land is not retained; but in 1758,
in addition to taxing slaves thirty-six shillings each and
land at the same amount for each one hundred acres; a tax
of eighteen shillings was also assessed upon every one hundred pounds at interest, four per cent. of the income was
levied upon annuities, and cattle, when a person owned over
thirty, were taxed two shillings and six pence a head.[2] In
proclamation money these taxes would be only one-fifth the
amounts stated in the law. Yet making allowance for the
difference in the value in money, it is evident that the ten
shillings tax would open the suffrage to some persons, par-

[1] McCrady, II, 326. See also *Statutes at Large,* IV, 31.
[2] Act of May 19, 1758; *Statutes at Large,* IV, 54.

ticularly in the towns, who did not possess the necessary freehold qualification.

It has been said that the causes for the passage of the law of 1759 have not been found by the writer. It is interesting to note, however, that only three years later, the Virginia legislature also passed an act which extended the suffrage; and the questions naturally arise, whether there were any conditions in the southern colonies in the fifteen years preceding the Revolution which called for an extension of the suffrage, and if so, in what way this extension of the suffrage affected the revolutionary movement in that part of the country? The records are not yet available for the preparation of answers to these questions.

Little need be said concerning the local suffrage of South Carolina, for, apart from the parish officers, there were absolutely no local elective officials. An instruction of May, 1671, had provided for the monthly election by the inhabitants of every town of "one or two of ye discreetest men" to "truck wth ye Indians for Beades;" [1] but this regular apportionment of the Indian trade does not appear to have been made. In 1697 the proprietors proposed the erection of Charleston into a municipal corporation,[2] but such a step was not taken until almost ninety years later, when both the proprietary and royal governments had been displaced.[3] Under both of these governments the affairs of Charleston were controlled by commissioners appointed by acts of the legislature, vacancies in whose numbers were sometimes filled by themselves or by the appointment of the governor.[4] Local officers to look after roads, bridges, and the navigation of small streams were appointed in the same way.[5]

It was in the parish alone, therefore, that any popular election for local officials took place, and this parish election system was a remarkably liberal one. Instead of the permanent close corporation of the Virginia parish, the South

---

[1] Rivers, *Sketch,* Appendix, 368.

[2] *Collections S. C. Hist. Soc.,* I, 142.

[3] The city was incorporated in 1783 by act of legislature; see *Statutes at Large,* VII, 97.

[4] *Statutes at Large,* VII, 53, 55, 59, 74, 89.

[5] *Ibid.,* 478, 480, 485, 495; IX, 49–57, 163, 184, 190, 203, 229, 246, etc.

Carolina vestrymen were chosen annually, and the ministers were elected by the people and not by the vestry.   Parishes in South Carolina were erected by the act of 1704,[1] entitled " An Act for the Establishment of Religious Worship in this Province, according to the Church of England, and for the erecting of Churches for the Publick Worship of God, and Ministers and the building convenient Houses for them."   The electors, both of the ministers and vestrymen, were to be conformists to the Church of England, inhabitants of the parish, and either freeholders or taxpayers of the parish.

" The severall rectors or ministers of the severall parishes shall be chosen by the major part of the inhabitants of the said parish, that are of the religion of the Church of England and conform to the same, and are either freeholders within the same parish, or that contribute to the publick taxes and charges thereof." [2]

No change in this method of electing vestrymen or ministers was made by the great Church Act of 1706,[3] nor by the subsequent acts relating to the subject during the colonial period.   The suffrage here was broader than in Maryland, where an elector must be a tax-paying freeholder of the parish; but it did not differ much from the freeholders and housekeepers of the Virginia parish elections.   The most marked distinction between the South Carolina vestry and those of her neighbors was in the fact of its annual election; and this proved a most desirable feature, by which the inconveniences, carelessness and even corruption of the North Carolina, Virginia, and Maryland vestries were avoided. To this annual election of vestrymen and the popular election of ministers much of the strength of the South Carolina church has been attributed; but there can be no doubt that other economic and religious influences aided what would otherwise have been only a piece of ecclesiastical machinery.   Perhaps the feature which made the South Carolina vestry government so successful as compared with

[1] Act of November 4, 1704, *Statutes at Large*, II, 236–246.
[2] *Ibid.*, 239.
[3] Act of November 30, 1706, *Statutes at Large*, II, 282–294.

that of North Carolina or Virginia was the fact that only members of the Church of England could vote for vestrymen or ministers.

In conclusion, then, we may summarize the suffrage provisions here noticed. South Carolina began with an electorate, which, on account of the ease of securing land, was practically synonymous with free manhood. Some merchants and artisans later settled in the colony, particularly in Charleston, and a tax-paying or personal property qualification was made an alternative with the freehold basis. From 1692 onward, with the exception of the interval from 1745 to 1759, the laws were so worded that landless men might vote, if they paid sufficient taxes or owned a certain amount of personal property. Perhaps unconsciously, the proprietors at first encouraged popular elections, by their anxiety to establish a parliament in the form provided for in the fundamental constitutions. Later they opposed a more popular elective system, and for this reason as well as others lost their province. The suffrage question comes very prominently to the front in colonial politics in South Carolina. On three occasions it is the principal theme before the people; first in the last decade of the seventeenth century in connection with the political status of the Huguenots; secondly, in the first decade of the eighteenth century when it took the form of irregularities in elections and an attempt to establish religious qualifications of representatives; and, thirdly, in 1716–1719, when there arose a popular demand for a method of election which would permit a more accurate representation of the community. Under the royal government the suffrage franchise did not become a cause of popular excitement. Three great laws were passed bearing upon the subject, those of 1721, 1745, 1759; but these laws do not appear to have been the result of popular clamor or interest.

The voter throughout the whole period must be a male person over twenty-one years of age; after 1716 he must be of the Christian religion, and of the white race. In 1717 apprentices and servants were prohibited from voting, and in 1718–19 the word " free" was inserted before " white man;" while in 1759 the word " Protestant" was substituted for " Christian." Before 1696–97 there was apparently no residence qualification upon voters, but from that year a residence of three months was required. This was raised to six months in 1716 and to one year in 1719, at which point it remained throughout the colonial period. The property qualification of fifty acres freehold prescribed by the fundamental constitutions may have been observed in the early years; but from 1692 to 1716 the elector was permitted an alternative of the ten pounds property (presumably real or personal). In the latter year the requirement was simply thirty pounds current money, but in 1717 this was changed to fifty acres of land or fifty pounds currency value in taxable property; and the latter alternative was again changed in 1718–19 to the payment of a tax of twenty shillings. In 1745 the tax-paying basis is abolished, and the fifty acres gives place to a settled plantation or three hundred acres of unsettled land or sixty pounds proclamation money value in town houses or lands. Lastly, in 1759 the unsettled freehold was cut down to one hundred acres, and the tax-paying basis was restored.

The student of the suffrage in this colony is impressed by the breadth of the suffrage in a community which possessed so many features of economic aristocracy. Frequent popular elections both in church and state were open to the freeholders and taxpayers of the colony upon a comparatively broad basis. And these elections, at first perhaps conducted by the subscribing of names to one sheet of paper or by proxy voting, soon came to be determined solely by written paper ballots deposited by the voter himself in some crude form of a ballot-box. The *viva voce* voting of the freeholder of New York or Virginia here gives way to the democratic ballot of the South Carolina taxpayer.

CHAPTER VI.

THE SUFFRAGE IN GEORGIA.

Peculiar circumstances attended the settlement of Georgia. The experience of the recent Indian and Spanish wars had demonstrated the weakness of the southern frontier,[1] and a plan which would populate this border land with English paupers and debtors, thus serving both utilitarian and charitable purposes, commended itself to the Crown as " highly becoming." As so frequently the case in philanthropic enterprises, the recipients of the charity in Georgia were expected passively to take what was given, and Oliver Twists were not included in the calculations of Oglethorpe or the other trustees. Thus it happened that a type of government similar to the petty military despotism in Old Virginia was established in another colony a century and a quarter after the Virginia settlement was made.

The royal charter of June 9, 1732, placed the colony in the control of the twenty trustees and their associates or successors, who, in their legislative powers, were restricted only by the necessity of submitting their laws for approval to the king in council, and the limitation that the laws, constitutions or ordinances be not repugnant to the laws of England.[2] During the term of twenty-one years, all persons in the colony were to be subject to laws made in this manner. The corporation had the right for the same period to appoint such governors, judges, magistrates or other civil and military officers as were thought fit and needful; at the end of twenty-one years the colony should be given a form of government and manner of passing laws determined by the king, and receive a governor appointed by the Crown.[3]

Under the terms of this charter the settlers received a

[1] Preamble to Georgia charter, Poore, *Charters and Constitutions*, I, 369.

[2] *Ibid.*, 373-374.

[3] *Ibid.*, 377.

surfeit of paternal legislation. The trustees met in London in July, 1732, to begin the work of organizing the colony,[1] and in the rules for settlement they never lost sight of the military purpose of the colony. The settlers were provided with tools and arms; their land allotments were to be laid out in the neighborhood of towns and must not exceed fifty acres in amount for each family; the lands were held on a military tenure, and to make this sure, they were entailed in the male line. The land must be cultivated within twelve months after the grant, and the settler was required to plant at least one hundred white mulberry trees for every ten acres that he cleared,[2] in order to encourage the silk culture, which was a favorite project of the trustees. Slavery was forbidden because it might injure the poor free laborers, and a little later thé manufacture or trade in rum or brandy was prohibited.[3]

The colony which settled at Savannah in 1733 was under the control of Oglethorpe. No provision was made for a general organization of the colony except in his person. A town court composed of three bailiffs and a recorder assisted by two constables and two tithingmen was established for Savannah before the expedition left England,[4] but this court possessed only judicial powers, while all other governmental authority rested in their leader. It is difficult to define the authority so exercised, for it extended to any economic, political or military policy which seemed necessary to Oglethorpe. There can be no question that in the main he used the authority with discretion, and on some occasions even called meetings of the inhabitants to discuss the affairs of the colony.[5] But generally he issued orders as would a military commander, without consultation with any one.[6] Such action, while it may have been necessary, often led to discontent among those who felt themselves injured by it.[7]

[1] Hugh M'Call, *The History of Georgia*, I, 16.
[2] *Ibid.*, 22.
[3] *Ibid.*, 25, 29.
[4] *Collections of Georgia Historical Society*, I, 95, 177; II, 282.
[5] *Ibid.*, II, 111, 239.
[6] *Ibid.*, 109; III, 73.
[7] *Ibid.*, II, 146-149; Stevens, *History of Georgia*, I, 220-222.

The single town court of Savannah was later joined by a second one at Frederica,[1] and both were supported by appropriations from the Trustees' treasury.[2] The officials of these courts were appointed by the Trustees, while the settlers exercised no share whatever in their government.[3] Next to Oglethorpe, by far the most powerful man in the colony, was the keeper of the Trustees' store, from which supplies were distributed to the inhabitants. This officer, sometimes also holding the position of bailiff of Savannah, possessed almost the power of life and death over the settlers; and he is described by one grand jury as having " the dangerous power in his hands of alluring weak-minded people, to comply with unjust measures, and also overawing others, from making just complaints and representations" to the Trustees.[4]

Oglethorpe's personal government continued until 1741, when the Trustees divided the province into two counties, established a president and four assistants as a governing board at Savannah, and promised the same form of government for Frederica.[5] But Oglethorpe retained his personal control of affairs in the south along the Spanish frontier, and the Frederica county organization was never established. Upon the General's return to England, the president and assistants at Savannah were, in 1743, declared the supreme political authority for the whole colony;[6] and in this form the government continued until the surrender to the Crown. Throughout the period of trusteeship there were no regular elections, either for local or general officers, and no lawful representative system whatever.

But if the Trustees did not grant a popular government, they could not prevent occasional meetings of the settlers, nor could they stifle the petitions of Englishmen seeking redress of grievances. Both the charity-settlers and the

[1] *Coll. Ga. Hist. Soc.,* II, 95, 292.
[2] *Ibid.,* II, 307; III, 90. Augusta may have received one magistrate (*ibid.,* II, 95).
[3] *Ibid.,* II, 160–161, 202, 233, 282.
[4] *Ibid.,* 141, 233.
[5] Stevens, I. 224–225; Jones, *History of Georgia,* I, 416.
[6] Stevens, I. 226.

volunteers found themselves narrowly hedged in by the
theoretical rules of the Trustees respecting land tenures, quit-
rents, the silk culture, the rum traffic, and the use of negro
slaves.   The multitude of grievances might, in other colonies where the danger of Spanish or Indian warfare did
not exist, and where the Trustees' store did not dispense
its blessings, have led to actual rebellion; but here it produced a great emigration to South Carolina, and called forth
a crop of protests, petitions and representations to the English authorities.

In the preparation of these petitions the colonists frequently used the old English institution of the grand jury,
which was as near as they ever reached to a legal representative body.   At other times the protests were the fruit of
simple gatherings of the freeholders and inhabitants.   In
July, 1735, only two years after the settlement, the freeholders signed a petition representing to the Trustees the
expensiveness of white servants, the profitableness of negro
slavery, and protesting against the acts of the store-keeper,
who had ruled all the other magistrates, so that they became
" in a manner but ciphers." [1]   In 1737 the grand jury again
protested against the acts of the store-keeper, Thomas Causton; they asked for more servants, and particularly they
pointed out " the many inconveniences, for want of a body
of the laws and constitutions of this province." [2]   In 1738
a still stronger movement led to the signing of a petition
by 117 freeholders and settlers, praying for a modification
of the land system and for the admission of negro slaves; [3]
and in 1740, twenty-four of the " most respectable" settlers
petitioned for the privilege of introducing slaves. [4]

The popular dissatisfaction reached a higher plane of
organization in 1741.   On the seventh of October, of that
year, a meeting " of Landholders, Settlers and Inhabitants"
was held at Savannah to discuss their grievances and the
best mode of obtaining redress.   The assembly appointed
Thomas Stevens as agent to represent the facts to various

[1] *Coll. Ga. Hist. Soc.*, II, 200–201; Stevens, I, 290.
[2] *Coll. Ga. Hist. Soc.*, II, 141, 211; Stevens, I, 290.
[3] *Coll. Ga. Hist. Soc.*, II, 217–222; Stevens, I, 279, 295, 297.
[4] Stevens, I, 291.

officials in England, and then selected a committee of correspondence composed of five persons. The proceedings of this meeting are signed by 123 persons, and letters favoring its actions were received from eighteen absentees.[1] In the instructions which the committee of correspondence gave to the agent, he was told to solicit " That a regular government be established in Georgia, as in other of his Majesty's provinces in America," [2] as well as the various economic reforms which had been previously demanded.

Gradually some of the reforms were granted. The new general government under president and assistants was an improvement over the local courts; the land laws were soon made less strict; and the prohibition of the rum trade was removed. Even the prohibition of slavery, the last ideal of the Trustees, was broken down by the hiring of slaves on long term leases from their Carolina owners.[3] Yet an account published in London in 1743 said the colony was a failure, and gave a list of the causes for its ill-success.[4] These were said to be (1) the too flattering descriptions of the land circulated in Europe; (2) the entailment of estates in the male line; (3) restrictions upon the sale of lands; (4) restrictions upon the size of land grants; (5) the various requirements with respect to the clearing, fencing and planting of lands; (6) higher quit-rents than the richest lands in America could bear; (7) the prohibition of negro labor; and certain political disadvantages which were expressed as follows:

"8. The denying us the privilege of being judged by the laws of our mother country; and subjecting the lives and fortunes of all people in the colony to one person or set of men, who assumed the privilege, under the name of a Court of Chancery, of acting according to their own will and fancy.

"9. General Oglethorpe's taking upon him to nominate magistrates, appoint justices of the peace, and to do many other such things, with-

---

[1] *Coll. Ga. Hist. Soc.,* II, 153–154; Stevens, I, 300; Jones, I, 416.
[2] *Coll. Ga. Hist. Soc.,* II, 155.
[3] For this gradual introduction of negroes, see M'Call, I, 206 ff.; Stevens, I, 285–312.
[4] *Coll. Ga. Hist. Soc.,* II, 262–263.

out ever exhibiting to the people any legal commission or authority for so doing." [1]

Popular elections and a representative system at last developed out of the widespread desire for the introduction of slavery. Early in 1749 another public meeting had been held, and another petition praying for liberty to introduce slaves was drawn up. The president and assistants called in some of " the principal People of the Colony," [2] and upon their advice drew up the petition and a set of proposed regulations governing the slave system. The petition was signed by the president, assistants and many of the inhabitants, and certified with the town seal of Savannah.[3] This meeting and petition are the true germ of popular government in the colony. When the action of the Georgia officers and inhabitants became known in England, the Trustees at last resolved to permit the introduction of slavery under certain restrictions. And upon sending their proposed regulations to the president of the colony they say, " as you took into Consultation with you upon this Affair several of the principal People of the Colony, when you propos'd the Regulations which occurr'd to you, you must assemble such again that they may see the Regulations upon which the Trustees think proper to form the Act." [4] In this manner, the slave question led to the first assembly of citizens which met under the authority and with the approval of the Trustees.

In October, 1749, a convention which met in accordance with this instruction was composed of about twenty-seven persons,[5] chosen from the different districts.[6] I have found no record of the method of choice in the localities, nor of the manner of assignment of representatives. In the absence of any law upon the subject, the elections, if held at all, must have been managed quite informally. The assembly

[1] *Coll. Ga. Hist. Soc.*, II, 262–263.

[2] Jones, I, 422.

[3] *Ibid.*, 422–423; Stevens, I, 311.

[4] Jones, I, 423; M'Call, I, 209; Stevens, I, 311.

[5] So says Stevens, and Jones, of course, follows him; M'Call gives only twenty-three representatives.

[6] M'Call, I, 209.

adopted substantially all the regulations suggested by the Trustees, and then the members signed their names to a paper requesting the introduction of slavery under these restrictions. The twenty-seven signers are said to be of the "highest respectability in the province." [1]

This extraordinary assembly was followed shortly by provision for an annual meeting of representatives, who were to meet not for purposes of legislation, but in order that the Trustees might be made acquainted with the state of the province, "the better to enable them to procure all the advantages they can for the good of the people, and provide for the welfare and security of the province." [2] The assembly was to meet for not longer than one month "at the most leisure time," in each year. Every village, town, or district having ten families settled within its limits, was entitled to send a representative, and those having thirty families could "depute two persons." Savannah should have four deputies; Augusta and Ebenezer each two, and Frederica, if thirty families were inhabiting there, the same number. [3]

The assembly could only "propose, debate, and represent to the Trustees what shall appear to them to be for the benefit, not only of each particular settlement, but for the province in general;" [4] since legislative power was by the charter vested solely in the Trustees. The representatives were to furnish an account of the population, land cultivation, negro servitude, and productions of the districts which they severally represented. No qualifications for the suffrage were set, but those of representatives were established in the strangest manner.

"From and after the 24th day of June, 1751, no person shall be capable of being chosen a deputy who has not one hundred mulberry trees planted, and properly fenced, upon every fifty acres he possesses; and that from and after the 24th day of June, 1753, no person shall be capable of being chosen a deputy who has not strictly conformed to

[1] Stevens, I, 312; Jones, I, 425; M'Call, I, 209 ff.
[2] Stevens, I, 245.
[3] Stevens, I, 246; Jones, I, 434–435; M'Call, I, 231.
[4] *Ibid.*

the limitation of the number of negro slaves in proportion to his white servants, who has not at least one female in his family instructed in the art of reeling silk, and who does not yearly produce fifteen pounds of silk upon fifty acres of land, and the like quantity upon every fifty acres he possesses." [1]

"Thus tenaciously," says Stevens, "did the Trustees cling to some of the original purposes of their settlement; and so strangely did they engraft upon the legislature of Georgia the unusual qualifications, not of freehold and income, but of mulberry trees and raw silk, as constituting eligibility to a seat in the assembly. This was sealed, and became the law of the Trustees, on the 27th of March, 1750." [2] In no other part of the American colonies shall we find a more absurd political qualification than this imposed by the philanthropic Trustees of Georgia.

But the government of the Trustees was fast approaching its close. It had proved a "philanthropic, agricultural, industrial, commercial, and governmental" failure.[3] Even before the Trust's twenty-one years of legal duration had expired, it felt the necessity of surrendering its authority to the Crown, and on June 23, 1752, the transfer to the Crown was completed, the last meeting of the Trustees was held, and their seal broken.[4] After this the Board of Trade recommended to the king that the colony be organized with a governor, an assembly, and courts of judicature, under regulations well adapted to the circumstances of the colony.[5] And accordingly, on August 6, 1754, the King in Council appointed John Reynolds as governor of the colony.

In the new governor's commission and instructions, the suffrage, for the first time in Georgia, was expressly defined. The electors of members of the "Commons House of Assembly" were to be freeholders who possessed at least fifty acres of land in the parish or district where they voted;

[1] Stevens, I, 247.
[2] *Ibid.* Compare the equally extreme measures taken by Frederick the Great to establish silk culture in Prussia.
[3] *Ibid.*, 313.
[4] Stevens, I, 252–258; Jones, I, 450–460.
[5] *Ibid.*, 381; *Ibid.*, 460.

while members of the assembly were required to possess at least five hundred acres of land in any part of the province.[1] The assembly was given legislative power similar to assemblies in other royal colonies. Now the silk-worm and mulberry tree prerequisites gave place to a rational qualification for suffrage or office-holding, and the old information-giving group of deputies was displaced by a truly representative legislative assembly.

The first assembly met in January, 1755, and was composed of nineteen members, who were apportioned among three districts, into which the governor, for convenience, divided the colony.[2] Some excitement was caused in the assembly by the actions of one Edmund Gray, who had fraudulently gained a representative's land qualification, and who even tried to assemble the freeholders in Savannah to intimidate the assembly. He and his friends were expelled from the legislature.[3]

The suffrage qualification came up for consideration in this first assembly, for it was found that the terms of the governor's instructions limiting the suffrage to those owning fifty acres of land would disfranchise many of the inhabitants in towns. Owing to the exposed situation of the colony, it had been the policy of the Trustees and of Oglethorpe to settle the people in towns, where they could be easily protected; and in carrying out this policy the fifty acres of each settler were often divided between a home lot in the town, a few acres in the commons, and the remainder in farm land near the town.[4] After the alienation of lands was permitted, it is probable that many owners of town lots did not possess any other land. To remedy the inequalities which the uniform suffrage requirement would produce, the assembly was forced to appeal to the English government, since no law in the colony could change the governor's instructions. The assembly said, in a memorial to the king, that according to the instructions

[1] Jones, I, 464.
[2] Stevens, I, 389, 392; Jones, I, 474.
[3] Stevens, I, 398–399.
[4] *Ibid.*, 107, 137. Compare Penn's apportionment of lots in Philadelphia.

"residents in towns having buildings and improvements greater in value than five hundred acres, were not permitted to sit in the Assembly; and freeholders of town lots liable to pay taxes for the support of government, were not permitted to vote for representatives, though the value of their one or two town acres greatly exceeded the fifty acres by which many others became qualified to vote."[1]

In England the Board of Trade considered this memorial during May and July, 1755,[2] and referred the matter to the lords justices. In November of the same year an additional instruction was prepared for the governor, according to which he was authorized to assent to a bill for ascertaining the qualifications of electors upon the condition that the bill be first submitted for approval to his Majesty, or that it contain a clause suspending the execution of the act until the king's pleasure should be known.[3] The power thus granted does not appear to have been exercised.

In 1761 an act was passed " To assertain the manner and form of Electing Members to represent the Inhabitants of this Province in the Commons House of Assembly."[4] The preamble states that the manner and form of choosing members had never yet been determined. The act does not change the property qualifications of voters as they had been in 1754. The suffrage clause reads:

"every free white man and no other who has attained to the age of Twenty One years and hath been Resident in the Province Six Months and is legally possessed in his own Right of fifty Acres of Land in the said Parish District or village for which the Member or Members is or are to be elected to represent in the General Assembly shall be deemed a person qualified for Electing a Representative or Representatives to serve as Member or Members of the Commons House of Assembly for the Parish District Town or village wherein he is possessed of the above Qualification."

[1] Stevens, I, 412; Jones, I, 489.
[2] MS. *Board of Trade Journals* (in Pa. Hist. Soc.), Vol. 63, pp. 184, 185–186, 276, 280.
[3] *Ibid.*, 320, 321, 324.
[4] Title only given in Watkins's *Digest*, 67; in full in Bishop, *Elections in American Colonies*, 279–287.

Thus in spite of the earlier protest of the townspeople, the old requirement was continued, and, indeed, retained without change until the Revolution.

The general conduct of elections was carefully defined by the act of 1761. The returning officer was to prepare a book and enter therein the names of all persons presenting themselves as candidates, leaving " a fair column" under each candidate's name. It was the duty of the officer to repeat distinctly the name of the candidate for which each elector voted, and then to enter the elector's name in the " fair column" under the candidate's name. Voters were forbidden to alter their votes after once casting them, and could not vote twice at " one and the same Election." Candidates were to be free-born subjects of Great Britain or the dominions belonging thereto, or naturalized persons, professing the Christian religion; they must be twenty-one years of age; residents of the province twelve months before the date of the election writ, and possessed of five hundred acres of land in the province. Either electors or candidates could be compelled to swear that they were properly qualified. The polls were to be open from nine in the morning until six in the afternoon on not more than two days; and fines were to be imposed for intimidation or bribery in elections.

This act is the only general election act passed in the colony of Georgia, and its suffrage provision of fifty acres of freehold, taken from the governor's instructions, is the only legal qualification for electors which the colony possessed. In the same way the elections for representatives are the only ones of which any record has been found; presumably all other officers were appointed by the Crown or the governor.[1]

[1] It is very much regretted that none of the original materials of Georgia history was accessible to the writer, except those published in the *Collections of the Historical Society*. It is believed that a much more detailed account of the suffrage and representation than that given above could be obtained from the known extant material. Unfortunately, I have not had the opportunity to inspect these manuscripts.

CHAPTER VII.

The Suffrage in New York.

I. *Under the Dutch*, 1613–1664.

1. The Provincial Suffrage.

About fifteen years of colonial life in New Netherland passed without any apparent popular participation in the government. Under the control of the New Netherland Company, the Dutch colony was merely a trading settlement, and during the early years of the West India Company no provision was made for giving the colonists a share in the government. It was not until the patroon concessions of 1629 were issued that we find evidence of a change of policy. By these concessions[1] broad feudal political and economic rights were given to persons bringing out a certain number of settlers. But in addition to the mediæval terms respecting patroons, the concessions also offered inducements to individual settlers, and among other privileges gave the colonies lying on each river or island the right to appoint deputies every two years to give information annually to the Commander and his Council.[2]

These provisions might have furnished the basis for a regular representative system had they been adhered to by the directors in New Amsterdam; but, in fact, it was thirteen years after the granting of the concessions before a partially representative body was called, and over twenty years until, in 1658, a truly representative assembly was summoned.

Three quasi-representative boards were erected by the directors,—" The Twelve Men" of 1642, " The Eight Men" of 1643–44, and " The Nine Men" of 1647–1650. The Twelve Men were selected to advise Director Kieft concern-

[1] O'Callaghan, *History of New Netherland*, I, 112–120.
[2] Articles XXI and XXVIII.

ing the impending war with the Indians, and, naturally, in this first and hasty election, we see no formal ideas of the suffrage. The twelve committeemen were chosen by a meeting "of all the masters and heads of families" of New Amsterdam and vicinity, which had been called by the director.[1] The board tried to induce the director to recognize them as a permanent part of the government, but he refused their demands, saying they had been chosen only to consult concerning the Indian affairs; but the director did promise that he would consult with persons among the commonalty regarding taxation and other public matters.[2] In this way the governor offered to recognize informally the wishes of the community, although he refused to provide a permanent representative system.

The recurrence of Indian troubles[3] again forced Kieft to call a general meeting of the settlers, in which, according to a document signed by those present, only forty-eight persons took part.[4] The commonalty, strangely, refused to select a committee to represent them, but asked the director to nominate persons from their number, who might be accepted or rejected by the meeting; and the director and council nominating eight men, the choice was accepted in a paper signed by twenty-eight persons.[5]

This meeting and the papers signed by those present show how slim was the attendance at such gatherings, and how narrow the occasional suffrage granted to the "masters and heads of families." O'Callaghan estimates the population in and around New Amsterdam at this time as about twenty-five hundred souls, five hundred of whom were men.[6] If these figures be correct, the meeting can scarcely be called a democratic one; and we have no proof that it was a representative body, although persons might have been present from the neighboring settlements. Apparently this meeting, like a later one, was composed only of "some of the most in-

[1] O'Callaghan, *New Netherland,* I, 241; Brodhead, *New York,* I, 317.
[2] *N. Y. Col. Doc.,* I, 202–203.
[3] *Ibid.,* 181–185.
[4] *Ibid.,* 191.
[5] *Ibid.,* 192; O'Callaghan, I, 283.
[6] O'Callaghan, I, 385–386.

fluential burghers and inhabitants" of New Amsterdam and its vicinity.[1]   It is thus rather difficult to interpret the real meaning of the word " commonalty," and the meagreness of the records leaves us in doubt whether participation in the meeting was limited by definite action of the director or by the reluctance of the people to attend.   A system of proxy voting would have solved the difficulty of inadequate means of transportation, but there is no evidence pointing to the existence of such a plan.   The method which arose naturally in Massachusetts and Maryland, and developed later on Long Island under the English, appears totally lacking in New Netherland.[2]

The Eight Men appointed by the director with the consent of the commonalty placed a broad construction upon their powers.   They expelled one of their number and elected another in his place; they passed local ordinances, adopted measures for the prosecution of the Indian war, and demanded that taxes be laid only with their consent.[3]   They wrote to the West India Company and the States General of the Netherlands and threatened to betake themselves to the English if their condition was not improved.[4]   The following year, 1644, the Eight Men, angered at Kieft's action in imposing unpopular taxes, sent a long protest to Holland, in which they spare no words to describe the director's lack of judgment in dealing with the Indians and his arbitrary rule over the Dutch.[5]   They say,—

[1] *N. Y. Col. Doc.,* XIV, 220.   Without doubt the difficulty of reaching New Amsterdam from the neighboring Long Island and mainland settlements would prevent a full gathering of even the heads of families.   Compare the reluctance to accept freemenship and perform political duties in Massachusetts and Maryland, *Mass. Col. Rec.,* II, 38; *Md. Archives, Proceedings and Acts of Assembly,* 1637–64, pp. 167, 170.

[2] Proxy voting existed in the English town of Gravesend under the Dutch rule (*N. Y. Col. Doc.,* XIV, 329), and may have been customary in other English towns, but it was not applied to the whole province (*Hempstead Town Records,* I, 409).

[3] O'Callaghan, I, 285–288.

[4] *N. Y. Col. Doc.,* I, 139–140, 190.

[5] *Ibid.,* 188, 209–213.

"It is impossible ever to settle this country until a different system be introduced here, and a new governor sent out with more people, who will settle in suitable places, one near the other, in the form of villages or hamlets, and elect from among themselves a Bailiff or Schout and Schepens, who will be empowered to send their deputies and give their votes on public affairs with the Director and Council, so that the entire country may not be hereafter, at the whim of one man, again reduced to similar danger."

With the composition and forwarding of their petition the work of the Eight Men ceased, and we hear no more of their organization. Kieft, however, called another meeting of the commonalty in August, 1645, to which he submitted the terms of a proposed treaty with the Indians, and assured them "that if any one could give good advice, he might declare his opinions freely." Only one person, a tailor, objected to the treaty.[1]

The petition of the Eight Men called forth proposals in Holland for greater political freedom in the colony. The Chamber of Accounts of the West India Company advised a formal representative assembly holding semi-annual meetings, and having power to advise concerning almost all public matters.[2] But the Chamber of Accounts was more liberal than the Board of XIX Directors, which was the real power in the West India Company. They did, indeed, compose new instructions to the director and council, but these gave no power to the deputies called by the director, except to inform him of the " State and condition of their Colonies." [3]

[1] Brodhead, I, 408.

[2] "As the respective Colonies are allowed by the 28th article of the Freedoms to delegate one or two persons to report their state and condition to the Director and Council, at least once a year, so are we of opinion that the said delegates should, moreover, assemble every six months, at the summons of the Director and Council, for mutual good understanding, and the general advancement of the public welfare, to aid in advising them, besides, upon all affairs relating to the prosperity of their Colonies, the conciliation of the Indians and neighbors, the maintenance of the Freedoms and privileges, the removal of abuses, and the support of the laws and statutes."—*N. Y. Col. Doc.*, I, 154.

[3] *N. Y. Col. Doc.*, I, 154.

The petition may also have played a part in deciding the company to recall Kieft and send out a new governor.

Stuyvesant had been in the colony but a short time when he, too, was compelled to call in the people to assist him in the wars with the Indians. He called together the people of Manhattan, Breuckelen, Amesfoort, and Pavonia, and directed them to choose eighteen persons from whom he and the council might select nine, " as is customary in the Fatherland." [1] After the election by the commonalty, Stuyvesant issued an ordinance in the nature of a charter of government. [2] In its preamble he says that he desired

"nothing more than that the government of New Netherland, entrusted to our care, and principally New Amsterdam, our capital and residence, might continue and increase in good order, justice, police, population, prosperity, and mutual harmony, and be provided with strong fortifications, a church, a school, trading place, harbor, and similar highly necessary public edifices, and improvements, to which end we are desirous of obtaining the assistance of our whole Commonalty, as nothing is better adapted to promote their own welfare and comfort, and as such is required in every well-regulated government."

But as " it is difficult to cover so many heads with a single cap, or to reduce so many opinions to one," he had directed a certain number to be chosen from the community. From this double nomination he now selected nine to act as the "Interlocuters in behalf of the Commonalty." The ordinance explained the duties of the Nine Men and the method of holding meetings. It provided for an annual change in the board upon the partial retirement principle of the Fatherland; six of the members were to lose their seats annually, and the old board, " without its being necessary to convene the entire Commonalty hereafter," should present twelve new names and the old nine members to the director for his choice of six new members.

"Thus jealously," says Brodhead, " did Stuyvesant hedge the meagre privileges he was forced to concede to the people. In the first election alone was the voice of the ' wavering

[1] Brodhead, I, 473; O'Callaghan, II, 36 (August, 1647).
[2] September 25, 1647; *Laws and Ordinances of New Netherland*, 75-78.

multitude' to be expressed; the Nine Men were to nominate their successors." [1]

We cannot here enter into the work of the Nine Men, nor look at the contest which they made for the rights of their board as granted by Stuyvesant in his ordinance.[2] When, however, they desired a delegation to Fatherland, Stuyvesant proposed a new representative assembly, perhaps hoping that the English towns on Long Island which enjoyed broad privileges might support his policy against the Nine Men.[3] This conference, composed of deputies from the "militia companies and the citizens," was scarcely a representative body, for it contained only seven militia officers and three citizens in addition to the company's officers.[4] The conference reached no definite conclusion, and the two sides seem anxious to increase their strength by inviting more deputies; the party of the Nine Men suggested the calling of two deputies from each village or colony in the province, while Stuyvesant proposed summoning merely deputies from the neighboring settlements.[5] No records of the projected assembly have been found.

In the following summer the Nine Men sent their famous remonstrance to Europe.[6] This document is invaluable to the student of colonial New York history, for it gives a remarkably full account of the country, its resources, trade, and political conditions.

The reasons for the declining prosperity of the province are stated to be wholly political:

"As we shall treat of the reasons and causes by which New Netherland has been reduced to its present low and ruinous condition, so we consider it necessary first to enumerate them separately; and, in accordance with our daily experience as far as our knowledge extends,

[1] *History of New York,* I, 475.
[2] *N. Y. Col. Doc.,* I, 315.
[3] *Ibid.*
[4] March 4, 1649; *N. Y. Col. Doc.,* XIV. 109-111; O'Callaghan, II, 90.
[5] *N. Y. Col. Doc.,* XIV, 112.
[6] *Ibid.,* I, 259-318, the three delegates bearing letters from the Nine Men, a petition on behalf of the commonalty and a voluminous remonstrance, left New Amsterdam on August 15, 1649.

we here assert in one word, and none better offers, that the cause is bad government with its attendants and consequences. With our best light we cannot perceive any other than this to be the sole and true foundation-stone of the decay and ruin in New Netherland. This government from which so much abuse proceeds is two-fold; to wit, in Fatherland by the Company, and in this country." [1]

The contest between the Nine Men and the director was for the time transferred to the halls of the States General, and that body considered a provisional order which would have established village governments, given a city government to New Amsterdam, made two members of the director's council elective, and provided for the continuance of the Nine Men for three years.[2]

But these proposals were met by the West India Company with a seemingly liberal set of concessions,[3] which actually made no mention of political privileges while they increased the economic inducements to settlers.[4] In the colony, too,

[1] *N. Y. Col. Doc.*, I, 295.
[2] *Ibid.*, 387–391.

> " The Council of New Netherland shall consist of a President or Director; a Vice Director and of three Councillors, one of whom shall be appointed on the part of their High Mightinesses and the West India Company, and the other two selected from the inhabitants of that country.
>
> " For which purpose the Director and Council shall be bound to call a meeting of the Patroons of Colonies, or their agents, and of the deputies of the Commonalty, to be held within the city of New Amsterdam for the purpose of nominating four qualified persons from whom two shall be selected who shall be thereunto qualified by their High Mightinesses and those of the West India Company. These two elected Councillors shall serve four consecutive years, but on the expiration of the aforesaid four years, one of the two may by lot continue two years more and the other retire in order to present two others in future, biennially, by a new nomination, in manner as aforesaid."

[3] Dated May 24, 1650; *N. Y. Col. Doc.*, I, 401–405.
[4] There can be no doubt that the West India Company did offer favorable terms to settlers. In 1650 it was said that the company had frequently transported the farmer and his family to New Netherland

Stuyvesant refused to commission new members of the board of Nine Men when a nomination was made to him in December, 1650,[1] thus ignoring the order of the States General of April 12, 1650, which directed the continuance of the Nine Men until further orders from the States General.[2]

The authority of the last of the three boards thus came to an end. The three bodies, the Twelve Men, the Eight Men, and the Nine Men, show a similarity in origin and in the reasons for their failure. Each was selected from the community of New Netherland, either by direct voice of the people or by the people ratifying the earlier choice of the director. The principle which underlay their origin was not a representation of localities, but of the whole community. On the other hand, the work of all three ceased when they came into conflict with the arbitrary power of the directors; no interference could be brooked with the authority of the petty sovereigns of New Netherland or the privileges of the honorable company which they represented. In the words of Director Kieft regarding the Twelve Men, which undoubtedly expressed his own and Stuyvesant's later opinion of the other boards as soon as their immediate advantage to the director ceased, the boards tended " to a dangerous consequence and to the great injury both of the country and of our authority." [3]

---

and given him there a farm and bouwerie, four horses, four cows, and sheep and pigs in proportion; the farmer to have the use of the cattle and their increase for six years; returning to the company the number he had received. The farmer bound himself to pay the company one hundred guilders and eighty pounds of butter yearly. (*N. Y. Col. Doc.,* I, 371.)

[1] In December, 1648, Stuyvesant renewed the board, putting in two new members; and apparently a similar renewal must have taken place in 1649, although I have found no record of the fact. In 1650 twelve nominations were made to Stuyvesant, but he refused to select new members, claiming the old board had exceeded its powers (*N. Y. Col. Doc.,* I, 439, 450, 452, 455; O'Callaghan, II, 89; Brodhead, I, 495).

[2] *N. Y. Col. Doc.,* I, 399.

[3] *Ibid.,* 203. Stuyvesant for a short time had the sympathy and support of the English on Long Island. In 1651, Gravesend and Hempstead

After the overthrow of the Nine Men, no such permanent boards were again established, but occasional meetings, partaking of the nature of pure representative bodies, were held, composed of deputies from the several towns and settlements. The first record found of such a meeting is that of one called by the director and council to meet on September 11, 1653. The burgomasters and schepens of New Amsterdam, on September 9, elected two persons to act as delegates to a " general assembly of the country," [1] but no other record of the meeting is known to the writer.

Later on in the same year two assemblies were held. The first one met in pursuance of a call of Stuyvesant to the " nearest subordinate colonies" to send deputies to meet two members of the council and discuss means for stopping the depredations of certain English thieves on Long Island.[2]

---

wrote to Holland expressing their satisfaction with the government of the directors.   These letters have a peculiar interest in view of the independent attitude shortly afterward taken by the Long Island towns.

> ". . . We clearly acknowledge that the frequent changeing a government or the power of electing a Governor among ourselves, which some among us, as we understand, aim at, would be our ruin and destruction by reason of our factious and various opinions, inasmuch as many among us be unwilling to subject themselves to any sort of government, mild or strong, it must, on that account, be compulsory or by force until the Governor's authority be well confirmed; for such persons will not only despise, scorn, or disobey authority, and by their evil example drag other persons along, whereby the laws would be powerless, but every one would desire to do what would please and gratify himself.   In fine the strongest would swallow up the weakest, and by means of elections or choosing, we would be involved in like inconveniences.   Moreover, we are not supplied and provided with persons qualified and fit for such stations.   Therefore, and seeing that we have nothing to bring forward against our present Governor, but on the contrary, truly, and in deed approving his public deportment in his administration, we request that he be still continued over us, and that no change be made."

[1] *Records of New Amsterdam*, I, 117.
[2] *N. Y. Col. Doc.*, XIV, 219.

In addition to the councillors and New Amsterdam deputies, only three towns, all English,[1] were represented. The attitude of the English was now far different from their humility of 1651; they demanded protection from the West India Company, and threatened if it were not granted to stop paying taxes; and they urged the New Amsterdam authorities to join them in an alliance for mutual protection.[2] The latter, however, suggested a full representation of all the neighboring towns and the sending of a remonstrance to officers of the company in Holland. The plan was adopted and tacitly accepted by Stuyvesant,[3] although the city magistrates and not the director invited the towns to send their deputies to the second meeting.[4]

Deputies came to the meeting of December 10, 1653, from four English towns, three Dutch towns, and from New Amsterdam, but the English delegates controlled the meeting.[5] The principal work of the assembly was the drafting and presentation to the director of a remonstrance which was " written in English, by the Deputies from the English villages." [6] The petition [7] recognized the divine and natural origin of " paternal government," but, while acknowledging the authority of the States General and the West India Company, the petitioners claimed the privileges in New Netherland which subjects of the Fatherland enjoyed. They were apprehensive of the establishment of an arbitrary government among them:

" 'Tis contrary to the first intentions and genuine principles of every well regulated government, that one or more men should arrogate to themselves the exclusive power to dispose, at will, of the life and property of any individual, and this, by virtue or under pretense of a law or order he, or they, might enact, without the consent, knowledge or election of the whole Body, or its agents or representatives. Hence

[1] Gravesend, Vlissingen (Flushing), Newtown.
[2] *N. Y. Col. Doc.*, XIV, 223–224; O'Callaghan, II, 238.
[3] *N. Y. Col. Doc.*, XIV, 231, 239.
[4] *Rec. of New Amsterdam*, I, 140; *N. Y. Col. Doc.*, XIV, 227–229.
[5] *N. Y. Col. Doc.*, I, 553; XIV, 233–236.
[6] *Ibid.*, I, 553. George Baxter of Gravesend was the author of the remonstrance; it was translated into Dutch before given to Stuyvesant.
[7] *Ibid.*, 550–552.

the enactment, except as aforesaid, of new Laws or orders affecting the Commonalty, or the Inhabitants, their lives or property, is contrary and opposed to the granted Freedoms of the Dutch Government, and odious to every freeborn man, and principally so to those whom God has placed in a free state on newly settled lands, which might require new laws and orders, not transcending, but resembling as near as possible, those of Netherland. We humbly submit that 'tis one of our privileges that our consent or that of our representatives is necessarily required in the enactment of such laws and orders."

These general statements were followed by a list of specific grievances.[1]

Stuyvesant's first reply to the petition was an evasive one,[2] but on December 12 he declared the assembly an illegal gathering.[3] The following day the meeting, now calling itself a "convention," replied that the director had given his consent to their gathering; and besides, the

"Convention had no other aim, than the service and protection of the country, the maintenance and preservation of the freedoms, privileges and property of its inhabitants, but not an unlawful usurpation of the authority of the said Honble Director-General and Council; on the contrary, their intention was to prevent illegal proceedings, *while the laws of Nature give to all men the right to gather for the welfare and protection of their freedom and property."* [4]

Stuyvesant gave a characteristic rejoinder to the last expressions of the convention. The "pretended Convention" was "actually declared to be illegal," and its members were called

---

[1] Among which were the absence of any protection by the Company, the enforcement of council orders which had never been published, the refusal to grant deeds and patents which had been promised, and the evidence of favoritism in the granting of lands.

[2] He demanded a better translation of the petition and copies for each member of the council; the assembly refused both demands.

[3] He claimed they had exceeded their authority, and that the Dutch towns had no right to send representatives (*N. Y. Col. Doc.*, XIV, 232). Since he had expressed his intention of giving them that right before the meeting (*Ibid.*, 223–4), his subsequent attitude must have come from chagrin that the Dutch deputies did not give him their support against the English.

[4] *Ibid.*, 237.

upon to disperse, and hold no more meetings, under pain " of our extreme displeasure and arbitrary correction." [1] The order was obeyed by the deputies, but their unredressed wrongs smothered for a time until they broke out into the flames of actual rebellion to Stuyvesant's rule. Naturally, the director had the last words in the controversy. In two papers [2] respecting the convention, he answered the complaints of the deputies. Replying to their demand for all the rights of subjects in Fatherland, he infers, in that case, they would have the right to send deputies to the States General, a line of reasoning which seems to him a *reductio ad absurdam.* Concerning their demand for more privileges, he said,—

"It ought to be remembered, that the Englishmen, who are the authors of and leaders in these innovations, enjoy more privileges, than the Exemptions of New Netherland grant to any Hollander."

And he hinted that their affinity for their own nation had led them to threaten to tax themselves and secure their own protection. Replying to the argument from the law of Nature, proof and explanation were demanded:

"The Director-General and Council think, that the authorities are appointed for these purposes, but not all men generally, for that would create confusion. The Lords-Directors resolved for this reason with the knowledge and consent of their High: Might: to appoint the Director-General and Council, giving them ample authority for the preservation and protection of the privileges, freedom and property of the Company and the good inhabitants and if necessary for the convocation of an Assembly of their subjects, but this authority was not conferred on the Burgomasters and Schepens, much less to *all men."*

After the dismissal of the assembly of 1653, Stuyvesant avoided giving the Englishmen an opportunity of again expressing their ideas. In February, 1654, when the opinion

[1] *N. Y. Col. Doc.,* XIV, 238.
[2] One of these is his "Deductions" upon their petition, sent to the Directors of the Company (*N. Y. Col. Doc.,* XIV, 233-236) ; and the other is a statement entered upon the Council Minutes of New Netherland (*ibid.,* 239-240).

of the localities was desired, Stuyvesant consulted with the New Amsterdam authorities and with "the friends" in the several villages.[1] In May of the same year, when an English fleet was feared, he called in the magistrates of the Dutch villages of Breuckelen, Midwout, and Amesfoort.[2]

When peace had been made with England, the Dutch tried to conciliate the English inhabitants, and even went so far as to offer remarkable concessions to new English settlers, who, it was hoped, would settle between the Delaware and Hudson rivers, and thus complete a line of settlements between the distant parts of the province.[3] The new agreement permitted the English settlers in case of disagreement between themselves and Stuyvesant or his successors to elect a chief or director for themselves, only requiring all writs to be issued in the name of the Netherlands.[4] But the English took a yard where the Dutch would have given them an ell. English settlers from Connecticut were coming down the Bronx, and in 1662 Connecticut claimed the entire Bronx and Westchester settlements, together with all the towns on Long Island, including those hitherto under the Dutch, and directed all of them to send deputies to the next general court.[5] A compromise was reached later, by which Stuyvesant yielded Westchester and eastern Long Island to Connecticut, while the English towns in western Long

---

[1] *Rec. of New Amsterdam,* I, 159.

[2] *Ibid.,* 201. The English on Long Island were found to be in correspondence with the authorities in Boston, and two of them were imprisoned by Stuyvesant. In March, 1655–6, the republic of England was publicly proclaimed in Gravesend (*N. Y. Col. Doc.,* II, 152; XIV, 246, 278, etc.; Brodhead, I, ch. XVII; Flint, *Early Long Island,* 277–278).

[3] O'Callaghan, II, 443.

[4] Dated February 14, 1661.

> "The said inhabitants shall have full liberty, after they have planted their colonie, in case of difference with the aforesaid Peter Stuyvesant, or any that shall survive him as Governor, by appointment of the States of Netherlands, to chuse a Director or Cheife; only they shall issue out all writs of what nature soever, in the name of the States Generall of the United Netherlands."

[5] *Conn. Col. Rec.,* 1636–65, 420–423; Brodhead, I, 703.

Island, hitherto under Dutch control, were to be independent of both Connecticut and New Amsterdam.[1] The inhabitants of these towns, perhaps familiar with the earlier promise made to intending Englishmen, now elected one John Scott as "president" and set up an independent government, until the decision of the king should be known.[2]

In the mean time, Stuyvesant, upon the suggestion of the New Amsterdam authorities,[3] had called together another assembly. This body, meeting on November 1, 1663, was more nearly representative of the Dutch population than any of the earlier assemblies or boards. Two delegates from each of eight Dutch towns, including New Amsterdam, were sent, and in one instance at least the election was with the consent of the people.[4] This assembly took no positive measures to support the Dutch authorities, but spent its time in complaining of the Company's neglect of the colony. Its only practical outcome seems to have been the appointment of a delegate to visit Fatherland and explain to the authorities the defenceless condition of the province.[5]

The continued aggressions of the English under Scott led Stuyvesant again to ask advice from the city officers, but he met with scant encouragement. They replied they were indifferent concerning the sovereignty of the country, whether it were held by Dutch or English. "We are of opinion," they say, "that the Burgher is not bound to dispute whether this be the King of England's soil or their High Mightinesses; but if they will deprive us of our properties, freedoms, and privileges, to resist them with our lives or fortunes."[6] But Scott's menacing attitude must

---

[1] O'Callaghan, II, 495.

[2] *N. Y. Col. Doc.*, XIV, 542, 544, 547–8, 551–2; O'Callaghan, II, 498–500; Brodhead, I, 723–28; Flint, *Early Long Island*, 282–286; Thompson, *Long Island* (second edition), II, 320; *Records of New Amsterdam*, V, 18–24.

[3] *Rec. of New Amsterdam*, IV, 318.

[4] O'Callaghan, II, 490, note 4. In the return from Boswyck, the magistrates of that town state that "the aforesaid magistrates have chosen and named two persons from the same [village], with the knowledge and consent of the majority of the inhabitants."

[5] *Rec. of New Amst.*, IV, 342.   [6] *Ibid.*, V, 20.

have seemed dangerous to the property and freedom of the Dutch, for shortly after this we find the New Amsterdam authorities advising the calling of another assembly.[1]

The last representative assembly of New Netherland met in New Amsterdam on April 10, 1664, and was composed of deputies from twelve Dutch towns.[2] The old dispute regarding the duty of the Company to protect the colony furnished the principal theme for discussion. Stuyvesant demanded supplies and military levies from the inhabitants; the deputies demanded the fulfilment of the company's promises. And with mutual recriminations the assembly closed its meeting without any action for the protection of the province. It was not long after this that the dreaded English attack came, and the fleet under Nicholls won an unexpectedly easy conquest. Since the Company gave itself " so little concern about the safety of the country and its inhabitants as not to be willing to send a ship of war to its succor in such pressing necessity, nor even a letter of advise,"[3] the people had carried out their threat, that they would not longer " dwell and sit down on an uncertainty," but would be obliged " to seek by submission to another government" [4] the protection which the Honorable Company refused.

2. The Suffrage in Local Elections.

A. *In the Dutch Towns.*

There was apparently but little popular political activity in the Dutch towns of New Netherland.[5] The development of these towns was slow, and often it was artificially encouraged by the New Amsterdam authorities.[6] The colonists

---

[1] *Rec. of New Amsterdam*, V, 33.

[2] O'Callaghan, II, 505–509.

[3] *N. Y. Col. Doc.*, II, 367–68.

[4] *Ibid.*, 375.

[5] This section merely summarizes the conclusions reached by the writer in an article in *Amer. Hist. Rev.*, VI, 1–18.

[6] *N. Y. Col. Doc.*, I, 160–162; *Laws and Ordinances of New Neth.*, 206, 234. 368.

lacked the common ownership of the land, the common political rights, and the intense religious interest which helped to form the New England town. The absence of these centralizing forces and the liberal policy of the Dutch West India Company in making large individual land grants greatly retarded the growth of towns among the Dutch. Many years usually intervened between the date of settlement of a locality and the time of its incorporation.

When the towns were incorporated, the town officers were a schout and several schepens, who were in some cases first selected by the local inhabitants,[1] but thereafter in all cases, it is believed, constituted a close corporation. The existing magistrates had the power to nominate a double number of persons from whom the director and council selected some to fill vacancies in the local magistracy. A number of these nominations have been preserved, and in no case is there evidence of popular election of the proposed magistrates.[2]

While, therefore, the evidence points to the absence of any regular popular elections, there were occasional meetings of the settlers to consider questions of local importance. We have records of such a meeting in Brooklyn in 1660, to which the magistrates " had convened all the inhabitants of the village of Breuckelen." [3] In 1663 the " town people" of Harlem were summoned in meeting to take measures to avert a threatened Indian attack.[4] Similar, but not frequent, instances are to be found concerning Bergen,[5] New Amsterdam,[6] and the Delaware settlements.[7] Stuyvesant, in writing to Holland in 1653, wishes to give the impression that popu-

---

[1] Stiles, *Hist. of Brooklyn*, I, 45; *Laws and Ordinances of New Neth.*, 335; Thompson, *Long Island* (second ed.), II, 155. In other cases even the first selection was made in the charter itself, *N. Y. Col. Doc.*, XIII, 196–198; *Laws and Ordinances of New Neth.*, 403, 458.

[2] *Amer. Hist. Rev.*, VI, 9, notes.

[3] *N. Y. Col. Doc.*, XIV, 479.

[4] Riker, *Hist. of Harlem*, 222.

[5] *N. Y. Col. Doc.*, XIII, 232, 319.

[6] *Records of New Amst.*, IV, 273; *N. Y. Col. Doc.*, XIV, 220.

[7] *N. Y. Col. Doc.*, XII, 151, 154–5, 308; *Pa. Archives*, Second Series, VII, 511.

lar elections were not uncommon, but his letter scarcely proves the fact:

> "It is untrue, that any Magistrates have been appointed against the laws of Netherland or against the wish of the people. . . . The Magistrates of New Amsterdam, before being installed and taking the oath in the presence of the Director-General, were each by name and surname and by his office proclaimed from the front of the Council Chamber, and the Community was called upon to express their objections. The same is usually done by the Director-General and Council at the installation of other, military officers. . . ." [1]

But in all these cases the popular action appears upon an exceptional occasion and does not enter as an integral part into the town life. Under such circumstances the suffrage was an accidental privilege rather than a definite right, and consequently we find among the Dutch no statements of the suffrage qualifications. Where popular elections did not take place, there could be no definition of the suffrage.

B. *In the English Towns.*

In the English towns which developed under the New Netherland jurisdiction, political practice was far more popular than in the Dutch settlements.[2] Director Kieft encouraged English settlers, and gave favorable charters to four English towns before a single Dutch village had been incorporated. In the charters of Newtown, Hempstead, Flushing, and Gravesend there is a degree of popular government never attained in the Dutch towns.[3] The towns received a definite tract of land, with power to build a town and fortifications, and to practise liberty of conscience.[4] Within the town the

---

[1] *N. Y. Col. Doc.,* XIV, 235.

[2] See *Amer. Hist. Rev.,* VI, 10–16.

[3] Newtown chartered, March 28, 1642; for charter, see O'Callaghan, *New Netherland,* I, 425. Hempstead chartered November 16, 1644; see Thompson, *Long Island* (second edition), II, 4–6. Flushing chartered October 10, 1645; see *Laws and Ordinances of New Netherland,* 48–51. Gravesend chartered December 19, 1645; see *Documentary Hist. of N. Y.,* I, 629–632.

[4] Gravesend charter.

patentees could erect a civil organization, hold town meetings, and elect three magistrates and a schout, who should be confirmed by the director. The Gravesend charter reads,—

" With libertie likewise for them, the sᵈ pattentees, theyr associates heyres etc to erect a bodye politique and ciuill combination amongst themselves, as free men of this Province & of the Towns of Grauesend & to make such civill ordinances as the Maior part of ye Inhabitants ffree of the Towne shall thinke fitting for theyr quiett & peaceable subsisting & to Nominate elect & choose three of ye Ablest approued honest men & them to present annuallie to ye Gouernor Generall of this Province for the tyme being, for him ye said Gouernᵣ to establish and confirme. . . ."

The Hempstead charter contained almost exactly the same terms, while the Newtown and the Flushing charters were somewhat less liberal. Some years after this Stuyvesant granted more restricted privileges to the English settlers at Westchester [1] and Jamaica,[2] in which he attempted to limit them to the customs of the Dutch towns.

We have considerable evidence of democratic political activities in these English towns. In the first place, their annual returns of elections to the director show that the officers were appointed in the town meeting by a popular vote and not by nomination of the magistrates.[3] In the second place, a number of orders of the town meetings are extant showing regular activity upon the part of these meetings, and throwing much light upon the details of town government.[4] There can be no doubt, with this evidence before us, that the English townsman exercised a regular and strong control over this town government through the popular elections and the town meetings.

In such cases the New England customs appear to have governed the suffrage conditions. The four early town char-

[1] March 16, 1656 (*N. Y. Col. Doc.*, XIII, 65–6).
[2] March 21, 1656 (*Ibid.*, XIV, 339–340).
[3] *N. Y. Col. Doc.*, XIV, 189, 296, 300, 329, 343, 345, 422, 424, etc.
[4] *Ibid.*, 128–129; 504–506; 529–530.

ters had implied that the original founders would be joined
by certain associates or followed by successors and heirs, and
that the political privileges granted would extend and descend to these persons.   Associates, upon receiving their lots
and rights in the common lands, obtained at the same time a
voice in the town meeting.[1]   The admission of such associates usually required the consent of the town meeting, and
in Gravesend none of the original twenty-eight owners could
sell his land until he had settled and built a house in the
town; while even after he had done so he must first " propound it to the towne in generall & in case the towne would
not buy," then he might sell to outsiders.[2]   It was expressly
stated, however, that the sale might not be made to one
" notoriouslie detected for an infamous person or a disturber
of the common peace."   Hempstead excluded " quakers and
such like," and required newcomers to show letters of com-
mendation and approbation from the authorities of the town
from which they came.[3]

The elections, especially after the Quaker difficulties had
arisen, were not always managed with decorum.   A party
of Dutchmen who had purchased lands and houses in Gravesend claimed to have been excluded from the suffrage,
although proxy votes were cast by the English for those in
confinement, for others who had left the town, and for con-
spirators against the government.[4]   "An honest Dutchman,
who was a hired man," was not permitted to vote in the place
of his master who was absent.   It is interesting to notice
that in this town of Gravesend occurs the only instance found
in all the colonies of woman suffrage.   In the summer of
1655, when the town had neglected to make its usual nomination of officers to the director, Stuyvesant wrote to Lady
Moody, the oldest patentee of the town, and the other inhabitants, directing them to perform their duty as required by
their patent; and a month later the names of the selected
nominees were sent to the director in a document signed by

[1] In Hempstead, *N. Y. Col. Doc.*, XIV, 529.
[2] *N. Y. Col. Doc.*, XIV, 128–9.
[3] *Ibid.*, 529.
[4] *Ibid.;   see* also *Laws and Ordinances of New Neth.*, 338.

Deborah Moody and John Tillton " as clerk in Behalf of the Rest." [1]

Stuyvesant, who followed Kieft, was opposed to the privileges which the latter had granted the English. In 1653 he wrote,—

"The English (on Long Island) do not only enjoy the right of nominating their own Magistrates, but some of them also usurp the election and appointment of such Magistrates, as they please, without regard to their religion. Some, especially the people of Gravesend, elect libertines and Anabaptists, which is decidedly against the laws of the Netherlands.

" . . . But if it be made a rule, that the selection and nomination shall be left to the people generally, whom it most concerns, then every one would want for Magistrate a man of his own stamp, for instance a thief would choose for Magistrate a thief and dishonest man, a drunkard a smuggler, etc. . . ." [2]

And in 1656, when Englishmen asked for town charters for settlements at Westchester and Jamaica, the director replied that, regarding both lands and election of magistrates, they might be placed upon " the footing and order in use in the villages of Middleburg, Breuckelen, Midwout, and Amesfoort," all of which had the limited privileges of the Dutch towns. [3] The same conservatism is shown in Stuyvesant's negotiations with some Milford inhabitants who proposed leaving their homes in Connecticut and making a settlement in what is now New Jersey. [4]

But while the director was opposed to popular government,

---

[1] *N. Y. Col. Doc.*, XIV, 527–529. See Flint, *Early Long Island*, 104–115, Brodhead, I, 411–412, for Lady Moody's settlement at Gravesend. Compare the demand made by Mrs. Margaret Brent for suffrage in Maryland. See Neill, *Virginia Carolorum*, 274–275, for sketch of life of Lady Moody.

[2] *Ibid.*, 235.

[3] *Ibid.*, 339–340. It must be noted that the towns of Jamaica and Westchester interpreted their charters very broadly, and held town meetings and popular elections in the same manner as the other English towns were accustomed to do (*N. Y. Col. Doc.*, XIV, 504–506, 509; Bolton's *Hist. of Westchester*, Revised edition, II, 279–281).

[4] *Ibid.*, XIII, 209–222.

he could not stamp it out in the English towns. We have abundant evidence of communal activity among the English settlers; their town meetings and popular elections were held almost continuously under the Dutch rule;[1] and at last their self-consciousness found expression in the union of six towns and the election of President John Scott.

C. *In New Amsterdam.*

Nearly forty years after the first settlement of New Netherland, a separate government was erected for the city of New Amsterdam. The first demand for a distinct city government was sent to Holland by the Nine Men in 1649, when their representatives were directed to ask for a " suitable municipal government." [2] It was urged that this, together with other reforms, would encourage the settlement of the colony and promote its prosperity. A committee of the States General shortly afterwards advised the establishment of a " Burgher Government" in New Amsterdam, consisting of a sheriff, two burgomasters, and five schepens.[3] The report was not adopted, but its consideration stirred up the West India Company, and on April 4, 1652, Stuyvesant was directed to erect a government similar to that of Amsterdam. The officers were to be those named in the provisional order of the States General, selected from the " honest and respectable" persons of the settlement. The directors querulously expressed the hope that some such might be found among the inhabitants.[4]

It was ten months after the dating of this instruction before Stuyvesant inaugurated the city government. He allowed no popular election of magistrates, although after the choice of the officers they " were each by name and surname and by his office proclaimed," and " the community was called upon to express their objections." [5] Stuyvesant does

[1] See Stuyvesant's rule forbidding town meetings in Flushing, *Laws and Ordinances of New Neth.*, 338.

[2] *N. Y. Col. Doc.*, I, 260.

[3] *Doc. Hist. of N. Y.*, I, 598; *N. Y. Col. Doc.*, I, 387–391.

[4] *Ibid.*, 599–600.

[5] *N. Y. Col. Doc.*, XIV, 235; O'Callaghan, II, 212–216; Brodhead, I, 548–540.

not refer to any objections, and it is unlikely, under the circumstances, that any were made.

Another three years passed before the director would agree to a method for renewing the magistrates, although the burgomasters and schepens had twice petitioned for a change.[1] When this was granted in 1656, it was so hedged about that it contained no provision for popular elections.[2] A double nomination was to be made annually by the magistrates, but the existing magistrates were always to be considered in nomination; the nominees must be well-qualified persons, favorable to the director and council; and a member of the council must be present at the meeting of the magistrates when they selected their nominees. Under this arrangement the local officials were annually elected until the coming of the English.[3]

The organization of the city government was soon made yet more aristocratic. Stuyvesant was not content with forbidding popular elections and compelling double nominations by the magistrates, nor even was the presence of the councillor at the selection sufficient for him. By ordinances of January 30 and February 2, 1657,[4] Stuyvesant limited narrowly the number of persons who could hold the municipal offices. The ordinances established two classes of citizens, one holding the greater burgherecht, and the other the smaller burgherecht. The first class was composed of those who had held colonial, municipal, military, or ecclesiastical offices, or the male descendants of such, or who had paid fifty guilders. The second class was made up of those born in the city, or those who had kept fire and light for a year and a half, or who kept shop and paid twenty guilders. The

---

[1] In 1654 and 1656; *N. Y. Col. Doc.*, XIV, 244; O'Callaghan, II, 311.

[2] *Records of New Amsterdam*, II, 16, 24–29, 282–286; O'Callaghan, II, 370.

[3] It is to be noted, however, that New Amsterdam was not given a separate schout or sheriff until 1660. (*Doc. Hist. of N. Y.*, I, 600.)

[4] *Laws and Ordinances of New Neth.*, 299–301. See J. F. Jameson, *Mag. Amer. Hist.*, VIII, 321, for a discussion of local government in Holland and the Netherlands. Also O'Callaghan, I, 391, II, 338–341; Brodhead, I, 452 ff. For the granting of the burgherecht, see *N. Y. Hist. Soc. Coll.*, 1885, 1–16.

tenure of municipal offices was limited to those possessing the greater burgherecht, who thus constituted a close hereditary office-holding class.

In conclusion, it may be said that regular popular suffrage was not practised among the Dutch of New Netherland. Neither in the local town governments, nor in the municipal government of New Amsterdam, nor in the colonial representative system, is there evidence of such suffrage. Occasional meetings of the "community" were held in New Amsterdam or in the villages, and in some cases a selection of magistrates by the officials was publicly announced to the inhabitants. But such cases cannot furnish a basis for a general system of elections. nor give rise to a definite theory of the suffrage. Again, the elective system of New Netherland was clogged by a process of double and triple nominations, by the arbitrary power of the director, and by the aristocratic classes in the city of New Amsterdam. The democratic practices of the English towns are in marked contrast to the ideas of Stuyvesant, but these towns are not an integral part of New Netherland. They are off-shoots from the New England town life, and they bear all the characteristics of the parent stem. The true Dutch towns are miniature reproductions of the institutions of the Netherlands, with their indirect and cumbrous elective machinery exercised by a commercial aristocracy.

II. *The Early English Period,* 1664–1691.

This is the period of struggle for the right of representation, during which no continuous representative system existed, although one assembly was held at the opening of the period and several near its close. We will but glance at the suffrage in connection with these assemblies, without taking up the details of the interesting contest between the colonists and James, Duke of York.

The Duke's patent had given him absolute power to govern all English subjects within his territory by such laws as he or his assigns should make. No mention was here made of the popular participation in the framing of laws which many earlier proprietors had been compelled to acknowledge. The

Duke was unrestrained in his power except by the feeble provision that his laws should be " as neare as conveniently may be" agreeable to the statutes of England. His control over commerce and his legal ownership of the land made the property and trade of the existing settlers insecure; while under the charter he need grant them no political privileges. We look in vain in this remarkable charter for any indication of popular government.

But the Duke must conciliate, at least in a degree, the inhabitants of his new territory, or its possession would be profitless to him. The terms of capitulation granted by Colonel Nicholls, the Duke's representative, to the Dutch inhabitants constituted a voluntary limitation of the proprietor's power. By these articles, of which there were three sets,[1] the Dutch were admitted as English denizens upon recognizing the king's authority. They were guaranteed in their lands and other property, and might, if they wished, leave the country within a limited time and take their property with them. To those remaining, the Dutch rules of inheritance were promised, and they were permitted freedom of conscience and worship. In all cases no sudden change in political organization was contemplated, and the existing officers were directed to continue the performance of their duties for a time at least.

On Long Island, where Nicholls wished to keep the good will of the English settlers, his promises were still broader. He is said to have written to certain prominent men promising that the English inhabitants of the island should have privileges equal to, if not greater than, those enjoyed by the other New England colonies.[2] In February, 1665, Nicholls proceeded to carry out his plans for a government of Long Island, although he may have previously erected Long Island, Staten Island, and the Bronx settlements into a county called Yorkshire. He now wrote to the towns re-

---

[1] The three sets were drawn respectively for New Amsterdam and its surrounding territories, for the upper Hudson settlements, and for the Delaware regions. See *N. Y. Col. Doc.*, II, 250–253; XIV, 559; III, 71–73.

[2] *Southold Town Records*, I, 357; *Rept. of N. Y. State Historian*, 1897, 240–242; *N. Y. Col. Doc.*, XIV, 555–556.

minding them of the many grievous inconveniences under which they had groaned, and explaining how the king at his own charge had shown his " signall grace and honor" to his subjects by conquering the Dutch, and by giving control of the land to the Duke of York. Nicholls then states his determination to settle " good and knowne Laws" for the country, with the best advice and information of a general meeting.[1]

This general meeting, called the Hempstead assembly, is the first representative body held under the English in New York. The representatives were to be chosen by the several towns, and Nicholls directed that the deputies be " chosen by the major part of the freemen only, which is to be understood, of all Persons rated according to their Estates, whether English or Dutch;" and he recommended that the people select " the most sober, able, and discreet persons without partiality or faction, the fruit and benefitt whereof will return to themselves in a full and perfect settlement and composure of all controversyes, and the propagacon of true Religion amongst us." Under this provision, it is believed that none but freeholders voted, although the phrase " rated according to their Estates" is not easily translatable at this late day; it surely excluded those who paid only poll-taxes.

Thirty-four deputies attended the meeting at Hempstead, and on March 1, 1665, the assembly accepted a code of laws which Nicholls had drafted, and which came later to be called the " Duke's Laws." This code made no provision for a general provincial organization except of the judicial circuits and the military companies; it omitted all reference to a general representative assembly, which was so distinctive a feature of the New England colonies, and was one of the privileges which the Long Islanders had expected to receive.[2] In spite of strong popular protests and numerous petitions, almost twenty years passed before the Duke agreed to an assembly.

At last, by the instructions given to Governor Dongan, on

[1] *N. Y. Col. Doc.,* XIV, 564.
[2] *Southold Town Records,* I, 358–359; *Easthampton Town Records,* I, 241; *Hempstead Records,* I, 260; *N. Y. Col. Doc.,* XIV, 631–2; *Report of State Historian for 1897,* 240–242.

January 27, 1682-3, formal provision was made for an assembly.[1]

> ". . . there shall be a General Assembly of all the Freeholders, by the persons who they shall choose to represent them in order to consulting with yourself and the said Council what laws are fitt and necessary to be made and established for the good weale and government of the said Colony and its Dependencyes, and of all the inhabitants thereof . . ."

The new governor arrived in the province in August, 1683, and shortly afterwards, on September 13, warrants were issued to the sheriffs of the province for the election of deputies to an assembly. These writs directed that the freeholders in the several towns should take part in the election,[2] and a few days later the council entered upon its minutes the order, "none but freeholders to vote at the election." [3] The writs further established a curious system of indirect voting for certain parts of the province. Each of the three ridings of Yorkshire was to send two delegates, New York City was to elect four, Esopus and Albany each two, and Staten Island, Schenectady, Pemaquid (Maine), and the islands (Martha's Vineyard, Nantucket, Gardiners, etc.) were each to send one. On Long Island, on the Esopus, and on the islands the various towns or settlements were to elect a certain number of committeemen, who should meet in the principal town and there elect the proper number of deputies from the riding or the district.[4] Thus this assembly differed from that of 1665 in the unit of representation, which in the

[1] *N. Y. Col. Doc.,* III, 331; *N. Y. Col. Laws,* I, 108-110.
[2] *Ibid.,* XIV, 770-771; *Journals of Legislative Council of N. Y.,* I, Introduction, xi.
[3] *Calendar of Council Minutes,* 33.
[4] Evidence of this method of voting exists in the records of East Hampton and Huntington.

> "At a Legall Towne meting there, [four persons] were chosen to meete at Southold uppon Wednesday next to Joyne with the Committee of ye other Townes in Chusing Two Representatives for this Rideing to Meete at York according to order." *East Hampton Records,* II, 134-5. See also *Huntington Records,* I, 372.

earlier one had been the town, but in the later body was a much wider district or territory, to which as yet no specific name was given.[1]

The assembly in its first act, which it called a "charter," provided for a general organization of government, and stated a number of specific rights of the citizen.[2]   Among the many other subjects treated in this remarkable act occurs the first general statement of the suffrage qualification:

" Every ffreeholder within this province and ffreeman in any Corpora-con Shall have his free Choise and Vote in the Electing of the Representatives without any manner of constraint or Imposicon.   (A)nd that in all Eleccons the Majority of Voices shall carry itt and by freeholders is understood every one who is Soe understood according to the Lawes of England."

The English practice at this time was that established by the acts of 1430 and 1432 fixing the qualifications of the suffrage as forty shillings income from freehold; and this remained the legal qualification in New York during the short existence of the representative system under Governor Dongan.   It is to be noted, however, that the provincial franchise included also freemen in corporations.   In 1683 this would have included New York City alone, where the Dutch burgherecht had been translated into the English free-manship, and continued under much the same privileges and restrictions.[3]

Dongan's second assembly was elected in 1685 in virtue of writs directed to the sheriffs of the counties, commanding the freeholders of each county to elect representatives,[4] presumably in accordance with the terms of the act just quoted.

In one county at least, the indirect system of voting established in 1683 was used again in 1685.   An entry in the Southampton records is as follows: " At a towne meeting held in Southampton with the rest of the county by the

[1] One of the acts of this first assembly was to divide the colony into twelve counties; *N. Y. Col. Laws,* I, 121; *N. Y. Col. Doc.,* XIII, 575.

[2] *N. Y. Col. Laws,* I, 111–116; the charter was subsequently vetoed by James, after he had become King; *N. Y. Col. Doc.,* III, 357.

[3] *N. Y. Col. Doc.,* III, 337. See *post.*

[4] *Journal of Legis. Council,* Introduction, xiv.

major voote of the pxoes of ye county major Howell was
chosen to be one of ye assemblymen for the County of Suffolk, And Mr. Joshua Hubert was the other." [1] This election was the last held under the government of James II.
The king soon discontinued the representative system, and
gave legislative power to the governor and his council.[2]

Under the usurper Jacob Leisler, who seized control of the
colonial government after the news of the English Revolution of 1688 reached New York,[3] there were occasional
popular elections, and a partially representative system was
established. Leisler, without doubt, felt the necessity of
strengthening his questionable authority by gaining the good
will of the people. This he did by procuring the popular
election of members of a council of safety; [4] but many of
the inhabitants were opposed to his authority and took no
part in the election. It is said that his followers were " some
of the meanest sort of the Inhabitants," [5] and according to
one account only one-third of the people participated in the
elections.[6] In New York City Leisler ordered that certain
officers, by charter appointive by the king's governor, should
be elected by the Protestant freeholders,[7] and sent writs
directing the popular election of justices and militia officers
in the counties, all of whom had previously been appointed
by the governor.[8] In February, 1689–90, Leisler took

[1] *Southampton Town Records,* II, 286.

[2] See commission and instructions of Governor Dongan, *N. Y. Col.
Doc.,* III, 369–375, 382–385.

[3] *Doc. Hist. of N. Y.,* II, 426; *N. Y. Col. Doc.,* III, 598.

[4] This committee was partially representative of the province, two
persons coming from each of the town or settlements of New York
City, Brooklyn, Flatbush, Flushing, Newtown, Staten Island, New Jersey, Esopus, and Westchester. But Albany, Ulster, and Suffolk Counties, and almost all of New Jersey were unrepresented, and many towns
in the several counties were individually opposed to the revolution.
See *Doc. Hist. of N. Y.,* II, 56, 427; *N. Y. Col. Doc.,* III, 585, 597, 609,
670, 737.

[5] *Ibid.,* 427.

[6] *N. Y. Col. Doc.,* III, 670.

[7] *Ibid.,* 675; *Doc. Hist.,* II, 35. The election was carried through by a
minority of the inhabitants.

[8] *Ibid.,* 655, 674–5.

another step in organizing the government by issuing writs for the election of " proper and fit" persons to act as representatives of the counties.[1] All the counties except one were represented in this assembly,[2] but " Suffolk County would not meddle with it." [3] The elections do not appear to have been fully participated in by the people. In New York City Leisler personally directed the elections, at which only a few persons, " all off his side," voted. " From the other Counties came Representatives onely chosen by a few people off their side and very weak men." [4]

Leisler failed in gaining the support of the influential inhabitants. His friends did not belong to the former governing class, but he must have gained adherents among the poorer classes, since his popular elections would admit them to a greater share in the provincial government. But a revolutionist is often forced to ignore the forms of law; and while Leisler attempted to maintain the elective system, yet his evident interferences in the system made the suffrage little more than a farce. The merchants of New York, in a petition to the king and queen, could find no better name for his followers " than a Rable, those who formerly were scarce thought fit to bear the meanest offices." [5] A gathering of freeholders on Long Island called Leisler a " Tyrant," who, they said, acted upon Catiline's maxim that " The Ills that I have done can not be safe but by attempting greater." [6] Thus, in spite of his democratic utterances, Leisler's acts were not accepted by the people of the province, nor approved by the English authorities, who, in November, 1689, commissioned a new governor for the colony.

If the Duke's laws made no provision for a general elective system, they did not lack rules for the local suffrage. The laws were drawn from New England sources, and yet it is remarkable that Nicholls cut out the whole subject of freemanship, both of the colony and the town. This principle,

[1] *Doc. Hist.*, II, 73.
[2] *Journal of Legislative Council of N. Y.*, Introduction, xxiv.
[3] *N. Y. Col. Doc.*, III, 717.
[4] *Ibid.*
[5] *Ibid.*, 748–9.
[6] *Ibid.*, 754–6.

copied from English corporation practice, received an extended connotation in America, and lay at the basis of local
and colonial suffrage in New England during Nicholls's
time. It must be remembered that Nicholls and his fellow-
commissioners were directed by their instructions to inquire
into this exclusive freemanship to which the king objected.[1]
His practical knowledge of the workings of the freemanship principle in New England must have determined Nicholls to omit it from his code. Although the word freeman
occurred scores of times in the New Haven and Massachusetts codes, from which Nicholls drew his legislation, yet it
is sedulously erased from the Duke's laws, and even the
allied subjects of residence and admission of inhabitants are
not mentioned.[2] The New England codes forbade a man
settling in a town without the consent of the local officers
or the town meeting; but this, too, savored of the freeman
idea and was rejected by Nicholls. In addition to fostering
political and ecclesiastical intolerance, the New England
freemanship, whether of town or province, was opposed to
the powers granted by charter to the Duke of York;[3] and
Nicholls also had the example of Stuyvesant before him in
opposing the freemanship idea.[4] Thus there were abundant
reasons for Nicholls's refusal to adopt the freemanship principle; his own experience in New England, his instructions,

[1] *N. Y. Col. Doc.*, III, 51–54, 57–63, 84, 110–113; *Records of Massachusetts Bay*, IV, pt. II, 129, 173–174, 186 ff., 200–211, 218 ff.

[2] The word *freeman* does occur once in the Laws, but in that case it
means *free man*, *N. Y. Col. Laws*, I, 36. The words freeman or freemen are used twenty-five times in the New Haven Laws of 1656, and
fifty-five times in the Massachusetts laws of 1660.

[3] By the Duke's charter he and his heirs are given power " to admit
such and so many person and persons to trade and traffique unto and
within the terrytoryes and islands aforesaid and into every and any
part and parcell thereof and to have possesse and enjoy any lands or
hereditaments in the parts and places aforesaid. . . ."

[4] " None of the Townes of N. Netherlands are troubled with inhabitance, the which doe not Lyke her or her Magistrates, beinge
reserved that they doe not admitt any inhabitance without approbation
and acknowledgement of the Director Generall and Counsell. . . ."
N. Y. Col. Doc., XIII, 211.

the Duke's charter, and Dutch custom were all opposed to the exclusiveness of the New England corporation.

But, although the laws made no provision for these subjects, there is reason to believe that the towns, at least in Long Island, acted upon the New England custom. The town books show many actions and by-laws of the town meetings relating to the admission of new inhabitants.[1] A person " not legally accepted" is ordered to leave Easthampton,[2] and a " notorious thief" is rejected as an inhabitant.[3] In Southampton, in 1676, after a division of the town lands had been made, the holders of the land could not sell or let them to any one except he were " approved of by ye Justices, the minister ye constables and overseers of ye town."[4] And in Hempstead no " unresident" person could settle in the town without the consent of the town.[5] It is evident from these few illustrations that the towns kept control of the admission of inhabitants, and even imposed severe conditions upon intending settlers, as when, in Southampton, they must be acceptable to four sets of officials, including the minister.

Since the Duke's laws omitted the subject of freemanship, it might be supposed that Nicholls would substitute some other form of qualification for the suffrage. But, in fact, he did not clearly define the voting class. The elective officers under the laws were constables, town overseers, gaugers of cask, militia officers, church wardens, and ministers.[6] In the case of militia officers alone the voting class is distinct, for these officers are to be elected by " the plurality of voyces of the Soldiers."[7]

In the suffrage for the other officers, four different expres-

---

[1] *E.g., East-Hampton Records,* I, 282, 288, 324; II, 175.

[2] *Records,* I, 371.

[3] *Ibid.,* II, 175.

[4] *Ibid.,* 255.

[5] *Ibid.,* 28.

[6] Other officers not mentioned in the laws were occasionally elected by the towns: see *Hempstead Records,* I, 228; *Huntington Records,* I, 359–360.

[7] *N. Y. Col. Laws,* I, 50. All persons over sixteen years of age, including servants, and excluding certain judicial and ecclesiastical officials and a few others, were to attend the militia trainings.

sions are used in describing the electors: "householders," "inhabitants householders," "freeholders," "Inhabitants freeholders, Householders." In spite of the seeming variety, it is believed that these phrases all refer to the same class of citizens;[1] and that the words "inhabitants" and "householders" are to be taken not in a substantive, but an adjective, sense, qualifying the word "freeholders." The word inhabitant meant a householder,[2] and the suffrage must have been limited to *inhabiting and householding freeholders.*

Although it is clear that Nicholls meant to limit the suffrage to freeholders, yet there is no statement of the size of freehold required; and perhaps the variance in local conditions made it impracticable to adopt a general qualification.

But the lack of definiteness led to many contests and disputed elections in the several towns. It was the natural tendency of the original proprietors in the towns to desire to

[1] The evidence for this belief is drawn from two sources: (*a*) the internal evidence of the Laws; and (*b*) the practice of the towns.

(*a*) From the Laws. In one place the Laws speak of the election of overseers by the "Housholders," and in another place, by the "freeholders;" and similarly the election of the minister is said to be by "the Inhabitants housholders;" and by the "Inhabitants freeholders housholders."

(*b*) From the town practice. The town records use the words as loosely as do the Laws. For instance, in Southampton the phrases occur, "inhabitants *or* freeholders;" "freeholders;" "freeholders *and* Inhabitants" (*Records*, II, 279, 295, 305; also I, 135–138 note). In 1672 an election in Hempstead was contested because persons had voted who were freeholders indeed, but held only small tracts, and it was maintained that a man must be not only a freeholder, but a freeholder of a certain number of acres, in order to possess the suffrage (*N. Y. Col. Doc.*, XIV, 667). In 1676 Andros granted a patent to the town officers of Southold, for themselves and "their associats, the freeholders and Inhabitants of the s^d Town," and subsequently these officers state, "All which freeholders we doe fully own . . . to be our onely associats" (*Town Records*, II, 8–12). The last case shows that the town officers believed *Inhabitants* to be a qualification of the word *freeholders;* a man must be an inhabitant *and* a freeholder to be qualified to vote.

[2] "He who hath a house in his hands in a town, may be said to be an Inhabitant." Jacob's *Law Dictionary*, London, 1797. See *post*, Chap. XI.

limit the right of suffrage to themselves or those who had an equivalent share in the town lands. As the towns increased in population, or lands were divided among the descendants of the early settlers, or poorer persons bought small tracts, there arose a class made up of freeholders, indeed, but freeholders who were not on a plane of economic or social equality with the original proprietors. Under these circumstances, a contest between the two classes was bound to occur, and the governor usually threw his influence on the side of the wealthier class.

As early as 1666 the Court of Assizes ordered that the " Dividing of Towne Lotts, thereby multiplying poor freemen and votes, to be rectified by the Sessions;" [1] but the remedy was evidently not satisfactory, for again in 1670 the Long Island towns petitioned for legislation against " divers poor inconsiderable persons, who though they have but a Small Portion of a Lott, yett Expect to give their votes in Town Courts equal with ye best freeholders." [2] The petitioners feared that this tendency might " in tyme prove to ye destruction of ye place, in that it will come to be governed by ye worst and least concerned of ye Inhabitants;" and again the Assizes referred the matter to the Court of Sessions. In the same spirit was the decision of the governor and council in 1680, limiting the suffrage in Flushing in public and town matters to those who held at least sixty acres of land, the proportion to which the original settlers were entitled. [3] And at a somewhat later period the voting upon land questions in Southampton was taken not by persons, but by " fifties," keeping up the equality of votes according to the original

---

[1] *Rept. of State Historian,* 1896, 341.

[2] *N. Y. Col. Laws,* I, 83.

[3] " Whereas the former constitution of the s^d Towne, at their first settlement, in the yeare 1654, was in dividing their home Lotts, into 4 acres a piece, then addicon of six acres, & after that 50 more to each Inhabitant None for the future shall be esteemed a Freeman of s^d Towne that hath not sixty acres of land within its limits, besides meadows . . . . . & such as shall have the like proporcon of land & no other other to be esteemed Freemen for votes in publick or other town matters." *N. Y. Col. Doc.,* XIV, 751.

proportion of fifty acres apiece.[1] But the governor's power was not always extended to the large landholders, and in a disputed election case in Hempstead in 1672 the smaller free-holders were upheld in their claim to the right to vote.[2]

It was the latter policy which was to be adopted as the general principle for the colony and local elections in the next period of New York history. The increase in the value of land and the growth of population would make the fifty or sixty acres requirement a burdensome one; and the later practice required the freehold to be of a certain value rather than of a certain size.[3] In some of the Long Island towns it is interesting to note a tendency towards proxy voting, but it does not appear to have become a general policy in any town.[4]

The provisions of the Duke's laws, which we have been discussing, did not at first hold good outside of Yorkshire;[5]

[1] Even fractions of a proportion were counted. The town meeting "having under the consideration the Laying out a division of Land proceed to a voote by proxees as followeth 64¼ fifties were for a division, 79¾ fifties were for no division." *Town Records*, II, 143, April 2, 1700.

[2] This election hinged upon the votes of certain persons who were said to "have small parcells of land & have no relation to the Towne, equall wth ye Ancient Inhabitants, some Lotts being divided into severall shares." The decision of the governor states that the claimants were "Capacitated by the Law to give their Votes as ffre-holders." *N. Y. Col. Doc.*, XIV, 667.

[3] See *post.*

[4] One case has already been referred to in the early history of Gravesend, *N. Y. Col. Doc.*, XIV, 529. In Hempstead, in 1684, we have the express provision "that it is agreed upon by the major vote that for the future none of the Inhabitants of this towne bring in any Vots more then their owne except it bee through Sixness or Lameness and if Soe then they Send and order on the publique towne meeting that they gave him that brings their vote their order soe to procede for them and noe other votes to be of any Effect;" *Town Records*, I, 409, April 18, 1684.

In Southampton, in 1700, voting on the public land matters was said to be by "proxees;" but this may have meant ballots (*Town Records*, II, 143).

[5] Long Island, Staten Island, and Westchester.

but they were gradually extended to the upper Hudson [1] and Delaware settlements, although it is believed they were never fully in force in the Delaware region.[2]   In New York City there were no elective offices until, in 1683, Governor Dongan granted limited privileges by which the mayor, recorder, sheriff, coroner, and town clerk were to be appointed by the governor, and the freemen in six wards elected their own aldermen, common councilmen, constables, overseers of the poor, assessors, scavengers, questmen, and other officers.[3] The word freemen was not here defined, but it may have had the meaning of the word in the Dutch days.   Three years later, when a formal charter was granted to the city,[4] Dongan permitted the popular election of aldermen, assistants, and petty constables, but the other municipal officers were chosen by the governor or the city authorities.   The elective officers were to be "chosen by Majority of Voices of the Inhabitants of each Ward;" a most vague provision, which later called for more precise definition.[5]   Similar provisions are found in the Albany charter of the same year.[6]

During the short period of legislative activity from 1683–85, there were few changes in the provisions of the Duke's Laws respecting local suffrage.   In one case we find the word freeman [7] linked with that of freeholder; in another case the word freeholders alone is used; [8] and in still another act the popular election of militia officers was discontinued.[9]

In concluding the subject of the local suffrage during the years 1665–1691, it may be said that while with two excep-

---

[1] See *Amer. Hist. Rev.*, VI, 717–718; Munsell's *Annals of Albany*, VI, 20; VII, 97; *Hist. Coll. of Albany*, IV, 390–509 *passim; N. Y. Col. Doc.*, XIII, 428, 438, 449, 459, 471.

[2] See treatment of Suffrage in Delaware.

[3] *N. Y. Col. Doc.*, III, 338–9.

[4] April 27, 1686, *Col. Laws*, I, 181–195.

[5] See *post*.

[6] *N. Y. Col. Laws*, I, 195–216; Munsell, *Annals of Albany*, II, 62–87.

[7] *Ibid.*, 131, chap. 9 of acts of March 1, 1683.   Assessors and treasurers were to be elected by the major vote of the freeholders and freemen of each city, town, and county.

[8] Act of October 21, 1684, *Col. Laws*, I, 143.

[9] Act of October 27, 1684, *Col. Laws*, I, 161.

tions the suffrage franchise was limited to the land-holding class, yet no definite amount of land was set as a necessary qualification. The exceptions to this qualification are to be found in the case of the freeman in New York City during the period 1683–1686, and the election of militia officers by all the soldiers down to 1684. The most difficult question is that arising out of the use of the word " inhabitants;" while the most picturesque features are to be found in the struggle of the small freeholders to obtain the franchise, and in the partial proxy system for the election of representatives.

III. *The Later English Period,* 1691–1775. •

1. The Provincial Suffrage.

The basis for the suffrage franchise in the royal colonies is to be found, first, in the commissions and instructions given by the English government to the colonial governors; secondly, in the laws passed by the colonial assemblies from time to time; and finally, in the local customs and interpretations which arose under these instructions and these laws. In New York, the commission of Governor Slaughter, of November 14, 1689, marks the legal beginning of a permanent representative system. The temporary instructions sent by William and Mary to Lieutenant-Governor Nicholson in July, 1689, did indeed authorize him to call to his assistance as many as necessary of the principal freeholders and inhabitants of the province.[1] But this vague provision would not have furnished an adequate basis for an assembly even if Nicholson had remained in control. And, as events proved, it was Leisler, and not the regularly commissioned governor, who attempted to revive the representative form of government. Since Nicholson did not have opportunity to carry out the power given to him, and since Leisler's assemblies did not possess royal sanction, we must date the revival of representation from Slaughter's time.

By this commission the governor could call assemblies of the " inhabitants being freeholders," according to the usages

[1] *N. Y. Col. Doc.,* III, 606.

14

of the other American plantations.[1]   The members of the
assembly were to be " duely elected by the Major part of the
Freeholders of the respective Countyes and places;" and legislative power was vested in the governor, council, and assembly.[2]   The phraseology of this document was closely
copied in the commissions of later governors,[3] and the English government contented itself with a general restriction of
suffrage to freeholders without attempting to define the
word.

The first assembly under Slaughter took up the question
and gave the word freeholder a legal meaning.   By the act
of May 13, 1691, it was provided

"That every freeholder within this Province and freeman in any
Corporation shall have his free choice & voat in the electing, of the
Representatives without any manner of Constraint or Imposition; and
that in all elections the Majority of votes shall carry itt, and by free-
holders is to be understood every one who shall have fourty shillings
P Annum in freehold." [4]

This act, it will be seen, is identical with the requirement of
1683, except that forty shillings income from freehold is
now expressed instead of giving a mere reference to the
English qualification.   The distinction between the county
and the borough suffrage, which was to continue so long
in New York history, is also established by this act.[5]

For a few years the colony enjoyed in comparative peace

---

[1] *N. Y. Col. Laws,* I, 221; *N. Y. Col. Doc.,* III, 623.

[2] The relation of the governor to the council in legislation later led
to disputes which were appealed to England for decision.

[3] In one commission, that of Governor Hunter, dated September 15,
1709, occur the words "assemblies of the Freeholders and Planters"
(*N. Y. Col. Doc.,* V, 92–98) ; but the latter word does not again occur.

[4] *N. Y. Col. Laws,* I, 244.

[5] Under the royal government the Long Island towns, for a time at
least, kept up the proxy, or indirect methods of election which they
had adopted in 1683, as the following extract shows: "At a towne
meeting (being legally Convened) ordered that by a Majr vote that
Capt John Wheeler should on ye 11th of ye Instant go to Southampton
[to] carry our Towne proxes for the electing of Representatives for
this County of Suffolk" (*East-Hampton Town Records,* II, 281; October 5, 1692).

its newly found privilege of representation, and apparently did not feel the need of an elaborate regulation of elections. But by 1698 serious election difficulties had arisen. We cannot follow all the party struggles which led to these disorders, but both sides seemed willing to adopt unscrupulous methods. In this year it was said that the representatives elected were mainly " men of no great figure, Taylors and other mean conditions;" [1] that the sheriff of Orange County had not permitted a single freeholder to vote, and yet had returned persons as legally members of the assembly; [2] and that eleven out of the nineteen members of the assembly held positions by disputed elections.[3] The governor was forced to dissolve the assembly; but in the succeeding election there was fighting in a number of places, not without some broken heads in consequence, and contested seats in the assembly.[4]

These disorders showed the need of a more comprehensive election law, and at the session of 1699 an act [5] was passed which remained in force without substantial change until the Revolution. In its preamble the act told the conditions which called for its passage:

" Whereas of late ye Election of ye Representives to serve in Assembly in ye respective Cittys & Countyes of this province have been managed with great ourage tumult & Deceit to ye grevious oppression And Depriving of ye Subject of his Chiefest Birthright in Chuseing of his Representatives in Assembly for Remedy whereof for ye time to come and y't ye Subject may freely enjoy his undoubted right of Electing his Representatives without Disturbance or molestacon. Bee it enacted," . . . etc.

The qualification for the suffrage was changed from the fifteenth century English law to one better suited to colonial conditions; that is, the forty-shilling income was changed to

[1] *N. Y. Col. Doc.*, IV, 384.
[2] *Ibid.*, 395; 384; Ruttenber, *History of the County of Orange*, 45-46.
[3] *Ibid.*
[4] *Ibid.*, 507; Smith, *History of New York*, 97, 99 (London edition of 1757).
[5] Act of May 16, 1699, *N. Y. Col. Laws*, I, 405 ff. Repealed by act of November 27, 1702, but the repealing act was disallowed by the Queen in 1708. *Cf.* English statute, 7 and 8 Wm. III., chap 25.

a requirement that the elector possess lands or tenements to the value of forty pounds, in freehold, free of all incumbrances, and have held them at least three months before the election.   Representatives were to have the same qualifications as electors, and both elector and elected must be over twenty-one years of age.   In case a poll were necessary, the sheriff was authorized to appoint sworn clerks to set down the name of each elector, the place of his freehold, and the name of the person for whom he should vote.   Any candidate might require any elector to take oath that he was a freeholder, that he had not been previously polled at the election, and had not procured his freehold in order to gain a voice in the election.   In New York City and Albany the suffrage was open to all freemen of the corporations who had resided in the city three months before the election.

This act did not provide for election by ballot, nor did it include the elaborate provisions against fraud and error which are to be found in the laws of Pennsylvania and Delaware.   Yet from 1708 to the Revolution it remained the principal election law of the colony.   Frequent legislation was had upon the subject of local suffrage, but the colonial elections were permanently limited to persons possessing forty pounds value of freehold, or holding freemanship in either of the two cities.

The act of 1699 did not have the quieting effect upon elections which its authors had hoped to gain from it.   The party troubles continued,[1] and in 1701 the legislature passed a number of partisan measures;   all of which, however, the succeeding legislature of 1702 repealed, together with the election act of 1699.[2]   But the repealing act in turn was dis-

[1] Smith's *Hist. of N. Y.* (London ed. of 1757), 99 ff; *Journal of Legislative Council of N. Y.,* I, 168-170;   *Colonial Laws,* I, 450-523; *N. Y. Col. Doc.,* IV, 958.

[2] *N. Y. Col. Laws,* I, 523.   The preamble to the repealing act is as follows: "For as much as Several Acts and Laws have lately been past in this Colony, with plausible and Colourable Titles and pretences, some of them Incongruous, and unjust in themselves, others to obtain private and Sinister ends, under the Cloak of publick good; many pretended Acts as Laws, by persons unquallified by Right or Law to sit or act in the Legislative power, and by Several as were not the

allowed by the queen on June 26, 1708, after the Crown had refused its consent to a number of other acts of the period, 1700–1702.[1] This disallowance of the repealing act restored legality to the act of 1699, and brought back to the statute-book a number of other laws, the principal among which for our purpose was one defining the nature of free-hold requisite for voters, and excluding Catholics from the suffrage.

The act of October 18, 1701, extended the word freeholder to include any person who held land for his life or his wife's life, and declared him legally qualified to vote if the land were in sufficient quantity. Mortgages upon his freehold should not debar a man from the suffrage, if he were in possession and derived an income from the property. In this form the freeholder clause remained unchanged until the Revolution, with the exception of a minor clause in an act of 1769, which provided that the holding of lands in trust for a corporation or for pious purposes should not qualify the trustee for the exercise of the suffrage.[2]

Choice of the People, and all of them, instead of being for the profit and advantage of the Subject, as they ought to be, have been and prov'd to the Distruccon of property, the confining and Enervating of Liberty, Ruinous to Trade, to the Impoverishing of the People, a Discouragement to Industry and hurtfull to the Settlement and prosperity of the Colony." (Act of November 27, 1702.)

[1] *N. Y. Col. Doc.,* IV, 1026; V, 48.

[2] Act of May 20, 1769, *Col. Laws,* IV, 1094. The act was subsequently disapproved by king, June 6, 1770. The contested election of 1737 led to a decision by the legislature that those who held freeholds of forty pounds, three months before election, could vote; but a grantee of a mortgage in fee forfeited, in possession of mortgaged premises for several years was not qualified by virtue of the mortgage (*N. Y. Col. Doc.,* VI, 56). Governor Cornbury in 1708 proposed a novel plan of representation based upon tax assessments. The governor had found difficulty in getting the assembly to pass a duty on certain goods which the English government desired taxed. The country districts, wanting cheap goods, refused to vote for the measure, so the governor urged giving to New York City as many representatives as the rest of the province possessed; and this would not be so unequal, he said, since the last assembly had put one-half the tax assessments upon New York City (*Col. Doc.,* V, 58). It is needless

After 1701 two more questions concerning the suffrage arose. One of these was the imposition of religious restrictions by the disfranchisement of Catholics and Jews, and the other was the question of non-resident and plural voting. Among the various acts which had been passed in 1701, repealed by the subsequent assembly, and restored by the disallowance of the act of repeal, was the act of October 18, 1701, already quoted, concerning freeholds. This act had a severe clause positively forbidding any papist, popish recusant, or any person refusing to take the various test oaths, from voting for representatives or for any other officer whatever.[1] The act, however, had no punitive provision respecting this clause, and it is to be doubted if it was strictly enforced.

Somewhat the same doubt surrounds the disfranchisement of the Jews in 1737. In that year a contest arose between two assembly candidates in New York City, Philipse and Van Horne, over the result of the election, and the dispute was carried to the assembly for decision. In the argument which arose, Mr. Smith, later chief-justice, acted as counsel for Van Horne, and urged that the apparent majority of votes for Philipse was gained through the votes of some Jews and some non-resident voters. Smith delivered an impassioned speech, in which he described the death of Christ at the hands of the Jews, and urged that the curse still clung to the race and rendered them unfit for political duties. So vivid was his description that the staid legislators wept, and the populace within hearing wanted at once to attack the Jews. The impression of the speech was so strong that the

---

to say that the English government did not adopt the suggestion of Cornbury.

[1] ".... from henceforth and for ever hereafter, no Papist, no Popish Recusant, or Such person or persons as shall refuse Upon the tender and demand of the Sheriff, or either of the Candidates, to take the Oaths appointed by Law to be taken instead of the Oaths of Allegiance and Supremacy, and to Sign the Test and Association, as Directed by Law in other cases shall be Suffered to give his or their Vote or Votes for any Representative or Representatives to Serve in this or any future Generall Assembly within this Province, or for any other Officer or Officers whatsoever." (*Col. Laws*, I, 452-4.)

assembly passed a resolve altogether disfranchising Jews and refusing to count their votes in the contested election.[1] Both the act of 1701 and the resolve of 1737 were unrepealed at the time of the Revolution, but the enforcement of either must have been left to the local officers, and it is perhaps impossible to determine to what extent Jews and Catholics were actually disfranchised.

The other phase of the suffrage, that of non-resident and plural voting, remains to be mentioned. As early as 1700 it was thought proper to permit a freeholder to vote in several counties if he held land in each; and to facilitate this plural voting, it seems to have been customary to hold the elections on different days in different counties.[2] In 1737, too, this right of non-residents was expressly affirmed by the legislature when objection was made to the counting of their votes in the disputed election case already mentioned. The decision of the legislature favoring non-resident voting, while in accord with the English practice, did not win popular favor, when the opinion was held " that a personal residence was as requisite in the elector, as communion of interests by a competent freehold." [3] This popular opinion may have been strengthened by the participation of absentee freeholders in the provincial elections, while they were excluded from the local town meetings and elections, where only inhabiting freeholders could vote.[4] The limitation to inhabitants in the one case would tend to create a popular sentiment in favor of the same test for all elections.

[1] *The Continuation of Smith's Hist. of N. Y.* (*Coll. of N. Y. Hist. Soc.*, 1826), 36–41; Dunlap's *Hist. of N. Y.* (N. Y., 1839), I, 318–319.

[2] In a petition against the actions of Lord Bellomont, March 11, 1700, it is said,—

"That soon after his Lordᴾ issued out writts for chusing a new assembly, and the Election was appointed to be upon the same day in all places except the two most remote counties whereby the best freeholders who had estates in several counties, were deprived of giving their votes at several elections," *N. Y. Col. Doc.*, IV, 621. See also Ruttenber, *History of Orange County*, 44–47; Bishop, *History of Elections in American Colonies*, 69.

[3] *Continuation of Smith's Hist.*, 37.

[4] See *post*, p. 219.

The non-resident voting was, however, continued, and tax-lists are extant for the city and county of New York for 1768 and 1769 in which the non-resident voters are particularly designated.[1]   In the latter year the subject came up for discussion in the assembly and council during the consideration of a new election law.   Mr. William Smith, Jr., in the council, in opposing certain parts of the proposed bill, said that so far as it casts doubts upon the suffrage of non-residents that it interfered with a right which " is essential to Liberty, clearly established by sound Exposition, and invariably followed."[2]   The bill passed, but was subsequently disallowed by the king, probably because it required the representative to reside in the district which he represented.[3]   An act of 1775 shows that the claim to vote more than once sometimes led to inconsistencies.   The freeholders of the town of Schenectady and the manors of Rensselerwyck and Livingston had claimed the right not only of electing the representative from those places, but also of

[1] See " A Copy of the Poll List of the Election for Representatives for the City and County of New-York; which Election began On Monday the 7th Day of March, and ended on Friday the 11th of the same Month, in the Year of our Lord MDCCLXVIII. Alphabetically Made." And similar list for election of Jan. 23–27, 1769. The non-resident voters are marked by the letters N R. In 1769 there were only six non-residents out of 1575 electors; in 1768 there were twenty-seven.

[2] *Journal of Legislative Council,* II, 1706, May 19, 1769. The bill also required representatives to reside in the district which they represented.   To this Mr. Smith said " incapacitating non-residents from representing their Electors is an alteration of the Election Act of 1699 (the first section of which is nearly similar to the Statute of the 8th of H. VI. cap. 7) is repugnant to the constant usage of Parliament, and the general practice of the assembly, for near seventy years past, abridges the Right of Electors in all the Counties, and may be very prejudicial to the City and County of New York in particular, where it is for many reasons most probable the greater number of non-resident Members would reside; and it is the more unreasonable with respect to the city since this Capital sends only four out of twenty-seven Members, tho' it bears one third part of the Burden in all Publick Levies."

[3] Act of May 20, 1769; disallowed, June 6, 1770.

having a part in the election of a representative for the city and county of Albany. The act significantly forbidding the exercise of such a plural suffrage "*in the right of such free-hold only,*" leads to the intimation that those who held free-holds in both parts might vote in each place.[1]

These illustrations are sufficient to show that throughout the colonial period the freeholder might, if he chose, vote in all the counties in which he possessed land;[2] while to make this possible the elections were sometimes held upon different days in different counties, or the polls were kept open for nearly a week, during which a freeholder might visit several counties and cast his vote in each.

Some few facts concerning the number of electors have been found. In 1735, in a disputed election for representative from New York City, when a poll had been demanded, and the inhabitants had been brought to the polls in coaches and accompanied with drums and musicians, it was found, at ten o'clock at night, that one candidate had received 413 and the other 399 votes; and this in an election when "the zeal of the friends of the candidates was so great that it was supposed every voter in the city was brought out."[3] If this supposition were true, there were over eight hundred voters in a population of about 10,000,[4] or eight per cent. of the population. A tax-list for 1761 shows 1447 voters in the city and county of New York;[5] and one for 1769 contains the names of 1515 electors.[6] In the latter case it is interesting to note that out of the 1515 electors 407 voted in the

---

[1] Act of April 3, 1775, Ch. 69; *Laws of New York, 1774–5,* 206–7.

[2] Early in the commonwealth period the suffrage was limited to inhabiting freeholders. The act of March 27, 1778 (chap. 16) provided that no one could vote in state elections unless he resided in the district in which he offered to vote. *Laws of the State of New York,* I, 28 (Albany, 1886).

[3] Valentine's *Manual of the Corporation,* 1869, p. 851.

[4] *Ibid.,* 1851, 352, gives the population of the city for 1737 as 10,664.

[5] "A Copy of the Poll List of the Election for Representatives for the city and County of New-York; which Election began on Tuesday the 17th Day of February, and ended on Thursday the 19th of the same Month, in the year of our Lord MDCCLXI. Alphabetically Made."

[6] Similar list for election of January 23 to January 27, 1769.

right of both freemanship and freehold, 506 were freeholders
only, and 602 were freemen only.   It would thus appear that
in New York City two-fifths of the electors of representatives
did not possess land, but voted in the right of their freemanship.

According to Valentine's Manual,[1] the population in the
year nearest to 1761 given therein (1756) was 13,040, and
in the nearest year to 1769 (1771) it was 21,863.   These
figures would make the voting class in the city at from
one-ninth to one-fourteenth of the total population; and,
taking into consideration the variation of dates, the electors
may have comprised about eight per cent. of the population,
while two-fifths of these electors did not possess real estate,
but voted in virtue of their freemanship alone.

The provincial suffrage during this period was first based
upon the English custom, but in a short time the qualification
was changed to a freehold of the value of forty pounds, or
the holding of freemanship in either of the two municipal
corporations.   Catholics were by statute early excluded from
the suffrage, and later Jews were disfranchised by resolution
of the assembly.   Non-residents could vote wherever the
freehold lay, and might thus cast several votes in different
counties.   Voting throughout all the period was according
to the English *viva-voce* plan.

2. The Local Suffrage.

The local franchise of the province of New York may be
divided into five classes: (1) County elections; (2) city
elections; (3) town elections and town meetings; (4) parish
elections; (5) the meetings of persons interested in the common lands of the town.[2]   A few words may be said about
each of these forms of suffrage.

1. *County Elections.*   The earlier county officers were appointed by the governor or by act of legislature,[3] but by an

---

[1] 1851, 353.

[2] There were no militia elections in New York during this period.

[3] Act of June 19, 1703, *Col. Laws,* I, 532–8; Act of October 13, 1713,
Col. Laws, I, 795–800.

act of October 6, 1708,[1] entitled an " Act to Relieve this colony from Divers Irregularitys and Extortions," the coroners were to be elected by the freeholders of the counties. In the elaborate act of 1703 which established the representative county officers,[2] all elections for the supervisors, assessors, and collectors were to be made by the freeholders and inhabitants of the respective towns; and while subsequent acts provided for the election of these officers in districts or precincts as well as in towns, yet the phrase " freeholders and inhabitants" is almost invariably used.[3] The use of a somewhat similar phrase has already been noted in the Duke's Laws, and it is believed that the class here described was *inhabiting freeholders,* as under the earlier code. The proof that the word inhabitant was meant as an additional qualification for the freeholder rather than as an additional class of voters is gained from the laws themselves and from the custom of the towns. In several instances the phrase " freeholders inhabiting within the said county" or district is used, thus giving clear evidence of the intention of the framers of the laws;[4] while an inspection of the town books of Hempstead shows that none but freeholders were permitted to vote in that town.[5]

[1] *Col. Laws,* I, 622.

[2] Act of June 19, 1703, chap. 133, *Col. Laws,* I, 539–542; the act of May 13, 1691 (*Col. Laws,* I, 237), was so vaguely worded that it led to many disputes.

[3] For the early laws on this subject see acts of November 12, 1709 (Ch. 212); November 25, 1710 (Ch. 225); December 10, 1712 (Ch. 257); October 23, 1713 (Ch. 270); October 23, 1713 (Ch. 271); July 21, 1715 (Ch. 297); July 3, 1718 (Ch. 354); June 24, 1719 (Ch. 397); June 24, 1719 (Ch. 380); etc.

[4] Acts of June 19, 1703 (Ch. 133); July 21, 1715 (Ch. 297 and Ch. 300); May 27, 1717 (Ch. 332). See also Bishop, *History of Elections in American Colonies,* 222–3.

[5] The legal phrase " freeholders and inhabitants" is often used by the town clerks; sometimes the term is simply " inhabitants;" but in Hempstead the words are so used that we can gather from them the idea that only freeholders could vote. Thus the records from 1685 to 1704 speak of matters being concluded by " mager" vote of the town; after 1704 the words " freeholders and inhabitants" are infrequently used, but the general term is merely " freeholders;" while after about 1750 the legal

The difficulty in picturing the voting class arises from the fact that the word inhabitant was never defined in the laws, and that the phrase was generally adopted by all officers and town clerks, so that it is almost impossible to find anything else than the single legal phrase. The same clause was used throughout the colonial period,[1] and even appears frequently in the returns for the election of deputies to the provincial convention of April, 1775,[2] although here, as in the town records of the colonial period, the word inhabitant is sometimes used. In elections for county officers, with the possible exception of those for coroner,[3] the franchise was restricted to inhabiting freeholders. No limitation of the necessary freehold, either as to size or value, having been found, it may be taken that any freeholder, of large or small estate, could vote in the county elections if he were an inhabitant of the county.

2. *City Elections.* In these elections the principal peculiarity lay in the freemanship. The old burgherecht of the Dutch New Amsterdam had continued under the English rule, and was well expressed in an ordinance of the mayor and aldermen in 1675–6:

"Ordered that noe person or Merchant whatsoever shall sell, or cause to bee sold, or put to sale any Goods, wares and Merchandizes by Retale upon paine to forfeit all such goods, wares and merchandizes unless

---

phrase is used almost exclusively. These variations were without doubt due to the idiosyncrasies of the clerks, but they show us that it made no difference whether the attendants at the town meetings and elections were called inhabitants or freeholders, or freeholders and inhabitants; and since this is true we are logically forced to the conclusion that the narrower term must be accepted. *Records of Hempstead,* II–IV *passim.*

[1] Acts of March 24, 1772, *Col. Laws,* V, 395, 403; act of February 8, 1774 (Ch. VIII); *Laws of 1774-5,* p. 12; act of March 19, 1774 (Ch. XLII), *Laws of 1774-5,* p. 70; April 3, 1775 (Ch. LXXVI), *Laws of 1774-5,* p. 212.

[2] *Journal of Provincial Convention,* April 20, 1775, I, 2–9. Elections were said to be by " freeholders and inhabitants," by " freemen, freeholders and inhabitants" (N. Y. City) ; " by inhabitants," and by " freeholders."

[3] The act of October 6, 1708, named only freeholders as electors of coroners.

such person or persons are Free-men or made Free or Burghers of this Citty, and settled housekeepers for the space of one year or given security for the same Unless by Special License from the Mayor and Aldermen with the approbacon of the Governor. And if any Person or Persons soe made free shall depart from this Citty by the space of six months Unless such Person or persons so departing shall during that time keepe fire and Candle Light and pay Scott and Lott shall Loose his and their freedome; and that all and every Merchant hereafter to be made free shall pay for the same, Six Bevers; And all Handecraft trades [men] and others to pay two Bevers for their being made freemen; (Unless by Speciall order of Court)." [1]

By the provisional charter granted in 1683 the beaver skins were commuted into pounds and shillings, every merchant or shopkeeper paying three pounds twelve shillings for his freedom, and every craftsman one pound four shillings.[2] Dongan's charter gave to the mayor, recorder, and aldermen the power to admit freemen, but to make no greater charge than five pounds [3] for the freemanship. Four days after the date of the charter the city authorities raised the fee to the limit permitted in the charter,[4] but in 1691 it was changed back to the sums required in 1683.[5] In 1694-5 [6] it was further provided that every apprentice should be registered with the city authorities, and upon completing a term of service of not less than four years should be made free of the city by his master, " if he have well and truely served him." Montgomery's charter of 1730 [7] made no change in the freeman qualifications; and the fees of 1683, with the extension to apprentices in 1695, continued the method of gaining the freemanship until the Revolution put a stop to the municipal activities. Some laws were passed during this period respecting the suffrage in the city. An act of 1702, called forth by the " great Strifes Debates & Suites" which had previously happened, required voting freeholders not only to hold land in the city, but also to reside therein, and

---

[1] *N. Y. Hist. Soc. Coll.,* 1885, 40–41.

[2] *Ibid.,* 45, 47.

[3] *Ibid.,* 48; *N. Y. Col. Laws,* 181–195.

[4] *Ibid.,* 48.

[5] *Ibid.,* 50.

[6] *Ibid.,* 52; January 16, 1694-5.

[7] *N. Y. Col. Laws,* II, 575–639.

gave freemen the right to vote only in the ward in which they resided, provided they had taken their residence in the ward three months before the election.[1]　By the Montgomery charter electors were spoken of as " ffreeholders or ffreemen Inhabitants of the said city," which was the requirement of the act of 1702; while vestrymen were subsequently elected by the " wards." [2]　An act of 1771 [3] identified the word freeholder as used in the charter with its use for the provincial suffrage, *i.e.*, forty pounds value of freehold; and required freemen to have held their freedom for three months and have resided in the ward one month.　This act also required electors to declare whether they voted as freeholders or freemen, a rule which had already been in use.[4]

The Albany charter of 1686, which remained the constitution of the city until the Revolution, prescribed that elective officers should be chosen " by the majority of voices of the inhabitants of each ward."　The mayor, recorder, and aldermen could admit freemen, but none could be admitted except natural born or naturalized subjects of the King of England; and they could not be compelled to pay more than three pounds twelve shillings for merchant right or thirty-six shillings for craftsman rights in the city.[5]　These sums were evidently retained in practice for strangers coming to the city, but for persons born in Albany the fee, in 1763, was reduced to two shillings,[6] and later was made still lower.'　The names of those admitted, except in a few instances, are not given in the records,[8] but occasional mention is made of fees accruing from the admission of freemen.[9]

[1] *N. Y. Col. Laws*, I, 490: disallowed by the queen, December 31, 1702.

[2] Acts of November 29, 1745, *Col. Laws*, III, 506; and of January 27, 1770, *Col. Laws*, V, 85.

[3] *Col. Laws*, V, 228; continued by act of March 9, 1774.

[4] See poll lists of 1768-69.

[5] *N. Y. Col. Laws*, I, 209, 210; Munsell's *Annals of Albany*, II, 79-80.

[6] Munsell, *Hist. Coll. of Albany* I, 144.

[7] *Ibid.*, 172, 199.　In 1769 it was reduced to one shilling six pence.

[8] Albany City Records are published in Vols. II-X of Munsell's *Annals of Albany*, and Vol. I of the *Hist. Coll. of Albany*.

[9] *Hist. Coll. of Albany*, I, *passim*.

The city elections are usually said to be by the " inhabitants,"[1] but it is believed that this meant inhabiting freeholders and freemen, and in one case the electors are distinctly so described.[2] A contested case in 1773 led to the adoption of rules regulating the suffrage, prescribing (1) that no alien could vote, no matter what his term of residence; (2) British subjects having resided six weeks in the city had the right to vote in the wards they inhabited; (3) no bond servant could vote during the time of his service; (4) the votes of persons who had been bribed were null and void.[3]

3. *Town Elections.* The earliest act upon this subject is that of May 6, 1691,[4] which authorized the holding of town meetings and gave to the freeholders at these meetings the right to make prudential by-laws and to elect certain local officers. Other early acts also used the word freeholders alone[5] in defining the suffrage. In an act of 1702,[6] later disallowed by the queen, the voters of Kingston (" Kings Town") are spoken of as " freeholders and freemen" of the town, but no other application of the word freemen to town voters has been noticed. After 1703 the term " freeholder and inhabitant" is generally used in the laws and town records, and is believed to have the meaning ascribed to it for county elections.[7]

[1] Munsell, *Annals of Albany*, VI, 266.   [2] *Ibid.*, 285.

[3] Munsell, *Hist. Coll. of Albany*, I, 254.

[4] " An Act for the Enableing each Respective Towne within this Province to Regulate their Fences and Highwayes and make Prudentiall Orders for their Peace and Orderly Improvements," *Col. Laws*, I, 225.

[5] Act of May 13, 1691, *Col. Laws*, I, 237; May 16, 1699, *Col. Laws*, I, 427. The act of October 18, 1701, makes no mention of an electoral class, merely providing for elections by the " towns."

[6] Act of May 1, 1702, *Col. Laws*, I, 488.

[7] See *Col. Laws*, I, 539, 1033; II, 130; III, 54, 320, 415, 947, 959, 1017; IV, 944, 977; V, 405. It is interesting to notice that when the legislators desired to express the class which we to-day would call inhabitants, they used other phrases in addition to the "freeholder and inhabitant" clause. Thus taxes were to be levied upon " all & every ye ffreeholders, Inhabitants Residenters and Sojourners of and in this Province" (Act of May 16, 1699, *Col. Laws*, I, 396–401). Other tax laws varied the wording somewhat, but almost invariably added another class to the free-

4. *Parish Elections.* Under the Duke's Laws, ministers had been elected by the towns, but by the act of September 22, 1693,[1] ten " vistry" men and two church wardens were to be elected in each parish in the counties of Richmond, Westchester, and Queens and in the city of New York by the freeholders of the city or county, and the minister was to be selected by the vestrymen. There are but few later acts concerning these elections, one of which used the phrase freeholders and inhabitants,[2] another " freeholders" alone,[3] and still another only " inhabitants." [4] It is most likely that these terms all refer to the class of local voters already mentioned. In New York City a later act provided for the election of vestrymen by " each ward," [5] but afterwards the word freeholder alone is used,[6] and again the qualifications of voters for other city elections are established for the city parish elections.[7] The apparent intention was to place the parish elections upon the same suffrage basis as the political elections of the towns and cities.

5. *Suffrage concerning Land Matters.* Still another division of the population for voting purposes existed. This arose out of the interest of certain persons in the unoccupied and common lands of the towns, which, having been granted to certain proprietors at the founding of the towns, continued as a distinct right of their descendants and successors. The laws [8] gave to those thus concerned the right to make rules relating to the common lands and in certain cases to divide the lands among themselves. The phrases used in the laws describing this class of persons are " proprietors."

---

holders and inhabitants. See Chaps. 8, 15, 20, 22, 29, 39, 43, 50, 51, 53, 56, 63, 71, 82, etc., of colonial laws.

[1] *Col. Laws,* I, 328.

[2] *Laws,* III, 429, referring only to Richmond County.

[3] *Col. Laws,* I, 440–1.   [4] *Laws,* V, 297.

[5] Act of November 29, 1745, *Col. Laws,* III, 506.

[6] Act of January 27, 1770, *Col. Laws,* V, 86.

[7] Act of February 16, 1771, *Col. Laws,* V, 228; revived and continued until 1780 by act of March 9, 1774, *Laws of N. Y. 1774–5,* 45.

[8] Acts of October 30, 1708, *Laws,* I, 633; of July 21, 1715, *Laws,* I, 882; of October 16, 1718, *Laws,* I, 1006; of February 19, 1756, *Laws,* IV, 41–3: and of January 27, 1770, *Laws,* V, 115.

" owners," " joint tenants," " tenants in common," etc., all
of which sufficiently mark off the owners of such lands from
those holding no share therein.

The body of tenants in common differed from the " freeholders and inhabitants" of the ordinary town meeting by
excluding some voters and including others not ordinarily
permitted to vote in the town meeting. Thus there can be
no doubt that there were freeholders in the towns who did
not enjoy the rights in the commons,[1] and, on the other
hand, non-resident freeholders may have been allowed to
vote on matters which so directly concerned their own property interests.[2] The matters were to be determined by the
owners resident in the colony, however,[3] thus ignoring any
proprietors, if there were such, resident in Europe. An
inspection of the records of Hempstead shows that frequent
meetings of the " freeholders and tennants in common of
the plain Land in the town abovesaid" were held, and by-
laws and regulations concerning the care and division of the
town land were adopted.[4] In such elections the proportions
of the early allotment of land were sometimes maintained,
as in Southampton, where the voting is said to be by
" fifties," and even portions of a " fifty" might be voted.[5]
A later act may have limited the voting in such elections to
those who held full shares according to the early division.[6]

While an effort has been made here to enumerate the
various forms of local suffrage, it will be noticed that the
elections mentioned were almost all made up of freeholders

---

[1] *N. Y. Col. Doc.*, XIV, 751. In the Southampton Records occurs the
phrase " those interested in the town lands," which may imply that there
were some not so interested, *Records*, II, 252.

[2] It must be admitted that no proof has been found for the latter statement except the negative evidence coming from the general omission of
the word "inhabitants" in connection with such meetings. See the
various references to the laws and to town action.

[3] Act of October 30, 1708, gave power to joint tenants *here residing*
by major vote to divide their lands.

[4] *Records of Hempstead*, IV, 86, 216, 219, 248, 351, 375, 446–448, etc.

[5] *Southampton Town Records*, II, 143. April 2, 1700. The term evidently referred to fifty acres.

[6] Act of October 16, 1718, *Col. Laws*, I, 1006.

and inhabitants, or, as we have interpreted the phrase, of inhabiting freeholders.   The variations from this rule are to be found in the city elections of New York City and Albany, and in the elections and meetings concerning common land. It is believed that the double qualification of freeholdership and inhabitancy was required in county, town, and parish elections from 1703 until the revolutionary period.

CHAPTER VIII.

The Suffrage in New Jersey.

New Jersey's history as a political organization begins with Stuyvesant's grant of a charter to the settlement of Bergen, on September 5, 1661.[1] Before that date, although some forty years and more had passed since the first settlement, there was no incorporation of the inhabitants either along the Hudson or on the Delaware. Indeed, the population was so small in numbers and so scattered geographically that it would be the height of archæological nicety to attribute any political activity to the settlers: Only one hundred and thirty-nine persons took the oath of allegiance to the new proprietors in 1665, after the coming of Governor Carteret to the colony,[2] and under the Dutch the number of heads of families must have been still smaller. And when the Dutch governor granted his charter in 1661, he gave to the residents of the Bergen territory a government similar to that which he had imposed upon other parts of the Dutch dominion; it consisted simply of a local court, composed of four officers, and possessing certain limited judicial, legislative, and administrative powers. In the selection of this court the people appear to have had no choice, for the yearly appointments were made by the New Amsterdam authorities from a double number of candidates proposed by the existing officers.[3] As this continued to be the method of government until the occupation of the country by the English, it is scarcely of moment to apply the word *suffrage* to conditions which were fixed first by a local close corporation, and in the last resort by the general officers at New Amsterdam. It is not until the coming of the English that any element of popular government appears.

By a hostile act against a friendly nation, Charles II. of

[1] *Laws and Ordinances of New Netherlands*, 403.
[2] *New Jersey Colonial Archives*, I, 48–51.
[3] *New York Colonial Documents*, XIII, 231.

England on March 12, 1663–64, made his well-known grant
to his brother, James, Duke of York, including within the
lands so bestowed not only Maine and Long Island, but also
that from the west side of the Connecticut River to the east
side of the Delaware,[1] and giving James full and absolute
power to govern the inhabitants of the ceded territory.
Before he had acquired possession the Duke had parted with
a large share of his grant to two noblemen, Lord Berkeley
and Sir George Carteret; and on June 24 granted them the
land between the Hudson and Delaware rivers "in as full
and ample manner as the same is granted unto the said Duke
of York."[2]　　And although Colonel Nicholls, the Duke's
governor at New York, strongly opposed the grant,[3] it remained valid, and soon was acted upon by the new proprietors.

In the winter of 1664–5 Berkeley and Carteret proceeded
to advertise their colony, and announced certain "Concessions and Agreements of the Lords Proprietors of the Province of New Cæsarea, or New Jersey, to and with all &
every the Adventurers and all such as shall settle or plant
there."[4]　Considering the close relations of the proprietors to
the king and the Duke of York, these concessions are remarkably favorable to the intending settlers.　The liberty of
conscience was guaranteed, the political privilege of a general legislative assembly and of chartered towns and cities
was promised, and the great inducement of cheap, almost
free, land was held forth.

Before mentioning the suffrage conditions as laid down
in the concessions, it will be proper to call attention to the
manner of obtaining land and the conditions imposed upon
the settlers therein.　During the whole colonial period freeholding was the most marked qualification for the suffrage
in New Jersey; and the question, therefore, naturally arises,
upon what conditions could land be obtained?　The pro-

[1] Leaming and Spicer, *Grants, Concessions, and Original Constitutions
of the Province of New Jersey,* 3; Poore, *Charters and Constitutions.*
I, 783.

[2] *Ibid.,* 8; Smith, *History of New Jersey,* 60–61.

[3] *New Jersey Col. Archives,* I, 46–48.

[4] Leaming and Spicer, 12–26.

prietary concessions gave to every free man going out before
January 1, 1665, one hundred and fifty acres for himself
and the same amount for every able-bodied servant, well
armed and provisioned, which he should bring with him; and
seventy-five acres for every weaker servant, male or female,
over fourteen years of age. And upon attaining his freedom
each Christian servant was to receive seventy-five acres. The
only conditions required of the settler were that he should
be fully armed, provisioned for six months, and that after
March 25, 1670, he should pay annually a quit-rent of one-
half penny for each acre which he had received. Settlers
who should come to the colony after 1666 would receive
smaller amounts of land, diminishing year by year, until by
1668 the amount for an able-bodied settler was to be only
sixty acres.

It will thus be seen that the settler needed little more
capital than sufficient to purchase his own equipment and
arms; the proprietors demanded no money payment for
lands, but at the end of five years—1670—the quit-rents
should become due. It was further provided that all subjects
of the King of England should be at liberty to plant and
become freemen of the province. Thus land was the cheapest
commodity in the country; and a community whose members
possessed thousands of acres of land might still be compelled
to take up a voluntary contribution of *nails* in order to roof
over the meeting-house.[1] Land was thus open to any free
English subject who could get out to the new country; and
its value must be expressed, not in terms of purchase money
paid to the proprietors, for there was none such, but in
terms of the cost of transportation of men, implements, and
cattle thither. Indeed, land in America sometimes had a
negative value, and it was necessary to pay persons to go
out to it; the owners hoping to be reimbursed by the growth
of the country and advancement of trade.[2] Once in America,
if the settler possessed a good character and was not politically or religiously obnoxious, it was an easy matter to get
land. Since agriculture was almost the sole occupation, he

[1] In Newark, April 17, 1669; *Town Records,* 18.
[2] See the inducements offered by the Dutch West India Company to
settlers; *N. Y. Col. Doc.,* I, 371. (March 4, 1650.)

who did not possess land was usually a vagrant and socially dangerous.   Hence, to the seventeenth and eighteenth century settler and statesman the possession of land meant little more than that the individual had a permanent and definite employment.

With this understanding of the ease of acquiring land and the universality of land-holding, we are ready to look at the first definite suffrage qualifications laid down in New Jersey. The concessions provided for an annual session of an elective assembly chosen by the freeholders of the province:

"The inhabitants being freemen, or chief agents to others of the Province aforesaid; do as soon as this our commission shall arrive, by virtue of a writ in our names by the Governor to be for the present (until our seal comes) sealed and signed, make choice of twelve deputies or representatives from amongst themselves; who being chosen are to join with the said Governor and Council for the making of such laws, ordinances and constitution as shall be necessary for the present government and welfare of the said Province.   But so soon as parishes, divisions, tribes and other distinctions are made, that then the inhabitants or freeholders of the several respective parishes, tribes, divisions and distinctions aforesaid, do by our writts, under our seals (which we ingage, shall be in due time issued) annually meet on the first day of January, and choose freeholders for each respective division, tribe or parish to be the deputies or representatives of the same: which body of representatives or the major part of them, shall, with the Governor & Council aforesaid, be the General Assembly of the said Province, the Governor or his deputy being present. . . ."

This regulation, made before the first body of emigrants to the new province had set out, provided for two kinds of assemblies: a preliminary representative body, chosen by the whole community of planters and settlers and their agents; and a permanent representative organization, elected by the freeholders and based upon geographical districts. The latter assembly, thus composed of governor, council, and house of deputies, was given large powers.   It could appoint its own meetings and adjournment, constitute courts, erect manors, hundreds, boroughs, towns and cities; it could levy taxes, organize and train the militia, and naturalize foreigners; it should determine the method of land allotment, and make provision for the support of government. The laws of the assembly must be consonant to reason and conform as nearly as convenient to the laws of England; and they must not be opposed to the interest of the Lords Proprietors nor repugnant to the Concessions; and lastly, the laws should remain in force only one year unless confirmed by the proprietors.

The Concessions had stated that the electors of the deputies in this assembly should be freeholders, but no definition or qualification of the word freeholder was given. Yet freeholder is a relative rather than a definite term, and particularly was the meaning of the word undetermined in 1665. It implied, however, certain legal proof of the right of possession, and often required the performance of express duties to the lord. In New Jersey these two qualifications of a freehold were translated into the terms " proprietary title" and " proprietary quit-rents;" and for over a hundred years they furnish the unchanging background for the history of the province. We must now notice how the question originated.

Before the news reached America that the Duke of York had ceded part of his territory to Berkeley and Carteret, Colonel Nicholls, whose orders had been to subdue and govern all the land described in the King's patent to the Duke, had made land grants in what is now New Jersey. The first of these grants was made by Nicholls to several Long Island inhabitants who wished to settle on the site of the later town of Elizabeth; and this grant was followed in the spring of 1665 by a patent for lands along the coast southward and westward of Staten Island, called the " Monmouth Patent." [1] When Governor Carteret arrived, in the summer of 1665, to take charge of the province for the proprietors, he

---

[1] For the Elizabeth-town settlement and claims see W. A. Whitehead, *A Review of some of the Circumstances Connected with the Settlement of Elizabeth, N. J.*, read before the N. J. Historical Society, May 20, 1869; also Whitehead, *East Jersey under the Proprietary Governments*, 42–45; Smith, *History of New Jersey*, 61–68.

For the Monmouth patent see Leaming and Spicer, 661–663; *N. J. Archives*, I, 43–46; Whitehead, *East Jersey*, 45–47, 61; Smith, *New Jersey*, 62.

found that settlements had been made under these patents; but for the time being the previous settlers appear to have recognized his authority, and no question of jurisdiction arose for several years.

The first three years of the provincial government were consumed by the governor and council in allotting land, surveying tracts, and organizing local governments; and not until April, 1668, did the governor issue a proclamation for the freeholders to elect their delegates to an assembly.[1] The elections were held accordingly, and ten deputies were selected from six towns;[2] and in May and November the governor, council, and deputies held sessions of the " Assembly" at Elizabeth-Town, at which a number of acts were passed. But no sooner was the representative system inaugurated than the question of the suffrage arose.

The governor in his writ had directed that all freeholders should take part in the elections, but now the disputed land-titles led to troubles at the elections. Many of the settlers on the Monmouth and Elizabeth-Town patents had refused to repatent their lands under the proprietors, and declined to take the oaths to the proprietors; and thus in a short time after Carteret had issued his writ for the first election the necessity arose for a definition of a freehold. The governor and council met the conditions boldly by refusing altogether the suffrage to those who would not take the oath of allegiance:

" Prohibition for those at Navesinks to bare any office or have any Vote in Election till they have taken the Oath.

" . . . No person or persons are to be admitted as a Freed man or Freholders of this Province of New Jersey . . . untill they have taken or subscribed to the Oath of Aleagance to our Soveraign Lord the King and his Successors and to be true and faithfull to the Interest of the Lords Proprietors. . . ."[3]

But it was difficult to enforce such a rule when voting was done in the towns without any control by the governor and

[1] *N. J. Archives*, I, 56; Whitehead, *East Jersey*, 59.
[2] Whitehead, *East Jersey*, 59, note 3.
[3] *N. J. Archives*, I, 58.

council. Naturally, the next step was to threaten the towns which permitted illegal voting. The inhabitants of Woodbridge had been granted a charter,[1] with the right to elect local magistrates and deputies to the assembly; but they had admitted some illegal voters to their town meetings, and now Governor Carteret threatens them with the forfeiture of their charter. This proclamation goes a step farther than the one to Navesinks, where the requirement was only the taking of the oaths, by demanding also the formal patenting of lands as a qualification for voting:

" Whereas I have Reseved information that ther are severall persons which you have Admitted to have ther voices in ye towne meetings, that have not any Land Surveyed and pattented according to theire Articles and the tenner of the Charter granted to your Corporation, But on the Contrary in Contempt doe Wilfully neglect the same, Against the Lords Proprietors Authority, and to the prejudice and hindrance of all other honest minded men, as also the indangering of the breach of your Charter by ye suffering of such malignant Spirits to live amongst you, or to have anything to doe in your publick afairs, for the preventing whereof I have thought good by the advise of my Counsell to signify this unto you; That all such persons that are not conformeable to the Tenner of your Charter, and that have not pattented their land accordingly are not from this day forward to [be] Accompted as freholders, and by Conciquence are not to have any ofice whatsoever; nor to have any vote or voice in your towne metings upon any publick busines whatsoever; nor yett to enjoy any lands within the bounds of your Corporation; but [it] shal and may be lawful for you to dispose of those lands intended for them for the other persons that will be obedient or submit themselves to the laws and government of the province. . . ."[2]

This was in October, 1670, and in the mean time the proprietary quit-rents had become due, March 25, 1670, and many of the inhabitants of the tracts granted by Nicholls refused to make the payments to the New Jersey proprietors. The Newark settlers had provided for the prompt payment of their rents,[3] but the Elizabeth-Town and Monmouth patent inhabitants refused to pay, claiming their prior grants.

[1] See charter in *N. J. Historical Society Collections*, I, 184.
[2] *N. J. Archives*, I, 63.
[3] *Newark Town Records, N. J. Hist. Soc. Coll.*, VI. 30.

Several irregular meetings of deputies were held during this period,[1] presumably to take general action against the proprietors. In May, 1672, representatives of five towns met at Elizabeth-Town, and, taking advantage of the absence of Governor Carteret in New York, they elected James Carteret, a son of the proprietor, Sir George Carteret, as " President of the Country."[2] Upon this the governor was compelled to return to England, where his actions were sustained by the proprietors, even against Carteret's own son.

Governor Carteret returned to the province with documents confirming his own authority, the rights of the proprietors, and vesting political power within the province in those only who held proprietary titles to their lands. The king sent over a letter directed to the governor and council of the province commanding all persons to yield allegiance to Berkeley and Carteret.[3] The proprietors forwarded " a declaration of the true intent and meaning of the Concessions," in which the old Nicholls patentees were expressly excluded from the suffrage:

" . . . no person or persons whatsoever shall be counted a freeholder of the said Province, nor have any vote in electing, nor be capable of being elected for any office of trust, either civil or military, until he doth actually hold his or their lands by patent from us, the Lords proprietors."[4]

These documents were published by the governor upon his arrival, and warnings sent to the towns to have their lands surveyed and registered.[5] But the process of reducing all the inhabitants to the rule of the proprietors was unexpectedly interrupted by the reconquest of all the region from the Delaware to the Hudson by the Dutch in the summer of 1673.

After the Dutch fleet had taken New York City, the New Jersey towns near New York sent commissioners to the

[1] Whitehead, *East Jersey,* 60, note 3; 66–69.
[2] *Ibid.,* 67.
[3] Leaming and Spicer, 38.
[4] *Ibid.,* 32–34; Whitehead, *East Jersey,* 71.
[5] *N. J. Archives,* I, 119.

Dutch officers at New Orange (New York), yielding their allegiance to the Dutch,[1] and receiving in return the same privileges as those granted to the Dutch towns.[2]   In the towns, where the charters of Governor Carteret had granted the local suffrage to all freeholders, the Dutch established the system of double nomination which had been such a distinctive feature of their earlier government in the New Netherland region.[3]   The Dutch retained control of their old territory only a few months, and in February, 1674, the New York, New Jersey, and Delaware lands were all restored to the English by treaty, occupation being taken by Edmund Andros for the English in October, 1674.

After the retrocession of the lands to the English, King Charles made a second grant to his brother James,[4] and James in turn made a second grant of New Jersey.[5]   But this new grant was made only to Carteret and did not include all the province, for as early as March, 1673, Berkeley had disposed of his undivided half of New Jersey to John Fenwick in trust for Edward Byllinge.[6]   The Duke of York thus recognized the division of the province, and in his grant to Carteret gave him the better part of the territory: that north of a line drawn from Barnegat Creek to a point on the Delaware below Renkokus Creek.   The division of the land made by this grant was naturally not acceptable to the successors of Berkeley, and on July 1, 1676, a quintipartite deed of division was drawn up between Byllinge and his

---

[1] *N. Y. Col. Doc.*, XIII, 473.

[2] *N. J. Archives*, I, 124.   At the time of the surrender to the Dutch, there were estimated to be 391 male inhabitants (freeholders?) in the province, of whom 327 took the oath of allegiance to the Dutch (*Archives*, I, 133).

[3] *N. Y. Col. Doc.*, XIII, 477; *N. J. Archives*, I, 126.   A most curious system of triple nomination and indirect election was established.   Each of the English towns in New Jersey was to elect two deputies; these deputies were to meet and to nominate three persons for schout (sheriff) and three for secretary, and from these nominees the Director and Council would select one for each office.

[4] Leaming and Spicer, 41–45.

[5] July 29, 1674. Leaming and Spicer, 46–48.

[6] Whitehead, *East Jersey*, 81.

assignees on one part and Carteret on the other, by which the share of the Berkeley claimants, now called West Jersey, was very considerably enlarged.[1]   From this time until the assumption of control by the Crown in 1702, New Jersey was divided into two political organizations, with distinct policies and development.   We must, therefore, turn our attention first of all to the continuation of the struggle between Carteret and his settlers in East Jersey, and then take a summary view of the suffrage as it existed in West Jersey under the proprietors.

Upon his return to the province after the Dutch occupation, Governor Carteret was again fortified with ample powers to bring the malcontents upon the Nicholls grants to terms.   A second letter from King Charles was obtained, acknowledging Carteret's title and commanding all to yield him obedience;[2] still more additional directions were made supplementary to the original Concessions.[3]   One year's time was given to the Nicholls patentees to repatent their lands, and at the end of that time, if the new registration were not made, the lands and homes of the occupiers were to be forfeited.   No one could vote nor hold office unless his land was obtained by the proprietary title; and the people of one of Nicholls's grants who had peaceably submitted were rewarded with greater political privileges in matters of local government.   Thus threats and hopes of rewards were both used to bring the obdurate settlers to a recognition of the proprietary rights.

The reasons for the refusal of the old settlers to take out new patents were threefold: the inconvenience of new surveys and registration, the fees and cost of repatenting, and the perpetual quit-rents which the new patents required. The governor made the matter as convenient as possible by appointing special days upon which inhabitants could take out their patents, and thus become " quallified as well for a Generall Assembly as Elective for other Offices." [4]   The

[1] Leaming and Spicer, 61–72.
[2] *Ibid.,* 49.
[3] *Ibid.,* 50–57.
[4] *N. J. Archives,* I, 176.

second assembly of the province met in the fall of 1675,[1] and from that time until 1688 frequent assemblies were held. Yet the electors and members of these assemblies appear not to have been always qualified according to the instructions of the proprietor;[2] many of the old inhabitants must still have refused to patent their lands under the proprietor; and yet the governor could not prevent their voting and even sitting in the assembly.

Other difficulties now beset the province. The Duke of York's governor in New York, Edmund Andros, claimed the right to levy customs duties upon all ships entering New Jersey ports; and in the conflict of authority which arose over the subject Andros entered New Jersey, seized Governor Carteret, and imprisoned him in New York.[3] A jury failed to convict Carteret, and the case was sent to England for the consideration of Sir George Carteret and the Duke of York. In the interim Andros ruled East Jersey, and permitted the inhabitants a privilege which his master had denied New York, a representative assembly. This assembly stood upon their rights under the concessions and as Englishmen when Andros tried to force the Duke of York's Book of Laws upon them:[4]

" 1680 New Jersey Assembly to the Go:
" June 2nd Wee the Deputies of the Freeholders of this Province of New Jersey doe expect that all privileges belonging to Inhabitants & Freeholders of the sd Province granted to them by Vertue of the Concessions made by the Ld John Berkeley & Sr George Carterett bee to all Intents & Purposes allowed & confirmed & maintained to the aforesaid Inhabitnts & Freeholders without any Infringment: one particular principal whereof is as of right belonging to every free borne Englishman, that there bee a Generall Assembly called once a yeare . . ."[5]

The independent attitude of the assembly was shown not only towards Andros, but also towards Governor Carteret when, after the disavowal of Andros's acts, he was reinstated

[1] Leaming and Spicer, 94.
[2] *N. J. Archives*, I, 364.
[3] Smith, *New Jersey*, 68; Whitehead, *East Jersey*, 93.
[4] *N. Y. Col. Doc.*, XIII, 541: *N. J. Archives*, I, 296-7; 305 ff.
[5] *Ibid.*, 311.

in authority. The assembly of October, 1681, appears to
have been under the influence of the settlers upon the Nicholls grants, and accordingly the session was a very stormy
one, in which the assembly protested against the orders of
the proprietors in 1672, which had limited political privileges
to those who held proprietary titles; and the governor denied
the right of many of the assembly to sit in the house at all
because they did not possess patents from the proprietors.[1]

This was the last assembly held under the authority of the
Carterets, and it was the most turbulent. Throughout the
whole period in which Sir George Carteret or his family held
East Jersey the province was in a state of turmoil over the
land question. The disputes arose out of the unfortunate
grants made by Nicholls, and their termination was not
reached until over fifty years had passed. The proprietors
used every means within their power to bring the Nicholls
patentees to terms. Forcible eviction was threatened, and
perhaps tried in a few cases; submission was encouraged by
granting additional privileges to those who had peaceably
acknowledged Carteret's authority; and as a last resort, in
the instructions of 1672 and 1674, the proprietor had directed
that those refusing to recognize his authority should be
debarred from political privileges, both in the towns and in
the provincial elections. But the situation was one in which
the possessor was stronger than the absent proprietor or his
governor in the colony; evictions were almost impossible
when such a large part of the population was concerned.
The occupiers retained possession, and in addition often exercised political rights. The whole situation is most interesting as showing the close connection between political privileges and land-holding; and it illustrates the difficulty of
enforcing abstract title rights in a new country.

After the death of Sir George Carteret in 1680, the trustees of his estate sold East Jersey at auction to William Penn

---

[1] *N. Y. Col. Doc.,* III, 293–300; *N. J. Archives,* I, 354–365. Concerning the additional instruction of 1672, the Assembly said: " The Lords
would likely neuer haue had a thought of such Contradicc'on of themselves had it not been a bratt begotten in New Jersey sent for England
to be borne and Retransported to New Jersey to be fed with the groanes
and Oppressions of the People." (*Archives,* I, 363.)

and eleven associates.[1]   And shortly after this each of the
twelve purchasers disposed of one-half of his share to
another, thus making in all twenty-four proprietors.   In
order to make their title to the province more secure, the
new proprietors obtained a new release from the Duke of
York[2] and a letter from the king recognizing their right
to their purchase.   Having thus settled their title, the proprietors appointed a governor, Robert Barclay, the famous
Quaker apologist, and Barclay in turn appointed a deputy
who was to reside in the province.

Following these first steps in provincial organization, the
proprietors of East Jersey issued a most remarkable political
code for the province, called " The Fundamental Constitutions for the Province of East New Jersey in America." [3]
This frame of government provided in elaborate terms for a
great council composed of the twenty-four proprietors or
their proxies and representatives of the freemen to the number of seventy-two or one hundred and forty-four.   A great
advance was made by the constitutions upon the subject of
the suffrage.   The old vague term " freeholder" was carefully defined, and non-freeholders who rented houses in
towns were allowed the privilege of voting:

" The persons qualified to be freemen, that are capable to choose and
be chosen in the Great Council, shall be every planter and inhabitant
dwelling and residing within the Province, who hath acquired rights to
and is in possession of fifty acres of ground, and hath cultivated ten
acres of it; or in boroughs, who hath a house and three acres; or have
a house and land only hired, if he can prove he have fifty pounds in
stock of his own." [4]

Thus a decided step towards political equality was proposed
by the proprietors, and the artisans and small freeholders of
the towns were placed upon an equality with the larger freeholders of the country districts; while the rights of the latter

[1] February 1 and 2, 1681–2; Leaming and Spicer, 73; Whitehead, *East
Jersey*, 103.
[2] Leaming and Spicer, 141–150.
[3] *Ibid.*, 153–166.
[4] Article III of the Constitutions.

were restricted by requiring the country freeholder to be in possession, and to have under cultivation at least ten acres of his freehold.[1] The proposed arrangement, which was nearer to political equity than the old qualifications, had one defect, for by it the freeholder must have "*acquired rights to*" his land; and this might lead, and indeed eventually did lead, to the old trouble concerning proprietary titles.

Among the proprietors, who were to constitute one house of the assembly, the suffrage qualifications were closely limited. No proprietor could retain his vote unless he kept at least one-fourth of his propriety; and as there were twenty-four proprieties at first, at least one-ninety-sixth of the whole province of East Jersey must be retained by each proprietor. If any proprietor thus forfeited his right to vote in the proprietary council, his right might be passed on to others who held the required amount, or after forty years had elapsed, and vacancies still appeared, then selections might be made from those possessing five thousand or three thousand acres of land. As an apologist for the Fundamental Constitutions says,—

"To avoid Lording over one another, No man can purchase above the 24th part of the Countrey; and on the other hand, least any should squander away their Interest, and yet retain the character of the Government that belongs to Property, and thence be capable to betray it, as not being bound by Interest, there must be a suitable quantity retained, otherwise the Title in the Government extinguishes in him, and passes to another, to be Elected by the Proprietors, that Dominion may follow Property, and the inconveniency of a Beggarly Nobility and Gentry may be avoided."[2]

Such was the seventeenth and eighteenth century conception of political rights; dominion should follow property, and the privilege of participating in government was conditioned

[1] The requirement that part of freehold should be cultivated is seen in Penn's Laws Made in England; in Markham's Frame for Penna.; Penna. Act of November 27, 1700, and January 12, 1705–6, and Delaware Act of 1734.

[2] George Scot in *Model of the Government of the Province of East-New-Jersey*, London, 1685; reprinted in *N. J. Hist. Soc. Coll.*, I, 239 ff; 269.

upon the antecedent participation in the wealth of the country; the politically efficient were those " bound by Interest." [1]

This proposed code never went into effect, for, although the proprietors thought they had granted many new privileges in the Fundamental Constitutions, the people and assembly did not view the code in the same light; further, the new frame was to go into effect only upon those who would submit to a new survey of their lands, accepting new titles, paying all old quit-rents, and who promised to make provision for the support of the government.[2] Such restrictions would have defeated a much better constitution than the Fundamentals of 1683. The governor in the province was compelled to retain the government under the Concessions of 1665, and in April, 1686, the assembly decidedly refused to accept the new frame. After that time it is supposed that no further action was taken towards the establishment of the code.[3]

But one more feature of a constitutional nature remains to be noted before the surrender of East Jersey to the Crown. Between 1686 and 1702 the province had passed through many experiences; comparative peace had reigned between 1686 to 1688, and then the land was turned over to Andros as part of his " Dominion of New England;" from 1689 till 1692 there was no general provincial government whatever; then came a few years of quiet until the arrival of Governor Basse in 1697. During all this time the only consecutive policy was the popular opposition to the proprietary quit-rents. So unsatisfactory and costly was the collection of the rents, that at last the proprietors proposed to commute them into a single payment, and then vest the land in fee in the holders.[4] At this point the proprietors used the same threats and promises which Carteret had employed in 1672 and 1674. It was provided that *when* the people have purchased at least one-half of the quit-rents and paid arrears of rents,

---

[1] *Cf.* the Virginia Bill of Rights of 1776: " All men, having sufficient evidence of permanent common interest with, and attachment to, the community, have the right of suffrage."

[2] Leaming and Spicer, 179–181.

[3] Whitehead, *East Jersey,* 133; 134, note 1.

[4] Leaming and Spicer, 214–219.

and the assembly has made provision for support of the government, *then* the governor may agree to a general law for the annual meetings of assembly, and the assembly may have the power to name a double number of candidates for local county offices, the governor selecting a single number for the offices; *but* if in any county or town a major part of the freeholders do not so commute their rents, then that town or county should not have the privilege of nomination of their officers by assembly, but the governor should appoint all local officers; *provided,* that such political privileges as were granted under these terms should continue only so long as the assembly made provision for the support of the government.[1]

It was but natural that Englishmen should reject such propositions as these; for, although the payment of the quit-rents may have been a reasonable, or at least a legal, claim of the proprietors, the conditioning of political privileges upon the payment of the rents was vicious in principle. These were the people who in 1680 had told Andros that it is a " right belonging to every free borne Englishman, that there bee a Generall Assembly called once a yeare;" and now their " birth-right privileges" must be bartered for quit-rents at the rate of a ha'penny an acre. Yet the colonists were ready to pay off the rents if an equitable agreement could be reached, and went so far as to send a special agent to England to confer with the proprietors.[2]   But in drawing up a statement of the rights of the subjects in 1699, the assembly omitted to give any other qualification of the suffrage than simple freeholdership,[3] thereby ignoring all the proprietary claims to rents or new surveys.

There followed several years of confusion and disorder. The governor appointed sheriffs and county officers in accordance with his instructions, but the people refused to obey them and violently attacked the justices and sheriffs, and even kept Governor Hamilton in confinement for several

[1] Instructions to Governor Basse, April 14, 1698, Leaming and Spicer, 214–219.
[2] Whitehead, *East Jersey,* 193.
[3] Leaming and Spicer, 368–372.

days.[1]   In these days, called the " Revolution," the governor
attempted to dispossess some of the settlers of their lands,[2]
and at last the people petitioned the king to take the government into his own hands.[3]   It was undoubtedly believed at
this time that with the overthrow of the proprietary government would go all the proprietary quit-rents and troubles
over the ownership of the soil.[4]   The transfer to the Crown
was made in 1702,[5] and after that change in authority the
suffrage dispute centred about other matters than the abstract
title to land.

We must now retrace our course to the year 1676, in which
the division of New Jersey into the two sections, East and
West Jersey, was made by the drafting of the quintipartite
deed.   In the western section, as in the eastern, the subject
of land titles was a perennial source of trouble, but there was
one difference between the two divisions in favor of West
Jersey.   In East Jersey the land troubles arose between the
settlers and the proprietors, giving rise to strong protests
and revolutionary acts against the proprietors on the one
hand, and to evictions and political disfranchisement of the
settlers on the other.   In West Jersey the land disputes were
generally among the proprietors or proprietary claimants
themselves, and there was no definite arraying of popular
classes against the large hereditary owners of the land.   And
it will be seen also that West Jersey enjoyed a larger measure
of local self-government and more freedom from European
restraint than was the case in East Jersey.   Thus, down to
the union of the two divisions and the assumption of control
by the Crown in 1702, the history of West Jersey shows less
turbulence and violence than is to be found in the eastern
section.

It is, of course, not our purpose to study in detail the land
disputes, but clearness demands that a short statement be
made of the title changes in West Jersey down to 1702.   In

---

[1] Whitehead, *East Jersey,* 215.
[2] *New Jersey Historical Society Collections,* V, 30.
[3] *Ibid.,* 30, 32.
[4] Whitehead, *East Jersey,* 214.
[5] Leaming and Spicer, 609–617.   The transfer papers were signed April
15, 1702, and accepted by the queen on April 17.

the year 1673 Lord Berkeley had sold his undivided share in New Jersey to John Fenwick in trust for Edward Byllinge; and a contest arising between Byllinge and Fenwick, William Penn was appointed arbitrator by a Friends' meeting in London, and Penn awarded an undivided tenth of West Jersey to Fenwick and the other undivided nine-tenths to Byllinge. After much pressure, Fenwick accepted this decision, while Byllinge turned over his nine-tenths to Penn, Laurie, and Lucas as trustees for his creditors. Fenwick then mortgaged his one-tenth to Eldridge and Warner on a one thousand-year lease for £110, and having thus disposed of his land, set sail for America; and, the only one of all the proprietary claimants upon the spot, Fenwick began granting lands without regard to the rights of Byllinge's trustees or his own mortgagees. In the mean time, sales of land having been made in England to so-called proprietors, it was proposed to divide the land into tenths, and a company of proprietors from Yorkshire agreed to settle upon one of these tenths, and a company from London upon another. The proprietors in England then elected Byllinge as governor and allowed him to appoint a deputy. In 1680, in order to make the title more secure, a new grant was obtained from the Duke of York, but this only complicated matters by granting the lands to the assignees of Fenwick and Byllinge, but the political power to Byllinge himself. Byllinge's power in the colony was not at first recognized, but later his governor was accepted. In 1683 Fenwick sold all his share in West Jersey except 150,000 acres to William Penn for ten shillings, and thus one of the most disturbing elements of the colony was quieted.[1] After Byllinge's death in 1687, Daniel Coxe, of London, already holding a large proprietary interest, bought the rights of Byllinge's heirs and claimed the sole political authority; but in 1692 Coxe transferred his interest to a company of proprietors, who styled themselves the West Jersey Society, and who appointed their first governor in the same year. This society retained the land and political rights until the surrender to the Crown in 1702,

---

[1] For the interesting personality of John Fenwick, see R. G. Johnson, *History of Salem* (*N. J.*); Shourds. *Fenwick's Colony; N. Y. Col. Doc.*, XII: *N. J. Archives,* I; Smith, *History of N. J.,* 79 ff.

when they yielded their political power, but their title to all unoccupied land is still (1904) valid, and the society keeps up its organization in West Jersey.[1]

Turning now to the subject of the suffrage in West Jersey, we need not mention the informal meetings held by Fenwick[2] in his colony, but must notice first of all the suffrage provisions in the first frame of government for West Jersey, called "The Concessions and Agreements of the Proprietors, Freeholders and Inhabitants of the Province of West New Jersey, in America."[3] This remarkably liberal constitution was drawn up in England, dated March 3, 1676–7, and was signed by one hundred and fifty-one persons, among whom were Penn, Laurie, Lucas, Warner, Byllinge, Olive, and Jennings, all greatly interested in New Jersey history. The Concessions partake of the nature of an agreement between the intending settlers and the English proprietors, and they appear to have been signed by Byllinge and his representatives, by the new purchasing proprietors, and by those about to sail for the colony.

The Concessions provided for the division of the country into tenths, and each tenth in turn into ten proprietaries, making one hundred proprietaries for the whole province, and determined the amounts of land which should be given to new settlers, tracts which were much smaller than those we have seen were granted to the settlers in East Jersey under the Concessions of 1665. They further provided for a temporary and permanent government by officers elected by the people. The temporary government was composed of commissioners elected by "the proprietors, Freeholders and Inhabitants" of each of the tenths, who were to govern and order the affairs of the province for the good and welfare of the people. The commissioners were to be elected by ballot:

"And the said Elections shall be made and distinguished by balloting Trunks, to avoid noise and confusion, and not by Voices, holding up of the Hands, or otherwise howsoever."[4]

[1] See *The Surveyors' Association of West New Jersey*, 118–144.

[2] *N. J. Col. Archives*, I, 225, 275.

[3] Leaming and Spicer, 382–411; *N. J. Archives*, I, 240 ff; Smith, *New Jersey*, 521 ff.

[4] Article III.

These commissioners were to continue to be elected by annual elections until " distinctions of tribes" occur, and then there was to be a " General, Free and Supream Assembly" composed of one member from each of the one hundred proprietaries, elected by the " inhabitants, freeholders, and proprietors."

The West Jersey Concessions of 1677 were more liberal to the settlers than were the Fundamental Constitutions of East Jersey of 1683. The assembly according to the latter was made up of two houses, one of which was composed solely of those holding definite proprietary interests in the province; while in West Jersey the proprietors did not retain to themselves any such share in legislation; for in references to the suffrage the three words, inhabitants, freeholders, and proprietors, are used, and no attempt is made to vest with superior political privileges those who hold title to the unoccupied land. The humblest freeholder and the greatest proprietor are on a political equality and each may in orderly fashion cast his vote into the " balloting trunk." The representatives thus elected were called the " trustees" of the people; they were directly responsible to their constituents, who had the power to instruct them upon public measures; and they were to be paid by the people of their several districts, that thereby each " may be known to be the Servant of the People."

This elective system was not set in operation until 1681, when Samuel Jennings, deputy governor under Byllinge, called an assembly, which soon showed itself stronger than the governor. Byllinge, under his second grant from the Duke of York of 1680, was claiming sole political authority of the province, and therefore the newly elected representatives, fearing perhaps the withdrawal of the old Concessions, drew up a formal set of conditions,[1] and refused to recognize Jennings as governor until he had accepted these fundamentals. This agreement provided for annual assemblies elected by the " free people" of the province; it took from the governor any veto upon acts of the assembly, compelling him to accept all acts passed by them; it forbade the governor

---

[1] Leaming and Spicer, 423–425.

to pass any law without the general assembly, and if he did so, he should be esteemed an enemy of the free people of the province and the law should be void; it made all offices elective or appointive by the assembly; it granted liberty of conscience, and no one was to be rendered incapable of holding office on account of faith; finally, this compact prohibited the raising of any tax by the governor.

After this first assembly, annual elections took place with considerable, if not complete, regularity until the cession to the Crown in 1702.[1] These assemblies exercised very broad powers. They elected the councillors, justices of the peace, land commissioners, constables, and other inferior officers; and in three years, 1683, 1684, 1685, even elected their governor, and compelled him to take an oath to observe the established constitution of the province.[2] This was self-government in practically complete form. The freeholders[3] elected the members of assembly, and the assembly elected all other provincial officers, while town officers were occasionally elected or nominated by the localities.[4] The tenths remained the unit of representation until 1694, when the county was substituted, Burlington and Gloucester counties sending twenty representatives each, Salem ten, and Cape May five. In 1699 this number of fifty-five representatives was found " burdensome and superfluous," and accordingly the numbers were changed to ten for Burlington and Gloucester counties, five for Salem and three for Cape May, all of whom were to be " sufficient freeholders." But in 1701 the old numbers were once more adopted.[5] It is not at all surprising that the number of representatives was felt to be too great, for an almanac of the time estimates that West

---

[1] Smith, *New Jersey,* 154; but Leaming and Spicer give no laws between 1685 and 1692.

[2] *Ibid.,* 164, 189, 190.

[3] By a law passed at the session of September 26–28, 1682, it was provided that elections for assemblymen should be by the " freeholders;" while the two other terms, " inhabitants" and " proprietors" are omitted from the clause, and were not reinstated thereafter (Leaming and Spicer, 455–6).

[4] Leaming and Spicer, 454, 494, 496.

[5] *Ibid.,* 533, 567, 581.

Jersey contained only eight hundred and thirty-two free-holders;[1] thus giving one representative to every fifteen voters.

Throughout the whole period of separate organization, the suffrage in West Jersey was exercised by those holding land, but beyond the simple word " freeholder" as used in the laws, no further qualification or explanation was given; and apparently no disputes occurred which might create the necessity for a clearer definition of terms.

After years of negotiations, the transfer of the Jerseys to the Crown was accomplished in 1702. As early as the year 1699 the proprietors had offered to surrender their governmental rights to the Crown, but they demanded many conditions and guarantees. Again in 1701 the proprietors of the two sections united in framing the conditions upon which they would yield to the king; and among the guarantees which they asked was one which gave the model for the later representative system of the royal province of New Jersey. East and West Jersey should be united, and a single assembly for both sections should meet alternately at Perth Amboy and Burlington. This assembly, the proprietors suggested, should be composed of thirty-six members: two elected by the " inhabitants householders" of Perth Amboy, two by those of Burlington, sixteen by the " freeholders" of East Jersey, and the same number by the freeholders of West Jersey; and membership in the assembly was to be limited to those possessing over one thousand acres of land, and the right of suffrage outside the two towns to those possessing a freehold of one hundred acres.[2] The proprietors further asked for a confirmation of their rights to the soil and quit-rents, the right to appoint the first governor, religious liberty for the inhabitants, the regular establishment of courts, and other privileges. But shortly after this the Board of Trade questioned the right of the Duke of York to alienate his rights in government, and advised the king to appoint a governor for the provinces without making terms with the existing proprietors.[3] The following spring the proprietors

[1] *N. J. Archives,* II, 305.
[2] Leaming and Spicer, 588, 591–3, 599.
[3] *Ibid.,* 603–9.

surrendered their political powers in both provinces to the queen without restriction or qualification.

After the surrender of the Jerseys to the Crown, we must look for the next constitutional expression in the governor's commission and instructions.   Lord Cornbury had already been appointed governor of New York, and in the fall of 1702 he was commissioned as governor over the neighboring province of New Jersey.   His commission [1] and instructions [2] show the influence of the demands made by the proprietors, and granted almost everything which they desired. The assembly was not so large as the proprietors had wished, but it was formed upon the plan suggested by them, and the qualifications both of members of the assembly and of voters were similar to those given in the petition of the proprietors.

The assembly was to be composed of twenty-four members, ten of whom were chosen by the freeholders of East Jersey and ten by the freeholders of West Jersey, two by the " inhabitants householders" of Perth Amboy and two by those of Burlington.[3]   No one could act as an elector unless he possessed one hundred acres of land in the section (East or West) in which he desired to vote, nor serve in the assembly unless he held one thousand acres in the section.   It will be seen that the new organization acted in two ways: en-

---

[1] December 5, 1702; Leaming and Spicer, 647–656; Smith, *History of New Jersey,* 220–230.

[2] November 16, 1702; Leaming and Spicer, 619–646; Smith, *History of New Jersey,* 230–261.

[3] The extension of the suffrage in Burlington and Perth Amboy was one of the requests of the proprietors' petition, and was one of the provisions of the proposed fundamentals of 1683 in East Jersey.   In the town charters (Newark, 1666; Bergen, 1668; Woodbridge, 1669; Monmouth, 1672) the word freeholders is always used (see charters in *N. J. Hist. Soc. Coll.,* I, 183, 184, 186; *Leaming and Spicer,* 663–4).   In the legislation concerning towns sometimes the word freeholder is used (Laws of May 26 and November 3, 1668); sometimes the word " inhabitant" (Ch. VIII of East Jersey Laws of 1686); sometimes the word "town" (East Jersey Laws, 1693, Ch. VIII, 1698–9, Ch. V).   In Burlington (West Jersey Laws, Ch. XIII of 1693) local matters were determined by " actual inhabitants who enjoy the fee simple of a house and land therein."   In all these there is no reference to " inhabitants householders."

larging the suffrage in the towns by allowing all inhabiting householders to vote, and limiting the suffrage in the country by substituting the new provision of one hundred acres in freehold for the indefinite term " freeholder," unqualified as to amount. No exact figures have been obtained showing the effect of the new qualifications, but there is no doubt that they were very unpopular, both on account of the restriction upon members of the assembly and upon voters in the country.[1]

Governor Cornbury arrived in New York in May, 1702, but his commission and instructions as governor of New Jersey did not reach him until the end of July, 1703.[2] Within a few days after the receipt of these papers, the governor visited New Jersey, and before a month had passed he had issued his writs for the election of members of assembly.[3] Some inconvenience and injustice were brought on in this first election under the royal government by the omission in the governor's instructions of any districting scheme, and accordingly the ten representatives from the two divisions of the province were elected at large, and the polls were held in one place, compelling some voters to travel over a hundred miles to the voting place.[4] If one were to believe all of Colonel Quarry's accounts to the Board of Trade, there was not a little corruption and undue influence at the polls of this first election. Surely no modern election expert could do better than to return as elected one who received only forty-two votes out of over four hundred; and the undefined powers of the sheriff of those days permitted him to adjourn the election and compel " several hundred of substantial housekeepers to sleep out of doors in an inclement season of the year" while waiting for their turn to vote.[5]

The assembly, meeting in November, 1703, soon adjourned till May, 1704, and in the fall a new election took

[1] *N. J. Archives*, III, 6, 28, 71, 84; *N. J. Hist. Soc. Coll.*, V, 49, 55; MS. *Board of Trade Journals* in Penna. Historical Society Library, November 20, 1705.

[2] *Ibid.*, II, 543, note.

[3] *Ibid.*, III, 5.

[4] *Ibid.*, III, 16, 28; XIII, 306.

[5] *Ibid.*, III, 15.

place. The members of the new assembly at once took up the consideration of the question of suffrage and elections. The governor had already written to the Board of Trade,[1] giving three objections to the qualifications as fixed in his instructions: that some were chosen to the assembly, but could not serve because they did not have one thousand acres of land, although possessing more than that value in land and goods; that some of those possessing the required amounts of land had not twenty shillings in money, " drive noe trade, and can neither read nor write, nay they can not answer a question that is asked them;" and that the instructions were faulty in not providing for elections in the counties instead of in the two divisions at large. Thus the governor pointed the way towards a more liberal policy, holding that property in goods was as sufficient a test of a man's interest in the state as was real estate, and even hinting that land itself was of little value as a suffrage qualification if the elector or elected was unable to read or write.

While the governor thus showed himself in favor of a personal property qualification as well as a landed requirement, the other opponents of the proprietary interest in the province were urging that the heavy land qualifications were " an infringement of the naturall right of the other Inhabitants and tend to enslave them." [2] Thus governor and antiproprietary party acted in harmony, and when the second assembly met, in November, 1704, they excluded three persons whose qualifications were not clearly shown, and then by a bare majority passed a new law entitled " An Act for altering the present Constitution, and Regulating the Election of Representatives to serve in general Assembly in this Province." [3] I have never seen a copy of this law, but it is frequently referred to in the correspondence of the day, in public discussions, and in the journals of the Board of Trade, and from these sources the two principal features of the act are obtained. These features were, first, the repeal of the

[1] *N. J. Archives,* III, 28.
[2] *Ibid.,* 37.
[3] *Ibid.,* 72; 88; the act is given by title only in Bradford's *Laws* (edition of 1717), 5.

clause of the governor's instructions requiring voters to possess one hundred acres, and members of assembly one thousand acres, and substituting for that provision the old vague
term " freeholder" without any additional qualification; and
secondly, the introduction of the governor's favorite theory
of the equality of land and personal property as the basis
for political qualifications.[1] The exact method by which the
equality of the two forms of property was obtained is not
stated in any of the documents of the period.

The new law attracted attention immediately both in New
Jersey and in England. The governor wrote to the Board
of Trade that it would be "more advantageous to the
Queen's service and the good of the country" than the old
method;[2] and three of the proprietors in England also memo-
rialized the Board, protesting against the high requirements
of Cornbury's instructions and asking that all freeholders
might have a share in elections.[3] The Board admitted two
of these petitioners personally to its meetings, and upon their
advice sent to the queen the draft of new instructions for
the governor.[4] On May 3, 1705, the new instruction was
approved by the queen in council.[5] It was a virtual compromise of the suffrage question. The desire of the more
popular party that all freeholders should be permitted to vote
was not granted, but the governor's proposal that personal
property be accepted in lieu of land was incorporated, and
the clause was so worded that any freeholder could vote who
had

" 100 Acres of Land of an Estate of Freehold in his own right within
the County for which he shall so Vote, or a personal Estate in Money,
Goods and Chattels to the Value of £50 Sterling."

[1] See *Archives*, III, 17, 84, 86–95; 126; MS. *Board of Trade Journals,*
April 13, 1705, Vol. 17, 357–8; November 20, 1705, Vol. 18, 108, 110,
114–5, 120; Leaming and Spicer, 657–660; *N. J. Hist. Soc. Coll.* V, 50.

The act was subsequently disallowed by the queen; see Bradford's
Laws (edition of 1732), 7.

[2] *Archives*, III, 71.

[3] *Ibid.*, 84.

[4] MS. *Board of Trade Journals*, April 13 and 16, 1705, Vol. 17, 357–8.

[5] *Archives*, III, 96–98.

It further gave the suffrage to the inhabiting householders of Salem, Burlington, and Perth Amboy, and changed the method of election of the assemblymen from the general ticket plan to a local election of two representatives for each county and two from each of the three towns.

But while the authorities in England were determining upon revising Cornbury's instructions and admitting smaller freeholders to the suffrage, action in opposition to the new law was taken by the West Jersey proprietors. On April 16, 1705, some of the English proprietors had spoken to the Board of Trade in favor of the new provisions, but on the succeeding day a protest was signed by nineteen of the proprietors of West Jersey against any extension of popular powers. These proprietors had been largely responsible for the clause in Cornbury's instructions which had required such large amounts of freehold for voting and holding seats in the assembly,[1] and undoubtedly the restriction would work in their interest. It was but natural, therefore, that they should object to a change in qualifications which would throw open these political privileges to irresponsible inhabitants. In their protest they give most explicit expression of their theories of government.

The proprietors urged[2] that the governor and assembly had no right to alter the qualifications established by the governor's instructions, but that these provisions were to be a " standing and unalterable" part of the constitution. They were, furthermore, perfectly in accord with the constitution of England, " where the electors of the knights of shires must have a certain fixed freehold, and the elected are generally the principal landed men of their respective county's." The new broad suffrage qualifications, too, were inexpedient, " for certainly those persons are fittest to be trusted with choosing and being legislators, who have a fixed valuable and permanent interest in lands, and must stand and fall with their country." " But money is an uncertain inter-

[1] It has already been noted that the qualifications set down in Cornbury's instructions were copied from the suggestions of the proprietors at the time of surrender. See also *N. J. Archives*, III, 139.

[2] Leaming and Spicer, 657–660: *N. J. Archives*, III, 86–95. There are important differences between these two copies of the protest.

est, and if it be admitted a qualification equal to land, an Assembly may be packed of strangers and beggars, who will have little regard to the good of the country, from whence they can remove at pleasure, and may oppress the landed men with heavy taxes." And finally, the protest expresses the alarms of the proprietors that the " Alteration now made was intended to put the election of Representatives into the meanest of the people who being impatient of any Superi^{rs,} will never fail to choose such from amongst themselves as may oppose us, and destroy our Rights."

Although this paper is dated the 17th of April, 1705, it was not received by the Board of Trade until the following September,[1] the delay being caused, perhaps, by the difficulty of obtaining signatures to the petition, for the proprietors were scattered through England and Scotland. The delay was costly to the proprietors, and in May the queen sent the new instruction to Cornbury, permitting him to extend the suffrage to *all freeholders who possessed either one hundred acres of land or fifty pounds personal estate.* In November, 1705, the subject again came up for consideration in the Board of Trade, and that indefatigable colonial agitator, Colonel Quarry, was asked for his advice.[2] Others of the proprietors were called in,[3] and in the following February, 1705–6, the Board wrote to Cornbury that they had no objections to the bill passed in November, 1704, except that it did not state the quantity of acres necessary to qualify electors and elected,[4] and they refer him to the new instruction recently sent to him for guidance.

After much more correspondence upon the subject, the tenor of the instructions was at last carried out by a law passed at a session of the legislature in the spring of 1709, during Governor Lovelace's short administration., This act gave definite legal form to the additional instruction sent to Governor Cornbury in May, 1705. It provided that electors in the counties and members of the assembly should be freeholders; electors possessing at least one hundred acres of

[1] *N. J. Archives,* III, 86.
[2] MS. *Board of Trade Journals,* November 20, 1705, Vol. 18, 108.
[3] *Ibid.,* 110, 114–5, 120.
[4] *N. J. Archives,* III, 126.

land or fifty pounds value of personal *and* real estate; and
assemblymen one thousand acres of land or five hundred
pounds value in lands and personal property.[1]   This law
referred only to voters in the *counties,* and did not mention
the qualifications for town residents; but in the instructions
to the governors down to and including Governor Franklin,
in 1762, the town suffrage is extended to " inhabitants householders."   No further change in the suffrage for the provincial assembly was made from 1709 down to the Revolution.
Householders in the two towns of Perth Amboy and Burlington[2] and freeholders in the counties as stated above
exercised the suffrage privilege.   The qualifications were undoubtedly liberal in 1709, but as the population of the province became more dense and a non-landholding class arose,
political theories changed also.   One of the first results of
the revolutionary spirit was the demand for the extension of
the suffrage,[3] and it was not long before this was accomplished.

As one passes from the view of the provincial organization
to the study of local government, an extension of the suffrage
is noticeable.   Thus, in Massachusetts and Connecticut the
suffrage was much broader in town elections than in the
colonial elections, and other colonies as well as old England
show the same principle.   New Jersey was no exception to
this practice.   The earliest legislation concerning town activity placed the control of local affairs in the hands of the
freeholders, but after the cession of the provinces to the
Crown a more liberal policy is apparent.   An act of 1709[4]
provided that poor officers should be elected in town meetings; and in 1709–10[5] the representative system of county

[1] Bradford's *Laws* (ed. of 1717), 5.

[2] For a number of years Salem also had separate representation in the
Assembly, but by new instructions to Governor Burnet in 1727, Salem
lost its representatives and was united with Salem county (*N. J. Archives,* XIV, 336–7).

[3] See *Extracts from the Journal of Proceedings of the Provincial Con-
gress of New Jersey,* Trenton, May, June, and August, 1775.   Burlington, Isaac Collins, 1775.   Reprint by Joseph Sailer, Woodbury, N. J.,
1835; pp. 75, 142, 228.

[4] Bradford's *Laws* (ed. of 1717), 31.

[5] *N. J. Archives,* XIII, 398, note; Bradford's *Laws,* 17.

government was established, but changed somewhat in 1714. By the last act " the Inhabitants of each Town and Precinct" within each county were to elect annually two " Freeholders," and these " chosen Freeholders" should meet with the justices to fix a county tax rate and appoint certain officers.[1] The term " inhabitant" here used occurs almost continuously from this time in the laws relating to local suffrage, although usually combined with the word " freeholder," the phrase " freeholders and inhabitants" being the most common form down to the Revolution.[2]

This phrase is not one peculiar to New Jersey, for it runs throughout a century of New York legislation, and in that province, it is believed, was applied only to *inhabiting freeholders.*[3] Such was not the interpretation, however, which was placed upon it in New Jersey. We have already seen that the governor's instructions granted the provincial suffrage to householders in three towns, and that the act of 1714, while giving local suffrage to " inhabitants," directed that the elected should be " freeholders." An act of 1717 expressly stated that the electors should be " freeholders and inhabitants, householders," and thereby accepted the English legal meaning of the word " inhabitants" as one who holds a house. That there were two forms of suffrage is also recognized by the assembly in laws relating to the important matter of the location of the county seats in new counties,[4] providing that the decision of this question should be left to those who were qualified to vote for representatives. But apart from these several instances, the word inhabitant,[5] or the phrase freeholder and inhabitant, is always used.[6]

It is quite possible, indeed, that the actual suffrage was not

[1] Bradford's *Laws*, 7.

[2] *Ibid.* (1717), 61, 66, acts of January, 1716–17; Nevill's *Laws*, I, 420, act of 1749; Nevill's *Laws*, II, 345, act of 1760.

[3] See chapter on New York.

[4] County of Cumberland, 1747, Nevill's *Laws*, I, 361; County of Sussex, 1753, Nevill's *Laws*, II, 20.

[5] See Nevill's *Laws*, II, 19.

[6] By the city charters of Burlington and Trenton, householders were permitted to vote in city affairs; *N. J. Hist. Soc. Proc.*, Sec. Series, IX, 158.

always limited even to householders, but that still less responsible persons occasionally voted in town elections. This must have been the case, else there would have been no reason for the law passed in 1766, which carefully defined the term " inhabitant." [1]   This act, which must serve as our strongest clue to the local suffrage qualifications before the Revolution, expressed in clear terms the meaning of the word. It was passed " for the better ascertaining what Persons Shall have a Right to vote at Town-meetings, and the Elections of the Township and Precinct Officers," and it prescribed

"that no Person or Persons, except in Towns corporate, shall have the Privilege to give his or their Voice or Vote at any Town meeting . . . unless the Person offering such Vote is a Freeholder, a Tenant for Years, or Householder & Resident, in such Township or Precinct; and all Powers given to the Inhabitants of this Colony at their said Meetings by any Act or Acts of the General Assembly of this Colony shall be understood to extend only to the Freeholders, Tenants for Years, or Householders, being Residents in such Township or Precinct, and no others; any Law, Custom or Usage to the contrary thereof in anywise notwithstanding."

It thus appears certain that non-freeholders voted and had the right to vote in local elections in the colonial period; and that throughout the whole period of royal government the householders of two towns (for a time also those of a third) had the right to a share in electing the provincial representatives from those towns. The usual statement, therefore, that the suffrage in New Jersey was limited to freeholders must be qualified in large measure by the admission of householders in certain towns for the provincial suffrage, and householders throughout the whole colony in local elections. We have seen that from the first years of the royal administration an effort was made to extend the suffrage to non-freeholders. This movement was unsuccessful so far as the assembly suffrage was concerned, but the advice of the governors and the public agitation led to the cutting down of the freehold

[1] Act of June 28, 1766, " An Act explaining the Right of voting at Town-Meetings, and the Elections of Township Officers;" Allinson's *Laws*, 287.

qualification to the lowest degree; for if a man possessed any amount, however small, of land in freehold he could vote for representatives, if he also owned fifty pounds personal property. The local suffrage was still wider; all freeholders, of whatever size holding, could vote; and the same privilege was open also to all resident householders. By these provisions the suffrage in New Jersey was placed on a broader basis than in the neighboring colony of New York; while, on the other hand, it was not so liberal as in Pennsylvania.[1]

[1] The Pennsylvania qualification was fifty acres of land, of which twelve were cleared, *or* fifty pounds personal estate, *Statutes at Large,* II, 212–221, Act of January 12, 1705–6. But in certain local matters *only freeholders* could vote, *Statutes at Large,* IV, 116, Act of May 10, 1729, and *Pamphlet Laws,* 112, Act of 1771, March 9.

CHAPTER IX.

The Suffrage in Delaware.

A noteworthy fact which becomes apparent in a study of the suffrage in the middle colonies is the weakness or total absence of popular government in those colonies which were founded by the Dutch and Swedes, and in its early development within the English colonies, both northern and southern. That wide territory which later included the colonies of New York, New Jersey, Pennsylvania, and Delaware, has few facts to give to the student of popular political institutions until after its conquest by the English. During the fifty years of occupation of the Hudson Valley and the forty years of settlement on the Delaware there is not as much political activity as is to be seen in the first few years of one of the spontaneous political organizations of Englishmen. In the insignificant settlements of Maine, in the New Hampshire towns, among the one hundred Englishmen at Plymouth, in the towns of Rhode Island, Connecticut, New Haven, and on Long Island, political organizations appear as surely as the English names and features.

The search for the conditions of the suffrage in the early years of the middle colonies is, therefore, largely a search for those occasional and irregular elections through which the will of the people may have been expressed. And yet this search is not altogether a waste of time, for, if it does no more, it will aid in an appreciation of those regular political forms which were later introduced by the English.[1]

The Dutch were the first to settle on the Delaware River, where before 1650 they had established three forts. The fort at Swaanendael, near Cape Henlopen, however, was de-

---

[1] It is not intended to draw the inference that there is nothing of value in the early settlements on the Hudson and the Delaware. There are, of course, many important social, economic or personal facts in connection with these settlements, but for the constitutional historian there is often little to describe beyond an arbitrary military government.

stroyed by the Indians in 1631; Fort Beversrede was an insignificant trading station within the present limits of Philadelphia, perhaps erected in 1633; and the third one near the present Gloucester, New Jersey, was occupied from 1623 to 1651. After the latter date the Dutch destroyed Fort Nassau in New Jersey, and, moving to the west bank of the river, built Fort Casimir, near the present Newcastle, Delaware, and within menacing distance of the Swedish Fort Christina. In these early attempts at Dutch occupation the government appears purely military, and the forts served to protect the few settlers around them and also to furnish a post for the Indian trade. As late as 1648 Fort Beversrede on the Schuylkill had, owing to the encroachments of the Swedes, scarcely land enough for a " little garden," [1] and their trade was similarly hampered by the Swedes. Until the Dutch conquest of the lands on the South River it is impossible to find any political organization among the Dutchmen on the Delaware.

A similar conclusion will be reached regarding the English settlements. Some New Haven men doubtless came to the Delaware and perhaps occupied land in what is now Philadelphia; [2] but their occupation was of short duration. So, too, the county palatine of Sir Edmund Plowden, including the Delaware lands, was never organized by its proprietor. [3]

Turning from the Dutch and the English, therefore, we may examine the political conditions in the Swedish settlements. With the intrigues for the formation of the Swedish South Company we are not here concerned, [4] but its charter, granted in 1626, shows a typical seventeenth century trading company, [5] with no recognition of the political rights of the

---

[1] *Pa. Archives,* Second Series, VII, 467.

[2] 1641–2; Hazard, *Annals,* 59–64; *Pa. Archives,* Sec. Series, VII, 462; Brodhead, *Hist. of N. Y.,* I, 322; Scharf and Westcott, *History of Philadelphia,* I, 67.

[3] Hazard, *Historical Collections,* I, 160–174; Hazard, *Annals,* 36–39, 108–112.

[4] See Jameson, *William Usselinx.*

[5] Jameson, *Usselinx,* 114–117; Hazard, *Annals.* 16–20; *N. Y. Col. Doc.,* XII, 7–15.

colonists. An extension of time was granted to this company in 1633,[1] and in 1638 some Swedish settlers arrived on the South River and settled within the present limits of Wilmington, Delaware. The early organization of these Swedes is not clearly shown in the few existing documents of this period, but the control of affairs in the colony was apparently vested solely in a governor. By 1642 two such governors had been displaced and a third appointed.[2] The instructions and commission of the latter, John Printz, do not show any formal sharing of authority between the governor and the people, although the governor is cautioned to conduct himself so that he may be able to answer for it before God, the Queen, " and every brave Swede." [3] Down to the close of the Swedish rule there is apparently no change from the arbitrary rule of the company's governors, and no participation on the part of the settlers in the government of the colony.

In September, 1655, Governor Stuyvesant, from New Amsterdam, entered the South River with a force of seven hundred men, a greater number, perhaps, than the entire Swedish population on the river. By the terms of the capitulation, which followed as a matter of course upon this military display, those Swedes desiring to remain and taking an oath of allegiance to the Dutch government were to be guaranteed their lives, property, and their religion.[4] A vice-director was appointed by Stuyvesant to take charge of the Delaware settlements, receiving power to " keep order, do justice, and administer it either in civil or military cases;" but he should be assisted by a council composed of two named persons, and two sergeants in the trial of military offences, or " two most suitable freemen" in civil cases.[5]

Under the Dutch rule there are indications of occasional

[1] Hazard, 30, 34; Jameson, *Usselinx,* 161.

[2] *Ibid., Annals,* 57, 59, 62.

[3] *Ibid.,* 63; Hazard, *Register of Penna.,* IV, 200.

[4] *Ibid., Annals,* 185–190; *Pa. Archives,* Sec. Series, VII, 483–487; *N. Y. Col. Doc.,* I, 607–8; XII, 102–106.

[5] Hazard, 205–206; *Pa. Archives,* Sec. Series, VII, 490–493; *N. Y. Col. Doc.,* XII, 113.

popular participation in the colony's affairs. Thus, as early as 1656 a local court was established for the Swedes, composed of a sheriff (schout) and commissaries,[1] and evidently modelled after similar courts erected in the Dutch towns of New Netherland.[2]   These officials were chosen by Stuyvesant, but there appears to have been some popular action concerning the selection.[3]   The friendly attitude of Stuyvesant towards the Swedes did not meet with the approval of the West India Company, and in 1661, after about five years had passed, the Swedish sheriff was discharged.[4]

In the meantime the Dutch vice-director and his councillors had been holding court at Fort Casimir, directing military affairs, deciding civil and criminal cases, and occasionally calling in the inhabitants to give assistance.[5]   On November 8, 1656, the "whole community" appeared, and selected four persons from whom the vice-director later chose two proper persons as inspectors of tobacco. After this election the fencing of their lands was advised by the vice-director, and the community proceeded to elect two persons to serve as overseers and surveyors of fences. Later, the building of a bridge and the cutting of palisades for the fort

[1] *N. Y. Col. Doc.*, XII, 151. This court met at Tinicum Island (*ibid.* 159), and its jurisdiction was recognized by the vice-director's court at Fort Casimir.

[2] *Amer. Hist. Rev.*, VI, 6–9; *Pa. Archives*, Sec. Series, VII, 531–2. Military officers were also appointed among the Swedes. The West India Company thought this dangerous, but Stuyvesant wrote, " We have thought the most suitable [form of government] would be a lenient method of governing them and proceeding with them, to win their hearts and divert their thoughts from a hard and tyrannical form of government, and considering this we granted to the Swedish nation, at their request, some officers, that in time of necessity, against the savages and other enemies, in case of defence, they might keep order, but we gave them no written document or commission, much less were any arms distributed among them;" *Pa. Arch.*, Sec. Series, VII, 571.

[3] Compare *Pa. Arch.*, Sec. Series, VII, 511, with *N. Y. Col. Doc.*, XII, 151.

[4] *N. Y. Col. Doc.*, XII, 233, 271, 338, 345; *Pa. Archives*, Sec. Series, VII, 555.

[5] See Minutes of Administration of Jean Paul Jacquèt, *N. Y. Col. Doc.*, XII, 133–162.

were agreed upon.[1] A similar meeting was held about two months later, on January 10, 1657, at which the attention of the inhabitants was drawn to the high prices which some traders had been giving to the Indians for skins; and afterwards the community set a fixed price in wampum upon furs, and agreed mutually not to give more than this amount; and those violating the promise were to be considered perjurers.[2] In these two meetings the people took a part in election and in legislation in a way which does not differ materially from the New England town meeting, except that the meetings were called at irregular intervals, records of these two meetings alone remaining, and they did not, consequently, form an integral part of the local government.[3]

Another change in the control of the Delaware settlements was under consideration while these events were happening. In December, 1656, the Directors of the Dutch West India Company informed Stuyvesant that the company had ceded Fort Casimir, thereafter to be called New Amstel, and the land below it to the mouth of the river to the city of Amsterdam, and that the city would soon take steps to enlarge the colony and send over a director to govern it.[4] To encourage emigration to the new colony, the city published a set of conditions under which settlers could enter the colony.[5] In addition to many economic inducements, these conditions also promised very favorable political privileges; there should be a " schout" or " head of justice" appointed by the director at New Amsterdam, three burgomasters appointed

[1] *N. Y. Col. Doc.*, XII, 154-5.

[2] *Ibid.*, 157.

[3] The government of the Company's colony at Altona (Wilmington) was mainly under the control of the vice-director. On April 28, 1660, an inhabitant came before this officer and said, " that we ought to make new Commissaries every year, pursuant to the custom of Holland;" he inquired " whether he and other freemen were to be treated forever as boys," and declared "that they should not always be ruled by such clowns," etc. (*N. Y. Col. Doc.*, XII, 308.)

[4] *N. Y. Col. Doc.*, XII, 131-33.

[5] Laws of New Netherlands, 239-248, 269-288; *N. Y. Col. Doc.*, I, 630-636; Hazard, *Annals,* 220 ff.

by the common burghers from among the " honestest, fittest
and richest," and five or seven schepens (magistrates) selected by the director from a double number nominated by
the " body of the burghers." [1]   After the colony numbered
two hundred families, it was to elect a common council, and
the popular elections were to give place to a close corporation.

The officers were chosen by the people for the first time
in 1657,[2] and subsequently there must have been other elections, for in June, 1660, we learn of a meeting of the " community," and an election of commissaries;[3] and in 1664,
at the surrender of the New Amstel authorities to the English, a number of " burgomasters" signed the articles of
capitulation for themselves and " all the Dutch and Swedes
inhabiting in Delaware Bay and Delaware River." [4]   But
promises of free land, free seed corn, exemption from taxes,
and the grant of political power did not make the New
Amstel colony a success.   The colonists deserted and went
to neighboring English settlements, and the city was unable to get any return for its invested capital.[5]   Conflicts
of authority also occurred between the representatives of the
city of Amsterdam and those of the West India Company;[6]
and in addition to these internal difficulties, the English in
Maryland claimed the whole territory and threatened to use
force against the occupants.[7]

Further inducements to settlers were offered by the city
in 1661 and 1663 by throwing open the trade with the
colony to all persons, by promising independence of the New
Amsterdam authorities, and by giving greater freedom in
local affairs.[8]   This policy of local independence did not conform to Stuyvesant's ideas of government.   He thought it

---

[1] One election is noted by Hazard, *Annals*, 239; *N. Y. Col. Doc.*, XII,
319.

[2] Hazard. *Annals*, 239.

[3] *N. Y. Col. Doc.*, XII, 319.

[4] *Pa. Archives*, Sec. Series, V, 544.

[5] *N. Y. Col. Doc.*, II, 202; XII, 271, 408.

[6] *Ibid.*, XII, 197–199, 232–4, 287, 314, 326, 408, etc.

[7] *Ibid.*, 261.

[8] *Ibid.*, II, 173–175; *Laws of New Netherlands*, 388, 447.

would encourage the officials in the city's colony in their past usurpations of authority; further, it would lead the other villages and colonies to demand like privilege, and, under the early exemptions, these could not be denied, for each colony was to possess as great privileges as any single one obtained.[1]

Shortly after this the West India Company transferred to the city of Amsterdam all its possessions on the South River, and in October, 1663, Stuyvesant at New Amsterdam signed the deed of cession.[2] The English conquest of 1664 prevented a further development of the city's schemes of colonization. Amsterdam, from the first, had offered greater inducements to settlers than those advertised by the West India Company. The colony was treated as a business venture, for the success of which all means must be used. In addition to granting religious liberty, trade privileges, and free land, a further promise of political privileges was made; and as the failure of the colony became apparent, the concessions to settlers were made more extensive. But neither a commercial company nor a single city could secure the colony against foreign attack, and the States-General of the Netherlands would not give the necessary protection.

After New Amsterdam had surrendered to the English in 1664, Sir Robert Carre was sent to the Delaware to reduce the Dutch settlements on that river. The terms of surrender were similar to those granted to the inhabitants of New Amsterdam and the Hudson Valley.[3] The Dutch and Swedes had their property rights secured to them; they were permitted to leave the region within six months, and if remaining and taking the oath of allegiance, they were entitled to enjoy commercial and religious liberty, and their officers and magistrates were to " exercise their Customary Power in Adminison of Justice wth in their precincts, for Six Months or until his Maties pleasure" be known.[4]

[1] *N. Y. Col. Doc.*, XII, 374.

[2] *Ibid.*, II, 199; XII, 449. For reasons for this transfer see *N. Y. Col. Doc.*, II, 201 ; XII, 440–442, and Brodhead, *Hist. of N. Y.*, I, 714–716.

[3] *Ibid.*, III, 71–73; *Pa. Arch.*, Sec. Series, V, 544; Hazard, *Annals*, 364.

[4] *Ibid.*

For several years after this surrender, a dual form of government existed within the Delaware settlements; an English military commander with a force of twenty soldiers possessed superior authority on the River; but the civil government in the respective plantations was continued, and only in cases of dispute was the commander to call to his assistance five named inhabitants to act as councillors. The council, in which the commander had a double vote in case of a tie, could decide civil suits, give advice concerning the Indian trade, and supervise the military protection of the several plantations.[1] But the commander did not often interfere with the Dutch officers, and as late as 1670 and 1671 we find references to schouts and commissaries, who have the duties of the old Dutch officers.[2]

In the spring of 1665 Col. Nicholls had issued his code of laws known as the "Duke's Laws," but the operation of these was limited for a time to Long Island, and they were only gradually extended to the Delaware lands, where they were never fully in force. In 1668 the first step towards the establishment of the laws was taken,[3] and in 1671 the militia provisions of the Laws were extended to the Delaware.[4] The following year, the governor at New York, in commissioning a justice of the peace for the Delaware lands, directed him to observe the laws established for the Duke's territories,[5] and at last the final step in the establishment of English laws on the Delaware came by an order from Governor Andros, dated September 22, 1676.[6] It provided

" 1. That the booke of lawes Established by his Royall Highnesse, and practiced in New Yorke, Long Island, and Dependences bee likewise in force, and practiced in this River and Precincts, Except the Constables Courts, Country Rates, and some other things peculiar to Long Island, and the Millitia as now Ordered to remaine in the King, but that a Constable in each place bee yearely chosen for the Preservacon of his Maties Peace with all other Power as directed by the law."

[1] *N. Y. Col. Doc.*, XII, 461–2; *Pa. Arch.*, Sec. Series, VII, 722–3.
[2] Hazard, *Annals*, 380, 383.
[3] *N. Y. Col. Doc.*, XII, 462.
[4] *Ibid.*, 487.
[5] *Ibid.*, 495.
[6] *Ibid.*, 561–63; *Pa. Archives*, Sec. Series, VII, 783–785.

The order recognized three courts, at Whorekill, Newcastle, and Upland, to be composed of justices of the peace, having limited criminal and civil jurisdiction, and possessing the power to make by-laws for their respective territories, not repugnant to the laws of the government. Taxes could not be levied, except in extraordinary cases, without the consent of the governor. A sheriff was to be appointed by the governor for the whole Delaware region.

The democratic features of the laws as they were put in force in Long Island were not introduced by this order into the Delaware settlements.[1] There were no town meetings or constables' courts, and it is believed that there were no regular popular elections. The order of Andros did, indeed, provide for the election of constables, but these officials, as well as other local officers, were actually appointed by the courts. The three courts furnish the most distinctive feature of political organization on the Delaware down to Penn's time, and they gave a model for the later county government of Pennsylvania and Delaware, Before the English conquest, there had been three Dutch local courts on the Delaware, one for New Amstel (Newcastle),[2] another at Christina (later called Altona, now Wilmington),[3] and the third near the mouth of the Schuylkill on Tinicum Island.[4] When the city of Amsterdam obtained control of the entire Delaware region it is believed that the separate court at Altona was incorporated with that of Newcastle, while a rudimentary form of government was established for certain new plantations near the Cape called the Whorekill settlement.[5] These courts with their schouts and commissaries must have been the "inferiour Magistrates" mentioned in the articles of capitulation in 1664, and they may have existed continuously from that time until the order of September 22, 1676, formally adopted their organization as the basis of government for the river, although the occasional refer-

---

[1] See *Amer. Hist. Rev.*, VI, 718–723.
[2] *N. Y. Col. Doc.*, XII, *passim.*
[3] *Ibid., passim.*
[4] *Ibid.*, 211, 310.
[5] *Ibid.*, 229–230, 450.

ences in the records do not furnish absolute proof of their continuous action.[1]

An inspection of the records of two of these courts furnishes no evidence of popular elections.[2]   Both at Newcastle and at Upland the court appointed constables, overseers of highways, under-sheriffs, church-wardens, church-elders, attorneys, viewers of tobacco, vendu-masters, and perhaps other officers.[3]   The commissions of the justices of the several courts were stated to run for one year or until superseded, but often a new commission was not issued until considerably longer than a year.[4]   The courts appear to have been permitted, like the old Dutch courts, to nominate a list of persons from whom the governor might choose the new justices.[5]   In all this political and administrative activity of the local courts there is nothing to remind one of the town meetings and popular elections which were carried on under the Duke's laws on Long Island.[6]   With the possible exception of the town officers of Newcastle,[7] it seems

[1] In 1660 we find a record of the Court at Tinicum Island (*N. Y. Col. Doc.*, XII, 311), and in 1672 a similar court was being held on the neighboring mainland at Upland (Chester).   It is believed that the latter was a continuation of the previous Dutch court, with its place of meeting changed between 1660–1672, from Tinicum Island to Upland.   In 1669–70, January 25, an officer to preserve the peace was provided for Whorekill (*N. Y. Col. Doc.*, XII, 472), and in 1672 there had been in existence for some time a schout and commissaries (*Ibid.*, 496).

[2] The records of the court at Upland from 1672 until Penn's occupation have been printed in volume seven of the Memoirs of the Hist. Soc. of Penna.   A transcript of the Newcastle records, beginning in October, 1676, and continuing until 1681, has been made from the originals and deposited in the Hist. Soc. of Penna.   The copy has been used by the writer.

[3] See *Newcastle Court Records* (Pa. Hist. Soc. copy), I, 54, 74, 109, 136, 145, 163, 217, 285, 302–3, 460; II, 31, 32, 99, 165–68, 224, 328, 349; *Upland Court Records*, 57, 104, 184, 194.

[4] *Newcastle Court Records*, I, 3–7, 189–193, 250–252, 416–417; II, 265–266; *Upland Court Records*, 37, 165.

[5] *Newcastle Court Records*, I, 403; *N. Y. Col. Doc.*, XII, 606, 650.

[6] Even the popular election of militia officers was apparently forbidden, for the militia was "to remain in the King." (*N. Y. Col. Doc.*, XII, 561.)

[7] *N. Y. Col. Doc.*, XII, 496.

probable that no elections by the people were held on the South River under the government of the Duke of York.

With the cession of the Delaware lands to Penn the history of the lower settlements is for a time overshadowed by that of their more prosperous neighbors in Pennsylvania. It is probable that the local government, both of Delaware and Pennsylvania, was largely influenced by the previous powers of the three courts on the Delaware, for Penn's frames and laws, while singularly explicit regarding a general representative system, were almost silent upon the subject of local government, and it is quite likely, although perhaps not demonstrable, that he drew upon the existing forms for his county government.[1]

It is not necessary here to review the various suffrage provisions of the Pennsylvania legislation from 1682 to 1702, for the province and the territories were under the same government during this time. But jealousies between the two sections soon arose, and in 1699 some of the lower counties refused to elect representatives; and during Penn's second visit the conflict of interests continued, until in the charter of privileges of 1701 he inserted a provision permitting the legislative separation of the province and territories. Renewed contests between the two sections took place after the proprietor's departure for England, and in 1702 the lower counties, as in 1699, neglected to elect representatives under the charter of 1701.[2] This was taken by the Pennsylvania delegates to mean a separation, and when in 1704 the three counties again asked for representation they were refused admission to the Pennsylvania assembly.[3] From this time, therefore, may be dated the legislative separation of the "Three Lower Counties" from the province.

---

[1] The records during the Duke of York's control at first speak of the three "courts," avoiding the word county, even going so far as to describe the physical bounds of the courts; but the word county came in, either accidentally or intentionally, about 1679 or 1680. (*Newcastle Court Records*, II, 129-130, 188, 199–202; *Upland Court Records*, 165.)

[2] *Votes of Assembly of Penna.*, I, I, Appendix, xiv–xxv; *Col. Rec. of Pa.*, II, 72–84, 128–140.

[3] *Ibid.*, I, II, 4.

Access to the early laws of Delaware has not been had, and the first election law examined is that of 7 George II. (1734).[1] This act, entitled "An Act for regulating Elections, and ascertaining the Number of the Members of Assembly," was passed, as its preamble states, because the existing election laws were "uncertain and deficient." It provided for an annual assembly composed of at least six persons from each county, and stated the qualifications of electors and elected in similar form to those of Pennsylvania. A voter must be (1) a natural born subject of Great Britain, or have been naturalized in England, in this province, or in Pennsylvania; (2) of the male sex; (3) of twenty-one years of age; (4) be a freeholder within this government holding fifty acres of land, with twelve acres cleared and improved, or be otherwise worth forty pounds lawful money; (5) a resident for the term of two years. The law imposed a fine of five pounds upon persons voting without proper qualification, and a fine of twenty shillings upon those neglecting to vote when possessing the qualifications, unless detained by sickness or other unavoidable accident. Giving or receiving bribes were punishable by a fine of five pounds, as was also the offering to serve for nothing or less than the legal allowance of representatives.[2] The act required the use of paper ballots except in the case of illiterate persons, who were permitted to vote "verbally;" it provided for election inspectors, the giving of certain oaths to electors, and for the continuance of the polls from day to day until all those present were polled; and it gave in full the several oaths of allegiance and adjuration which must be taken by members of the assembly. Subsequent acts of 1766[3] and 1772[4] slightly changed the mode of choosing election inspectors, but the principal features of the act of 1734 continued without material change until the Revolution.

[1] Printed code of 1741, p. 76; code of 1752, p. 118.
[2] A person so elected was disqualified for office for the year in which the election took place.
[3] November 1, 1766, Adams' *Laws*, I, 429.
[4] June 13, 1772, Adams' *Laws*, I, 500; made perpetual by act of September 2, 1775.

An idea of a colonial election can be drawn from the words of the act of June 13, 1772. The sheriff of each county was required to furnish a ballot-box for each hundred, with the name of the hundred painted on the outside of the box. On election day the sheriff delivered these boxes to the inspectors for the respective hundreds, who evidently sat together in some convenient place in the county town. The elector presented his ballot to the inspector of the hundred in which he dwelt, and the inspector called aloud the name of the voter presenting his ballot, and then deposited it in the proper box. After the election was completed, and it might last several days, the sheriff must open each box separately and compare the number of ballots it contained with the number of persons who had been announced as voting in that hundred. When these were made to tally all the ballots were placed in one box and counted by the election clerks. There was a penalty of twenty shillings for voting more than once or even offering to do so.[1]

An early act [2] changed the term of sheriffs and coroners from three years to one year and provided for the election of a double number, from whom the governor should choose one to serve, or, if he neglected the duty, at the end of six days the person having the highest number of votes was to fill the office. The act of 13 George II.[3] shows in its preamble that in Delaware, as in Pennsylvania, the office of sheriff was much sought after. Candidates are said to "make it their frequent Practice to engage Persons to vote for them, by giving them strong Drink, and using other Means, inconsistent with the Design of free Voting at Elections; by Means whereof many unguarded Persons are drunk and disorderly more particularly at the Time of Elections; whereby great Confusions and Mischiefs arise." Steps were taken to prevent such evils by disqualifying the sheriff for three years after he had served three terms in succession; and by imposing a fine of ten pounds for giving any reward or promise of reward, and five pounds for receiving any such bribe.

[1] Adams' *Laws*, I, 500.
[2] Code of 1752, p. 29 (date not given).
[3] Code of 1741, p. 108; code of 1752, p. 133.

Many of the local officials were appointed by the county courts,[1] and in the few cases of election, the qualifications of the provincial suffrage are prescribed for local electors.[2] One exception to this rule existed in the borough suffrage ot Wilmington as determined by its charter of November 16, 1739.[3] The borough charter provided for two burgesses, six assistants, one high constable, and one town clerk, all of whom were to be annually elected by ballot by the inhabitants.   The suffrage was extended to all freeholders and to those housekeepers who had resided one year in the borough and hired a house and ground of the yearly value of at least five pounds.   The inhabitants were permitted to appoint other necessary officers and in town meetings to make convenient rules and ordinances, provided they were not repugnant to the laws of the " territories." [4]

Although the Delaware territories had a greatly varied history from the Swedish and Dutch settlements down to the Revolution, yet their population was small and economically homogeneous.   Racial differences existed, but these apparently did not influence politics.   Thus the suffrage question was never a vital one in this province as it was in New England or Maryland.   For fifty years of the early settlements there were no regular elections, and not until the act of 1734 was the subject carefully defined; but the act of that year remained almost unchanged down to the Revolution.   In local matters, while the levy court and the hundred organization are interesting forms of local government, they do not furnish anything of interest to a study of the suffrage.   Delaware's franchise laws followed closely those of Pennsylvania, with compulsory voting, and fines for neglect, as a most striking innovation.

[1] See acts of 15 Geo. II (code of 1752, pp. 200, 214, 220) ; 25 Geo. II (Adams, I, 316) ; November 1, 1766 (*ibid.*, 429) ; November 25, 1775 (*ibid.*, 544).

[2] Act of 16 Geo. II (code of 1752, p. 231).

[3] See *The Ordinances of the City of Wilmington, Delaware, to which are prefixed the Original Borough Charter and the Acts of the Legislature, now in force, relating to the City,* Wilmington, 1872.

[4] This charter is closely similar to those granted to Chester, Bristol, and Lancaster in Pennsylvania, see *post.* 296–297.

CHAPTER X.

The Suffrage in Pennsylvania.

Before King Charles's grant to William Penn, the Delaware lands were described as an "appendage of New York," and while a number of Dutch, Swedish, and English settlers had established themselves upon the soil of the present Pennsylvania before Penn's assumption of control, yet they had always been subject to some distant authority,—the Swedish governor at Christina, the Dutch director at New Amsterdam, or the Duke of York's deputy at New York. Among these early diverse racial elements there were no closely settled towns as in New England, few common interests, and consequently little common political activity. The court at Upland, in existence only a few years before Penn's grant, was the most dignified political body, which, throughout the first forty years and more of European settlement, met within the present limits of Pennsylvania. Popular suffrage was rarely exercised during this period, and never was permanently established. The few instances in which it occurred will be found mentioned in the articles upon the colonies of Delaware and New York.

Penn's charter from the king, therefore, furnishes us with a logical starting-point for a view of the suffrage in Pennsylvania. Within this charter distinct provision is made for popular legislative assemblies in which the inhabitants may join with the proprietor in the making of laws:

"Wee . . . Doe grant free, full & absolute power, by vertue of these presents to him & his heires . . . to ordeyne, make, Enact & vnder his and their Seales to publish any Laws whatsoever, for the raising of money for the publick vse of the said province, or for any other End appertayning either vnto the publick state, peace, or safety of the said Countrey, or vnto the private vtility of perticular persons, according vnto their best discretions, by and with the advice, assent and approbacon of the freemen of the said Countrey, or the greater part of them, or of their Delegates or Deputies . . ."[1]

[1] *Charter and Laws of the Province of Pennsylvania, 1682–1700,* 81.

The proprietor fully approved of this clause of the charter, and shortly after obtaining the legal title to the land he wrote a letter to the inhabitants promising them broad powers in self-government:

". . . I hope you will not be troubled at your change, and the king's choice, for you are now fixed at the mercy of no governor that comes to make his fortune great; you shall be governed by laws of your own making, and live a free, and, if you will, a sober and industrious people. I shall not usurp the right of any, or oppress his person. God has furnished me with a better resolution, and has given me his grace to keep it. In short, whatever sober and free men can reasonably desire for the security and improvement of their own happiness, I shall heartily comply with, and in five months resolve, if it please God, to see you. . . ." [1]

The same faith in popular government is also to be seen in the promise made in Penn's Proposals to Adventurers that even the matter of the division of lots and land tracts shall be left "to the majority of votes among the adventurers." [2] But it was his intention that he should be on the ground before the calling of the assemblies, for in his commission to his deputy, Markham, he expressly forbids his representative to call the people in assemblies. [3]

In the months immediately following the receipt of his grant, Penn and his friends were engaged in outlining a plan of government for the new colony. After many drafts [4] a "frame" of government was issued on April 25, 1682, comprising 24 numbered sections. [5] The frame enacted that "the government of this province shall, according to the powers of the patent, consist of the Governor and freemen of the said province; in form of a Provincial Council and General Assembly, by whom all laws shall be made, officers chosen and publick affairs transacted." The council was to consist of seventy-two members, and the assembly of two hundred members elected by the freemen; but the first assembly should be composed of all the freemen. The elec-

---

[1] Hazard, *Annals of Pennsylvania,* 502.

[2] *Ibid.,* 511.

[3] *Charter and Laws, 1682–1700,* Appendix, 470.

[4] See Shepperd, *Proprietary Government in Pa.,* 225–250, for a description of the extant manuscripts of these frames.

[5] *Charter and Laws, 1682–1700,* 91–99.

tion of councillors and assemblymen was to be by ballot, but the Frame did not give the qualifications of electors. This was added in a code of forty numbered sections called "The Laws agreed upon in England." [1] It is here that we first find a definition of the word *freeman*. That the royal charter had used it synonymously with *freeholder* is proved by the fact that the assembly is spoken of in one instance as made up of the freemen and in another case as composed of the freeholders.[2] The Frame had used only the word freemen, but by the Laws a freeman is declared to be one who (*a*) has purchased one hundred acres of land, or the heir of such an one; or (*b*) who has paid his passage across the Atlantic and taken up one hundred acres at the rent of one penny an acre, and cultivated ten acres thereof; or (*c*) who has been a servant and becoming free, has taken up fifty acres and cultivated twenty; or (*d*) who is an inhabitant, artificer, or other resident paying scot and lot to the government. All such freemen could vote for or serve in the Council or Assembly.

The qualifications in this clause may have been intended to distinguish between the county and the town suffrage. Scot and lot is a vague term, but its use here might mean a tax paid only in the towns; so that in the country districts of Pennsylvania where nearly every reputable citizen would be a freeholder the holding of land was to be a requisite to voting; while in the towns, where intelligent "artificers" might live and pay taxes, but frequently hold no land, the qualification of electors was changed to fit their conditions. In some of the other colonies a similar provision was made in order to meet the difference between the economic conditions of the towns and the country.[3] The clause, however, was never enacted in this form in Pennsylvania.

Another of the laws made in England added further restrictions upon the elector by requiring him to be twenty-one years of age, not convicted of ill-fame or of unsober or dishonest conversation, but professing faith in Jesus Christ.

[1] May 5, 1682, *Charter and Laws*, 99–103.
[2] Compare the phraseology of Lord Baltimore's patent.
[3] See N. Y., N. J., Va., etc.

When Penn arrived in the province he issued writs for the first assembly, not calling all the freemen, but directing the "freeholders" of the counties to elect seven representatives for each county.[1] This was a departure from the primary assembly of all the freemen which the frame directed should be first called, and also at variance with the representative organization as laid down in the frame. The motives of Penn in calling a representative body instead of a gathering of all of the freemen do not appear.

Foremost among the acts of the first assembly appears "An Act for Naturalization."[2] This had a marked bearing upon the suffrage, since it determined the manner in which a large number of foreigners might obtain freemanship. It was provided that all foreigners over twenty-one years of age holding land in fee should be held as freemen, if within three months they would *solemnly promise* allegiance to the king and fidelity to the proprietor. The assembly also went on to debate "what Persons are fit to be elected, as also who are fit to make Election."[3] The fruit of this debate is seen in a few changes which the Great Law [4] made in the laws agreed upon in England. Both electors and elected must now believe in "Jesus Christ to be the son of God, the Saviour of the World;" but they were freed from the clause requiring a definite part of their lands to be cultivated. All freeholders must indeed have their lands "seated" or settled, but no longer need they have ten or twenty acres under cultivation. Those paying scot and lot retained their right to vote. These provisions—one hundred acres of land seated, or fifty acres for freed servants, and the payment of scot and lot—continued in force until all the proprietary legislation was set aside by Governor Fletcher in 1693.

[1] *Charter and Laws*, 472. The preface to Vol. I of the *Votes of Assembly* says that this first assembly was attended by "so many of the Freemen as thought fit to attend" (*Votes*, I, p. iii) ; but the writ proves that the assembly was a representative and not a primary organization ; and the *Votes* themselves on the first page record an undue election for one of the Newcastle members.

[2] *Ibid.*, 105 ; *Votes*, I, I. 4.   [3] *Votes*, I, I. 4.

[4] Chapters II and LVII, *Charter and Laws*, 108, 121.

While there was no change in the legal qualifications of the suffrage [1] in the period of ten years, yet several interesting administrative facts may be mentioned. Both the frame of 1682 and that of 1683 required the election of representatives by ballot, but this appears not always to have been carried out, and we are unfamiliar with the actual details of the process when the balloting-box was used.

As early as March, 1682–3, a question in the assembly was settled by a bean ballot, which is described in the following words: "the Number of Votes was decided by Beans, put into the Balloting-Box; and by the major Votes, it was carried in the Affirmative." [2] A contested election case in Philadelphia in 1689 shows a lack of uniformity existing in election procedure. There appears no objection to ascertaining the election upon the "view" of the sheriff, by the acclamation of the electors, except, as in this case, where a number of unqualified persons mingled with the electors and by acclamation carried the election of their candidate. The petitioners to the council aver that fifty or sixty "Welsh men" and persons "out of Jarsey" had elected a councillor who would not have received a majority of legal votes had a poll or ballot been taken. Yet in the new election which was ordered the sheriff stated in his return that the freemen were not willing to vote by ballot, preferring by voice to elect their councillors. [3] The second election was questioned also when the returns were sent to the council, because it was not taken by ballot. And again there appeared great confusion of thought and practice. One member said that the ballot was only used when doubt existed as to the candidate receiving the majority of votes (voices); another stated that the ballot was used only in Philadelphia County, while in other places "we are elected by vote." But this was denied by a third member who said that at Upland (Chester) and all the lower counties the election was made by putting black and white beans into

---

[1] The frame of April 2, 1683, did not change the suffrage conditions, although it greatly modified the organization of the legislature.

[2] *Votes*, I, I, 8. [3] *Col. Rec.*, I, 268, 279, 281–2.

a hat, " which is a ballotting in his sense."[1]   Among the patent reasons for neglect of the ballot was the desire to finish the elections in a short time in order that the farmers, who often travelled many miles to vote, might return home in good season.   Another reason without doubt was the fact that many of the electors could not write out their ballots, and must either have the ballot written for them or, by voting *viva voce*, proclaim to the other electors their inability to write.

In 1692 Penn was dispossessed of his government, and Governor Fletcher, of New York, was commissioned royal governor of Pennsylvania and the " Countrey of Newcastle," with as great powers as those he possessed in New York,[2] including the power to call assemblies elected by the majority of the freeholders.   The sole change in the suffrage by this royal assumption of control is found in the omission of the scot and lot inhabitants and in the removing the requirement of a definite size of freehold.   Fletcher appears unwilling to enlarge or limit the terms of his commission in this respect, and although in the " Petition of Right" he agreed to eighty-six chapters of the statutes passed before his time, yet Chapter II of the Great Law of 1682, giving the property qualifications of voters, was omitted, while Chapter LVII, containing the religious qualification, was retained.   The natural inference to be drawn from this omission is that Fletcher did not care to add the scot and lot payers to the freeholders of his commission nor to restrict the latter word to those possessing one hundred acres or more of settled land.   There can be no doubt, however, that little actual change in the suffrage was made by the omission of the previous qualifications.   The scot and lot voters must have been few in number and confined to Philadelphia County, where the city of Philadelphia and the bor-

[1] West Jersey had advanced to a more definite method, for as early as September, 1683, it was provided that votes were to be given in writing upon pieces of paper (*Leaming and Spicer*, 478).   Compare also the corn and bean ballot in Mass. and Conn., and the ballot in South Carolina.

[2] October 21, 1692, *Pennsylvania Col. Rec.*, I, 352–7; *New York Col. Doc.*, III, 856–860.

ough of Germantown, the only incorporated places in the province,[1] were situated.

Penn's province was restored to him by the Crown on August 20, 1694,[2] and shortly afterwards Penn commissioned William Markham as his governor. After a long contest with the assembly,[3] Markham issued a new frame of government, the third which the province had received.[4] Markham's frame restored the term freeman, which had been changed by Fletcher's commission to freeholder, and defined the term in a manner which was but slightly changed down to the Revolution:

" 3. And to the end, It may be known who those that in this Province & territories have right of, or be deemed freemen to Choose or to be Chosen to serve in Council and assembly as aforesaid:

" *Be it Enacted by the authority aforesaid,* That no Inhabitant of this ·Province or Territories, shall have right of electing or being elected as aforesaid, Unless they be free Denizens of this government and are of the age of Twenty-one years or upwards, and have fifty acres of land, ten acres whereof being seated and cleared, or be otherwise worth fifty pounds lawful money of this government Clear estate, and have been Resident within this government for the space of two years next before such election."

Here for the first time we have a definite suffrage provision clothed in a modern phraseology and adapted to the needs of a community which was receiving large numbers of foreign immigrants into its midst. The voter must be a free denizen of the government; that is, if foreign-born he must have become naturalized and taken the oaths or affirmations of allegiance to the Crown and fidelity to the proprietor; he must be twenty-one years of age and have resided in the province at least two years. The old mediæval

[1] The charter of 1691 to Philadelphia, may or may not have been in force in 1693. The exact status of affairs under this charter has not yet been determined by local historians. Germantown received the first borough charter granted in the province, in 1689. *Penna. Archives,* I, 111–115; Holcomb, *Johns Hopkins University Studies,* IV, 158.

[2] *Charter and Laws,* 245.

[3] See Shepperd, *Proprietary Government in Pa.,* 278–283.

[4] During session of assembly, October 26–November 7, 1696.

alternative to the freehold—the scot and lot—was changed to a definite personal property qualification.

Three years after the granting of Markham's frame a most interesting contest arose over the neglect of the suffrage by certain counties. Fines for refusal to hold office and perform political duties were common in the early history of almost all the colonies, and in a number there existed punishments for individual neglect of the suffrage,[1] while Massachusetts fined towns refusing to elect representatives; but it was left for the Pennsylvania legislature of 1699 to exceed all other legislation of this nature. The three lower Delaware counties were growing restive under the increase of wealth and population in the three Pennsylvania counties, and feared an early increase in the number of counties in the province, with a consequent breaking down of the equality of representation between the province and the territories.[2] In 1699 the freemen of Newcastle County, duly warned by the sheriff, met for purposes of election, but utterly refused to make any selection of representatives. This refusal was termed by the assembly a great contempt of the governor and the authority of the government and " a most manifold Slight of that inestimable priviledge of being represented in Legislation by reason of their owne choice."[3] The assembly then proceeded to force the " inestimable priviledge" upon the people by placing a penalty of one hundred pounds fine upon any county refusing to elect representatives, and providing that the sum could be levied by distress and sale of the goods of any four or more inhabitants of the county, who should be reimbursed by a county tax upon all property. Heavy fines were also imposed upon individual sheriffs neglecting their duties in elections, and upon representatives refusing to serve when elected.[4]

The Delaware members attended the sessions of the next two assemblies, but their attendance must have been due more largely to the presence of the proprietor than to the threats contained in the law of 1699. Penn, himself, recog-

[1] Early Md., Mass., Del., Va., etc.
[2] *Votes,* I, I, 130.
[3] *Charter and Laws,* 278.
[4] *Ibid.,* 279.

nized the differences between the two sections in his charter of 1701, and made provision for the legislative separation of the territories from the province, a permission taken advantage of by the lower counties in 1702.

The assembly meeting in the fall of 1700, under the direction of Penn, revised and re-enacted the laws of the province,[1] making little change in the suffrage conditions. Fifty acres of freehold or fifty pounds of personal estate were retained as stated by Markham's frame, but it was now required that twelve acres of the freehold, instead of ten, should be cleared and improved.[2] An act for naturalization, passed at the same session, put this power into the hands of the proprietor or his governor.[3] Penn's new frame of government, signed October 28, 1701, did not specify the qualifications of electors, but referred to the act of November 27, 1700. It reinstated, however, the former religious qualification for office-holders, requiring their belief in Christ as the Saviour of the world.[4] This test was strengthened beyond the terms of the charter by later action. As early as 1703 [5] the members of assembly took the various English tests, either by oath or affirmation, against the political or spiritual control of the Pope, denying the doctrine of transubstantiation, and denouncing the adoration of the Virgin and the practice of the mass.

For several years after Penn's departure for England, the subject of the suffrage does not appear in any of the records. The attention of the legislature, however, was called to the conduct of elections in 1705 through a petition from Philadelphia County, setting forth how an election had been determined first by the " vote" (*viva voce*), and, as the

---

[1] *Statutes at Large*, II, 3–141.

[2] *Ibid.*, 24.

[3] *Ibid.*, 29. Both of these acts were repealed by the Queen in Council, February 7, 1705–6. The reason given for repealing the election act was that it provided for advertisement of elections on trees or houses as well as court houses. " It ought to have been ' churches, chapels, and public meeting-houses !'" (*Statutes at Large*, II, Appendix, 465.)

[4] *A Collection of Charters and other Publick Acts Relating to the Province of Pennsylvania*, Philadelphia, B. Franklin, 1740.

[5] *Votes*, I, II, 1.

time grew late, the country people set out for their homes, but that afterwards the ballot-box was called for, and by the votes of servants and unqualified persons, the candidate of the country people was set aside.[1]   The episode led to a new and comprehensive election law, the terms of which appear to have called forth considerable debate in the assembly. Among the questions discussed was that of allowing the qualified inhabitants of the city of Philadelphia to vote for the two city members and for the eight county members as well, thus giving them a double vote.[2]   A proposal to require fifty pounds *value* of real estate in the counties and fifty pounds of personal property in the city was voted down,[3] and the qualifications as laid down in the act of 1700 were adopted.[4]   The act itself, consequently, is of more value in the making, and as showing new administrative provisions to protect the suffrage than because it introduces new qualifications.[5]

It is not our part to analyze the election laws of the colony, but reference may be made to some of the important provisions of this first general election law.   The legislature is composed of eight members from each county and two from the city of Philadelphia.   Electors are to be native or naturalized citizens, twenty-one years of age, residents of the province for two years, and possessing fifty acres of freehold, twelve of which is cleared, or fifty pounds personal property.   Fines are imposed upon those voting who do not possess these qualifications, as also for bribery or voting more than once.   Elections are to be by written ballots deposited in boxes, with the polls open from ten in the morning till two in the afternoon, and adjourning from day to day.   Provision is made for judges, inspectors, and

[1] *Penna. Magazine of History and Biography*, II. 452.
[2] *Votes*, I, II, 69.
[3] *Ibid.*, 76.   A requirement of £50 value of real estate would have been almost prohibitive, for as late as 1775, in Philadelphia County (outside the city), the wealthiest and most populous county in the colony, there were only 147 persons assessed at over £50 out of a total rateable population of 6941 persons.
[4] *Ibid.*, 70.
[5] *Statutes at Large*, II, 212–221 ;   Act of January 12, 1705–6.

clerks of election; for returns by indenture to the governor and the assembly, and for fines upon those refusing to serve after election. The provisions of this act furnished the outline for all subsequent laws upon the subject in the colony. There were frequent changes in the method of selecting the election officials, particularly after the counties were divided into voting precincts, but the main provisions of the act of 1706 remained unchanged.

At the same session of assembly an act was passed regulating the elections of sheriffs and coroners,[1] which soon became a source of trouble. The act prescribed the method of electing these officers, but it did not state exactly the qualifications of electors at such elections. It was doubtless understood that the body of electors was the same for sheriffs and coroners as for representatives, since the former officers were to be elected in a double number after the election of assemblymen had taken place. From this double list of nominees the governor should choose one for each office, or, if he neglected this duty, then the person having the highest number of votes should assume the position.[2] The voters in this act were described as " freemen and electors," " freemen and inhabitants," and " freemen or electors," apparently making a distinction between the words freeman and elector. It was this ambiguity which led to disorders at elections and to the participation of many poorer people in the balloting for sheriffs and coroners. In January, 1713–14, a petition from Philadelphia called attention to the defects of the law,[3] but the assembly gave no redress. The following year the assembly was compelled to set aside both the persons receiving an apparent majority,[4] and two years later they passed an act limiting the suffrage for sheriffs and coroners to those qualified to vote for representatives.[5]

---

[1] Act of January 12, 1705–6, *Statutes at Large*, II, 272–5.

[2] Compare the common Dutch practice of double and triple nominations (*American Historical Review*, VI, 712–713).

[3] *Votes*, II, 146; *Statutes at Large*, III, 138.

[4] *Ibid.*, 159, 166.

[5] *Ibid.*, 213; *Statutes at Large*, III, 138–140; act of August 24, 1717. This act required each voter to present on one piece of paper the names

Exactly the same misinterpretation was made regarding the choice of election inspectors under the act of 1706, by the mingling of unqualified persons among the electors and their taking part in the *viva voce* vote for inspectors.[1]   Petitioners from Chester County first called the attention of the assembly to the abuse in 1726, and although a supplementary act was passed the following year,[2] yet great disorders occurred in 1739,[3] and the machinery of election was thereafter frequently changed in detail in order to adjust it to these conditions.[4]

From 1706 onward the interest in the suffrage in Pennsylvania centres not in the electors but in the masses of non-voters, who, legally disqualified, used every possible means to influence the elections.   One sees them frequently in the background of the election picture with sticks or stones or even " billets of wood," instead of the forbidden ballots, trying by physical means to express their opinions. From the point of view of the ruling class they are " servants," or " great numbers of disorderly persons," or " an outrageous Multitude," who, by " their rude and disorderly behaviour" disturb the elections, or who " presumed to vote when they did not have the right so to do."   Mention has already been made of their place in the city election of 1705, and how their interference in other elections compelled greater and greater stringency and accuracy of statement in the election laws.

---

of eight persons for representatives, two names for coroner, and six names for assessors of the county. The act of March 20, 1724–5 changed this from one piece to three distinct papers, one for each of the three classes of officers voted for. (*Votes*, II, 309; *Statutes at Large*, IV, 10.)

[1] *Statutes at Large*, IV, 331.

[2] *Votes*, III, 8, 9, 14, 25, 31; *Statutes at Large*, IV, 77; *Col. Rec.*, III, 277-8.

[3] *Ibid.*, 324, 337; *Statutes at Large*, IV, 331.

[4] *Statutes at Large*, IV, 375; V, 16, 153, 465; and *Pamphlet Laws,* acts of March 4, 1763, February, 1766, February 26, 1773. In one of these laws occurs the only instance known of the application of the term " hundred" to a political unit in Pennsylvania history (*Statutes at Large*, IV, 331) ; the hundred being a subdivision of the county for purpose of choosing election inspectors.

If our space permitted, it would be interesting to note the part played by these persons in a number of later contested elections. In 1739 Chester County sends up its protest against them;[1] and in 1742 it is Philadelphia which objects to its "bloody election" and the interference of a band of "strange sailors."[2] In 1749 Lancaster County has a great scandal, unqualified persons and even boys voting, some casting three, five, or ten ballots, and the total of votes cast perhaps more than doubling the number of voters at the election.[3] The following year, York County has its turn, and recounts a sorry story of the sheriff driven from the ballot-box and the polling place by a "multitude of People, chiefly Germans."[4] In 1752 Bucks County sent its petition against "able Freeholders greatly questioned, and others (perhaps making a better Figure) though insufficient, accepted" as electors; and York County again had a protest, this time against candidates "laying open the Public Houses at the Time of Election."[5] In almost every one of these cases the assembly tried to patch up the election law at the point where its weakness had admitted the unqualified persons. After 1752, frequent changes were made in the law for the choice of inspectors of election,[6] and at last these officers were required to use the constables' lists of taxables to aid them in judging of the qualifications of voters.[7] This machinery of election must have become more closely adapted to the wishes of the legislators, for in the later years there is little record of election disputes, and Acrelius, in 1758, in describing the method of election in the province, makes no reference to the excluded classes, although he gives a circumstantial and detailed account of elections.[8]

That the disqualified class was a large one is a patent

[1] *Votes*, III, 324, 337; *Col. Rec.*, IV, 335; *Statutes at Large*, IV, 331.
[2] *Ibid.*, 497–506, 521 and appendix; *Col. Rec.*, IV, 620–638; *Statutes at Large*, IV, 375; *Penna. Mag. of Hist.*, V, 11.
[3] *Ibid.*, IV, 117–126; Mombert, *History of Lancaster County*, 150.
[4] *Ibid.*, 150, 152; *Col. Rec.*, V, 468.
[5] *Ibid.*, 204–5; *Statutes at Large*, V, 159.
[6] Acts of March 11, 1752; September 29, 1759; March 4, 1763; February 8, 1766; February 26, 1773.
[7] Acts of March 11, 1752, and February 8, 1766.
[8] *Memoirs. Penna. Historical Society*, XI, 119–121.

fact; but it is difficult to arrive at any definite conclusion concerning the proportion which the voting class bore to the whole male population. An inspection of assessment lists may give some clue to the size of the class exercising the suffrage. The Historical Society of Pennsylvania has three tax-lists in its general collections—one for the county of Philadelphia for 1693,[1] another for Chestnut, South, and Middle wards of the city for 1754,[2] and the third for Chestnut, Lower Delaware, and Walnut wards of the city for 1767.[3]

In 1693 the suffrage was based on the instructions to Governor Fletcher, which limited the franchise to freeholders. Unfortunately, the tax-list of that year does not show the property upon which the assessment was made, and hence does not give the exact number of freeholders.[4] The list shows one hundred and eighty-six persons paying

[1] "By Virtue of a Law made at Philadelphia by a Gen[ll] Assembly held the 15th May, 1693. For Granting One penny per pound To King William & Queen Marey, etc."

[2] "A Tax of two pence in the pound and six shillings per head Laid on the Estates of the Freeholders & Inhabitants of the City of Philadelphia. . . . Assessed the 20th day of Aug. 1754."

[3] "We the subscribers Overseers of the poor have laid the following Tax of two pence in the pound and six shillings p. head on the Estates and Inhabitants of the City of Philadelphia."

Dated December 12, 1767.

	Total.	Men.	Women.	Poll tax.
* City	356	342	14	77
Northern Liberties	61	59	2	28
Oxford Township	32	31	1	9
Cheltenham	23	23	..	8
Bristol Township	16	16	..	5
Germantown Township	51	50	1	11
Plimouth Township	2	2	..	1
Byberry	18	18	..	3
Upper Precinct	5	5	..	1
Dublin	27	27	..	1
Passiunk, Wiccaco, Moyamensing	27	27	..	9
Beyond Schuykill	18	18	..	1
Welsh tract	69	67	2	24
Total	705	685	20	186

poll-tax out of a total male taxable population of six hundred and eighty-five; but even this does not give us a clue to the suffrage, for the least amount of property assessed was thirty pounds; those having less than that being taxed on the head, among whom must have been many small freeholders. We are forced to turn from this to the second one of 1754.

At this time, under the act of 1706, those inhabitants had the right to vote who held fifty acres of land or fifty pounds value of property, real or personal. The tax-list gives us the taxables for Chestnut, South, and Middle wards of the city of Philadelphia. It may be taken for granted that no one held fifty or more acres in any of these wards,[1] and that the distinction between the voting and non-voting classes can be based upon the value of the property held.[2] The list shows a total of four hundred and eighty-six male taxables, of whom sixty-three, or about 13 per cent., were assessed for fifty pounds or over. The list of 1767[3] shows fifty-three out of three hundred and sixty-four male taxables possessing fifty pounds or over; a proportion of nearly 15 per cent.

It is difficult to determine at this late day what relation the assessed value of property bore to its market value, and

[1] Penn's final plan of division of city lots gave two acres in the city to each purchaser of one hundred acres in the country.

[2] Summary of Philadelphia City taxables for 1754:

	Men.	Women.	Taxed on Poll.	Males assessed over £50.
Chestnut Ward	99	14	19	22
South Ward	142	10	22	17
Middle Ward	245	22	30	24
Total	486	46	71	63

[3] Summary of Philadelphia City taxables for 1767:

	Men.	Women.	Taxed on Poll.	Males assessed over £50.
Chestnut Ward	114	11	36	20
Lower Delaware	139	13	43	20
Walnut Ward	111	21	32	13
Total	364	45	111	53

it is not clear whether the assessment lists were made the sole basis for the voting privileges, since the laws of 1752 and 1766 stated that the tax-lists were to be given to the election inspectors to enable them " the better to judge of the quali- fications of the electors." [1]   But making all possible allow- ances for these elements of error, the fact is apparent that only a small minority of the male inhabitants of the city of Philadelphia were legally qualified for exercising the elec- toral franchise.

Access has also been gained to two other assessment lists, from which some valuable deductions may be made.   One of these is for certain farming districts in Philadelphia County, showing not only the value of the estates but also the exact number of acres of land owned by each freeholder in the spring of 1776.   Another is a list of the taxable in- habitants for the whole city and county of Philadelphia for the year 1775.[2]   From these lists a valuable comparison can be made showing the extent of the suffrage in a populous farming community and in the city of Philadelphia.

The list for 1776 gives us the taxable inhabitants of twelve townships in the northwestern part of Philadelphia County.[3] showing the nature and amount of each taxable's estate. By a count of the names and estates here given, it appears that among fourteen hundred and fifty-five male taxable in- habitants, seven hundred and forty-three, or a little over 50 per cent., owned fifty or more acres of land.   It must be remembered, too, that this was a populous district, near the city of Philadelphia, where, if anywhere in the colony, farms would be small.   In the back counties where land was cheap and farms large, the proportion of voters to the whole male population may have been even higher.   Such a proportion, making one person in every two taxable males a voter, would

[1] *Statutes at Large*, V, 156; VII, 37.

[2] " A tax of three Pence in the Pound and Nine shillings per Head laid on the Estates of the Freeholders and Inhabitants of the City and County of Philadelphia for paying Assembly Mens Wages, Building and Repairing of Bridges, Destroying Wolves, Foxes and Crows, and other Exigencies of the County for the ensuing Year.

Assessed the 31st day of March, 1775."

[3] The following table gives a summary of the taxable inhabitants of these townships according to the assessment of 1776:

give us perhaps one elector in every ten or twelve of the population.

On the other hand, those who were qualified to vote under the fifty pounds clause in the country must have been very few in number. In 1775 the twelve townships mentioned contained only fourteen persons who were assessed for fifty pounds or over. In places more distant from the centre of wealth and population, the proportion owning that amount was even smaller. An assessment list of Berks County for 1774 shows only twenty-nine taxables assessed for fifty pounds or over out of a total taxable population of three thousand eight hundred and eighty-five, or not one in a hundred! Evidently, if the assessment lists were used as the law directed to determine a man's qualification for the suffrage, very few received that privilege under the fifty pounds provision.[1]

TAX OF 1776.	TOTAL TAXABLE INHABITANTS.	WOMEN TAXABLES.	MALE TAXABLES.				PERSONS ASSESSED FOR £50 OR OVER.*
			Men having over 50 acres.	Men having under 50 acres.	Men paying poll taxes.	Total male taxables.	
Frankford and New Hanover..	183	4	98	74	7	179	0
Douglas township............	159	3	77	66	12	156	2
Upper Hanover township......	130	1	74	35	20	129	1
Limerick township...........	139	4	76	40	19	135	0
Upper Salford township......	108	2	52	31	23	106	0
Lower Salford "	79	1	42	23	13	78	0
Frederick "	71	3	33	28	7	68	0
Perkiomen and Skeipack township	97	0	61	23	13	97	3
Franconia township	78	3	47	15	13	75	0
Bristol "	88	3	28	44	13	85	4
Norriton "	120	0	39	58	23	120	1
Providence "	232	5	116	85	36	227	3
	1484	29	743	520	199	1455	14

* The figures of last column are taken from the list of preceding year (1775). It is unlikely that any considerable change took place.

[1] "A Register of the Eighteenth 18 Penny Provincial Tax and a County Tax, Assessed and Laid on the Inhabitants of the County of Berks, in the Month of December, A. D. 1774." I have used the MS. transcript in the Pennsylvania Historical Society.

While, however, the fifty acres requirement was met by nearly one-half of the adult male population in the country districts, it would be almost prohibitive in the city and boroughs, where the franchise would of necessity be based upon the value of estates rather than their area. The tax-lists lead to the belief that fifty acres of land and fifty pounds estate were by no means equivalent terms; and the franchise was more widely extended in the country than in the city of Philadelphia or the boroughs.[1]

A tax-list for 1775 gives the value, but not the size of the estates of all taxable inhabitants of the city and county. Taking the figures from this list,[2] it is clear that the suffrage was

[1] The restriction of the suffrage in the city has been ascribed to the desire of the ruling party to keep control of the government, by limiting the voters in Philadelphia and the number of representatives in the western counties. (C. H. Lincoln, *The Revolutionary Movement in Penna., 1760–1776*, 45; and *Penna. Mag. of Hist.*, XXIII, 27 note.)

[2] The following table gives a summary of this tax-list.

CITY.	TOTAL TAXABLE INHABITANTS.	FEMALE TAXABLES.		MALE TAXABLES.			
		Over £50.	Under £50.	Over £50 estate.	Under £50 estate.	Poll tax.	Total male taxables.
Dock Ward................	891	9	29	87	597	169	853
Walnut Ward..............	96	2	2	10	67	15	92
South Ward...............	153	5	2	16	97	33	146
Middle Ward	362	7	19	43	225	68	336
Chestnut Ward............	103	3	4	14	68	14	96
Lower Delaware Ward......	132	3	3	15	80	31	126
High Street Ward..........	161	3	9	18	109	22	149
North Ward	410	6	20	46	262	76	384
Mulberry Ward	1121	6	36	65	916	98	1079
Upper Delaware Ward	196	0	5	21	140	30	191
Total for city.............	3625	44	129	335	2561	556	3452
County outside city.........	6941	..	..	147*	5789*	1005	..
Entire city and county.......	10566	44	129	482	8350	1561	..

* Female taxpayers have not been distinguished in the county; but the number is so small as to be insignificant.

far more restricted in the urban than in the suburban and rural districts. In the city for the year 1775 out of a total of three thousand four hundred and fifty-two male taxables, there were only three hundred and thirty-five persons who were

TAXABLES, COUNTY OUTSIDE CITY.

TOWNSHIP.	Over £50.	Under £50.	Polls.	Total.
Abington	3	113	18	134
Blockley...............................	1	107	26	134
Bristol	4	74	16	94
Byberry	o	76	16	92
Cheltenham	2	85	22	109
Douglas................................	2	152	9	163
Frederick	o	90	7	97
Franconia	o	68	12	80
Frankford and New Hanover	o	165	16	181
Germantown	12	391	79	482
Gwinedth	o	111	27	138
Hatfield...............................	o	73	9	82
Harsham...............................	1	93	31	125
Kingsessing	10	66	9	85
Lower Merion	2	136	54	192
Lower Dublin	3	153	46	202
Lower Salford	..	58	20	78
Limrick	1	127	19	147
Moyamensing..........................	2	69	7	78
Montgomery...........................	1	73	12	86
Manor of Moreland	..	236	51	287
Marlborough,..........................	1	78	12	91
Norriton	1	96	20	117
Northern Liberties, West Part...........	18	430	41	489
Northern Liberties, East Part	25	498	52	575
Oxford	6	118	17	141
Plymouth.............................	1	74	26	101
Providence............................	3	197	30	230
Passyunk..............................	4	82	9	95
Perkiomen and Skippack................	3	85	18	106
Roxborough...........................	5	83	19	107
Southwark............................	24	680	67	771
Springfield............................	1	74	12	87
Tonamencin...........................	..	66	23	89
Upper Hanover........................	..	102	22	124
Upper Salford	..	87	21	108
Upper Merion.........................	1	82	21	104
Upper Dublin.........................	2	94	23	119
Whitemarsh...........................	6	135	38	179
Whitpain	..	99	13	112
Worcester.............................	2	113	15	130
	147	5789	1005	6941

assessed for fifty pounds or more; or scarcely one taxable male in ten by this assessment had the proper qualification for the suffrage. It is recognized that there may be some elements of error in this list; the property may have been purposely undervalued, some of the city inhabitants may have owned fifty acres or more in the country, and some personal property may not have been assessed at all. But making allowance for such errors, it is still believed that the proportion of voters to non-voters in the city is relatively small.

Looking over all of these assessment lists, it would appear that one man in every two taxables had the right to vote in the country districts; and estimating the taxables at one-fifth of the total population, we would find the franchise conferred upon one person in ten of the entire population of the farming communities. In the city of Philadelphia, on the other hand, where the fifty pounds clause would be the only qualification, but one taxable in ten possessed the requisite amount of property; or, using the same proportion of taxables to the whole population, only one person in fifty of the city population was shown by the tax assessments to be qualified for the suffrage. There is thus a remarkable difference between the number of legal voters in the country and in the city in Pennsylvania. It may be further noted that the limited suffrage in Philadelphia does not compare favorably with the municipal franchise in New York, where the voting class, owing to the admission of inhabitants as voters, must have been several times larger than that in Philadelphia. The laws of Pennsylvania undoubtedly worked to the disadvantage of the mechanics and artisans of the city.

We have hitherto been discussing the suffrage for the colonial legislature, but we may glance rapidly at a few instances in which the local suffrage qualifications varied from the provincial requirements.

The early history of local institutions in Pennsylvania is still involved in considerable obscurity, although some short studies of the subject have been made.[1] Setting aside the

[1] E. R. L. Gould, *J. H. Univ. Studies*, I; W. P. Holcomb, *Penna. Boroughs, J. H. Univ. Studies*, IV; Howard, *Local Const. Hist. in U. S.; Allinson and Penrose, Phila.*, xv–xliii.

conditions in the Swedish and Dutch days, and even those under the Duke of York's government, there still remain several problems in connection with the early history of institutions. Prominent among these is the question of the origin and functions of the Pennsylvania township. There is a strong contrast between the sturdy and com-pact New England town corporation and the vague and indefinite township in Pennsylvania in the seventeenth and eighteenth centuries. In New England the town is usually erected in a definite way, has precise boundaries, fixed powers, and distinct individuality. In Pennsylvania it is difficult to determine how the township began, and often we learn it is in existence in an accidental way by occasional references, rather than see its beginning in a formal act of incorporation. In a similar manner the functions of the early township, and even the titles of its officials, are lost in a fog of ambiguity which the light of occasional statutory provisions renders the more confusing. It is much to be desired that a comprehensive review of all the extant material on the subject should be made.[1]

Somewhat less obscurity surrounds the erection of the counties and the early years of Germantown borough,[2] but the political history of Philadelphia from 1682 to 1701 is

---

[1] It cannot be denied that some features of a democratic town organization did exist in Pennsylvania. A town book of Darby, 1682–1804, is extant, which shows a communal activity in the election of officials and the making of by-laws which savors strongly of New England practice. (See transcript of this volume in the Historical Society of Pennsylvania.) The phrase town meeting was sometimes used with reference to the gathering of the people for elective purposes. Certain returns of elections of town constables and overseers of the poor made to the Lancaster County court show this use of the words. The township of Bartt elected their candidates "by a towns meeting;" in another case the wording is "The township of derry Being met they chuse Adam Bame and John fleming or either of them to serve as Constabel for the Ensuing year Chosen by us." In other returns the election is said to be by the "freeholders," or by the "inhabitants." (See the MS. returns bound up with "Lancaster County Court Papers, 1752–1782," folios 141–171, in Historical Society of Pennsylvania.)

[2] 1689–1691.

almost a blank.[1] In glancing at some variations of the local suffrage from the normal we cannot make a study of local institutions, but must content ourselves with a few references to the statutory provisions on the franchise.

By the king's charter to Penn the proprietor was given

> "free and absolute power to Divide the said Countrey, and Islands, into Townes, Hundreds and Counties, and to erect and incorporate Townes into Borroughs, and Borroughs into Citties, and to make and Constitute ffaires and Markets therein, with all other convenient privilledges and immunities according to the merit of the inhabitants and the ffitness of the places."

It further provided that Penn should have authority to erect manors and establish upon them courts-baron and view of frankpledge.

We need not here examine the details of the survey of Penn's "great town,"[2] for these early acts are of an agrarian rather than a political nature. On March 24, 1681–2, Penn gave a charter to a "Free Society of Traders" who were privileged upon their lands to establish a manor by the name of Frank, and to hold courts of general sessions, courts-baron and -leet and view of frankpledge.[3] According to the constitution adopted by this society, a plural system of voting was to be put in force.[4] Penn's frame of 1682, the laws made in England, and the Great Law of December, 1682, neglect the whole subject of local government, with the exception of provisions for court procedure. Apparently, the counties of Philadelphia, Chester, and Bucks in the province, and of Newcastle, Kent, and Sussex in the territories were erected shortly after Penn's arrival in the province;[5] for we see the county organization sufficient by November 18, 1682, to warrant the proprietor in sending writs to sheriffs in six counties directing the election of seven assemblymen in each county.[6]

---

[1] See Allinson and Penrose, *Phila.*, xlv–7; *Penna. Magazine of History and Biography*, XV, 344; XVIII, 419.

[2] Hazard, *Annals*, 528, 594, etc.   [3] *Ibid.*, 541–550.

[4] *Ibid.*, 552; Hazard, *Register of Penna.*, I, 394.

[5] *Ibid.*, 605.

[6] *Ibid.*, 603; but see also *Charter and Laws*, Appendix, 472–3; *Votes*, I, I, 1–3.

In the somewhat voluminous legislation of March, 1682–3, and the two succeeding years, many details of local administration were given over to the county courts, including the levying of county taxes, the laying out of roads to public landings, and the appointment of viewers of pipe-staves, overseers of highways, and viewers of fences.[1] There is only one provision for the election of local officers, which is in Chapter 88 of the laws of 1692–3, requiring each *town* to choose one or two able persons to weigh bread exposed for sale.[2] No definition is given of the word town, nor of electors therein. It may be that town meant no more than a populous locality, and the subsequent use of the term would seem to justify this theory.[3]

The sheriffs and coroners by the frame of 1682 were to be appointed by the proprietor in the first instance;[4] but by the frame of 1683, sheriffs, coroners, and justices of the peace were to be appointed by the governor from a double nomination made by the assembly.[5] The new charter of 1701 placed the election of the sheriffs and coroners in the hands of the freemen of the respective counties, who should select a double number of candidates for those offices.[6] From this time down to the Revolution, county officials were elected by those qualified to vote for representatives,[7] and although attempts at voting were occasionally made by per-

[1] *Charter and Laws,* 133, 136, 139, 146, 178.

[2] *Ibid.,* 135.

[3] See the use of the word in acts of May 10, 1698, *Charter and Laws,* 276, and of November 27, 1700, *Statutes at Large,* II, 65–68. Seven towns are named: Bristol, Philadelphia, Germantown, Darby, Chester, Newcastle, and Lewes; of which it is believed that only two, Philadelphia and Germantown, had received any corporate power at this time. Yet Darby was holding regular meetings.

[4] *Charter and Laws,* 97.

[5] *Ibid.,* 159.

[6] Poore, *Charters and Constitutions,* II, 1538.

[7] *Charters and Laws,* 256; *Statutes at Large,* II, 34, 272; III, 138; IV, 10, 77, 331. An act of March 9, 1771 (*Pam. Laws,* p. 112), permitted *all* freeholders to vote for freeholders to audit the accounts of the overseers of the poor. This may have been an extension of the suffrage similar to that mentioned in the townships, since it neglected the fifty acres limitation.

sons not so qualified, yet the legislature by increasingly strict laws prevented their interference.

In the townships the officers were often appointed by the county court, or, where elective, the suffrage qualifications were apparently the same as those for electors of higher officers. Only one case has been found where the township suffrage differed expressly from the provincial suffrage. This is in a law providing for the erection of pounds in each township which directed that the election of a pound-keeper should be by those who are " owners or possessors of land" in each township.[1] This law, like the case mentioned in a previous note, by removing the fifty acres qualification, must have given the suffrage to small freeholders.

Pennsylvania, like many other colonies, possessed the local unit called the borough. Four places received borough charters during the colonial period, namely, Germantown, 1689; Chester, 1701; Bristol, 1720; Lancaster, 1742.[2] Of these, Germantown alone was constituted a close corporation without any popular elections; a reason, perhaps, why the charter was permitted to lapse by non-user in 1706.[3] The charters of Chester, Bristol, and Lancaster show strong similarities to one another, and all of them contain provisions for popular elections, and even seem to permit popular town meetings.[4] These charters established a new class of voters

[1] *Statutes at Large,* IV, 116, May 10, 1729.

[2] There is some proof that Philadelphia had a borough organization before 1691, but almost nothing is known of this government; Allinson and Penrose, *Philadelphia,* 4.

[3] See charter in *Pa. Archives,* I, 111–115. For description, see W. P. Holcomb, *Pennsylvania Boroughs, J. H. Univ. Studies,* IV, 158.

[4] See Chester charter in J. H. Martin, *History of Chester,* 111–113; Bristol, in Hazard, *Register of Penna.,* III, 312–314; Lancaster, in Mombert, *History of Lancaster County,* Appendix, 141–146. For boroughs in general, see Holcomb, *op. cit.* The following extracts will give an idea of the provisions for popular elections and town meetings:

> " And we do . . . grant full power and authority for the Burgesses, Constables, assistants and freeholders, together with such inhabitants, housekeepers within the said borough, as shall have resided therein at least for the space of one whole year next preceding any such election as is herein after directed, and hired a house and ground within the said borough of the yearly

in borough elections by extending the suffrage to house-holders as well as freeholders. In the first two charters, those of Chester and Bristol, the word householder is un-defined and unlimited; but in Lancaster the power of par-ticipation in elections was given to the freeholders, and to the " inhabitants, housekeepers within the said borough,"* who had resided in the borough one year before the election and who rented a house and ground of the annual rental of five pounds or upwards.

A similar advance in definition was made in the term town meeting, which in Chester and Bristol passed without comment, but in Lancaster is to be composed of the " inhabi-tants." These provisions of the borough charters are of interest because they give us the closest approximation to democracy which was made by the province of Pennsylvania. Mr. Holcomb has written of the political activities of one of these boroughs,[1] but the part of the town meeting in all three might with profit be made the subject of further study. The town meeting feature reminds us of New England prac-tice, while the householder suffrage is remarkably similar to that in use in many of the English boroughs.

Philadelphia possessed a more restricted suffrage than the boroughs, and she lacked altogether the town meeting which was their peculiar political feature. The charter of 1691,[2] of somewhat doubtful authenticity, and that of 1701 [3] both erected a municipality in which popular suffrage played no part. The mayor, recorder, eight aldermen, and twelve com-mon councilmen formed a close corporation, with power to

value of *five pounds* or upwards" to hold annual election on September 15 for above officers.

" And it shall and may be lawful for the said burgesses, high constables and assistants for the time being to assemble town meetings as often as they shall find occasion: At which meet-ings they may make such ordinances and rules, not repugnant to, or inconsistent with the laws of the said province, as to the greatest part of the inhabitants shall seem necessary and con-venient for the good government of the said Borough."

[1] Bristol, *op. cit.*

[2] Allinson and Penrose, *Phila.*, xlvii–lii.

[3] *A Collection of Charters and Other Publick Acts relating to the Province of Pennsylvania.* B. Franklin, Philadelphia, 1740, 35–42.

fill vacancies in their own number and to elect annually a mayor from among themselves.[1] Although the charter mentioned no popular election except for the county officers and coroner, yet it stated the qualification of electors and elected as laid down in the law of 1700. Subsequently, when the functions of the municipal authorities were found inadequate, the legislature, instead of increasing their authority, diverted a portion of municipal administration to elective or appointive boards. In the cases where these officials were elective, it is believed that the qualification was always identical with that for electors of representatives,[2] the description usually being "those of the inhabitants and freeholders of the said city who are qualified to elect and be elected to the assembly."

Still another type of municipality starting in the colonial period of Pennsylvania history was to furnish a model for a number of strange municipal corporations which grew up around the city of Philadelphia. Penn's plot for the city contained only eighteen hundred and twenty acres, which was laid out with about a mile on the Delaware front and over two and a half miles back to the Schuylkill. Population centred in the early years along the Delaware and soon outgrew the narrow limits set by the proprietor, while the back lots of the city were undeveloped. A large population thus settled to the northward and southward of the old city, and in these places there developed that abnormal municipality, *the incorporated district.* The district had greater powers than a township, it was somewhat greater and somewhat less than a borough, and it was inferior to the city in dignity, although often its political activities almost paralleled those of the city—Philadelphia. Nine of these districts, in addition to six boroughs and thirteen townships, were consolidated in 1854, when the bounds of the city were extended

---

[1] This charter is even less popular in its terms than that granted by Dongan to New York. See *ante;* also *Amer. Hist. Rev.,* VI, 702; *N. Y. Col. Laws,* I, 181–195.

[2] See acts of June 7, 1712; May 10, 1729; May 1, 1739; January 3, 1742–3; February 9, 1750–51; August 16, 1756; February 17, 1762; March 26, 1762; May 30, 1764; February 18, 1769; March 9, 1771.

to those of the county.[1] Only two of the districts, South-wark and Northern Liberties, were erected by the legislature in colonial times. The act of March 26, 1762, gave the bounds of the district of Southwark and provided for the election of certain officers—regulators of streets, assessors, and supervisors of streets—by the freeholders and other inhabitants of the district who were qualified by law to elect assemblymen. The act of March 9, 1771, provided for regulators of streets in the Northern Liberties, but it required their appointment by the county commissioners instead of by popular election. The subsequent history of these districts belongs to the commonwealth period, and must be put aside for the present.[2]

In conclusion, it may be said that the local suffrage varied but slightly from the colonial franchise. In Philadelphia apparently there was no variation whatever; in the towns and counties there was an infrequent substitution of the general term freeholder for the fifty acres or fifty pounds clause, while in the three boroughs occurred the greatest deviation by the inclusion of the householders within the voting class. There was no clear demarcation in Pennsylvania between the rural and the urban population as in New York, nor the distinction between the voting class in town affairs and that in provincial affairs as seen in the New England corporations. Pennsylvania was content with practically one test of the suffrage for all elections, and that, as already shown, was the holding of fifty acres of land or of fifty pounds estate; while outside of Philadelphia the latter was so infrequently held that we may declare the suffrage, except in the city, to be based practically on fifty acres of freehold.

[1] These districts were Southwark, Northern Liberties, Kensington, Spring Garden, Moyamensing, Penn, Richmond, West Philadelphia, and Belmont.

[2] No study of the incorporated districts of Philadelphia County has, so far as known, ever been made. Their organization, powers, and growth were remarkable, and deserve a place in the history of our institutions. The material for such a study is extant, see *Report on the Public Archives of the City and County of Philadelphia*, by Herman V. Ames and A. E. McKinley, *Report of American Historical Association*, 1901, Vol. II, 231–344.

CHAPTER XI.

The Suffrage in Massachusetts.

I. *The Colony of Massachusetts Bay.*

The colony of Massachusetts Bay, while in English theory only the settlement of a trading company, was in reality a great Puritan commonwealth. Its legal basis is to be found in the royal charter of 1628-9; its practical strength lay in the solidarity of feeling among the Puritans. These two factors, so diverse in their nature, and exercising such a determining influence upon the church and state of the Puritans, were united in the fixing of the qualifications for the suffrage franchise. The English corporation principle of freemanship, established by the charter, proved admirably adapted to the religious exclusiveness which the Puritans deemed necessary to the success of their state. Under no other form of organization could their religious and ecclesiastical ideals have approached so close to realization; and this organization, unwittingly, the Puritan-hater, Charles I., had prepared for them. It will be well, therefore, before investigating the suffrage conditions of the colony, to notice the aims of the founders in making their settlement, and the terms of that charter which they forced to do service for a state instead of a business company.

There can be little doubt to-day that the religious motive was the principal force in the establishment of the colony. The "Conclusions for New England," probably the work of John Winthrop, circulated after May, 1629, state that

"All other churches of Europe are brought to desolation, & o^r sinnes, for wch the Lord beginnes allreaddy to frowne upon us & to cutte us short, doe threatne evill times to be comminge upon us, and whoe knowes, but that God hath provided this place to be a refuge for many whome he meanes to save out of the generall callamity, & seeinge the Church hath noe place lefte to flie into but the wildernesse, what better worke can there be, then to goe & provide tabernacles & foode for her against she comes thether." [1]

The failure of other colonies, it was said, came about because their " mayne end was carnall and not religious." [2] Winthrop again, in his " Model of Christian Charity," written on board the *Arbella,* says,—

" For the worke wee have in hand, it is by a mutuall consent, through a special overvaluing providence and a more than ordinary approbation of yᵉ Churches of Christ, to seek out a place of cohabitation and Consorteshipp under a due form of Government both civill and ecclesiasticall." [3]

Said Francis Higginson, the famous Puritan minister,—

" We do not go to New England as Separatists from the Church of England, though we cannot but separate from the corruptions of it; but we go to practise the positive part of the Church reformation, and. to propagate the Gospel in America." [4]

From their words at this early stage, as well as their acts later, it is plain that the establishment of a church discipline and organization according to the prevalent principles of Puritanism was the dominant motive for the founding of the colony.

To the group of persons thus imbued with religious zeal for their peculiar faith, Charles I. gave added strength and definite legal standing by the grant of a charter of incorporation. The king, " for divers good Causes and consideracons," on March 4, 1628–9, erected twenty-six named persons, and " all such others as shall hereafter be admitted and made free of the Company," into a corporation by the name of " The Governor and Company of the Mattachusetts Bay in Newe-England." [5] The officers, " elected and

---

[1] Winsor, *Memorial History of Boston,* I, 105.
[2] Ellis, *The Puritan Age in Massachusetts,* 48.
[3] Winsor, *Boston,* I, 142.
[4] Ellis, *op. cit.,* 55.
[5] Poore, *Charters and Constitutions,* I, 932–942. The king confirmed the land grant previously made by the Council for New England to six of the incorporators.

chosen out of the freemen of the saide Company" annually, were to be a governor, a deputy-governor, and eighteen assistants. The officers might meet monthly, and every quarter there was to be " one greate generall and solempe assemblie" of the company. These meetings, called general courts, were empowered to admit new freemen; they could elect and constitute fit officers for the management of the concerns of the company; and could make laws and ordinances " for the Good and Welfare of the saide Company, and for the Government and ordering of the saide Landes and Plantacons, and the People inhabiting and to inhabite the same," with the restriction that such laws should not be contrary to the laws of England. One further feature of the charter transformed these rules for the organization of a trading company and its colony, otherwise so unimportant, into terms of the highest political significance. The absence of any stated meeting place for the company is now believed to have been the result of conscious endeavor upon the part of the petitioners for a charter.[1] The omission of any place of meeting in England made possible the holding of company meetings in New England, and brought about the identification of the company and the colony.

Connecting these unintentionally broad terms of the charter with the determined group of men who were to administer them, it is apparent that the charter gives abundant foundation for the establishment of a political commonwealth. Furthermore, the principle of freemanship, and the grant to the company of the power of admitting new freemen, made the leaders of the enterprise hope to restrict its membership to persons who were in religious accord with themselves. Thus the Puritan theocracy was nurtured under the very terms of the royal charter.

After the decision to remove the charter and the company was reached in the summer of 1629; after the new and more determined officers had been elected in the fall; after the *Arbella* with the charter and the new officers had arrived in New England;—after these steps had been taken there arose the question of the relation of the settlers in America to the recently arrived governor and company.

[1] Ellis, *Puritan Age,* 47; *Mass. Hist. Soc. Proc.,* 1869–1870, 172–175.

Up to this time the colony had been governed by officers chosen by the company in England, and the settlers had as yet no voice in their government. But they did not intend long to remain disfranchised.[1]

The first meeting of the company in America, held on October 19, 1630, was made up of the freemen, not numbering more than fifteen persons, and the settlers of the colony, who attended as a matter of privilege and not of right. At this meeting two distinct influences appear to be at work. The first of these was an effort to open the freemanship of the company to many of the settlers; and the second, an opposite tendency upon the part of the leaders of the enterprise to make the government more aristocratic than the terms of the charter provided. The two movements may have been connected with one another, for the immediate acceptance into the freemanship of the one hundred and more persons who expressed a desire for it[2] would have outweighed in voting power the small number—only fifteen or twenty—of company freemen who had actually come to America.[3] The extension of the freemanship was apparently not granted at this time, and the less than a score of freemen kept their rare dignity until the following spring. But evidently in fear of a sudden extension of the franchise, it was propounded at the October meeting that the freemen elect the assistants only, the latter elect the governor and deputy-governor, and that these officers with the assistants make laws and choose all other officers. The matter was submitted, not to the few freemen alone, but to all the people assembled to witness the first general court of the company: "This was fully assented vnto by the genall vote of the people, and ereccon of hands."[4] Thus there began

---

[1] Were they familiar with the lenient course pursued in Plymouth for the admission of partners?

[2] Palfrey, *History of New England*, I, 322; Hutchinson, *History of the Colony of Massachuset's Bay* (London, 1765), I, 25, says 109 freemen were admitted at this court; but I have followed the inference of Palfrey that they only asked for admission, and did not receive it at this time.

[3] Palfrey, I, 313, 323.

[4] *Records of The Governor and Company of the Massachusetts Bay in New England*, I, 79 (quoted hereafter as *Mass. Col. Rec.*)

that aristocratic tendency which later developed into the attempt to retain the assistants for life;[1] which could speak of an office as a freehold,[2] and lead to the establishment of a standing life council.[3] " Democracy," said Cotton, " I do not conceive that God ever did ordain as a fit Government either for Church or Commonwealth." [4]

In the spring of 1631 occurred the first annual meeting of the court for elective purposes, and, it is believed, the first admissions of freemen upon this side of the Atlantic. At the meeting of May 18 the freemanship was conferred upon one hundred and eighteen persons.[5] But by far the most noted action of the court at this session was the adoption of a rule requiring all persons admitted to the freemanship in the future to be church members. Of the more than a hundred new freemen made at this court, it has been estimated that at least one-half—perhaps three-quarters—were members of some church.[6] But, not satisfied with this proportion, the leaders of the Puritan experiment adopted for the future a definite religious test:

"And to the end the body of the comons may be pserued [preserved] of honest & good men, it was likewise ordered and agreed that for time to come noe man shalbe admitted to the freedome of this body polliticke, but such as are members of some of the churches within the lymitts of the same." [7]

It is likely that the recent demands for admission to the freemanship had aroused the founders of the movement to the danger which might come to their ecclesiastical ideals if those who were not church members should get a voice

[1] *Mass. Col. Rec.*, I, 87.

[2] Winthrop, *The History of New England from 1630 to 1649* (ed. Savage, 1853), I, 132.

[3] *Mass. Col. Rec.*, I, 167, 264; Winthrop, I, 302.

[4] Winsor, *Memorial History of Boston*, I, 161. For estimates of this aristocratic spirit see Doyle, *Puritan Colonies*, I, 103-104; Palfrey, I, 322, 349; Haynes, *Representation and Suffrage in Massachusetts, Johns Hopkins University Studies*, XII, 383-385.

[5] *Mass. Col. Rec.*, I, 366.

[6] Palfrey, I, 348, note.

[7] *Mass. Col. Rec.*, I, 87.

in the government. The picture of the narrow company freemanship blossoming out into a democratic government was one that does not appear to have come to the originators of the plan for the emigration to America.[1] But the recent applications for freemanship showed a breadth of political desire which argued ill for the ideals of the company unless they were well guarded; and in what better way could this be done than by limiting the political power to members of the churches? Cotton believed that " None are so fit to be trusted with the liberties of the commonwealth as church-members; for the liberties of the freemen of this commonwealth are such as require men of faithful integrity to God and the state to preserve the same." [2] The two principal liberties of the freemen, he states, are the election of magistrates and the choice of deputies. " Now both these liberties are such as carry along much power with them, either to establish or subvert the commonwealth." The Massachusetts Company as originally established had been a Puritan enterprise, and when its charter became the frame of government of a state, the integrity of the new controlling forces could be maintained only by the exclusion of non-Puritans. " The franchise was not one dependent upon social rank, nor upon pecuniary means, but upon hearty sympathy and accord in the religious intent of the enterprise." [3]

• Aside from the inequality inflicted upon open dissenters, there were, as Mr. Ellis has pointed out,[4] evident evil consequences of the religious qualification: the exclusion of many persons of upright lives who refused to rise before the congregation and make that public description of religious experience which was a prerequisite of church-membership, and the absence of any means for excluding hypocrites who entered the church for selfish and political reasons. Another and more practical source of irritation lay in the difficulty of determining what constituted church-membership. Con-

[1] Compare Winsor, *Memorial History of Boston*, I, 161.
[2] Palfrey, I, 345, note.
[3] Winsor, *Boston*, I, 150.
[4] *Ibid.*, 151.

troversies arose both over the meaning of the word church
and of the word member.

The early extreme congregationalism [1] led to the introduction of beliefs which differed greatly, or appeared to
differ, from those of the founders of the colony. Heresies,
more or less pronounced, arose in many congregations, until
the churches appeared more corrupt than the state.[2] The
church consequently, as the source of citizenship, must be
guarded and purged by the authority of the state; in self-
protection the civil authority was compelled to define orthodoxy and make provision for the punishment of heresy.
Such a position was but the logical outcome of the religious
qualification upon the suffrage.[3] As early as March 3,
1635–6, the general court had found " by sad experience
that much trouble and disturbance hath happened both to
the church & civill state by the officers & members of some
churches, wch have bene gathered within the limitts of this
jurisdiccon in a vndue manner, & not with such publique
approbacon as were meete." [4] To avoid such troubles in
the future the court ordered that no company of persons
should be recognized as a church unless the approval of the
magistrates and of the elders of the greater part of the
churches in the colony had first been obtained. The political
effect of the restriction [5] is seen in the further provision

"that noe p'son, being a member of any churche which shall hereafter
be gathered without the approbacon of the magistrates, & the greater

[1] The early doctrine of the settlers was that seven or more Christians
could by covenant enter into church association, taking for their guide
in faith and organization the Bible, and selecting their own ministers,
who, although owing their authority to God, obtained their official position by the choice of the congregation (*ibid.*, 163).

[2] Winthrop said in 1637, " Whereas the way of God hath always been
to gather his churches out of ye world, now ye world, or civill state,
must be raised out of ye churches," quoted in Winsor, *Boston*, I, 165.

[3] Palfrey, I, 432.

[4] *Mass. Col. Rec.*, I, 168.

[5] On the other hand, the religious side of the controversies of the
time is found in the eighty-two erroneous opinions declared heretical
by the gathering of the clergy in 1637 at Cambridge (Winthrop, I,
284).

pte of the said churches, shalbe admitted to the ffreedome of this comonwealthe."

Not content with the refusal, for the future, to admit members of irregular churches, the dominant party desired to exclude at once the members of such churches who were already freemen. Williams was exiled and Salem punished for accepting him as minister, but the Wheelwright affair led to a much wider forfeiture of political rights. Winthrop says the general court found " upon consultation, that two so opposite parties could not contain in the same body, without apparent hazard of ruin to the whole;" [1] and accordingly, seizing a slight pretext, the court proceeded to banish, disfranchise, or disarm the principal persons connected with the movement.[2] And to prevent any further petitions or discussions upon the matter, the court ordered that the punishment of disfranchisement, fine, imprisonment, or banishment could be inflicted upon any person " openly or willingly" defaming any court of justice or its proceedings or magistrates.[3] Temporarily, at least, the measures for attaining religious conformity were successful; [4] the state had purified the ecclesiastical source of citizenship; it had exercised its " power and libertie to see the peace, ordinances and Rules of Christ observed in every church according to his word." [5] A definition of the word church was thus obtained, which was made more precise later by the action of the Cambridge Synod of 1646 and 1647.[6] The meaning of church-membership, however, was not determined until 1662, when the Half-way Covenant was adopted.[7]

Membership in the church was not the only formal requisite for admission to the freemanship, although it was, indeed, the greatest practical limitation upon the suffrage. The church-member who desired to participate in the politi-

[1] I, 244.
[2] *Mass. Col. Rec.,* I, 205–211.
[3] *Ibid.,* 212–213.
[4] See Palfrey, I, 505–511, for a justification of the course of Massachusetts towards the Antinomians.
[5] *Mass. Body of Liberties* of 1641, section 58.
[6] Winthrop, II, 264, 269, etc.; Palfrey, II, 170–187.
[7] See *post.*

cal life of town or colony must be proposed to the general
court or some special court, and by that body be formally
admitted as a freeman,[1] and before acceptance he was compelled to take an oath of fidelity to the Company.   Freemanship did not follow *ex officio* from the relation of church-
membership.   Indeed, it is quite apparent that many members of the church did not desire the freemanship; being
willing, perhaps, to forfeit their political rights in order to
be freed from the duties of freemen.   In 1643 the churches
were instructed to deal with their members who refused to
" take their freedom;"[2] a few months later we learn of such
a "defect" of freemen at Marblehead that the general court
authorized the choice of a non-freeman for constable.[3]   In
1647 the court found that there were " many memb[rs] of
churches, who, to exempt y[m]selves from all publike service
in y[e] comon wealth, will not come in to be made freemen." [4]
Accordingly, all church-members, non-freemen as well as
freemen, were rendered liable for service in town offices and
as jurymen, and placed under the penalty of a fine for
refusing to accept such positions.   It is thus quite apparent
that many churchmen were not members of the political
corporation.

Not always was the formal process of admitting freemen
retained by the general court.   In 1641 the right was given
to " every Court within this Jurisdiction where two Magistrates are present," to admit as freemen " any Church Members, that are fit to be Freemen," giving them the oath and
certifying their names to the secretary at the next general
court.[5]   For about twenty years the county courts exercised
this right; but in 1664 the power was revoked and admissions for the future were to be made by the general court
alone.[6]   In addition to granting this authority for a time

[1] *Mass. Col. Rec.*, I, 117.   [2] *Ibid.*, II, 38.
[3] *Ibid.*, II, 57.   [4] *Ibid.*, 208.
[5] *The General Laws and Liberties of the Massachusetts Colony* (1672),
38; Ernst, *Constitutional History of Boston*, 16.
[6] Code of 1672, 56; *Mass. Col. Rec.*, IV, Part II, 118.   It is to be
noted, however, that the revisers of the laws in 1672, although printing
the repealing act of 1664, yet permitted the clause of 1641 to stand on
another page of their revised code.

to county courts, the general courts occasionally delegated to individuals the right of accepting freemen and administering to them the oath of fidelity. In 1647 "Mr Pinchin" was authorized " to make freemen in the towne of Springfeild, of those that are in covenant & live according to their p'fession;" [1] and in the same manner the commissioners sent by the court to obtain the submission of the Maine settlements were empowered to admit freemen and give the necessary oaths.[2] These settlements were so distant from Boston that there could be no hope of having the inhabitants appear personally before the general court. In all other cases, except during the period 1641 to 1664, the general court alone exercised the right of admitting freemen to the company.

An oath to be administered to all freemen had been prescribed before 1634; [3] in April of that year the assistants ordained an inhabitants' oath to be taken by all residents not enfranchised, but who were above the age of twenty years and either householders or sojourners in the colony.[4] In May a new freeman's oath was established, and the obligation of those who had taken the former oath was made to conform with the obligations imposed by the new one.[5] It

[1] *Mass. Col. Rec.*, II, 224.

[2] *Ibid.*, IV, Pt. I, 122 ff.; 128; 157; Williamson, *History of the State of Maine*, I, 334–357, 391.

[3] The date of the first form of freeman's oath is uncertain, *Mass. Col. Rec.*, I, 353.

[4] *Ibid.*, 115.

[5] *Ibid.*, 117.

" The Oath of a Freeman.

" I, A. B., being by Gods providence, an inhabitant & ffreeman within the jurisdiccon of this comonweale, doe freely acknowledge my selfe to be subiect to the goverm^t thereof, & therefore doe heere sweare, by the greate & dreadfull name of the euerlyving God, that I wilbe true & faithfull to the same, & will accordingly yielde assistance & support therevnto, with my p'son & estate, as in equity I am bound, and will also truely indeav^r to mainetaine & preserue all the libertyes & previlidges thereof, submitting my selfe to the wholesome lawes & orders made & established by the same; and furth^r, that I will not plott nor practise any evill against it, nor consent to any that

seems probable that from the first also an age requirement was established according to English precedent. In
1641 the Body of Liberties made one and twenty years
" the age for giving of votes, verdicts, or Sentence in any
Civill courts." [1] Admission to the freemanship at this time,
therefore, was dependent (1) upon age, (2) church-membership, (3) formal proposition to the general court, (4)
acceptance by that body or some delegated authority, (5)
the taking of a freeman's oath.

It is regretted that the demands of space will not allow an
examination of the representative system, as it was through
the growth of this system that the suffrage was given
a practical value to the outlying settlements; but the omission may be pardoned in view of the many accounts of the
system which have been written by local and general historians.[2] Reference should be made, however, to the method
of balloting. At the outset the Massachusetts Company did
not adopt the ballot in its elections, as we have seen that
the London Company did many years earlier,[3] but held its
elections in London by " erection of hands." [4] As early as
1629 the ballot was used in the church at Salem, and shortly
after the transmission of the charter to New England it
was adopted in the Company's elections. It was originally
used in the election of governor, the first occasion probably
being the election of May, 1634; [5] and in September, 1635,

---

shall soe doe, but will timely discover & reveale the same to
lawfull authority nowe here established, for the speedy preventing thereof. Moreouer, I doe solemnely bynde my selfe, in
the sight of God, that when I shalbe called to giue my voice
touching any such matter of this state, wherein ffreemen are
to deale, I will giue my vote & suffrage, as I shall iudge in
myne owne conscience may best conduce & tend to the publique
weale of the body, without respect of p'sons, or fav^r of any
man. Soe helpe mee God, in the Lord Jesus Christ."

[1] Body of Liberties, Sect. 53.

[2] See particularly G. H. Haynes, *Representation and Suffrage in
Massachusetts, 1620–1691, J. H. U. Studies*, XII, 374–460.

[3] See *ante*, pp. 18, 22.

[4] Lechford, *Plain Dealing*, 23.

[5] In the margin of the account of this election in Winthrop's history
occur the words " chosen by papers" (I, 132).

was extended to the elections of deputies to the general court. Up to this point the ballot only served the purpose of keeping the freeman's vote a secret from his fellows; it did not relieve him from the necessity of journeying to the capital city to cast his ballot. In a few months, however, the natural step was taken of permitting the freemen to cast their votes for company officers in their own towns, and transmit the ballots to the general court at Boston. This is what the men of the times called proxy voting, and it differed from the system adopted in most of the colonies outside of New England by requiring the transmission of the actual ballots to the general returning body, instead of forwarding a mere statement of the votes cast. In March, 1635–6, it was first applied to six frontier towns to enable them to retain their freemen at home " for the safty of their towne." [1] In a contemplated special election in the following December, this privilege was extended to any of the freemen " if they thinke not fit to come in p'son." [2] In March, 1636–7, the court, considering " the greate danger & damage that may accrue to the state by all the freemens leaveing their plantations to come to the place of elections," made this a permanent order, each freeman having the liberty to send his vote " by proxie," and the town deputies were directed to carry the ballots (proxies) to the meeting of the general court. [3] In 1640 and the following year a somewhat reactionary spirit is seen from the democratic method of " proxing." The candidates for magistrates were to be nominated by the deputies and the freemen merely given the right to choose among the nominees; [4] but this order was limited to one year and apparently was not extended. In 1641 the court proposed a true proxy system of indirect voting, according to which the several towns were to choose one elector for each ten freemen, and these electors in turn were to make the elections; [5] but this was

---

[1] *Mass. Col. Rec.,* I, 166.

[2] *Ibid.,* 185. Vane having been prevailed upon to remain in the colony, the election did not take place (Winthrop, I, 207–208).

[3] *Ibid.,* 188. In 1639 the freeman's choice in election between " person or by proxie" was more definitely stated (*ibid.,* 277).

[4] *Ibid.,* 293.　　　　　　　　　　[5] *Ibid.,* 333.

not satisfactory to the freemen, and no action was taken upon it. The method of sending to Boston the ballots or proxies of those who did not attend the court of elections in person was continued thereafter with but slight change until the surrender of the charter. After 1643 the votes for assistants,[1] but not for the other officers, were given in " Indian beanes, the white beanes to manifest election, the black for blanks." [2] Later, an attempt was made to do away altogether with the personal attendance of freemen at the election, and permit the voting only by papers and corn and beans in the several towns. This proved unpopular,[3] and in November, 1647, it was changed slightly so that none should " deliver in their votes at ye dores" of the general court except those who were made free upon election day.[4] In 1663, when the admission of freemen upon election day was prohibited, it was again ordered that none should cast their votes personally at Boston except members of the general court.[5] But again the freemen showed their desire to attend personally, and within a year the law was repealed.[6] From this time onward the freeman could attend the general court of election in person or he could send his paper ballot for the officers, and corn and beans for the assistants.[7]

We must now notice the size of the disfranchised class under the church-membership restriction, and shall trace the agitation for an extended suffrage until that question was taken up by the king himself, and English authority was brought to bear upon obstinate Massachusetts. Among

[1] Many different plans for the nomination and election of assistants were tried (see Haynes, *op. cit.,* 400–405).

[2] *Mass. Col. Rec.,* II, 42. The code of 1660 (p. 29) provided that " the freemen shall use Indian Corn & Beanes, the Indian Corn to manifest Election, the Beanes contrary."

[3] Winthrop, II, 311.

[4] *Mass. Col. Rec.,* II, 220.

[5] *Ibid.,* IV, Pt. II, 86.

[6] *Ibid.,* 134.

[7] The order of 1663 is interesting also because it permitted a freeman to vote in his town without attending personally at the election. He could " send his vote, sealed vp, in a note directed to the deputy or tounsmen." An act of 1738 required personal attendance (*Session Laws,* 681–683).

the one hundred and eighteen admitted at the first court of election in 1631 we have noticed that fully one-half were members of the church; but the new religious qualification soon led to the exclusion of more than one-half of the adult males. Among recent writers we have such expressions as, " At no period were the freemen any considerable proportion of the population;" [1] and " the number of freemen appears to have been from one-twentieth to one-tenth of the population." [2] Lechford, writing as early as 1640, asserts that three-fourths of the people were not members of the church and consequently not eligible for the freemanship.[3] A better idea of the extent of the franchise can be gained by comparing the number of arrivals in the colony with the actual admissions to the freedom of the company. Hutchinson [4] estimates that by the year 1640 the immigrants numbered about 21,200 persons. During the same period 1148 persons were admitted as freemen,[5] or about one person in every twenty who entered the limits of the colony. Taking the adult males at one-fifth of the population, these figures would seem to bear out Lechford's estimate previously given. Naturally such a restriction, in a new country where actual social and economic equality was more closely approximated than in England, would lead to discontent among the disfranchised and agitation for an extension of the suffrage. The disfranchised classes at first appear through their occasional illegal action at elections. At times they cast ballots in the elections; [6] at other times they were even chosen by the freemen to serve as deputies; [7] and in 1643 the general court was compelled to order the infliction of a fine of ten pounds upon non-freemen who took part in elections, as well as upon freemen who cast more

---

[1] Weeden, in *Amer. Antiquarian Society Proceedings*, 2d Series, IX, 348.

[2] Ernst, *Constitutional History of Boston*, 17.

[3] *Mass. Hist. Soc. Coll.*, 3d Series, III, 73.

[4] *History*, I, 93.

[5] See lists of freemen in *Mass. Col. Rec.*, I, 366–379; *New England Historical and Genealogical Register*, III, *passim*.

[6] *Mass. Col. Rec.*, I, 221; IV, Pt. I, 93; 147.

[7] *Ibid.*, I, 174; IV, Pt. I, 263.

than the legal number of ballots.[1]   By 1640 Lechford in his *ex parte* statements could claim that "the most of the persons at New-England are not admitted of their Church and therefore are not Freemen;"[2] "the people begin to complain, they are ruled like slaves;"[3] and "it is feared, that Elections cannot be safe there long, either in Church or Common-wealth." The growing strength of the feeling in favor of the disfranchised class is seen in the proposition made in the general court in March, 1643–4, "for yielding some more of the freeman's privileges to such as were no church members that should join in this government."[4] But the proposal came to naught "for want of opportunity of meeting, etc."[5] Later in the same year the opposition of the ruling parties to the non-freemen is seen in the strange refusal of the magistrates to publish their reasons for opposing a standing council proposed by the deputies.[6] Rather than gain popularity among the disfranchised classes, although they were largely in the majority, the magistrates were willing to have their actions misunderstood by the whole community.

Two years later, in 1646, the claims of the non-free were taken up by a group of agitators who desired to overthrow the ecclesiastical basis of the state and the extreme congregationalism of the churches, and be "wholly governed by the laws of England."[7] A plan was laid for the presentation of petitions to the general courts both of Plymouth and Massachusetts,[8] and for an appeal to the houses of Parliament if the demands should not be granted in New England.

---

[1] *Mass. Coll. Rec.*, II, 48.

[2] *Plain Dealing*, p. 23, in *Mass. Hist. Soc. Coll.*, 3d Series, III.

[3] *Ibid.*, 39.

[4] Winthrop, II, 160.

[5] *Ibid.* Unfortunately, we are not informed what were the reasons included in the "etc."

[6] They feared that such a publication "would cause a public breach throughout the country," and that the "non-members would certainly take part with the magistrates (we should not be able to avoid it), and this would make us and our cause, though never so just, obnoxious to the common sort of freemen" (Winthrop, II, 170–171).

[7] Winthrop, II, 261.   [8] Hutchinson, *History*, I, 145.

The petitioners to the Massachusetts court in May, 1646, while expressing their desire for a government according to the laws of England, yet aver that they cannot discern such a form to be in existence in Massachusetts in spite of the terms of the charter and the character of the settlers as Englishmen. They continue,—

"Whereas there are many thousands in these plantations, of the English nation, freeborne, quiett and peaceable men, righteous in their dealings, forward with hand, heart and purse, to advance the publick good, knowne friends to the honorable and victorious Houses of Parliament, lovers of their nation, &c., who are debarred from all civill imployments (without any just cause that we know) not being permitted to bear the least office (though it cannot be denied but some are well qualifyed) no not so much as to have any vote in choosing magistrates, captains or other civill and military officers; notwithstanding they have here expended their youth, borne the burden of the day, wasted much of their estates for the subsistence of these poore plantations, paid all assessments, taxes, rates, at least equall, if not exceeding others."

Therefore the petitioners request that

"civil liberty and freedom be forthwith granted to all truly English, equall to the rest of their countrymen, as in all plantations is accustomed to be done, and as all freeborne enjoy in our native country." [1]

The petitioners, most of whom were Presbyterians, also desired that members of the Church of England [2] or Scotland should be admitted to the communion of the New England churches; or, if these civil and religious privileges were refused them, that they should be freed from the heavy taxes imposed upon them. Should they fail of redress in America, the signers of the petition threatened to appeal to Parliament, who would, they hoped, "take their sad condition into consideration." Their closing sentiments, together with this threat, were not likely to gain for the

[1] Hutchinson, *A Collection of Original Papers Relative to the History of the Colony of Massachusetts-Bay*, Prince Society Reprint, I, 218–219; Hutchinson, *History*, I, 145–147.

[2] It will be remembered that at this time Presbyterianism was by act of Parliament the lawful religion of England.

petitioners the desired rights; in case their prayer should be granted, they expressed the hope of seeing

"the then contemned ordinances of God highly prized; the gospel, then dark, break forth as the sun; christian charity, then frozen, wax warm; jealousy of arbitrary government banished; strife and contention abated; and all business in church and state, which for many years had gone backward, successfully thriving."[1]

Means were taken by the leaders of the movement to spread copies of their petition throughout the colony, in neighboring provinces, and even to as distant places as the Dutch settlements, Virginia, and the Bermudas.[2] Support was found, we are told, mainly among the weaker classes. Young men and women " are taken with it,"[3] and those " of a linsey-woolsey disposition; some for prelacy, some for Presbytery, and some for *Plebsbytery*, but all joined together in the thing they would, which was to stir up the people to dislike of the present government."[4] Later a petition addressed to Parliament was drawn up and signed by twenty-five non-freemen for themselves and " many thousands more."[5]

In a community where such severe measures had been taken against the Antinomians and other dissenters; within a body of men who had so boldly transferred their charter from England, and who had recently refused to relinquish that charter upon the demand of Charles I.,—in such a community the attitude of the ruling classes towards the petitioners was a foregone conclusion. Formal consideration of the demands of the petition was denied at the time, and a law, already drawn up and about to pass, for allowing non-freemen equal participation with freemen in all town affairs, and perhaps imposing a property qualification upon voters in colonial elections, was also deferred

[1] Hutchinson, *History*, I, 147.
[2] Palfrey, II, 168.
[3] Hutchinson, *Papers* (Prince Soc.), I, 249.
[4] Palfrey, II, 169, note 2, quoting Johnson's *Wonder-Working Providence*, 202.
[5] Hutchinson, *History*, I, 147.

until the next session of the general court.[1]   A synod of the clergy, however, was called to give more definite form to the congregational system.[2]   In the meantime the petitioners continued their popular agitation, and when the court met in the fall of 1646 it was in a mood for the thorough suppression of the movement.

The court drew up a long reply to the charges made in the petition, showing by parallel columns the similarity between the English laws and those of Massachusetts;[3] and pointing out twelve false charges made in the petition. The petitioners were arraigned as authors of " diverse false and scandalous passages in a certain paper . . . against the churches of Christ and the civil government here established, derogating from the honor and authority of the same and tending to sedition." [4]   Later the petitioners were fined and prevented from sailing to England [5] with petitions from the non-freemen.   After this the movement gradually subsided; the leaders were disgraced and soon were scattered in England or America.[6]   At the election in May, 1647, " great laboring there had been by the friends of the petitioners to have one chosen governour, who favored their cause. . . . but the mind of the country appeared clearly, for the old governour was chosen again, with two or three hundred votes more than any other." [7]

But the olive-branch was linked with the sword of compulsion; the measure which had been postponed in the previous year was taken up again, and while no change was made in the colony elections, the proposed extension of the suffrage in town affairs was now adopted by the general court.   An order of September, 1635, had directed that none but freemen should have a voice in town affairs, such as the receiving of inhabitants and the laying out of town-lots; [8]

[1] Winthrop, II, 262; the language is slightly ambiguous.
[2] Palfrey, II, 170–174.
[3] Hutchinson, *Papers* (Prince Soc.), I, 223–247; Winthrop, II, 284.
[4] Palfrey, II, 175.
[5] Winthrop, II, 291 ff.; Palfrey, II, 176–178.
[6] Palfrey, II, 179.
[7] Thus modestly does Winthrop refer to his re-election (II, 307).
[8] *Mass. Coll. Rec.*, I, 161.

but the court now took into its consideration "ye usefull ptes & abilities of div^rs inhabitants amongst us, wch are not freemen." [1]   Accordingly the freemen of the towns were empowered to admit any inhabitants, being non-freemen, to the privileges of voting and jury service, if such inhabitants had taken the oath of fidelity to the government, had reached the age of twenty-four years, and were not under conviction of evil carriage against the government or the churches.[2]   It is difficult to tell how far the agitation played a part in securing this concession to the non-freemen.   Winthrop mentions an apparently wider reform than this which was set aside in May, 1646, because of the popular petition,[3] and it seems probable that the cause of an extended suffrage was injured rather than advanced by the popular appeal which had been made.   However, the liberty which was granted, united with the severe measures against the petitioners, appears to have quieted for a time the popular clamor.

For ten years the records do not show any determined effort to extend the franchise, and when a new interest was shown the attack on the exclusiveness of the freemanship was not made upon the political side, as it had been in 1646, but upon the ecclesiastical side.   We have noticed the attempt, about 1636, to extend the suffrage by the organization of new churches composed of those who, on account of dissentient views, could not enter the regular churches. The movement was met by a severe method of regulation of new churches and by the exclusion from the franchise of members of irregularly organized churches.   About 1657 a new attack upon the stronghold of privilege was made through the effort to extend the meaning of the term churchmember.   From Hartford, in Connecticut, there spread to the other colonies a controversy as to whether those who had been baptized and still recognized the obligations of baptism were to be accounted members of the church, or, if church-membership came only after evidence of regeneration, acceptance of the applicant by the congregation, and

[1] *Mass. Coll. Rec.,* II, 197 (general court of May 26, 1647).
[2] *Ibid.*   [3] *Ibid.,* II, 262.

continuance in full communion with the church.[1] A synod of Massachusetts and Connecticut ministers meeting in Boston in June, 1657, permitted what was called the Half-Way Covenant. Baptized persons, recognizing their obligations and being of good character, were permitted to bring their children to baptism; but the baptized were not admitted to full communion, nor, apparently, were they allowed to have a voice in the choice of church officers nor in civil elections in Massachusetts.[2]

This solution of the religious question might have introduced a broader basis for the suffrage in Massachusetts had a political interpretation been given to the synod's decision. This was not done, however, and when, upon the proposal of some inhabitants of the county of Middlesex, the general court was compelled to decide the question, it gave its authority to the narrower interpretation of the franchise:

"No Man whatsoever, shall be admitted to the Freedome of this Body Politick, but such as are Members of some Church of Christ and in full Communion, which they declare to be the true intent of the ancient Law."[3]

Thus the matter of the suffrage stood when the colony entered upon its contest with Charles II. shortly after his accession to the throne.[4]

[1] Palfrey, II, 487; Doyle, *Puritan Colonies*, II, 192.

[2] *Ibid.*, II, 489. Cp. Haynes, *Representation and Suffrage in Mass.*, J. H. U. *Studies*, XII, 424, with Lauer, *Church and State in New England, ibid.*, X, 140–142.

[3] Code of 1672, 56; *Mass. Col. Rec.*, IV, Pt. I, 420. It is interesting to notice the retention of this clause in the code of 1672 after the nominal extension of the suffrage in 1664. Randolph bases his charge that none but church-members can be freemen upon this and another clause, both of which were directly opposed to the act of 1664 admitting non-church-members (*Randolph Papers*, Prince Society, II, 293, III, 35).

[4] Besides requiring the voter to be a communicant of the church, the general court, in 1654, had ordered that no man, even a freeman, should serve as deputy in the court if he be "unsound in judgment, concerning the main points of christian religion as they have been held forth and acknowledged by the generality of the Protestant Orthodox writers, or that is Scandalous in his conversation, or that is unfaithfull to this Government." A fine of five pounds was to be levied upon every freeman knowingly making choice of any such person (Code of 1660, 25).

There were, however, two cases in which the attitude of the Massachusetts general court differed from its uniform policy towards dissenters; one showing greater leniency, and the other more harshness than was its usual custom. Instances of the first arise out of political considerations in connection with the Massachusetts claims to the territory of New Hampshire and Maine. Under the colonial interpretation of the charter of 1629 the Massachusetts jurisdiction included practically all the scattered settlements to the northward, but the inhabitants of these places were Episcopalians, or even religious exiles from Massachusetts.[1] It would be unwise as well as hazardous to the claims of Massachusetts to attempt to reduce these distant settlements to religious conformity as well as political subjection. The general court in 1642 accordingly admitted to the freedom of the colony all those in the New Hampshire settlements who had " liberty of freemen in their severall townes," and gave them the privilege of sending a deputy to the court, " though they bee not at p'sent church members."[2] About ten years later, when the Maine settlements were brought under the Massachusetts jurisdiction, the inhabitants were given the freedom, although they did not belong to any orthodox church.[3]

On the other hand, a strict policy of repression was adopted towards Quakers and Baptists, which while excluding them from the suffrage as a matter of course, also inflicted upon them more severe penalties. In 1647 Jesuits found within the province after being banished were to be subject to the death penalty;[4] and in 1653 the penalty of disfranchisement was inflicted upon a freeman because he

---

[1] Winthrop (*History*, II, 100) says the inhabitants of Gorges' province were not admitted to the New England Confederation because "they ran a different course from us both in their ministry and civil administration."

[2] *Mass. Col. Rec.*, II, 29; see for negotiations with the New Hampshire people, *ibid.*, I, 276, 324-5, 332, 342; II, 5, 41, 43; Palfrey, I, 587-594.

[3] *Mass. Col. Rec.*, IV, Pt. I, 122, 128, 157 ff.; Hutchinson, *History*, I, 177.

[4] *Mass. Col. Rec.*, II, 193.

had criticised certain ecclesiastical laws.[1]   In the fall of 1656 the court imposed penalties of whipping, imprisonment, hard labor, and banishment upon Quakers, and almost as severe punishments upon those who should defend their heretical opinions.[2]   In 1663 a more general rule was enacted, after experience had proved that there were in the colony many enemies " to all government, civil and ecclesiasticall, who will not yield obedience to authority, but make it much of theire religion to be in opposition thereto." [3] Accordingly the church-membership provision was extended by requiring all freemen to be not only members of the church, but also regular attendants upon the public worship:

" All persons, Quakers or others, wch refuse to attend vpon the publick worship of God established here, that all such persons, whither freemen or others, acting as aforesayd, shall & hereby are made vncapable of voting in all civil assemblyes during theire obstinate persisting in such wicked wayes & courses, & vntill certifficate be given of theire reformation."

From this time onward church attendance was required of all freemen, and it is significant that the clause disfranchising those who refused to attend the church was retained in the legal code as late as 1672,[4] and was not repealed down to the time of the forfeiture of the charter.   The action against the Baptists, while not leading to the extreme of the death penalty, was almost as rigorous as that directed against the Quakers.   As early as 1644 the sentence of banishment was passed against the Baptists,[5] and in 1665 five persons were disfranchised for professing the doctrines of the Anabaptists.[6]

[1] *Mass. Col. Rec.*, IV, Pt. I, 155, 194.

[2] *Ibid.*, 277; the death penalty clause came two years later (*ibid.*, 346).

[3] *Ibid.*, IV, Pt. II, 88–89.

[4] Code of 1672, 48.   This was one of the bases of Randolph's claim that none but church-members could be freemen (*Randolph Papers*, II, 293; III, 35).

[5] *Mass. Col. Rec.*, II, 85.

[6] *Ibid.*, IV, Pt. II, 290–291.   Later they were ordered to leave the colony (*ibid.*, 373) ; but the order was not enforced and the sect shortly came to be tolerated (Palfrey, II, 486).

Upon the restoration of the Stuart monarchy the Massachusetts General Court had written, in December, 1660, to King Charles II. praying for a continuance of their charter.[1] To this address the king sent a favorable reply, promising the inhabitants that he would not come behind any of his predecessors in a just encouragement of the colony, and that they should be partakers in his late promises of liberty towards tender consciences.[2] In spite of a second and still more humble and supplicatory letter from the general court,[3] the king, June 28, 1662, was ready to suggest changes in the government of New England by which members of the Church of England at least should be granted political and ecclesiastical privileges. In a letter of that date, while again promising protection and granting pardon for all offences against himself committed in the colony, Charles required and charged the people of Massachusetts to grant liberty of conscience to those who desired the use of the Book of Common Prayer; he directed the colonists to take the oath of allegiance, ordered that all justice should be administered in his name, and that laws repugnant to his authority should be repealed. He then ordered the abolition of the religious qualification upon the suffrage.

"Wee assuring ourself, & obleiging & comanding all persons concerned, that, in the election of the Gouernor or Asistants, there be only consideration had of the wisdome, virtue, & integrity of the persons to be chosen, & not of any affection wth refference to their opinions & outward professions, & that all the freeholders of competent estates, not vitious in conversacon & orthodoxe in religion, (though of different persuasions concerning church gouerment,) may haue their votes in the election of all officers, both ciuill & military."[4]

The royal letter caused great disappointment in the colony,[5] where the kind words of the king's first letter had led the colonists to hope for freedom from any English inter-

[1] *Mass. Col. Rec.,* IV, Pt. I, 450.
[2] Palfrey, II, 494–495.
[3] *Mass. Col. Rec.,* IV, Pt. II, 32.
[4] *Ibid.,* 164; Hutchinson, *Papers* (Prince Soc.), II, 100–104.
[5] Palfrey, II, 528.

ference. To carry out the king's commands would mean the overthrow of the Puritan theocracy; and the authorities, not openly refusing to obey, temporized with the matter. Beyond directing that writs should run in the king's name none of the royal orders was immediately executed by the general court.[1]

The four royal commissioners sent to New England in 1664, besides their other duties,[2] were directed to confer with the Massachusetts government on the king's letter of 1662 and to obtain a more reasonable compliance with its demands.[3] The commissioners' instructions were explicit upon this point.[4] The king deemed it "very scandalous" that any man should be debarred from the practice of religion according to English laws by those who had been given liberty to adopt what profession they pleased in religion; he now demanded,

" in a word, that persons of good & honest conversation who have lived long there may enjoy all ye priviledges ecclesiasticall & civill wch are due to them, and wch are enjoyed by oth^rs, as to choose and be chosen into places of government & the like; and that differences in opinion doe not lessen their charity to each other, since charity is a fundamental in all religion."

With these instructions upon the suffrage question the commissioners arrived in Boston in July, 1664.[5]

[1] In May, 1663, however, a committee of magistrates, deputies, and elders was appointed to " consider the perticulars relating to extending the liberty of certeine of the inhabitants in point of elections;" and any of the elders or freemen were privileged to hand to the committee their advice in writing upon the subject, in order that something might be agreed upon " if it be the will of God, that may be satisfactory and safe, as best conducing to his glory and this peoples felicity." No action appears to have been taken by this committee, and Massachusetts had made no further compliance with the king's commands when the royal commissioners reached Boston in the summer of 1664 (*Mass. Col. Rec.,* IV, Pt. II, 74).

[2] For general accounts of the commission see Palfrey, II, 574-634; Doyle, *Puritan Colonies,* II, 140-152; Deane, *The Puritan Age,* 502-520.

[3] *New York Colonial Documents,* III, 61-63.

[4] *Ibid.,* 51; 57-61.   [5] Palfrey, II, 579.

A few days after their arrival the general court met in special session and, at last alive to the necessity of some compliance with the royal demands, passed an act for the extension of the suffrage to non-church-members. This law, so famous for its formal compliance with the king's letter, and for its practical disobedience of his commands, is as follows:

"This Court doth Declare, That the Law prohibiting all persons, except Members of Churches, and that also for allowance of them, in any County Court, are hereby Repealed.

"And do also Order and Enact, That from henceforth all English men, presenting a Certificate under the hands of the Ministers or Minister of the place where they dwell, that they are Orthodox in Religion, and not vicious in their lives, and also a Certificate under the hands of the Select Men of the place, or of the major part of them, that they are Free holders, and are for their own proper Estate (without heads of persons) rateable to the Country in a single Country Rate, after the usual manner of valuation in the place where they live, to the full value of *ten shillings*, or that they are in full Communion with some church among us; It shall be in the liberty of all and every such person or persons, being twenty-four years of age, Householders and settled Inhabitants in this Jurisdiction, from time to time to present themselves and their desires to this Court for their admittance to the Freedome of this Common-wealth, and shall be allowed the privilidge to have such their desire propounded, and put to vote in the General Court, for acceptance to the Freedome of the Body politick, by the sufferage of the major part, according to the Rules of our Patent." [1]

By this act the church-membership restriction was technically abolished, but a mere list of the requirements imposed upon those who desired admission under the terms of the act, and not being in communion with some church, shows how very slightly was the door to the freemanship left ajar. The applicant must be (1) twenty-four years of age, (2) a settled inhabitant (regularly admitted by some town), (3) a householder, (4) a freeholder, (5) a payer of taxes upon property, (6) orthodox in religion, (7) not vicious in life; (8) he must present a certificate from all the ministers of his town proving his religious and moral qualifications, (9) and a certificate from the majority of

[1] Code of 1672, 56; *Mass. Col. Rec.*, IV, Pt. II, 118.

the selectmen of his town that he was a freeholder and a tax-payer to the amount of ten shillings, not including his poll-tax; and (10) finally, he must be accepted by the vote of the majority of the general court. Yet, said the court, in a letter to the king in October, 1664, this was the "utmost" they could do to satisfy his majesty and still retain consistency "with conscience of our duty towards God, & the just libertyes & priviledges of our patent."[1] Even after several persons had been admitted to the freedom under this plan, it was but natural that the royal commissioners should consider it merely a subterfuge by which "they might evade the King's letter in that poynt."[2]

Finding that the law of 1664 would not give the extension of the suffrage which they had expected, in February, 1664-5, the commissioners asked the general court to invite all the inhabitants of the colony to come up to the annual elections in the following May.[3] When the court refused to call the people together, the commissioners even resorted to the means of writing letters to non-freemen in the country, asking them to attend the election.[4] In spite of all their efforts, the commissioners were unsuccessful in arousing the popular clamor which they hoped would overawe the oligarchy. The assembly did not change its attitude except, if anything, to become more independent. In the correspondence between the court and the commissioners the former asserted that the oath of allegiance was administered, and that justice ran in the king's name. They quietly, but firmly, refused to grant the use of the Prayer-Book or "haue the same set vp here: we conceive it is apparent that it will disturbe our peace in our present enjoyments."[5] They even had the audacity to declare that they had conformed to the king's request in the matter of the suffrage:

"Touching civil libertjes.

"To elect or be elected, vnto civil offices, the quallifications mentioned in his majestjes letter, being orderly euidenced to us, are accepted, as may appeare by our late lawe & practise therevpon."

[1] *Mass. Col. Rec.,* IV, Pt. II, 129.
[2] *N. Y. Col. Doc.,* III, 84.   [3] *Mass. Col. Rec.,* IV, Pt. II, 173.
[4] *Ibid.,* 174.   [5] *Ibid.,* 200.

This reply called forth a sarcastic rejoinder from the commissioners, in which they expressed admiration for those who came to America to establish liberty of conscience, and later denied it to others, in order that their own enjoyments might not be disturbed.[1] Their opinions upon the new freemanship law were not hidden in sarcasm:

"You have so tentered the kings quallifications as in making him only who payeth ten shillings to a single rate to be of competent estate, that when the king shall be enformed, as the trueth is, that not one church member in an hundred payes so much, & y^t in a towne of an hundred inhabitants, scarse three such men are to be found, wee feare the king will rather finde himself deluded then satisfied by your late act."

The commissioners now took up the printed law-book of 1660 and advised over a score of changes in it. In these suggestions they no longer speak for the whole body of dissenters or non-church-members, but they are content to ask that the restriction upon freemen be so changed that it will comprehend members of the Church of England.[2] The last features of the controversy are the report of the commissioners concerning Massachusetts[3] and a narrative drawn up by the general court recounting the facts of their intercourse with the commissioners.[4] Neither of these adds anything to the suffrage controversy; the court claimed it had repealed the obnoxious freemanship law, while the commissioners again alleged that the new act was of no value, its practical effect being to retain the old religious limitation.

Having seen the controversy between the commissioners and the court about the act of 1664, we may now look at such facts as illustrate the administration of this law. The terms of the law seem designed to keep out rather than admit to the suffrage those who were not members of some regular church. Bearing in mind the uncompromising character of the New England ministers, it would seem to be almost

[1] *Mass. Col. Rec.*, IV, Pt. II, 204–205.
[2] *Ibid.*, 210 ff.
[3] *N. Y. Col. Doc.*, III, 110–113; Hutchinson, *Papers* (Prince Soc.), II, 146–147.
[4] *Mass. Col. Rec.*, IV, Pt. II, 218 ff.

impossible for a person not belonging to the church to obtain a certificate of orthodoxy in religion from the ministers of his town. But even if this were possible, there were still the inhabitancy, the householder, the freeholder, and the tax-paying qualifications to be met by the applicant, in addition to the age requirement of twenty-four years. Of these qualifications the most difficult, next to the religious one, was that requiring the candidate for the freemanship to pay at least ten shillings, besides the poll-tax, in a single country rate. It is not easy to-day to catch the meaning of this tax qualification. The unit of taxation was a levy of one penny on the pound of all real and personal property,[1] and this was called a rate; when one rate did not yield a sufficient income, several, even twenty, might be laid.[2] A man paying ten shillings taxes at the rate of one penny on the pound would possess one hundred and twenty pounds value of taxable property. Such an amount was an unusual possession at that time and for many years afterwards, and in the colony at large the statement of the royal commissioners may have been near the truth, that " not one church member in an hundred payes so much," and " in a towne of an hundred inhabitants, scarce three such men are to be found." [3]

Several tax-lists for the town of Boston are extant for the years 1674, 1676, and 1687,[4] which throw some light upon the amount of assessed property held by citizens of that town. The list of 1674 [5] shows ninety-nine persons out of six hundred and seventy-four as paying ten shillings or more upon a single country rate. An incomplete list for 1676 [6] gives forty out of one hundred and ninety-seven male taxables as possessing one hundred and twenty pounds

[1] *The Book of the General Lavves and Libertyes,* 1660, 14; Code of 1672, 22–26. The laws, unfortunately, do not give a fixed valuation of land as was the case in Connecticut, but only of domestic animals.

[2] *Laws of New Hampshire* (1904), I, *Province Period, 1679–1702,* 335, 367, 433, 450.

[3] *Mass. Col. Rec.,* IV, Pt. II, 204–205.

[4] *First Report of the Record Commissioners of the City of Boston,* 1876, 22–133.

[5] *Ibid.,* 22–59.   [6] *Ibid.,* 66–67.

or more of taxable property. These lists show a far larger proportion of people possessing the property qualification than the commissioners claimed; one person in five or seven is very different from the three in a hundred claimed by the commissioners' report.[1] The list for 1687,[2] however, varies considerably from the earlier one, and shows a general lowering of the assessment values. Out of twelve hundred and thirty male tax-payers in that year, only thirty-four persons were rated for ten shillings or over. This brings up quite close to the commissioners' estimate of one in thirty-three of the population. The facts given in these lists show that the tax-paying qualification at best would have included only a small proportion of the population of Boston.

But the best testimony to the strictness of the new law is to be seen in the few cases of freemen admitted upon certificate. In the fall of 1664 six persons were given their freedom upon presenting certificates that they were qualified according to the law;[3] but this comparatively good beginning was not maintained, and from 1665 to 1680 inclusive only fourteen cases of such admissions have been noted.[4] It is not, of course, certain that the records have expressly stated all the cases where certificates were presented, and it is possible that others of the recorded admissions may have been upon certificate and no mention made of the fact. But, looking no farther than the face of the records, it is apparent that only about twenty persons were admitted to the free-manship under the new law.[5] Had the number of persons

[1] Allowance must be made for the wealth of Boston and also for the fact that these lists very likely did not include all those taxed on the polls alone; probably the country districts would show a much lower proportion of qualified persons than these lists give for Boston.

[2] *First Report of the Record Commissioners of the City of Boston,* 1876, 91–133.

[3] *Mass. Col. Rec.,* IV, Pt. II, 134.

[4] *Ibid.,* 145, 146, 285, 408; V, 264, 279.

[5] One of these certificates has been preserved in *Mass. Hist. Soc. Proc.,* 1st Series, XII, 105:

" Certificate of John Wilson and Hezekiah Usher.

" These do testifie vnto the honoured Gen. Court yᵗ mʳ John Tuttle, William Hasie, and Benjamin Muzzie of Boston—

so admitted been much greater, it is inconceivable that the Massachusetts agents later, in justifying their course before the Committee of Trade and Plantations, would have used no stronger word than " several" in describing the number of non-church-members who had been made free.[1]   It seems highly probable that the new qualification was used only as a means of evading the king's instructions,[2] and did not result in any appreciable extension of the suffrage.[3]

After the contest with the royal commissioners the colony entered upon a period of ten years of political peace and

---

Rumnie marsh, are vpon Good testimony of others, and my owne knowledge or experience both orthodox in the Christian Religion, and of unblameable conversation, as I do believe, and doe humbly comend them therefore vnto the Acceptance of the hon. Court, into the Society and Companie of our freemen, according as they expresse their desires therevnto, and Aymes at the Common Good therein.   JOHN WILSON SENIOR.

"2ᵈ d. of the 3m. 65.

" Mr John Tuttle, William Hasie and Benjamin Muzzie, are raiteable acording to the Law made for admitance of Freemen: 2.: May 1665.   HEZEKIAH VSHER."

[1] *Randolph Papers*, Prince Society, II, 283, III, 8.
[2] *N. Y. Col. Doc.*, III, 84.
[3] It must be noted, however, that the total number of admissions to the freemanship—presumably all church-members except the twenty already mentioned—was considerably greater in the years succeeding 1664 than in those immediately preceding, as the following figures show :

1645–1649 admissions were		230
1650–1654 "	"	146
1655–1659 "	"	64
1660–1664 "	"	48
1665–1669 "	"	305
1670–1674 "	"	415
1675–1679 "	"	271
1680–1684 "	"	397

The writer at first supposed that this increase in freemen was due to the new law, but later investigation disclosed no connection between this number of freemen and the law of 1664.

ecclesiastical quiet. The attitude towards the Quakers and other dissenters had changed somewhat, so far as religious tolerance was concerned, but this lessening severity did not extend to the admission of the non-conformists to the free-manship. When, in 1670, a request came from the county of York (Maine),—one of the places whose freemen had been admitted without reference to church-membership,—that the number of their freemen be increased, they received the reply,—

"this Court declares, y^t it is the best expedient to obteine the ends desired that those parts furnish themselves wth an able, pious, & orthodox minister, & commend that to them, according to the order of the County Court." [1]

Such language gives slight evidence of a compliance with the king's desires, and it shows that the only practical way of making freemen was still that established by the law of 1631. A similar vigilance is seen in the attempt to abolish election mistakes, frauds, and deceits in 1673,[2] and in the order of the same year that those who were desirous of becoming freemen under the act of 1664 should be proposed at one annual court of election and the question of their admission not put to a vote until the following year.[3]

After ten years of comparative quiet upon the suffrage question, the matter was taken up anew by the English government, and the interference from England was aided by the vehemence and persistency of the English agent in the colonies. Edward Randolph was not a man of statesmanlike character, nor, indeed, was his mission one which required such qualities; he was rather a political detective, who, for the use of the English authorities, ferreted out the political irregularities of the Massachusetts commonwealth. With the many topics of dispute—the Maine and New Hampshire question, the enforcement of the navigation acts, the judicial and oath controversies—we are not here con-

[1] *Mass. Col. Rec.,* IV, Pt. II, 452.
[2] *Ibid.,* 553.
[3] *Ibid.,* 562. This act was repealed ten years later (*ibid.,* V, 385). I have found no evidence in the records to show the reason for the act.

cerned; and our account of Randolph must be limited to his attitude towards the suffrage question.[1]

Almost immediately upon his arrival in New England he found evidences of the irregularities which it was his business to discover, and which undoubtedly did exist. In June, 1676, he writes that the officers of the colony are mainly " inconsiderable Mechanicks;" that confiding church-members are alone capable of election; and that the clergy generally are inclined to sedition, although some " Civil Gentlemen" abominate " the Hypocrisy of their Pharisaicall Sanhedrim."[2] By the following October he did not deal in such generalities, but now stated that no one could be admitted a freeman or have any vote unless he were a church-member in full communion. He had now discovered that the oaths of supremacy and allegiance were not taken, but that an oath of fidelity was imposed upon all persons under penalty of a fine for refusal; he believed he saw that the freemen made only one-sixth of the male population, and that only interest and design had drawn most of the people into church-membership.[3]

Randolph's letters were considered by the Committee of Trade and Plantations in England, who thought the colony had technically abolished its earlier freeman law at the demand of the king, but that the practice all along had been in accordance with the earlier narrow custom.[4] The agents of Massachusetts were called in to explain the conduct of the colony, and they replied that they knew of no such practice; "that several are freemen who are not Church-members, and that 'tis not the point of opinion in Religion, but the number or defect of Votes, that prefers one and lays by others."[5] In April, 1678, Randolph was back in England, laying his charges before the committee. The Massachusetts agents offered to show that his charges were falsehoods,[6] but Randolph replied by quoting their own law-book of 1672, and at the request of the lords of the committee he read the laws refusing freemanship to all not

[1] For an elaborate account of Randolph, see the Prince Society's edition of the *Randolph Papers*, I; and Palfrey, III, 280–397.

[2] *Randolph Papers*, II, 206, 207.

[3] *Ibid.*, 226, 235.

[4] *Ibid.*, 281.

[5] *Ibid.*, 283.

[6] *Ibid.*, 285.

in full communion with some orthodox church and forbidding any person from voting who was not an attendant upon the established public worship.[1]   The committee were much impressed by Randolph's case; they seemed "very much to resent" the action of Massachusetts, and instead of favoring the colony they expressed the opinion that "the whole matter ought seriously to be considered from the Very Root."[2]

Later the colony agents replied to the iterated statements[3] of Randolph respecting the limited suffrage.   Although by charter they had absolute power to admit any freemen they saw fit, yet, they aver, an express law had been made by which "others besides churchmembers are capacitated to be made ffreemen, upon which law severall considerable persons have been admitted, & any others may be from tyme to tyme, if they please to offer themselves."[4]   But such replies were justly held to be subterfuges, and failed to satisfy either Randolph or the English authorities when all were looking for points of attack upon Massachusetts.   Randolph, back again in America, wrote in 1679 in favor of a broad extension of the franchise by admitting as freemen all inhabitants who had taken the oath of allegiance, and excluding from the suffrage or office all refusing to take the oath.[5]   Such a radical change was not adopted by the English committee, but in May, 1679, they advised the king to direct "that there bee noe other distinction in making Freemen than that they bee men of competent Estates ratable at ten shillings, according to the Law of the place,"[6] and this feature was shortly afterwards incorporated into a royal letter to the general court.[7]   The court later replied[8]

---

[1] *Randolph Papers*, II, 293.   I do not know whether it was intentional or not that these laws were permitted to stand in the law-book of 1672, after the passage of the freeman act of 1664.

[2] *Ibid.*, 296.   [3] *Ibid.*, 311, 313, 318.
[4] *Ibid.*, III, 8.   [5] *Ibid.*, 35.
[6] *Ibid.*, 45.

[7] Hutchinson, *Papers* (Prince Society), II, 259.   Hutchinson, in a foot-note, says, "They seem to have held out till the last in refusing to admit" those who were not church-members or did not obtain a certificate from the minister of the town.

[8] June 11, 1680; *Mass. Col. Rec.*, V, 287, 288.

that no person was incapacitated for the freemanship who was a freeholder, ratable to the value of ten shillings, not vicious in life, and also orthodox in religion; and they expressly stated—for the first time—that to be of a different opinion upon matters of external worship, and particularly to desire to worship according to the rules of the Church of England, was not the form of heterodoxy which their law provided against. This is the most liberal statement on the subject which I have found; but even this shows no intention to make the property qualification of the non-church-members any lower than the extreme requirements of 1664. A perfectly frank statement would have said that these strict property conditions were not applied to " Congregational men," but only to those not in communion with the established churches.

In the midst of the attacks upon the company's charter there appears to be no intention on the part of the colonial leaders of changing the suffrage conditions. In August, 1682, when Randolph was again writing against the influence of the Independent ministers,[1] the Massachusetts agents in London were reiterating their usual part-truth, "There is noe other distinction vsed in makeing of ffreemen Then that they be ffreeholders of Tenn Shillings ratable Estate, and of the Protestant Religion."[2] Even after the court learned how sharply the proceedings against the colony were being pushed in England, the agents were instructed:[3]

" It being of the essentialls in our charter to vse our owne liberty wth respect to freemen, this Court hauing repealed that law that appointed a yeares probation, so as now wee haue fully complyed with his majeties former letters and comands in this matter, yow are not to make any alteration of the quallifications that are required by law as at present established."

Up to the last the form of political qualification which, in spite of all denials, actually favored church-members was

[1] *Randolph Papers,* III, 186, 187.
[2] *Ibid.,* 192. In February, 1682–3, the general court repealed the law requiring applicants for freedom who were not members of the church to undergo a year's probation before acceptance into the corporation; but this was as far as they would go (*Mass. Col. Rec.,* V, 385).
[3] March 30, 1683; *Mass. Col. Rec.,* V, 389.

upheld by those directing the policy of the colony. The overthrow of the religious system did not come until the company's charter was declared forfeited by the English Court of Chancery in 1684, and all political activity under the charter ceased two years later by the appointment of a president and sixteen councillors for Massachusetts, New Hampshire, Maine, and the King's Province.[1] Thereafter, until the overthrow of the government of Andros in the spring of 1689, Massachusetts was without any popular elections except those in the towns for local officers.

It would be interesting, if possible, to determine the number of freemen in Massachusetts immediately before the revocation of the charter, but it is doubtful if the material exists for an exact account. Palfrey estimates the freemen as numbering between one thousand and twelve hundred persons in 1670;[2] another writer believes the freemen made up about one-fifteenth of the entire population in 1679;[3] while Randolph, writing in 1682, states that there were eighteen hundred freemen,[4] and that they made up less than one-eighth of the (male?) inhabitants.[5] At an election for the nominations of magistrates in 1676, under the code of 1672,[6] each freeman voted for eighteen persons; and the highest number of votes cast was thirteen hundred and twenty, for John Leverett.[7] This would show that there were at least thirteen hundred freemen, and probably considerably more than that figure. It is not likely that every freeman gave one of his eighteen votes for Leverett, nor is it probable that every freeman took part in the nomination for magistrates. To place the number of freemen in 1676 at about fifteen hundred would, therefore, not seem an over-estimate. Votes for the nomination of magistrates in 1683 and 1686[8] show a smaller number of freemen participating than in 1676, a result perhaps to be attributed to

[1] Palfrey, III, 484.
[2] *New England*, III, 41, note 3.
[3] Ernst, *Constitutional History of Boston*, 17.
[4] *Randolph Papers*, Prince Society, III, 172, 173.
[5] *Ibid.*, 186, 187.
[6] Code of 1672, 47.
[7] *New Hampshire Hist. Soc. Coll.*, III, 99.
[8] Hutchinson, *Papers* (Prince Society), II, 282, 285.

the uncertainty concerning the company charter in the later years.[1] Taking these several instances, it appears that about thirteen hundred freemen actually participated in the annual nominations for magistrates. The population of the colony, at the lowest estimate, was twenty-five thousand in 1670; and allowing for the increase in population in the following years, we shall not be far wrong if we count the voting freemen as one-twentieth of the entire population, or one-fourth or one-fifth of the adult males.[2]

With the seizure and arrest of Andros and his associates in April, 1689, the popular forms of government were restored. It was not, indeed, thought best to have an election for colony officers in May, but delegates to conventions were elected by the several towns; and the second convention agreed to a policy similar to that adopted in the other colonies of New England,—that of restoring to office the magistrates who had been deposed by the recent coercive measures of James II.[3] Later the convention became bolder, taking the name of general court, and in the spring of 1690 providing for a regular colonial election.[4]

At an early point in the revolution against Andros there are indications of a change in sentiment upon the suffrage question. The charter officers were restored and the old forms revived, but the struggle with the Stuarts and their governors had brought the freemen and non-freemen more closely together. A broadside, evidently printed before the political question had been solved in May, 1689, expressed the opinion that the officers elected in 1686 would have the power and will " to take in Free men under qualifications of Sobriety, and some Interest in the Country by Estate." [5] In February, 1689–90, when the determination to hold an election in May had been reached, a change in the suffrage

[1] In 1683 there were 26, and in 1686, 32 nominees. Adding together the votes for all of these and dividing by eighteen, the number for which each voter could ballot, and taking it for granted that each freeman did vote for eighteen, it appears that there were 1260 voters in 1683 and 1305 in 1686.

[2] Compare Palfrey, III, 41, note 3.

[3] *Ibid.*, 589.

[4] *New Hampshire Provincial Laws* (1904), I, 349, 353.

[5] *Mass. Hist. Soc. Proc.*, 1st Series, XII, 118, 119.

qualifications was also adopted by which the old requirement of a minister's certificate was abolished, and a comparatively low property or tax-paying qualification imposed:

"It is Ordered by this Court, That the Clause in the Law title Freemen, referring to Ministers giving Certificate to Persons Desiring their
Freedom, be and hereby is repealed, And the Sum of Ten shillings is
reduced to ffour shillings in a Single Country Rate (without heads of
Persons) Or that the Person to be made free have houses or Lands of
the Cleer Yearly Value of Six Pounds Freehold w'ch Value is to be
returned to the Court by the Select men of the Place, or the Major
part of them who also are to Certify that such Person is not vicious
in Life."[1]

The effect of this act was not to repeal the clause under
which since 1631 adult male church-members had been admitted to the freemanship, but to lower the restrictions
imposed by the act of 1664 upon the admission of those who
were not members of the church.

There is abundant proof that the act of February,
1689–90, resulted in an immediate extension of the franchise. The records of the court[2] in the few succeeding
weeks give the names of nine hundred and nine new freemen.[3] This figure becomes significant when it is noted that
the number of freemen admitted during the two months of
March and April, 1690, was greater than the entire number
of admissions in the twelve years from 1674 to 1686 under
the old charter and suffrage provisions. Of the new admissions it is also interesting to notice that over half—four
hundred and ninety-three—were plainly admitted by virtue
of the new property and tax-paying qualifications, while
only two hundred and ninety-three were accepted because
of their church-membership; and of the remaining ones,

[1] *New Hampshire Provincial Laws*, I, 355; *New England Historical
and Genealogical Register*, III, 346; Sewall's Diary in *Mass. Hist. Soc.
Coll.*, 6th Series, I, 107. The income qualification of this act required
non-church-members to possess an income from freehold three times
as great as that required by the English forty-shilling qualification.

[2] The legislative records of the Inter-charter period have recently
been published in Vol. I of the *New Hampshire Laws, Provincial
Period*.

[3] *Ibid.*, 363–471 *passim*.

the basis for whose admission is not stated in the records, it is probable that a majority also came in under the terms of the new law. The revolutionists in Massachusetts, like Leisler in New York, granted an extension of the suffrage in order to strengthen their cause; but in the former colony they still retained the favoritism shown to the members of the church. It was not until the passing of the new charter of 1691 under the royal seals that the suffrage was established uniformly upon a property basis, and the peculiar political privileges of the church-members, after sixty years of practice, were at last abolished. A man's political rights, for the future, were to rest upon the ownership of wealth, not upon the possession of an orthodox Christian character. The ideal of the founders was a noble one, but two facts in the English world of the time made the attainment of the ideal impossible. The first of these facts was the lack of religious homogeneity in the English nation, and the growing toleration which came in spite of all the adverse legislation of the Cavalier Parliament. The religious restrictions imposed by Massachusetts were more far-reaching than those in England, and came into conflict with the less severe policy of the Stuarts. The second fact is to be seen in the anomaly of disfranchising members of the Church of England in an English colony. The English Parliament had indeed attempted to prevent non-conformists from voting in English elections, but it was not the more likely to relish the disfranchisement of Episcopalians by a non-conformist English colony. Had church-membership in New England carried with it orthodoxy in the English sense, it is possible the home government would not so strongly have opposed the religious qualifications; but the exclusion of Episcopalians from political power was as obnoxious to the Englishman of 1691 as it had been in the days of Charles I. and Charles II.

II. *The Plymouth Colony.*

Plymouth colony is the first of the many New England settlements whose political organization may be called indigenous; not in the sense that the type of government founded was un-English, but that it had no organic or legal

22

connection with the English government. Within the
limits of every one of the New England colonies there
appeared bands of settlers who had voluntarily united for
purposes of settlement, and who were compelled by force of
circumstances to form political associations. The most cele-
brated of such associations is that formed on board the
Mayflower on November 11, 1620. The Pilgrims were
already united by social and religious ties, and in their joint
endeavors to defray the cost of the expedition they had
formed a quasi-corporation of an economic nature. But
the political organization which should have been derived
from the Virginia Company, upon whose land they intended
to settle, was of no value when the Pilgrims found themselves many miles away from the lands of the Virginia
Company, and with no possibility of reaching the place of
their intended settlement. The political consequences of the
mistake of selecting so northern a settlement were seized
upon at once by "some of the strangers amongst them,"
who in "discontented & mutinous speeches" asserted that
they would "use their owne libertie" on shore, and that
there was none who had power to command them.[1]   To
curb such spirits, and also because it was felt that a political
association of the colonists would be as "firme as any
patent, and in some respects more sure," the *Mayflower*
compact was composed and signed.

The words of this document are known to almost every
American, but no excuse need be given for repeating here
the political phrases of the compact. The subscribers agree
that they do

"by these presents solemnly & mutualy in ye presence of God, and one
of another, covenant & combine our selves togeather into a civill body
politick, for our better ordering & preservation & furtherance of ye
ends aforesaid; and by vertue hearof to enacte, constitute, and frame
such just & equall lawes, ordinances, acts, constitutions, & offices, from
time to time, as shall be thought most meete & convenient for ye generall good of ye Colonie, unto which we promise all due submission
and obedience."[2]

[1] Bradford, *History of Plymouth Plantation*, 53.
[2] *Ibid.*, 54.

Under this association the government of Plymouth colony was administered for over seventy years. The patent from the Council for New England, obtained in 1621, gave a legal title to the land so unexpectedly occupied, but it did little more in a political way than to confirm the existing government. The self-incorporating body by this patent attained legal position, but no real change was made in the administration of government in the little colony. Bradford's anticipation that the personal compact would be "more sure" than any patent later received its justification, for no colonial political organization of the seventeenth century had as long a lease of life as did the government inaugurated so humbly in the *Mayflower* cabin.

Funds for the transportation of the Pilgrims had been obtained by the formation of a stock company in London, composed of certain capitalists and the emigrants. The shares were placed at ten pounds, and any free man going to the colony was entitled to one share without making a money subscription.[1] Perhaps one-quarter or one-fifth of the stock of the undertaking was represented by shares issued in this way to the settlers; the remainder of the capital—that is, four-fifths of seven thousand pounds—was furnished by London capitalists.[2] All the property of the enterprise was to be held in common, and at the end of seven years was to be distributed *pro rata* among the stockholders, both in England and the colony. In 1623 the London adventurers sent out some colonists who were not incorporated into the organization as stockholders, but who came out at their own risk and expense, and hence did not form a part of the communistic enterprise. These "particulars" were "yet to be subjecte to ye generall Government,"[3] although not sharing in the common duties or advantages.[4] While subject to the laws and regulations of the colony, it does not appear that these "particulars"

[1] Bradford, 28, 29.
[2] Doyle, *Puritan Colonies*, I, 42.
[3] Bradford, 100.
[4] *Ibid.*, 104, 123.

had any share in elections or government; and it is not to be wondered that they formed a discontented faction.[1]

These conditions, together with the desertion of some from the "generality" to the "particular" state, and the fear of the rapidly approaching time when all property must be distributed share and share alike, led to the proposal on the part of the colonist stockholders to purchase the shares of the London capitalists. Accordingly, in 1626, a contract was executed[2] for the extinction of the claims of the Londoners. The purchase outright by the colonists gave them entire control of the property of the colony, and permitted them to admit to their membership new proprietors upon their own terms. The effect upon the colony was much the same as that which followed the transfer of the Massachusetts charter to New England; it removed the directing power in the colony's affairs from England to America and identified the economic trading company activity with the political organization. The purchase led to another development,—an extension of the franchise in the colony.

Up to this point the community of goods and of political privileges, based respectively, as we have seen, upon the commercial contract made in London and upon the civil compact made on the *Mayflower,* was limited to those who became stockholders of the enterprise. Now that the colony had achieved self-ownership, the stockholder theory was not abandoned, but simply extended to include all the responsible inhabitants, whether they were "particulars" or of the "generality." The attitude of the colony was a more liberal one than that adopted in Massachusetts four years later. "For sundrie reasons," which, unfortunately, Bradford does not enumerate, it was determined to admit "into this partnership" all heads of families and those free single young men who were able to govern themselves and their affairs, and accordingly "be helpfull in ye comone-welth."[3] Each free single man was to receive one share, and heads of families were given one share for themselves and for

[1] Palfrey, I, 219; Bradford, 123.
[2] *Ibid.*, 143, 144.   [3] *Ibid.*, 145.

each person in their families. Upon this basis the lands, houses, and cattle were divided, and incidentally political privileges were now conferred upon many who previously as "particulars" did not participate in the government. Thus the inhabitants acquired possession of the lands of the colony; and partnership in the economic sense, which at first seemed the stronger of the bonds uniting the settlers, gradually gave place under the extension of private ownership of lands to the more modern feeling of political association.[1]

The new patent from the Council for New England, obtained in January, 1629–30, empowered Bradford and his heirs, associates, and assigns to incorporate themselves and the inhabitants of the colony under "some usual or fit name and title," and to make ordinances and constitutions for themselves, not contrary to the laws of England or to any frame of government established by the Council.[2] But this patent, like the earlier one, simply placed the duty of organizing the government upon the settlers, and left the *Mayflower* compact and the partnership arrangement of 1627 as the real bases of government.

By the codification of 1636 and the legislation of the two succeeding years, the civil and constitutional organization of the colony is evident for the first time. The class of freemen is now distinct; they are to meet annually for the purpose of electing the governor, assistants, constables, and other inferior officers,[3] and are subject to a fine for absence from election or refusal to hold office.[4] New freemen were admitted by a vote of the general court, composed of all the freemen;[5] or, later, by the representative courts. No

---

[1] At what point the word freeman was first applied to the partners does not appear from the records. It is used in 1633 and occurs frequently in the legislation of 1636, and probably was adopted from the Massachusetts use of the word (*Plymouth Records, Court Records,* I, 5).

[2] Hazard, *Historical Collections,* I, 298–304.

[3] *Records of the Colony of New Plymouth, Laws,* 7, 10.

[4] *Ibid.,* 10. The fine for neglecting to vote was re-enacted in 1660 and changed from three to ten shillings (*Records, Laws,* 84, 127).

[5] *Ibid., Court Records,* I, 32, and *passim.*

general qualifications appear to have been required of applicants for the freemanship except the taking of an oath of allegiance to the king and of fidelity to the government.[1] It is apparent, however, that the freemen did not, as in early Maryland, include all the *free men.* Notwithstanding the generous extension of political and economic rights in 1627, the existence of a non-enfranchised class is plain by 1636. The laws of that year established an inhabitant's oath, similar to that for freemen;[2] jury service was required of freeholders who were not freemen as well as those who had been admitted,[3] and no person could be admitted as an inhabitant, or be permitted to become a housekeeper, or to build a cottage, without the consent of some of the magistrates.[4]

As in early Connecticut, so in Plymouth, the suffrage was controlled largely by placing restrictions upon the admission of inhabitants rather than by expressing definite qualifications for the freemanship. Thus, in the absence

---

[1] *Records of the Colony of New Plymouth, Laws,* 8. In requiring the oath of allegiance to the king the government of Plymouth differed from that of Massachusetts. The oath is as follows:

"You shall be truly loyall to our Sov. Lord King Charles his heires & successors. You shall not speake or doe, devise or advise any thing or things act or acts directly or indirectly by land or water, that doth shall or may tend to the destruccon or overthrow of this prn't plantacons Colonie or Corporacon of New Plymouth, Neither shall you suffer the same to be spoken or done but shall hinder oppose & discover the same to the Govr & Assistants of the said Colony for the time being or some one of them. You shall faithfully submit unto such good & wholesome laws & ordnances as either are or shall be made for the ordering & governmt of the same, and shall endeavor to advance the growth & good of the several Colonies wthin the limits of this Corporacon by all due meanes & courses. All wch you promise & swear by the name of the great God of heaven & earth simply truly & faithfully to p'forme as you hope for help fro' God who is the God of truth and punisher of falsehood."

[2] *Ibid.,* 9, 12.
[3] *Ibid.,* 11.
[4] *Ibid.,* 26, 108, 109.

of any express restrictions upon the freemanship, the terms of admission of inhabitants into the colony became more important than they were in the Massachusetts Bay colony. The matter was not left with the several towns, but was controlled by the general government, and without the permission of some of the magistrates none could be admitted. By "lamentable experience" the general court had discovered that unworthy persons were sometimes admitted when such power was left to the local inhabitants.[1] In 1640 the court ordered that no new inhabitants be admitted into Yarmouth "except they bring certificate from the places whence they come, vnder sufficient mens hands of the s'd places, of their religious and honest carriage, wch certifycate shall first be allowed by the gou'n^r and assistants before such p'sons be admitted there."[2] An inhabitant's oath had been required as early as 1636, and in 1644 the court ordered that no person should be considered an inhabitant unless he took the oath of fidelity.[3] Between 1658 and 1662 residents who refused to take the oath of fidelity might be fined annually;[4] and in the former year, when many had "crept into some townshipes" contrary to the "ancient and wholsome" law of 1636–7, all not formally admitted were required to gain the approbation of the governor and at least two of the assistants; or, failing in that, to depart the colony.[5] In 1678 additional steps were taken for enforcing the law of 1636–7 in order to prevent "prophanes Increasing in the Collonie which is soe provoakeing to God and threatening to bringe Judgments vpon vs."[6] Fines were to be imposed upon residents who remained without permission, and upon persons entertaining such residents. The act concludes with the injunction to the magistrates,—showing the retention of a religious qualification at this late

---

[1] *Plymouth Records, Court Records,* I, 120.

[2] *Ibid.,* 142. See *Court Records,* III, 165, for permission to settle in a town.

[3] *Plymouth Records, Laws,* 43.

[4] *Ibid.,* 109, 118, 129. For infliction of fine, see *Court Orders,* III, 139, 176, 181, 191.

[5] *Ibid., Laws,* 118.

[6] *Ibid.,* 248.

date,—that they "wilbe carefull, that whom they accept off, are p'sons orthadox in theire Judgments." Thus to become a legal inhabitant a man must take the oath of fidelity, and must be accepted by the magistrates; and to obtain the approval of the latter a certificate of religious character might be required or some proof of orthodoxy in belief. While there was no religious qualification for the freemanship, the character of a man's religious belief might procure his admission or exclusion from the colony.

This question of inhabitancy in Plymouth is significant, not only because there were few restrictions upon the freemanship itself, but also on account of the political privileges which were granted to inhabitants who were not freemen. As early as 1636 non-freemen appear to be associated with the freemen in town affairs,[1] but their most valuable privilege came in the association with the freemen in the election of deputies to the representative courts established in 1638. The town deputies were to be chosen by the freemen and "such as are not ffreemen but haue taken the Oath of fidelitie and are masters of famylies and Inhabitants of the said Townes as they are to beare their [part] in the charges of their Committees so to haue a vote in the choyce of them."[2] But the delegates chosen must be freemen, and the magistrates and deputies were empowered to dismiss any deputy who was "insufficient or troublesome." Under this provision non-freemen participated in the election of representatives throughout the colonial period, although only freemen took part in the election of magistrates.[3]

The scrutiny required by law before the admission of inhabitants was not always exercised,[4] and in 1658 an order of court recognized the fact that "the Number of freemen in many places is but smale and the Inhabitants of the townshipes many more whoe haue equall voates with the freemen in the choise of Deputies;" by the weakness or prejudice of these inhabitants, the court stated, "it hath or

[1] *Plymouth Records, Laws,* 18.

[2] *Ibid.,* 31.

[3] The similar provision in Connecticut colony from 1639 to 1662 may have been introduced from Plymouth.

[4] Compare *Laws,* 118.

may come to passe that very vnfitt and vnworthy p'sons may be chosen." To prevent such evils the magistrates and deputies were again empowered to exclude objectionable members.[1] The more natural policy of limiting the suffrage was adopted in 1669, when it was provided that none should vote in town meetings but freemen, or "ffreeholders of twenty pounds ratable estate and of good conversation haueing taken the oath of fidelitie."[2] A few years later, in 1678, it was found "that the voateing of p'sons that haue not taken the oath of fidelity, doth much obstruct the carrying on of religion in the publicke weale." Accordingly, the exclusion from town meetings of those who had not taken the oath was reaffirmed, and the clerks of the towns were directed to keep the names of the men of their towns who had taken the oath.[3]

We must now notice what requirements were imposed upon applicants for the freemanship, after having become inhabitants of the colony. Three formalities cut off the non-free from the franchise,—the proposal of the applicant's name to the general court, his acceptance after a term of probation, and the taking of the oath of freeman by him after the court had voted to admit him.[4] For a number of years there appears to have been no formal method of proposing the names of applicants; and the term of probation was not a fixed one, but usually lasted until the next meeting of the court, which might not be a longer time than three or four months. A change in the method of admission did not come until June, 1656, when it was ordered that future candidates for the freemanship should be "such as shalbee alsoe approued of by the freemen in such townes wher they liue," and propounded to the court by the deputies of their respective towns.[5] Thus the approbation of the

[1] Compare *Laws*, 92.   [2] *Ibid.*, 223.   [3] *Ibid.*, 248.

[4] See *Records, passim*, for instances of each of these features.

[5] *Ibid., Court Orders,* III., 101; also *Laws*, 65, 68. Compare this custom with the relation of town freemanship to colony freemanship in Rhode Island, where the colony resigned almost entirely to the towns the prerogative of admission to the franchise. Plymouth never went so far in her local privileges. The Plymouth law was re-enacted in almost the same words in June, 1674 (*Records, Laws*, 236).

select class of freemen of a man's own town must first be obtained before his name could be proposed for admission to the colony court. Even this restriction did not seem sufficient, and two years later the applicant was required to "stand one whole yeare propounded to the Court," and then to be admitted if the court " shall not see cause to the Contrary." [1]

In the meantime, following the leadership of her stronger neighbors, Plymouth began a policy of religious restrictions which, while never so exclusive as those of Massachusetts and New Haven, yet departed from the more tolerant practice of the early settlers. In June, 1650, the features of the Massachusetts conformity act of 1635–6 were adopted by Plymouth. The new order provided

" That forasmuch as there are Risen vp amongst vs many scandalvs practises which are likly to proue destructiue to our churches and Common peace; That whosoeuer shall heerafter set vp any churches or publicke meetings diverse from those allreddy set vp and approued without the concent and approbacon of the Gouerment or shall continew any otherwise set vp without concent as aforsaid shalbe suspended from haueing any voyce in towne meetings and p'sented to the next general court to Receue such punishment as the court shall think meet to Inflict." [2]

A few years later, in 1659, during the first invasion by the Quakers into New England, Quakers and sympathizers with them were disfranchised in Plymouth. " Noe Quaker Rantor or any such corupt p'son" could be admitted to the franchise; [3] and freemen who were found to be Quakers or " manifest Incurragers" of them were to be disfranchised. Linked with the Quakers in exclusion from the freemanship were " opposers of the good and whosome lawes of this Collonie or manifest opposers of the true worship of God or such as refuse to doe the Countrey seruice being called thervnto;" and joined with them in incurring the pains of disfranchisement after admission were " such as shall contemptuously speake of the Court or of the lawes thereof

[1] *Records, Laws*, 79. Compare with similar feature in Connecticut.
[2] *Ibid.*, 57.
[3] *Records, Court Records*, III, 167; *Laws*, 100.

and such as are Judged by the Court grosly scandalouse as lyers drunkards Swearers &c." [1] The association of the Quakers in the minds of the legislators with such classes shows that the opposition to them was grounded not so much upon a religious fear as upon the political necessity of maintaining the purity of the body politic. Not until July, 1681, were the Quakers restored to a more favorable position. Then certain Quakers dwelling in Sandwich were given liberty to vote in the disposal of lands and the choice of rators or assessors.[2]

The royal commissioners to New England inquired into the condition of Plymouth as well as the other colonies, and were favorably impressed by the attitude of the authorities. To the four propositions of the commissioners [3] the general court responded in May, 1665. The reply to the first was that they had been accustomed to require all householders to take the oath of loyalty to the king. To the second, the court said it had been the constant practice

"to admitt men of competent estates and ciuell conversation, though of different judgments, yet being otherwise orthodox, to bee freemen, and to haue libertie to chose and bee chosen officers both ciuell and milletary." [4]

The reply to the third proposal was worded more guardedly; the court would "most hartily rejoyce that all our naighbours, soe quallifyed as in the proposition, would adjoyne themselves to our societie;" but if differing beliefs made this impossible, they would not deny the liberty of establishing other societies, where an able preaching minister was supported and regular Sabbath worship established; but they inferred that where by reason of the paucity and poverty ("pausette and pouertie") of the population

[1] Cases of disfranchisement both before and after 1659 are common in the Plymouth records. The causes of disfranchisement were drunkenness, lewdness, accepting Quakerism or sympathizing with Quakers, and opposing the government (*Court Records*, I, 132; III, 167, 176, 189).

[2] *Court Records*, VI, 71.

[3] *Ibid.*, IV, 85, 86.

[4] *Ibid.*

two congregations could not be maintained, it was not intended to root out the present organization. There are, the court added, " other places to accommodate men of different pswasions in societies by themselves." To the fourth proposal the court expressed itself not conscious of any laws derogatory to the king's dignity, but promised to repeal or alter them if any should be found.

These answers and the general attitude of the court pleased the commissioners, and they wrote in their narrative,—

" They are here constrained to perswade men, sometimes to compell them, to be free men, soe far are they from hindering any." [1]

Such a comment from those who were looking for irregularities means more than it would from the colonists themselves. Plymouth possessed fewer natural advantages and less wealth than did the neighboring colonies, and consequently there were not the same inducements for settlers to enter the colony. Thus she retained a greater economic and religious homogeneity than Massachusetts or Connecticut, and it is noteworthy that the records of Plymouth do not show the restless activity of a disfranchised class which is seen in Massachusetts and New Haven. Perhaps the commissioners were right in their statement of the difficulty of obtaining freemen.

But the test of such a statement would be found in the actual number of freemen and their proportion to the whole population. In 1634 it is probable that considerably more than a majority of the adult male taxpayers were freemen.[2] By 1638 the whole number of freemen was one hundred and twenty-three;[3] and forty-four more were added within the next five years.[4] In 1643, therefore, not allowing for deaths, there were one hundred and sixty-seven freemen, at

[1] Hutchinson, *Papers* (Prince Society), II, 145.
[2] There were sixty-eight freemen in 1634 and only eighty-six male taxables in the preceding year, but it is probable that the number of males was greater than the number of taxables (Palfrey, I, 344).
[3] *Court Records*, I, 52.
[4] *Ibid.*, 126–161 *passim;* II, 8–52 *passim.*

a time when the males between the ages of sixteen and sixty numbered six hundred and forty.[1] It accordingly seems probable that the freemen at this time made up about one-fourth of the adult male population. Yet sixteen years later, upon a matter submitted to the freemen, only one hundred and seventy-four freemen voted.[2] In 1670 the number of freemen had increased to three hundred and fifty-nine[3] in a population estimated at five thousand.[4] This would give one freeman to fourteen persons of the population, and make the freeman class one-third or one-fourth of the adult male population. Apparently, therefore, the enfranchised class in Plymouth was slightly larger than in Massachusetts, and somewhat smaller than in Connecticut[5] at this time.[6]

III. *The Northern Territories: New Hampshire and Maine.*

Little need be said in this connection of the suffrage in New Hampshire. The facts of interest during the independent existence of the colony will be told in their proper place, while under the rule of Massachusetts, her policies dominated the New Hampshire towns. Some of the New

[1] *Records*, VIII, 187.

[2] *Court Records*, III, 174.

[3] *Ibid.*, V, 274.

[4] Palfrey, III, 35.

[5] The writer cannot agree with Goodwin (*Pilgrim Republic*, 415) that the proportion of freemen in Massachusetts was "a half greater" than in Plymouth.

[6] Plymouth, like her neighbors, developed a system of so-called proxy voting, but the records are meagre in their descriptions of it, and apparently it never possessed the features of a true proxy which are to be found in early Rhode Island and Maryland. The "proxy" was simply the written ballot of the freeman who did not desire to attend personally the annual court of elections. The ballot was handed by the freeman to the town deputy after the latter's election in the town meeting, and by the deputy the actual ballot was taken, together with a list of the names of those so voting, to the general court of elections. There the freemen present first gave their votes and then, in an orderly fashion, the deputies presented the ballots of those who had decided not to attend (*Plymouth Records, Laws*, 79–80, *Court Orders*, II, 118).

Hampshire settlements had, indeed, been founded by dissenters from Massachusetts, and at the time of incorporation with Massachusetts, those who had been formally admitted as inhabitants or " freemen" of the New Hampshire towns were granted the Massachusetts franchise.[1] But this practice, apparently, did not continue after the union, and the same rules were applied to applicants for the freemenship from these towns as were imposed upon those in Massachusetts proper.

In Maine, on the other hand, there was a longer independent existence before the union with Massachusetts, and a greater variation from the prevailing New England idea of freemanship. From the time of the unfortunate Popham colony on the Kennebec in 1607 for almost thirty years there was no regularly organized government in Maine, and the scattered settlements under different grants were practically self-governing communities. The first government worthy of the name was that established in 1636 by William Gorges, a nephew of the proprietor, at Saco.[2] This was followed four years later by a more formal organization under the new charter granted by the king in 1639 to Gorges. The charter gave to the proprietor wide palatine powers similar to those granted to Lord Baltimore, and, as in the case of the latter, the inhabitants of the colony were to be joined with the proprietor in the making of laws. The legislative power was to be exercised by the proprietor " with the assent of the greater parte of the Freeholders of the said Province and Premisses for the tyme being (when there shal bee any) whoe are to bee called thereunto from tyme to tyme."[3] In March, 1639-40, Gorges executed papers for the establishment of government under the charter by erecting a council of seven named persons, and eight representatives of the freeholders elected from four counties.[4] The small village of Agamenticus (York) was first erected into a borough, and then in 1642 was made a city

[1] *Mass. Col. Rec.,* II, 29.

[4] Williamson, I, 281. The first meeting under Gorges's frame of
[3] Poore, *Charters and Constitutions,* I, 776.

[4] Williamson, I, 281. The first meeting under George's frame of government appears to have been a pure democratic meeting (*ibid.*).

with a mayor, recorder, twelve aldermen and twenty-four common councilmen, all annually elected by the citizens and freeholders.[1]

After the death of Gorges in 1647, some confusion arose in the colony, and in July, 1649, a popular convention, meeting at Gorgeana (York), established a popular government based upon a general compact:

"We, with our free and voluntary consent, do bind ourselves in a body politic and combination, to see these parts of the Country and Province regulated, according to such laws as have formerly been exercised, and such others as shall be thought meet, but not repugnant to the fundamental laws of our native Country."[2]

A governor and five or six councillors were to be elected annually and the choice determined "by most voices." Apparently, therefore, popular government existed among the settlers of the Gorges tract for a number of years before the union with Massachusetts. During this period, when any qualifications for the suffrage were expressed, and such was not often the case, the franchise was limited to freeholders, except in the case of the city of Gorgeana, where "citizens" could vote.

In addition to the Gorges colony there were a number of other settlements in the Maine territory, but their scattered inhabitants owed relationship to various proprietors, or to the colony of Plymouth, and political association was of the most rudimentary kind. Only among the settlers of the Lygonia patent do popular meetings appear to have played a definite part in the government.[3] At best the forms of government only were a little further developed in the Gorges lands and the colony of Lygonia than in the weak

---

[1] Palfrey, I, 527; Williamson, I, 287. Palfrey estimates that two-thirds of the adult males must have been favored with places of authority under this charter; and it was the foolishness of the proprietor in bestowing such an organization upon a frontier village, together with their heterodoxy in religion, which led to the exclusion of the Gorges settlements from the confederacy of New England colonists in 1643 (Winthrop, II, 100).

[2] Williamson, I, 326.

[3] *Ibid.*, 327, note.

settlements to the eastward of them; the real administration of government throughout all the country was crude and uncertain. It is probable that many welcomed the claims of Massachusetts as a means to a better regulation of society.[1]

In 1651 the Massachusetts general court took steps to assert the authority over the Maine settlements which it claimed was its right under the charter of 1628–29; and in the following year the nearest Maine settlements gave in their submission. The agreement with the inhabitants of Kittery Point included the following article relating to the franchise:

"7. That all the present inhabitants of Kittery shall be freemen of the countrye, and, having taken the oath of freemen, shall have libertye to give theire votes for the election of the Gouernor, Assistants, and other generall officers of the countrye."[2]

Similar terms were granted to Gorgeana (York), Wells, Saco, Cape Porpus, and, in 1658, to Lygonia.[3] It will be seen that the Massachusetts authorities by these articles admitted the inhabitants to the freemanship without referring to the religious question, and, as many of the Maine settlers were not Puritans, it was the wisest plan to adopt. It is hardly likely that the inhabitants of the northeastern settlements would so readily have submitted had their subjection included a religious as well as a political dependence upon Massachusetts. Yet there was no guarantee in the articles that the lenient policy would be continued; only the "present" inhabitants were given these terms. For the future the same religious restrictions governed the admission of freemen from the North as from the rest of the colony. The early liberalism may have led the inhabitants to think they would receive similar treatment in the future; but in 1670, when complaining of the lack of freemen, the inhabitants of York County were advised by the general court to obtain an orthodox minister as the best way to increase

---

[1] Williamson, I, 333.

[2] *Mass. Col. Rec.*, IV, Pt. I, 122 ff.

[3] *Ibid.*, 128, 157 ff., 357 ff. Williamson estimates that 150 persons took the freeman's oath in the first instance, and that they represented a population of about 2100 (I, 356, note).

the number of freemen among them.[1] No further concession was made to the New Hampshire and Maine settlers.
Until 1679, in New Hampshire, and during the entire
colonial period in Maine, the basis of representation and
the suffrage in the northern settlements was the legislation
of the colony of Massachusetts.

IV. *Under the Charter of 1691.*

For three years after the revolution of 1689 in Boston
the government of Massachusetts was carried on without
express legal sanction upon the principles of the old charter. We have already noted how the revolution resulted in
an extension of the suffrage during this inter-charter period.
It now remains for us to note the granting of the new charter and consider the suffrage provisions under its terms.
After the accession of William and Mary, Mather and other
agents worked to the utmost to obtain the restoration of the
old charter.[2] But in this they failed, and the king would
consent to the granting of a charter only where a closer connection should be maintained with England.[3]

The charter of October 7, 1691,[4] established a new
corporation, stripped of the commercial characteristics of the
old company, and gave it the name of the " Province of the
Massachusetts Bay in New England." The new government included the Bay colony, Plymouth, Maine, and the
scattered settlements from the Kennebec to Nova Scotia.
Its principal officers—governor, deputy-governor, and a
secretary—were to be appointed by the king; a council of
twenty-eight members was to be elected annually by the
assembly; and the representative assembly was to be composed of two deputies elected " by the Major parte of the
Freeholders and other inhabitants of the respective Townes
or Places who shall be present at such Eleccons."

The religious qualifications for the suffrage were abolished by the new charter, and at last the colony was given

---

[1] *Mass. Col. Rec.*, IV, Pt. II, 452.
[2] Palfrey, IV, 61–70.
[3] *Ibid.*, 71–75.
[4] Poore, *Charters and Constitutions*, I, 942–954.

a uniform property qualification. According to the terms of the copy of the charter which Governor Phipps brought to Boston on May 14, 1692, it was provided that

" noe Freeholder or other Person shall have a Vote in the Eleccon of Members to serve in any Greate and Generall Court or Assembly to be held as aforesaid who at the time of such Eleccon shall not have an estate of Freehold in Land within Our said Province or Territory to the value of Forty Shillings per Annu. at the least or other estate to the value of *Forty pounds* Sterl'." [1]

But this copy did not agree with that which passed the great seal on October 7, 1691, which required the voter to possess an income of forty shillings from freehold land or other estate to the value of *fifty pounds*.[2] The practice of the colonial government was based upon their copy of the charter, while the English government, throughout the colonial period, attempted to enforce the fifty pounds provision of the charter as enrolled in London.[3] Aside, however, from this controversy, the charter basis of the suffrage is interesting because it gave the rational dual qualifications,—those of real estate and of personal property. The antiquated forty-shilling freehold requisite, now two hundred and fifty years old, was joined with the alternative of the possession of forty or fifty pounds value of other property. This was as great a compromise as seventeenth century statesmen could admit to their favorite English doctrine of the representation of real estate. Yet it was more favorable than the requirements which the freemen of Rhode Island placed upon applicants for the freemanship, or those imposed upon New Hampshire by the royal commissions and instructions to her governors; and it was identical with the qualifications in force in Connecticut after 1702.

Since the royal charter of 1691 continued as the frame of government of the colony until the Revolution, its express

[1] Poore, I, 949.
[2] Ellis Ames in *Mass. Hist. Soc. Proc.*, 1868, 370–375, has pointed out the probable cause of the discrepancy, which he ascribes to a change in the English copy just before passing the great seal, while the copy made ready for Phipps was not changed in a corresponding manner.
[3] J. F. Jameson, *New England Magazine*, Jan., 1890, 486.

provisions for the suffrage furnish the sole legal basis of the franchise during the eighteenth century. There are no further changes in the formal qualifications of voters to be noted, except a naturalization act of February, 1730–31, which only indirectly affected the suffrage, through its exclusion of foreign Catholics from the rights of citizenship.[1]

We may, therefore, glance at some facts bearing upon the size of the voting class in Massachusetts during the eighteenth century. In the election of May, 1692, a few days before Governor Phipps arrived with the new charter, only about one thousand freemen took part in the election of magistrates;[2] which, accepting Palfrey's estimate of the population at the time,[3] would show only one voter to sixty persons in the population. This extremely small proportion, after the recent enlargement of the freemanship, can be explained only on the ground of a lack of popular interest in the election, perhaps resulting from the belief that the existing government was only temporary and must soon give place to the organization under the new charter.[4] Some idea of the proportion of voters after the charter was established can be gained from the records of the town of Boston. In 1703 only two hundred and six persons[5] voted for the representatives of Boston out of a population of about seven thousand;[6] or one person in thirty-five. During the ten years, 1745–1754, which may be taken as fairly normal election years, the average population of Boston has been estimated at 15,731 persons.[7] The records of the town show

---

[1] *Session Laws,* 447. By this act "all Protestants of foreign Nations" who had resided within the province for one year could be granted all the privileges of natural-born subjects of the king of England.

[2] *Mass. Hist. Soc. Coll.,* 3d Series, X, 120. The total number of votes cast for twenty-one candidates was 16,197. If each freeman voted for sixteen,—and that many are marked as elected,—the number of voters would be about one thousand.

[3] *New England,* IV, 135.

[4] Governor Bradstreet, on May 4, 1692, had taken the oath of office "for this year, or until there be a settlement of government from the crown of England" (Palfrey, IV, 89).

[5] Samuel Sewall, *Diary, Mass. Hist. Soc. Coll.,* 5th Series, VI, 79.

[6] *Report Boston Record Commissioners,* I, 4.

[7] *Ibid.*

exactly the number of voters in the annual elections for the representatives to the general court during this period.[1] The greatest number of voters at any election was 723 in 1748;[2] the least was 327 in 1752; and the average for the ten years was 502, or a little more than three per cent. of the population. In the years following down to the Revolution there was practically no change in the population of Boston,[3] and little variation in the size of the voting class. The average number of voters in the decade, 1755–1764, was 611,[4] or very nearly four per cent. of the population; while in the decade, 1765–1774, immediately preceding the Revolution, the average number of voters had shrunk to 555,[5] or about three and one-half per cent. of the population. The greatest number of voters at any Boston election appears to have been in 1763, when 1089 persons balloted,[6] or about six and one-half per cent. of the population. It is interesting to notice that the lack of contests led to a diminution in the number of electors; and in the years immediately preceding the Revolution, when the popular representatives received almost unanimous elections, the size of the voting class was smaller than in earlier years when local questions had aroused the interest of the people.[7]

It has been estimated that the potential voters, that is, all those who possessed the right of suffrage, made up about

[1] *Report Record Com.*, XIV, 72–255 *passim.*

[2] *Ibid.*, 148.

[3] *Ibid.*, I, 4.

[4] *Ibid.*, XIV, 255–305 *passim;* XVI, 10–113 *passim.*

[5] *Ibid.*, 141–278 *passim;* XVIII, 21–166 *passim.*

[6] *Ibid.*, XVI, 88. This election appears to have been overlooked by Ernst, who gives the figure 723 as probably the greatest number of voters (*Const. Hist. of Boston*, 47), a number surpassed on several occasions; and by Hart, who names 916 as the number of voters in "the most crowded town meeting ever held in Boston before the Revolution" (*Political Science Quarterly*, VII, 322).

[7] In 1771 the number of voters was 410, every one of whom voted for Thomas Cushing and John Hancock, 403 for Samuel Adams, and 399 for James Otis (each elector voting for four persons). In 1773 and 1774 almost the same unanimity existed. On the other hand, the election of 1772, contested somewhat, called out 723 voters (*Report of Record Com.*, XVIII, 53, 78, 129, 166).

sixteen per cent. of the population of Massachusetts at the close of the colonial period and the beginning of the national epoch.[1] And accepting this figure, it appears that only one out of four or five of the qualified voters actually exercised his right. This indifference was only slightly lessened in the votes upon constitutional questions in 1778–1780,[2] and in the ten years, 1780–1789 the actual voters numbered about three per cent. of the population.[3] It was not until after the adoption of the national constitution, and the introduction of party ideas and machinery that the voting class was considerably enlarged.[4] Just why the number of actual electors was so much smaller proportionately in Massachusetts than in New York or Virginia is not at once apparent. It is probable, however, that the solidarity of sentiment in New England did not develop that vigilance upon the part of the elector which was a natural outcome of the jarring factions of New York City; and the town meeting itself probably became so effective a political machine that attendance was not esteemed important or interesting as it was upon the Virginia election day. Whatever the cause, the citizen of Massachusetts does not appear to take as great an interest— measuring interest by the exercise of the suffrage franchise—in his colonial elections as is shown in some of the colonies outside of New England.

V. *Local Suffrage.*

A. *Town Elections.*

A general feature, if not indeed a universal one, in the early town life, both in Plymouth and the Bay Colony, was the common ownership of the town lands.[5] There is some

---

[1] J. F. Jameson, *New England Magazine,* Jan., 1890, 486; G. D. Luetscher, *Early Political Machinery in the United States,* 12.

[2] Jameson, *op. cit.,* 487, 488.

[3] *Ibid.*

[4] For a careful and interesting study of the causes leading to the growing participation in politics of the potential voters, see Luetscher, *Early Political Machinery.*

[5] Scarcely a topic of Massachusetts history has called forth so much discussion as the question of the origin and early organization of the

doubt about the relationship of the New England town to the English parish; it can be proved, perhaps, that the church congregation was not the common unit of colonizing force; and the question of priority between towns and the general government may not at present be determinable; but it is clear that in almost all the New England towns there was an economic partnership, which, by actual occupation, or purchase from the Indians, or, most commonly, by grant from the central colonial government, received a permanent basis in the common ownership of a tract of land. The land obtained in one of these ways was subsequently apportioned, in part or wholly to the original partners and to those who had later been joined with them. The individuals forming such a quasi corporation were the " commoners," and, originally, were the sole " inhabitants." To these original inhabitants others were added by the vote of the town, who might be admitted upon equal terms or only rent land and houses, or being freeholders yet not obtain rights of commonage. Thus an early equality of rights gave place to an economic and political diversity; and the term inhabitant came to include not only the original commoners and their successors, but also freeholders who had no rights of commonage, and householders who were only renters.

This term, " inhabitants," has given the Massachusetts historians a great deal of trouble. Since the colonial records did not frame a definition of it, recourse has been had to the English meanings of the word; but the writers have been unable even to agree upon this, and Coke has been quoted against Coke.[1] In Massachusetts the word possessed no

---

Massachusetts towns. The controversy has been complicated by the meagreness of the records, the failure of contemporary writers to define their terms, and the desire of recent writers to support personal historical theories. The present writer does not profess to have the fulness of information necessary to decide the questions in dispute, nor is this work the proper place for such a discussion. All that can be done here is to summarize the results of the local investigators and test the facts of local suffrage in Massachusetts in the light of the experience of other colonies.

[1] Channing, *J. H. U. Studies*, II, 444; C. F. Adams, *Mass. Hist. Soc. Proc.*, 2d Series, VII, 178; Goodell, *ibid.*, 213. The intricacies of the

fixed meaning. It cannot be held with Channing that an inhabitant was universally a householder or one who manured land in the town;[1] nor is it possible here to make the word synonymous with freeholder alone;[2] upon occasions the word received both a wider and a narrower interpretation than the English uses. The general court in 1634 imposed an oath upon inhabitants,[3] and by an order of April 1, required every " man of or above the age of twenty yeares, who hath bene or shall hereafter be resident within this jurisdiccon by the space of sixe monethes, as an householder or sojorner, and not infranchised," to swear that he was an inhabitant of the colony, that he would acknowledge the authority of the established government, and would respect its laws. According to this rule, therefore, the inhabitants included sojourners as well as householders.[4] On the other hand, the town of Hampton, New Hampshire, in 1662, while a part of the Massachusetts Bay colony, voted in town meeting that " no man shall be judged an inhabitant in this town, nor have power or liberty to act in town affairs, or have privilege of commonage, either sweepage or feedage, but he that hath one share of commonage, at least, according to the first division, and land to build upon."[5] Other records show various qualifications imposed upon town voters. Almost invariably the voter must previously have been accepted or " settled" in the town by vote of the town meeting or select-

---

subject of inhabitancy cannot be fully appreciated until one has perused the account given by Mildmay in *The Method and Rule of Proceeding upon all Elections . . . within the City of London* [1743], and the extensive notes by H. K. S. Causton in his edition of Mildmay (1841), pp. xxxvi, 53 ff. note, 92 ff. note. See also the ambiguous language of the act of Parliament, 26, Geo. III, ch. 100.

[1] *Op. cit.*

[2] *Mass. Hist. Soc. Proc.*, 2d Series, VII, 203. Chamberlain believes that the inhabitants " included all male adults who, either by general laws or town regulations, were permitted permanently to reside within the town limits, irrespective of their ownership of lands" (*ibid.*, VII, 241).

[3] *Mass. Col. Rec.*, I, 115.

[4] It should be stated, however, that the later custom called this the " resident's" oath.

[5] *New Hampshire Provincial Papers*, I, 153.

men.[1]   In Haverhill he must also obtain the town's consent to his voting in town meeting,[2] unless he possessed the qualifications imposed by the general colonial ordinance;[3] while in Watertown he could be accounted a "townsman" or voting inhabitant if he had received a share in the land dividends or was admitted with the consent of the town.[4]   On the other hand a person who had "sojourned in other mens houses" for two years in Charlestown was spoken of as an "inhabitant," and was expressly permitted by the general court to purchase land in the town.[5]

It can readily be understood that such variations in local custom, linked with the different names applied to the voters in town meetings,—as inhabitants, freeholders, freemen or townsmen,—would lead to difficulties in making generalizations respecting the suffrage in towns.   We shall be near the truth if we think of the suffrage in these Massachusetts towns as exercised by the householders who were also heads of families.[6]   There may have been some voters, who, by local consent or by the general laws, did not fall within the class of householders, but their numbers must have been few and their influence slight.[7]   The ancient English meaning of the

[1] *Dorchester Records*, in *Boston Rec. Com. Rept.*, IV, 8; Bond, *History of Watertown*, II, 998; Coffin, *Newbury*, 23; Chase, *Haverhill*, 89. A most interesting statement of the principles of the early land grants is to be found in the order of Watertown (Bond, II, 996), that "Those ffreemen of the Congregation shall build and dwell upon their Lotts at ye Towne Plott, and not to alienate them by selling or Exchanging them to any forrainer, but to ffreemen of the congregation, it being our real intent to sitt down here close togither, and therefore, these Lotts were granted to those ffreemen yt inhabited most remote from ye meeting-house, and dwell most scattered."

[2] Chase, *Haverhill*, 89.

[3] See *post*.

[4] Bond, *Watertown*, II, 998.

[5] Corey, *History of Malden*, 81 (1640).

[6] This opinion is based not upon any express stipulation found in the town records or the laws, but upon the general sense and spirit of the town regulations.

[7] C. F. Adams has pointed out that under Article XII. of the Body of Liberties of 1641 all the men (not servants) of the colony had the right to attend any public meetings or courts, and there in an orderly

word *inhabitant,* as equivalent to householder,[1] was the common, although perhaps not universal, acceptation of the word in Massachusetts.

But while the towns had considerable volition in fixing the local suffrage, the central government did not hesitate to legislate upon the subject. Mention has already been made of the provisions of the Plymouth laws upon the subject, and it remains now only to summarize the legislation of the Bay Colony. About four years after the restriction of the free-manship to church-members, a policy of almost equal severity was adopted with reference to the local suffrage. In September, 1635, the general court ordered

"that none but ffreemen shall have any vote in any towne, in any accon of aucthoritie, or necessity, or that which belongs to them by vertue of their ffreedome, as receaveing inhabitants, & layeing out of lotts, etc." [2]

By this law and future legislation the freemen were given entire control of town affairs. They had the power to dispose of town lands; to make ordinances and enforce them by fines; and to elect their town officers.[3] Later they obtained the power of fixing the price of labor in the towns,[4] and of taxing all inhabitants.[5] For twelve years the free-men retained these exclusive privileges, but in 1647 some political rights were restored to the town inhabitants. The general court "taking into consid^{r}ation ye usefull pts &

way to make propositions; and that the *viva voce* voting in the town meeting would give considerable opportunity for such persons to take part in the town affairs (*Mass. Hist. Soc. Proc.,* 2d Series, VII, 206). On the other hand, it should be remembered that voting by "papers" was early introduced into some of the town elections. It is found in 1659 in Dorchester (*Boston Rec. Com. Rept.,* IV, 99); before 1637 in Newbury (Coffin, *Newbury,* 19); by 1682 in Haverhill (Chase, *Haver-hill,* 137); and in the Plymouth Colony towns in 1643-4 (*Records, Laws,* 42).

[1] H. Cox, *Antient Parliamentary Elections* (London, 1868), 178, 179.
[2] *Mass. Col. Rec.,* I, 161.
[3] *Ibid.,* 172
[4] *Ibid.,* 183.
[5] *Ibid.,* 231.

abilities of div^rs inhabitants amongst us, wch are not freemen, w^ch, if imp'ved to publike use, ye affaires of this Comon
wealth may be ye easier carried [to] an end," impowered the
freemen of the respective towns to choose any non-free inhabitants, having taken the oath of fidelity and being over
twenty-four years of age, to be jurors and voters in the
town meetings, provided they had not been detected or convicted of evil carriage against the government or churches.[1]

In 1658 the qualifications of such non-free voters were
stated more definitely and at the same time made more rigid.
Thereafter town voters were

"all Englishmen, that are settled Inhabitants and householders in any
town, of the age of twenty-four years, and of honest & good Conver-
sations, being Rated at twenty pounds estate in a single Country Rate,
and that have taken the Oath of Fidelity to this Government, and no
other (except freemen) may be Chosen Select men, Jurors, or Constables, and have their vote, in the Choice of Select men, . . . as also
where no Select men are, to have their vote in ordering schooles,
hearding of cattle, laying out highwayes, and distributing Lands."[2]

The lines were drawn still more closely in 1670, when the
property qualification of non-freeman voters was raised to
eighty pounds taxable estate, but those at the time possessing
the right to vote were not to be deprived of it.[3] Finally, in
March, 1680–81 it was provided that any of the inhabitants
of a town, although not possessing the right to vote, could be
chosen by the qualified electors to fill any of the town offices;
and after election and officiation in the position, such inhabitants for ever afterwards should have free liberty to
vote or to be chosen into any town office.[4]

After the receipt of the charter of 1691 it became necessary

[1] *Mass. Col. Rec.*, II, 197. Any one convicted as above could vote
again if the court sentencing him saw fit to restore him to his former
liberty. The majority of the selectmen must be freemen.

[2] *Ibid.*, IV, Pt. I, 336; Code of 1660, 76. The proviso was still
retained that a majority of the selectmen must be freemen.

[3] Code of 1672, 147, 148.

[4] *Mass. Col. Rec.*, V, 306. This has been wrongly interpreted as
doing away altogether with the property qualification for non-free
town voters (Ernst, *Const. Hist. of Boston*, 22).

to set a new qualification for the local suffrage. In the fall of 1692 a law was passed which gave the local franchise to "freeholders and other Inhabitants of each Town Ratable at Twenty Pounds Estate, to one single Rate besides the Poll." [1] In 1700 it was enacted that no person, coming to reside in a town, although otherwise qualified, should be allowed to participate in town elections until he had applied to the selectmen of the town for admission as an inhabitant, and had been accepted by the town authorities; [2] and in 1722, when a question had arisen whether the twenty pounds qualification applied to freeholders as well as other inhabitants, the general court ordered that the fixed property qualification be required of all town voters.[3] After this date there was no change in the local suffrage qualification, although a number of administrative features were introduced; at twenty pounds taxable property the qualification remained during the entire provincial period.

B. *Church Elections.*

According to the theory of church organization adopted by the Puritans the members of the church possessed the right to choose their own ecclesiastical officers. But this wide liberty early brought too great a diversity of opinions and doctrines among the clergy, and led to the limitation, both in Plymouth and Massachusetts, of the choice of the church to "approved" ministers,[4] that is, those acceptable to the ruling religious classes. The inevitable evils of association of town and church called forth the following enactment in Massachusetts, which gives the ideal of ecclesiastical elections in the colony:—

[1] October 12, 1692, *Session Laws*, 37.

[2] May 29, 1700, *Session Laws*, 203, 204. "No person whatsoever coming to reside or dwell within any Town in this Province, (other than Freeholders or Proprietors of Land in such Town, or those born, or that have served an Apprenticeship there, and have not removed and become Inhabitants elsewhere) shall be admitted to the privilege of Election in such Town (though otherwise qualified)," unless he shall apply for and obtain the approbation of the selectmen.

[3] May 30, 1722, *Session Laws*, 367.

[4] *Plymouth Records, Laws*, 67.

"Every Church hath free liberty of Calling, Election and Ordination of all her Officers, from time to time, provided they be able, pious, and Orthodox: For the better explanation of the said Law, and as an addition thereunto, this Court doth Order and Declare, and be it hereby Ordered and Enacted, that by the Church, is to be meant, such as are in full Communion only; . . . and that no Inhabitant in any Town shall challenge a right unto or act in the Calling or Election of such Officer or Minister, until he be in full communion, upon the penalty of being accounted a disturber of peace and order." [1]

Under the charter of 1691 a change was made in the method of choosing the minister. This may have been due to an appreciation of the inconsistency in permitting a choice by the church-members only, and the collection of church-rates from all the town inhabitants. The new act of 1692 provided that orthodox ministers could be chosen in each town by the " major part of the Inhabitants" in town-meeting, and that all the town should be obliged to pay towards his support. [2] Not six months later this election by town meeting was changed to a choice by the " major part of such Inhabitants as do there usually attend on the Publick Worship of God, and are by Law duly qualified for Voting in Town Affairs." [3] In 1695 another change was made. [4] The minister was first to be chosen by the church, and then submitted to the qualified inhabitants of the town; [5] and in case of disapprobation by the town, a council from the neighboring churches could decide finally.

The injustice of excluding any of the qualified taxpayers from a voice in the choice of minister was thus avoided. On the other hand, early in the eighteenth century, certain dissenting sects were released from taxation for the established ministers upon condition that they would support and regularly attend public worship according to their own beliefs. To allow these persons to participate in the town elections of ministers would be equally unfair; and in 1728 an act which

[1] Code of 1672, 46.

[2] *Session Laws,* 35.

[3] February 8, 1692–93, Reprint of 1699, 39, 40.

[4] May 29, 1695, *ibid.,* 81.

[5] Members of the church might, of course, vote in the church election and in the town election.

exempted them from paying church taxes, also debarred them from voting in the towns upon any church matters.[1]

C. *Militia Elections.*

The Puritan colonies, with the exception of New Haven,[2] granted wider privileges in the choice of militia officers than in any other form of popular elections. Almost universally the choice of these officers was left to all the soldiers of the company or regiment. Thus Massachusetts in 1636 provided that a colonel and lieutenant-colonel should be chosen by the " men" of each regiment and submitted to the general court for approval; while the officers lower in rank were to be nominated by the respective towns, and the council was directed to select the incumbent from the names submitted to them.[3] The elective process is made more definite by an order of March 9, 1636–7, which provided that

" All persons of any trayned band, both freemen & others, who have taken the oath of residents, or shall take the same, & being no covenant servant in household wth any other, shall have their votes in nomination of those p'sons who are to bee appointed captaines, or other inferior officers of the same band, p'vided they nominate none but such as shalbe freemen; for it is the intent & order of the Court that no person shall henceforth bee chosen to any office in the comonwealth but such as is a freeman." [4]

It was provided in 1647 that all freemen whether exempt from militia service or not, should have a vote in the choice

[1] May 29, 1728, *Session Laws,* 405.

[2] See *post.*

[3] *Mass. Col. Rec.,* I, 187.

[4] *Ibid.,* 188. This liberal suffrage was not extended to the choice of sergeant-major-general, who, in 1643, was to be chosen by the body of freemen at the annual court of elections, nor to the election of the sergeant-majors in the shires. In the latter case the deputies were to nominate to their towns suitable freemen for the position, and the freemen of the towns were to vote by ballot for these nominees or for any other freemen (*ibid.,* II, 49, 50). Two years later the sergeant-majors could be chosen not only by freemen, but by " all yt have taken ye oath of fidelity, or shall take it before ye election (except servants or unsetled p'sons)" (*ibid.,* 117).

of military officers.[1] After 1656, a similar privilege was extended to householders; and the militia suffrage until abolished by the general court was extended to every freeman, householder, and listed soldier who had taken the oath of fidelity.[2]

There was some doubt, however, as to the right of the general court to delegate the choice of militia officers to the voters; and in 1669 " the Court considering the direction" of the patent, ordered that all commissioned officers except the major-general and " Admiral by Sea," should be chosen by the general court; and the inferior officers appointed by the commissioned officers.[3] In this way popular elections for militia officers were discontinued, although at a later date the committee upon militia in each town was authorized to present to the general court the names of two or three proper persons for each office. Formal militia elections ceased in 1669, not to be resumed for over a hundred years.

In Plymouth military officers above the grade of sergeant were to be chosen by the towns in a plural number and selections made by the general court; the inferior officers were to be appointed by the higher officers with the " consent of the Body" (of the soldiers?).[4] In practice even the higher officers appear to have been chosen by the train bands;[5] but not until 1667 was the following order concerning these elections passed: " In reference to milletary concernments It is enacted by the Court that noe single p'sons vnder twenty yeares of age either children or servants shall voate as to that accompt or any that are not settled Inhabitants of that place and have taken the oath of fidelitie." [6] This continued the basis of such elections until the province charter of 1691 gave the appointment of military officers to the governor and council.

[1] *Mass. Col. Rec.*, I, 191, 222.
[2] Code of 1660, 56.
[3] *Mass. Col. Rec.*, IV, Pt. II, 422; Code of 1672, 116.
[4] *Plymouth Records, Laws*, 39.
[5] *Court Records*, III, 89.
[6] *Plymouth Records, Laws*, 219.

D. *Voting concerning Land Matters.*

It has been noted already that the Massachusetts town life had its origin at about the same time as the common ownership of lands; in some cases the land ownership antedated town organization, but almost universally the political and economic community developed together. At first the commoners probably constituted the entire body politic of the town; and, until such time as the non-commoners acquired an undue influence over land matters, the subject of the common lands was discussed in open town meeting.[1] Early or late, however, the distinction between the civil and the property rights of the inhabitants was established. The separation of the commoners from the non-commoners in the settling of land matters did not come at any one time throughout the colony; but each town worked out its own solution of the problem. It might come almost at the beginning of town life, or it might be deferred for several generations after the founding of the town; it might be accompanied with compromise grants of land to non-commoners, or it might leave the latter altogether beyond the pale of participation in the common lands.[2] Thus in Watertown as early as 1635 the rights of commonage were restricted to those already possessing that right or purchasing it from a former holder;[3] in 1651 an agreement was made between Charlestown and the settlers of Malden that the rights of commonage in the latter place should be limited to the existing number of dwelling-houses;[4] in Dorchester in 1642 a question of land cultivation in "the necke of Land" was settled by a vote of the original lot-holders in the "neck," and where a man had purchased more than one lot he was entitled to a proportionate voice in the management of the commons.[5] On the other hand, in Haverhill the town legislated upon land matters for fifty years after

[1] Egleston, *J. H. U. Stud.*, IV, 581, 582.
[2] *Ibid.*, 585, 586.
[3] Bond, *Watertown*, II, 995.
[4] Corey, *Malden*, 110.
[5] *Rept. Boston Rec. Com.*, IV, 49, 99.

the settlement,[1] and frequent contests took place between the proprietors and the non-commoners.

The general court early passed orders regulating the care of common lands. Thus, in 1643, it placed the direction of common fields, that were fenced and used for the raising of grain, in the control of " those who have the great^r quantity in such feilds;" [2] and after a short interval in which the decision of these matters was left to the selectmen or freemen of the towns,[3] this principle of voting in proportion to the share held, was re-affirmed.[4] By later orders of the court the number of voters upon matters relating to the town commons was limited to the original proprietors or their successors and such as had received grants from the town or had purchased another person's share.[5] In Plymouth, on the other hand, not until 1682 were meetings of land proprietors distinct from the towns legally authorized.[6]

But no uniform method of voting upon such matters appears to have been adopted before 1692. The Plymouth order of 1682 appears to have provided for a majority vote according to the number of proprietors,[7] and within the Massachusetts towns also it was sometimes the individual, not the amount of his interest, which determined the vote.[8] But as time went on the property interest became stronger; the town meetings and the non-commoners lost their share in the control of land affairs, and at last these matters came to be settled in distinct meetings of the proprietors, where each man was entitled to an influence proportionate to the amount of his interest in the lands. The transition from the individual to the property basis is shown in a law of 1692 which provided for voting in proprietors' meetings according to each man's interest, where such interest had

---

[1] Chase, *Haverhill*, 204, 215, 251 ff.
[2] *Mass. Col. Rec.*, II, 39; 10 May, 1643.
[3] *Ibid.*, 49; 17 Oct., 1643.
[4] *Ibid.*, 195; 26 May, 1647.
[5] *Ibid.*, IV, Pt. I, 274, 275, 417.
[6] *Plymouth Records, Laws*, 257.
[7] *Ibid.*
[8] Corey, *Malden*, 368, 376; Coffin, *Newbury*, 140, 144.

been determined; and for voting as individuals where no such determination had been reached.[1]

Thus the cycle of change was completed; the control of the land, originally obtained by a group of partners, was returned to them or to their lawful successors. The confusion of economic and political interests in the early activity of the towns gave way to a distinct separation of the two phases of town life; and even the equal sharing of all proprietors was displaced by an influence graded according to wealth. The participation of all the inhabitants in the use, control and ownership of land—that economic democracy so common in the colonies—was giving way to the *laissez faire* doctrine of private ownership of land. The communal lands were divided into shares, distributed to the proprietors, or to the freeholders, or, in a few cases, to all the inhabitants; and the village community based upon land ceased to exist. The town abdicated to its citizens the control of the commons.

[1] *Session Laws*, 1692, 38.

CHAPTER XII.

The Suffrage in New Hampshire.

New Hampshire's earliest political organization had its origin, as was so frequently the case in New England, in the voluntary association of actual settlers. English patents and non-resident proprietors played only a meagre part in the early government of the colony. Of the four principal settlements, one, Hampton, was from the first considered part of Massachusetts and was settled in order to hold the northern territory;[1] the other three, Dover, Exeter, and Strawberry Bank (Portsmouth), were self-originative political entities. Exeter was settled by Wheelwright and his fellow-Antinomians from Massachusetts, and on July 4, 1639, they adopted the following interesting basis of government:

"Whereas it has pleased the lord to move the heart of our Dread Soveraigne Charles, by the grace of god King of England, Scotland France & Ireland, to grant license & liberty to sundry of his subjects to plant them selves in the Westerne partes of America; Wee his loyall subjects, brethren of the church of Exeter, situate & lying upon the river of Piscataquacke wth other inhabitants there considering wth our selves the holy will of god and our owne necessity that we should not live wth out wholsome lawes & civil government amongst us, of w^{h} we are altogether destitute, doe in the name of Christ & in the sight of god combine our selves together, to erect & set up amongst us such government as shall be to our best discerning, agreeable to the will of god, professing our selves subjects to our Soveraigne Lord King Charles according to the libertys of our English Colony of Massachusetts & binding our selves solemnly by the grace & helpe of Christ & in his name & feare to submit our selves to such godly & christian laws as are established in the Realme of England to our best knowledge, & to all other such lawes w^{h} shall upon good grounds be made & inacted amongst us according to god y^{t} we may live quietly & peaceablely together in all godlyness and honesty."[2]

[1] J. Dow, *History of the Town of Hampton*, 6–9.
[2] July 4, 1639; C. H. Bell, *History of the Town of Exeter*, 15; *New Hampshire Provincial Laws*, I, 744.

370

The inhabitants near Dover, under the Hilton patent, also found themselves without an adequate organization, and, in 1640, adopted a frame similar in its political features to that of Exeter, but lacking the frequent allusions to the Deity which the Exeter document contained.

"Whereas sundry mischiefs and inconveniences have befallen us, and more and greater may, in regard of want of civil government, his most gracious Majesty having settled no order for us to our knowledge: We, whose names are unwritten, being inhabitants upon the river Piscataqua, having voluntarily agreed to combine ourselves into a body politic, that we may the more comfortably enjoy the benefit of his Majesty's laws, together with all such laws as shall be concluded by a major part of the freemen of our Society, in case they be not repugnant to the laws of England, and administered in behalf of his majesty. And this we have mutually promised and engaged to do, and so continue till his excellent Majesty shall give other orders concerning us. . . ."[1]

In a similar manner the settlers at Strawberry Bank (or Portsmouth) appear to have formed an organization,— although the text of the agreement has not been preserved,—and elected a governor and two assistants.[2] At the same time they chose an Episcopal minister, made a grant of land for glebe purposes, and appointed two church-wardens.[3]

These agreements and the simple rules exacted under them contain nearly all the political activity which New Hampshire produced before the union with Massachusetts; and these associations, it is interesting to note, were not entered upon until a number of years after the first settlement in 1623. It is remarkable also, that these documents, so far as preserved, do not ignore the English king and government as was done in several cases in New Haven and Rhode Island, but explicitly affirm the allegiance due to the monarch. No general government was erected by these local agreements, as was the case in Connecticut; the

[1] Oct. 22, 1640; *New Hampshire Provincial Papers*, I, 126; *N. H. Laws*, I, 746.

[2] N. Adams, *Annals of Portsmouth*, 26, 27; *N. H. Laws*, I, 744.

[3] Adams, *Portsmouth*, 27.

inhabitants might be called freemen of the distinct towns, but not of a larger political entity.

In Dover and Portsmouth the inhabitants were not content with their indigenous governments, which do not appear to have been well administered;[1] and as early as 1639 they made overtures to Massachusetts for a union with that colony. Legal, ecclesiastical, and even forcible contests occurred in the New Hampshire towns;[2] and, tired at last of their own disorder, Dover and Portsmouth, in June, 1641, accepted the terms of Massachusetts for admission into the Bay colony.[3] The settlers were to be accounted inhabitants of Massachusetts; local courts were established for the towns; the inhabitants were exempted from any public charges except for purposes directly affecting themselves; and " also the inhabitants there are alowed to send two deputies from the whole ryver to the Court at Boston."[4]

At first the Massachusetts authorities would have extended their principle of religious restrictions upon the suffrage to the new territory, and in May, 1642, it was provided " that it shalbee in the power of any Co^{r}t there to admit & sweare freemen, so they bee qualified according to law."[5] But such a policy would have been almost a prohibitive one, and in the fall of the same year a more liberal rule was adopted according to which

"all the p'sent inhabitants of Pascataq [= Dover and Portsmouth] who formerly were free there shall have liberty of freemen in their severall townes to manage all their towne affairs, & shall each towne send a deputy to the Gen^{r}all Court, though they bee not at p'sent church members."[6]

A year later, Exeter also was admitted as a Massachusetts town,[7] the excommunicate Wheelwright going in exile into the Maine territory.[8]

[1] J. Belknap, *History of New Hampshire*, I, 54.
[2] Palfrey, *New England*, I, 587–592.
[3] *Mass. Col. Rec.*, I, 324, 332.
[4] *Ibid.*, 342.
[5] *Ibid.*, II, 5.
[6] *Ibid.*, 29.
[7] *Ibid.*, 37, 38, 43.
[8] Palfrey, I, 593.

For almost forty years the New Hampshire settlements remained under Massachusetts jurisdiction, during which time the laws of the latter colony were enforced in the northern towns. No further concessions in the matter of the suffrage appear to have been granted; and the qualifications of the voters in Massachusetts were required of voters in the New Hampshire towns, except in the case of those who were not church-members at the time of the union.[1]

In 1677, partly through the instrumentality of Edward Randolph, a decision was obtained from the English chief justices to the effect that the New Hampshire towns were outside the jurisdiction of Massachusetts, and also that Mason had no political rights in the settlement.[2] This decision left it to the Crown of England to give a proper form of government to the colony. Accordingly, in September, 1679, a commission was executed for a president and six named councillors; and these officers were given the privilege of adopting " such rules and methods (as to the persons who are to chuse their Deputies and ye time and place of meeting) as they shall judge most conveinent." [3] In exercising this power President Cutt and his council adopted a novel and by no means popular method of determining the voters in the four towns. After obtaining from the town selectmen a list of the names and estates of the inhabitants, the president and council proceeded to select by name from the lists those persons who should be privileged to vote in the first election for assemblymen.[4] No general qualifications for voters were stated, but the simple will of the governing board gave the right of the suffrage to one man and withheld it from another. The proportion of voters, 209 out of a population of about four thousand,[5] was not in itself so low as to cause dissatisfaction, but the arbitrary method of selecting the voters, and the evident dis-

[1] See *ante* under Maine.
[2] Belknap, *New Hampshire*, I, 164–169.
[3] *N. H. Provincial Papers*, I, 373; *N. H. Laws*, I, 6.
[4] *N. H. Laws*, I, 11–15 note, 779. Seventy-one persons were named as voters in Portsmouth, 57 in Hampton, 20 in Exeter, and 61 in Dover; or 209 in all.
[5] *Ibid.*, lix, 776.

appear satisfied with the Massachusetts form of government. The petition of February, 1689–90, for the union was signed by three hundred and seventy-two persons,[1] who must have included the greater part of the freeholders of the four towns.

In 1692 the government was resumed by the Crown, and again in his commission the royal governor was directed to assemble the deputies of the freeholders;[2] indeed, he was specially instructed to " take care that the members of the Assembly be elected only by freeholders, as being most agreeable to the custom of England, to which you are, as near as may be, to conform yourself." [3]   In spite of this provision, and a similar one in the commission and instructions of Governor Bellomont,[4] the elections do not appear to have been limited to freeholders.   In 1697 writs of election specified the " freemen" of the towns as electors;[5]   and in another case described the voters as " Freeholdrs and other Inhabitants of their several Towns, duly qualified." [6]   The earliest law extending the suffrage to non-freeholders which has been noticed is one of August, 1699.[7]   This retained the English qualification of forty shilling freehold, but linked with it a personal property alternative:

" No person Inhabiting within this Province, other than Freeholders of the value or income of *Forty shillings per Annum* or upwards in Land, or worth *Fifty Pounds* sterling at the least in personal Estate, shall have any vote in the Election of Representatives, or be capable of being Elected to serve in the General Assembly."

It was the same qualification as that set by the Massachusetts provincial charter.[8]

[1] *N. H. Prov. Papers,* II, 46. It is interesting to notice that Massachusetts permitted a certain degree of local legislation and representation in the assessing and collection of taxes (*N. H. Laws,* I, 482).

[2] *N. H. Prov. Papers,* II, 58.

[3] *Ibid.,* 64; *Laws,* I, 510.

[4] *Laws,* I, 614, 623.

[5] *N. H. Prov. Papers,* II, 237, 263.

[6] *Ibid.,* 283, 284.

[7] *Ibid.,* III, 216, 217.

[8] For election writ under this law referring to " Freeholders and other Inhabitants," see *N. H. Laws,* I, 637.

For almost a generation there was no change from this law. But in 1727 a new and comprehensive election law, narrowing the suffrage qualifications, was passed. This act provided for triennial meetings of the legislature; required members of the legislature to possess three hundred pounds value of real estate; and declared that

"no person shall have the liberty of voting in the choice of representatives, other than such who has a real estate of the value of fifty pounds within the town, parish, or precinct where such election shall be."[1]

But a landholder might vote in a place even if he were not an inhabitant, and, presumably, could vote in several towns if he held land in each. After the passage of this act, and it was not modified during the provincial period, no landless man could vote, and no freeholder unless he held land to the value of fifty pounds.

The facts of local suffrage in New Hampshire do not differ much from those of Massachusetts. Before the first union with the latter colony there were no general elections, and the towns were practically independent. Under the rule of Massachusetts her laws respecting local suffrage were enforced among the northern towns. Not until after 1680, therefore, need we note any forms of local elections. Under Cutt's Code, which applied the term freemen to the provincial elections, the same name was given to the voters in the towns, but no explanation or definition of the term was made.[2] Later, under the rule of Andros, local elections were the only ones permitted throughout the Dominion of New England, and these were to be held by the " inhabitants" of the several towns.[3] The same term is applied to town voters as late as 1694,[4] two years after the assembly had limited the local suffrage to freeholders. It is likely that these variations in terminology did not connote for

[1] *Acts and Laws of His Majesty's Province of New-Hampshire,* Portsmouth, 1771, p. 166.

[2] *N. H. Prov. Papers,* I, 403; *Laws,* I, 32, 33. The voters were simply " ye freemen of each Towne."

[3] *Conn. Col. Rec.,* III, 427–429.

[4] *N. H. Prov. Papers,* II, 73, 131, 132, 330.

different classes throughout the towns. Probably both freemen and inhabitants were nearly identical with the class of
freeholders.

In 1692 the assembly excluded from voting in town meetings all who were not freeholders,[1] and even required the
land-holding qualification in the elections of ministers, a
most unusual provision.[2] In 1718 and 1719 the assembly
adopted a large part of the Massachusetts legislation concerning local elections.[3] By the laws of these years the local
suffrage was extended to " freeholders and other inhabitants of each town rateable at twenty pounds estate, to one
single rate, beside the poll." The Massachusetts restriction
upon strangers was adopted *verbatim;* only after formal
admission by the town or the selectmen might a stranger,
although otherwise qualified, be admitted to a vote in town
affairs.[4] In a similar way the voting in meetings of land
proprietors was modelled upon the laws of Massachusetts;
and where the individual's interest in the common lands
had been ascertained the votes were to be proportioned to
this interest; where the proportion had not been determined,
each proprietor had an equal voice with all the others.[5]
These laws gave a basis for voting in local elections which
was changed but slightly before the Revolution. The only
important change was the substitution, in 1770, of a tax-
paying qualification in place of the property-holding qualification (£20) of the law of 1719. The new act provided
that every male person who paid thirty shillings taxes, including a poll-tax of eighteen shillings, should be " deemed
a legal voter in all affairs of the town or parish, where he
dwells, except chusing Representatives." [6] This in turn
was reduced in 1772, when a general reduction of the taxes
took place, to the payment of eighteen shillings taxes, including the poll-tax of twelve shillings.[7]

[1] *N. H. Prov. Papers,* III, 167.
[2] *Ibid.,* III, 189, 190. The latter act was repealed by the queen in
1706.
[3] *Acts and Laws of New Hampshire* (1771), 71, 123, 136–141.
[4] Taken from Massachusetts act of 1700. See *ante.*
[5] Massachusetts act of 1692. See *ante.*
[6] *Acts and Laws of New Hampshire* (1771). *Temporary Laws,* 38.
[7] *Temporary Laws,* 58.

The close relationship of New Hampshire to Massachusetts is seen not only during the formal union of the two colonies, but also in the frequent adoption by New Hampshire of the laws of her stronger neighbor. There is, consequently, little of novelty to be noted in New Hampshire legislation. The most striking cases appear in the legislation of Cutt's assembly in 1680, where the exclusion of all but Protestants from the suffrage comes at a remarkably early date in colonial history, when usually it makes its appearance after the Revolution of 1688. The age requirement of twenty-four years, also contained in this code, was without doubt adopted from the Massachusetts law; but it had a widely different application from its use in that colony. In Massachusetts it simply applied to the small number of non-church-members who might be admitted to the franchise; in New Hampshire it was universally applicable. But these features were of slight duration. Another divergence from Massachusetts custom continued until Revolutionary times. This was the absolute limitation of the assembly suffrage after 1727 to freeholders possessing fifty pounds value of real estate. The province had adopted at first the qualification of the Massachusetts charter,—forty shillings freehold or fifty pounds personal estate; but this was narrowed down to the class of freeholders alone; and with this restriction was continued for almost fifty years of colonial history.

CHAPTER XIII.

THE SUFFRAGE IN CONNECTICUT.

I. *The River Towns to 1662.*

The settlers in the Connecticut valley were staunch Puritans; they had formed a part of the political and ecclesiastical life of Massachusetts; and in transferring their place of abode to the western valley they often retained their church organization and followed the advice of their pastors.[1] Yet in spite of the place which religion occupied in their lives,—and we cannot say it was less than in the lives of the Puritans they left behind in Massachusetts,—the Connecticut settlers did not adopt the Massachusetts limitation of political power to church-members. The laws of the Bay formed the model for much of the later legislation in Connecticut; the land system, the town organization, and the general government were drawn largely from Massachusetts experience; but the feature of a formal ecclesiastical restriction of the suffrage was not carried westward.

There is not, however, any evidence that the suffrage question was one of the reasons for the emigration to the Connecticut.[2] Winthrop does not mention this motive; and the apparent reasons for the exodus are the desire for more land, the favorable reports of the Connecticut country, the opposition to the measures of the ruling party in Massachusetts, and, perhaps, a covert antagonism between the two pastors, Cotton and Hooker.[3] The latter, indeed, in his famous sermon in 1638, said, " The privilege of election, which belongs to the people, therefore must not be exercised according to their humors, but according to the blessed

[1] Judge Chamberlain, in *Mass. Hist. Soc. Proc.*, Second Series, V, 271.
[2] C. F. Adams, in *Mass. Hist. Soc. Proc.*, Second Series, VII, 180 note.
[3] Winthrop, *History of New England*, ed. by Savage, I, 160; Trumbull, *History of Connecticut* (ed. of 1898), I, 37-38; Doyle, *English Colonies in America, Puritan Colonies*, I, 154-155; Palfrey, *History of New England*, I, 449-450.

will and law of God;"[1] and a scholarly commentator says Hooker was " forging out a practical method of theocratic government."[2] The essential point of difference between the two colonies,—and the point which gave the greater practicability to the Connecticut constitution,—was the absence of any formal qualifications upon the colony freemanship, and the granting to the towns the right to admit or reject their own inhabitants. And since these town inhabitants, as we shall see, had the right to vote for deputies in the general court, although forbidden to vote for other colonial officers, the disfranchised and discontented portion of the population would be smaller than in Massachusetts.

For several years the history of the Connecticut valley is the story of feeble frontier settlements and trading forts which, after receiving the rapid influx of population from Massachusetts, were temporarily under the control of constables and commissioners appointed by that colony.[3] To these appointive officers there were later added certain " committees" or representatives of the several towns.[4] The records are so meagre that we cannot discern the method of choice of these representatives, nor is any distinct political qualification evident, before the adoption of the fundamental orders of 1638–9.[5]

It is, therefore, to those orders that we must look for the earliest requirements for the suffrage. The orders erected a " Publike State or Comonwelth" composed of freemen, whose affairs were directed by a governor, six magistrates, and two general courts every year composed of these officers, together with deputies sent from the several towns.[6]

[1] Palfrey, I, 537 note.

[2] Weeden, in *Amer. Antiquarian Soc. Proc.*, Second Series, IX, 347.

[3] For analysis of the early governments, see Andrews, *River Towns of Connecticut*, *J. H. U. Studies*, VII, 23–24.

[4] *Ibid.*, 24; *Public Records of the Colony of Connecticut, 1636–1665*, 9–13 (quoted hereafter as *Conn. Col. Rec.*).

[5] One writer believes that freemanship of the community antedated the adoption of the constitution of 1638–9 (Bronson, *Chapters on the Early Government of Connecticut*, New Haven Hist. Soc. Papers, III, 303).

[6] See the orders in *Conn. Col. Rec., 1636–1665*, 20–25.

Within the commonwealth thus erected by the " Inhabitants and Residents" of the three towns, there appear to be two classes of voters, which for many years afterwards were kept distinct.

The first class is that made up of those who were members of the corporation-commonwealth. The corporation was erected in a bold, naïve way, upon the model of that of Massachusetts, but without regard to the English theory that rights of incorporation must flow from some higher authority than the members of the company. With such an organization, even when self-instituted, there naturally goes the idea of membership, or, in the language of the time, freemanship. Hence the fundamental orders recognize the existence of freemen, give them a share in the government, and provide for the admission of new freemen. Unfortunately we do not know the number of freemen at the beginning of the new government, nor the class from which they were drawn. The surmise of Bronson [1] that the class of freemen antedated the making of the constitution does not seem justifiable. There were " Inhabitants and Residents" in the three towns, and it is likely that a more or less formal test was required before new inhabitants were admitted into the towns, but the writer has found no evidence of the existence of a community freemanship distinct from that of the towns. So far as the extant documents show, some of the inhabitants and residents of the towns erected themselves into freemen of their home-made corporation.

By the first fundamental, freemen only were permitted to vote in the election of the governor and the magistrates,[2] but other qualifications were added in order to limit the meaning of the word freemen. Thus, since an oath of fidelity was administered to all male persons over sixteen

[1] *Op. cit.*

[2] The wording of the clause is as follows: " wch choise shall be made by all that are admitted freemen and haue taken the Oath of Fidelity, and doe cohabitte wthin this Jurisdiction, (hauing beene admitted Inhabitants by the maior prt of the Towne wherein they liue,) or the mayor prte of such as shall be then prsent" (*Conn. Col. Rec., 1636–1665*, 21).

years of age,[1] it was *a fortiori* required of all freemen and voters. And in this connection it should be mentioned that the mere taking of the oath of fidelity did not make a man or a boy a freeman.[2] The taking of the oath was a compulsory matter with all males over sixteen years of age dwelling within the jurisdiction, while the freemanship was a privilege conferred by the express vote of the general court. In addition to taking the oath of fidelity, the applicant for freemanship must previously have been regularly admitted into some town of the jurisdiction by the vote of the townspeople; and at the time of election must dwell (" cohabitte") within the commonwealth. Thus four formal qualifications were imposed upon these electors of the governor and magistrates: an oath of fidelity, actual residence in the jurisdiction, legal inhabitancy of one of the towns, and admission by the general court to the freemanship.

The second group of voters, the electors of the town

[1] *Conn. Col. Rec., 1636–1665*, 62.

" The Oath of a Freeman.

" I, A. B., being by the Pruidence of God an Inhabitant wthin the Jurisdiction of Conectecott, doe acknowledge myselfe to be subiecte to the Government thereof, & doe sweare by the great & fearefull name of the euerliueing God, to be true & faythfull vnto the same, & doe submitt boath my prson & estate thereunto, according to all the holsome lawes & orders that there are, or hereafter shall be there made, & established by lawfull authority, & that I will nether plott nor practice any euell [evil] agt the same, nor consent to any that shall so doe, but will tymely discouer the same to lawfull authority there established; & that I will, as I am in duty bound, mayntayne the honner of the same & of the lawfull magestratts thereof, prmoting the publike good of yt, whilst I shall soe continue an Inhabitant there; & whensoeur I shall giue my voate or suffrage touching any matter wch conserns this Comon welth being cauled thereunto, will giue yt as in my conscience I shall judge, may conduce to the best good of the same, wthout respect of prsons or favor of any man. Soe helpe me God in or Lord Jesus Christe."

[2] A writer, usually careful in his judgments, has fallen into this error (*J. H. U. Stud.*, VII, 85). See also Trumbull, *History of Connecticut*, I, 75 (New London edition of 1898).

deputies to the general courts, was not so limited as was the first group. The deputies were to be chosen, according to the seventh fundamental, "by all that are admitted Inhabitants in the seu^rall Townes and haue taken the oath of fidellity," but the express proviso was added that no one "be chosen a Deputy for any Generall Courte wch is not a Freeman of this Comonwelth." Freemanship was required of the representative, but not of the elector. The latter must simply be a regularly admitted inhabitant of the town wherein he voted. It is well to remember, however, that the word *inhabitant* had a much narrower connotation at that time than it has to-day. In New England, and in almost all the colonies, the English legal meaning of the word was attached to it,—that is, an inhabitant meant a householder, usually the head of a family, and under American conditions it was frequently synonymous in practice with freeholder.[1] At this early period the inhabitant was not merely a resident of the town, he was the responsible head of a family, formally admitted by the town into participation in the town political and economic activities. Upon these two bases of freemanship and inhabitancy the elections for the colonial officers and for the town representatives respectively rested during the period that the constitution of 1639 was in operation.

We must now note those conditions which in law or fact were imposed upon applicants for inhabitancy in the towns and for the freemanship in the commonwealth. As early as 1643 the general court interpreted the clause of the fundamentals giving the suffrage for deputies to admitted inhabitants, by declaring that such inhabitants were those only who were "admitted by a generall voate of the mayor p^rte of the Towne that receaueth them." [2]   Hence the actual restrictions upon inhabitants were left to the votes of the respective town meetings.[3] That religious conformity was

[1] See *ante*, Chap. I and Chap. XI.

[2] *Conn. Col. Rec., 1636–1665*, 96.

[3] The code of 1650 provided for the disfranchisement from town or colony elections of persons who were "fyned or whipped for any scandalous offence;" they could be restored to their privileges by action of the court (*Conn. Col. Rec., 1636–1665*, 559).

sometimes one of these restrictions there seems no doubt,[1] and particularly does this appear to be the case in view of the emigration of church congregations from Massachusetts to Connecticut. At Wethersfield, where, in 1640, there were only seven formal members of the church,[2] it is likely the other inhabitants were members of some church in New England, but had not yet organized themselves into church fellowship owing to the quarrels among the seven claiming to be the church.[3] In the early days, too, admission as an inhabitant of a town was contingent upon a man's ability to enter into the economic life of the community. The inhabitants who planned the settlement of Wethersfield required their fellow " adventurers" to settle within the town before a certain date if they did not want to forfeit their interest in the town " devident." [4]

In Hartford the recipient of a grant of land was required to build upon it within twelve months after the grant; if he removed within four years his lands were to be forfeited to the town; but a sale was permitted either to the town or to a person approved by the town.[5] In Middletown a fixed term of residence and the erection and occupation of a tenantable house were required to hold title to town lots.[6] That the towns exerted their privilege of refusing inhabitants is shown by the town records of Hartford,[7] but after admission there does not seem to be any way of excluding an inhabitant, for the Hartford town meeting offered ten pounds to an objectionable man and his wife if they would remove from the town.[8]

[1] *New Haven Hist. Soc. Papers*, III, 315; Andrews, *J. H. U. Stud.*, VII, 83.

[2] Trumbull, I, 92–93.

[3] New Haven would not have received some twenty-two of the Wethersfield men had they not been members of some "approved" congregation.

[4] *Conn. Col. Rec., 1636–1665*, 4.

[5] *Hartford Town Votes*, I, 1 (printed in Vol. VI of the *Connecticut Historical Society's Collections*).

[6] *Conn. Col. Rec., 1636–1665*, 249.

[7] *Hartford Town Votes*, I, 132, 148, 171, 196.

[8] *Ibid.*, 148.

25

Such restrictions were not, however, always enforced. Before 1657 many objectionable persons seem to have been adopted by the towns as inhabitants,[1] and the presence of these persons led the general court to make the first property qualification upon the suffrage. The restriction was not made upon the freemen, but applied only to the " admitted inhabitants," to whom was given the right to vote for town deputies. The seventh fundamental, by an order of the court of February 26, 1656–7, was interpreted as granting the suffrage only to " householders that are one & twenty yeares of age, or haue bore office, or haue 30l. estate." [2] This limitation conformed to the English custom in respect to age and householding, but it went beyond that in the establishment of a legal property qualification for inhabitancy. In this form the suffrage for representatives was continued until 1662, when the terms of the new charter restricted such elections to the freemen alone.[3]

It has been seen that the fundamentals gave to the general court the power of admission of freemen. That body sometimes exercised the power directly and sometimes delegated it to specific persons or officers. As early as October, 1639, Governor Haynes and a Mr. Wells were appointed by the court to confer with the planters at Pequonnocke (Stratford), and were empowered to administer the oath of fidelity to them and to " make such free as they see fitt." [4] A similar authorization was made shortly afterwards.[5] In 1646 a general power of admitting freemen was delegated to any three magistrates, who were required to demand a certificate of the good character of the applicant; but their power was limited to the time intervening before the next meeting

[1] *New Haven Hist. Soc. Papers*, III, 301.

[2] *Conn. Col. Rec., 1636–1665*, 293. By the code of 1650 the court had declared twenty-one years to be the legal age for giving of votes or performing legal acts (*Rec. 1636–1665*, 510).

[3] In 1660 the towns were forbidden to admit as inhabitants any persons but " such as are knowne to be of an honest conversation" (*Conn. Col. Rec., 1636–1665*, 351).

[4] *Conn. Col. Rec., 1636–1665*, 36.

[5] *Ibid.*, 47.

of the general court.[1] The records do not show how many were admitted as freemen in this manner, but their number may have been considerable, for it does not seem probable that the twenty-three names of admitted freemen given in the records represent all the acceptable persons who came into Connecticut from 1639 to 1649. The order of the general court in 1657 requiring the town deputies to prepare a list of the names of freemen in their respective towns seems to point to the conclusion that the colony records are not complete on the subject.[2]

Perhaps it was some irregularity in the use of the delegated power of admitting freemen which led the court in 1657 to enact that "those and only those" who were approved by the general court should be made freemen. Applicants were further required to have "an affirmatiue certificate vnder the hands of all or the major part of the deputies in their seuerall townes, of their peaceable and honest conuersation."[3] It seems impossible to determine whether or not the admission of freemen by the magistrates continued up to the time of this act. The fact that 140 freemen were admitted within the fifteen months following the passage of the act indicates either a large increase in the class of persons qualified for freemanship, or a sudden desire for that privilege, or that the general court was exercising a function which previously had been performed by the magistrates.[4] The writer is inclined to accept the latter view.

In 1657 the court had imposed a property qualification upon voting inhabitants in the towns. Two years later, by an order of March 9, 1658–9, a similar restriction was placed upon the freemanship. An order of that date provided

[1] *Conn. Col. Rec., 1636–1665*, 139. The same order authorizes the administering of the oath of fidelity to all male persons over sixteen. years of age.

[2] *Conn. Col. Rec., 1636–1665*, 290.   [3] *Ibid.*

[4] This number is more than half the entire number of recorded admissions between 1639 and 1662. The greatest number admitted at any previous session of the court was in May, 1654, when thirty-six freemen were accepted (*Rec.*, 256).

> " That for the future none shalbe prsented to be made free-
> men in this Jurisdiction, or haue the priuilidge of freedome
> conferd vpon them, vntil they haue fulfild the age of twenty
> one years and haue 30l. of proper personal estate, or haue
> borne office in the Comon wealth; such persons quallified as
> before, and being men of an honest and peaceable conver-
> sation, shalbe prsented in an ordrly way at the General Court
> in October, yearly, to prvent tumult and trouble at the Court
> of Election." [1]

The reasons for the passage of this act are not given in the
contemporary documents.   Apparently it was called forth by
the rapid growth of the freeman class which had taken place
in the preceding two years.   The natural feeling may also
have arisen that the freemen voters should not possess a
lower qualification than that which had lately been imposed
upon those voting by right of inhabitancy.

The property qualification thus established was not identical with that imposed upon town inhabitants.   In the latter
case the requirement was thirty pounds " estate;" while in
the new act it was the same amount of " proper personal
estate."   This has been interpreted by students of the period
as meaning a real estate qualification for town inhabitants,
and a personal property requirement for the freemanship.[2]
Mr. Bronson [3] has pointed out that thirty pounds of personal
property was a comparatively large sum for that time, when
the average property of a taxable person was sixty pounds,
made up largely of real estate.   The new qualification must,
indeed, have been a very high one, for it practically prohibited further accessions to the freemanship.   Within the
next two and a half years, or until the charter went into
operation in October, 1662, there are only three recorded
admissions of freemen.   The one hundred and forty admissions in the fifteen months preceding the passage of this
act, and the three freemen admitted in the two and a half
years following, give us a very definite idea of the success
of the new restrictive legislation.   If the ideal of the general

[1] *Conn. Col. Rec., 1636–1665,* 331.

[2] Bronson, *New Haven Hist. Soc. Papers,* III, 315;   Andrews, *J. H.
U. Stud.,* VII, 87.

[3] *Op. cit.*

court was the exclusion of all other persons from the freemanship, that ideal was attained. In justice to the framers of the law, however, it may be believed that the operation of the act was more exclusive than they desired. At least we must remember that one of the first acts under the new charter was the passage of a law putting the freemanship on a far less aristocratic basis.[1]

While there was no formal religious qualification for voters in Connecticut, yet, on the other hand, there was no such separation of church and state as was established by Williams in Rhode Island. Hooker, indeed, had said that the privilege of election, although given by God to the people, " must not be exercised according to their humors, but according to the blessed will and law of God." [2] " To the first settlers in Connecticut," says a late writer, " civil and ecclesiastical affairs were convertible terms. The township and the church were coterminous : the town, by which term, as distinguished from the territorial *township,* was meant the body of voters within the township, settled civil and ecclesiastical affairs indifferently in the same town meeting ; and as about all the voters were at first church-members and agreed closely in creed and methods, the dual system produced little friction for a time." [3] Palfrey thought it reasonable to believe " that church-membership—or, to speak more precisely, a religious character in the candidate, such as naturally led to church-membership, and was commonly found in union with it—was also in Plymouth and Connecticut much regarded by the electors as a qualification of candidates for citizenship." [4] It is almost the universal opinion of Connecticut historians that the actual administration of the freeman principle in that colony led at first to virtually the same restrictions upon the suffrage as existed in New Haven or Massachusetts.[5]

[1] See *post,* 408.
[2] Palfrey, *New England,* I, 537.
[3] Johnston, *Connecticut,* 220.
[4] Palfrey, *New England,* II, 8.
[5] A further proof of this opinion is to be seen in the proposition of Connecticut made during the negotiations with New Haven that candidates for freemanship be " men of a religious carriage, visibly soe" (*New Haven Col. Rec., 1653–1665,* 495).

The number of original freemen in 1639 is not known, but their number was increased very slowly. Out of a total increase in population between 1639 and 1662 of about 3000 persons, only 229 are recorded as having been admitted to the freemanship.[1] That is, for twenty-three years only one person in thirteen of the new population was made a freeman of the corporation. In the first ten years there are only twenty-three recorded admissions; and of the remaining ones, more than half were admitted by the general court, between 1657 and 1659. Yet it is probable that, owing to the more liberal town suffrage, and the right of town inhabitants to vote for the town representatives in the general court, the limitations upon the freemanship were not felt so heavily as in Massachusetts. It is plain, too, that Connecticut was looked upon as more liberal than New Haven. Evidently, Hooker's plan of theocratic government was more practicable than those of Cotton and Davenport.

II. *The Suffrage in New Haven before the Union with Connecticut.*

The well-known peculiarity of the New Haven colony is the limitation of political power to those who were church-members. In New Haven, even more fully than in Massachusetts, did the church-members control the entire life of the community. In Massachusetts although participation in the colonial elections was granted only to freemen, yet non-freemen were sometimes given a part in the choice of town or militia officers; but in New Haven the attempt was made to limit the suffrage under any or all conditions—with the single exception of proprietary claims to lands—to those who were members of some approved church. In no other settlement on the continent was the theoretical ideal of a community of church-members so nearly attained; nowhere else were the lines between political power and disfranchisement so clearly and sharply drawn. Yet it must be said that New Haven was content with her religious qualification;

---

[1] Bronson, *op. cit.*, 313. There may have been others admitted in the irregular way by officers of the company, but no record has been found of such persons.

this was the supreme test of good citizenship, and it was the only one. She did not link to it any freehold or personal property prerequisite; all were invited " to come in by the doore" of the church: [1] every one was discouraged from " disorderly or uncomely attempts to climbe up another way."

The New Haven towns, like many other examples in America, appear to have sprung from the voluntary and spontaneous association of a group of Englishmen. The first compact may have been of a business nature when the friends contributed according to their ability towards the common expenses; or it may have been of a religious character, the brotherhood bond of members of a common church. Such voluntary economic or ecclesiastical associations before actual settlement are to be seen in the cases of New Haven proper,[2] in Milford,[3] Guilford,[4] and Southold.[5] But the purely personal compact of business copartners, or the friendly tie of common church-membership must be replaced either before [6] or soon after settlement by a more formal organization both of church and state. The association must be changed from a voluntary personal one to a more definite political organization whose jurisdiction in civil and religious affairs would be co-extensive with the territory of the town.[7] This transition was accomplished first in the town of New Haven according to a method later adopted in the neighboring towns.

The meeting of the New Haven planters on June 4, 1639, which tradition says was held in Mr. Newman's barn, acting under the advice of Minister Davenport, took the first steps for the " settling ciuill Gouernm^t according to God." [8]

---

[1] *New Haven Colonial Records, 1653–1665,* 403–404.

[2] *New Haven Hist. Soc. Papers,* I, 12.

[3] Atwater, *History of New Haven Colony,* 155.

[4] Steiner, *History of Guilford and Madison, Conn.,* 29; Atwater, *New Haven,* 161.

[5] *Ibid.,* 171–173.

[6] See grant of " civil power for the administration of justice and the preservation of peace" in Guilford; Steiner, *Guilford,* 29.

[7] Compare C. F. Adams, *The Genesis of Massachusetts Towns,* Mass. Hist. Soc. Proc., Second Series, VII, 179–187.

[8] *New Haven Col. Rec., 1638–1649,* 11 ff.

Here the well-known queries of Davenport were unanimously answered in the affirmative by the body of planters. It was agreed that " the Scripturs doe holde forth a perfect rule for the direction and gouernmᵗ of all men in all duet[ies] wᶜʰ they are to performe to God and men as well in the gouᵣmᵗ of famylyes and comonwealths as in matters of the chur[ch]." So likewise all accepted the earlier covenant they had made that the rules of scripture should be observed in all " publique offices wᶜʰ concerne ciuill order, as choyce of magistrates and officers, makeing and repealing of lawes, devideing allottmᵗˢ of inheritance and all things of a like nature." Upon the third query all expressed themselves as desirous of admission to church-fellowship as soon as they were fitted therefor by God; and the fourth inquiry that such a civil order should be established as would secure the purity and peace of the religious ordinances was with equal unanimity adopted.

In the fifth question there lay the whole theory of New Haven theocratic government: " Whether Free Burgesses shalbe chosen out of chur. members?" The question was carried unanimously; but one man, perhaps Samuel Eaton,[1] after the vote was taken, expressed a partial dissent from the decision. The objections were answered by Davenport and Theophilus Eaton, whose arguments called forth expressions of approval from some who owned they had not previously been quite fully satisfied of the justice of the restriction. And then by a second unanimous vote, this time undoubtedly with more spirit,

> " Mr. Robᵗ Newman was desired to write itt as an order wherevnto euery one thatt hereafter should be admitted here as planters should submitt and testefie the same by subscribing their names to the order, namely, that church members onely shall be free burgesses, and thatt they onely shall chuse magistrates & officers among themselues to haue the power of transacting all the publique ciuill affayres of this Plantation, of makeing and repealing lawes, devideing of inheritances, decideing of differences thatt may arise and doeing all things or businesses of like nature." [2]

[1] Atwater, *New Haven*, 99.
[2] *New Haven Col. Rec., 1638–1649*, 15.

This restriction of freemanship to church-members must be read in the light of the unanimous expression of the desire to enter church fellowship. All the adult planters were willing to enter the church when its organization should be completed, and in the light of this feeling the church-membership provision was not a limitation upon any of the men gathered in Mr. Newman's barn. Should all carry out their desire to enter the church, the suffrage would be co-extensive with the free planters. It would be, most likely, with respect to new-comers, that the rule would work hardship. The original settlers possessed a solidarity of feeling which had been the real reason for their previous association; but would new arrivals or a rising generation pay such regard to the religious tenets which persecution had brought into the foreground of the Puritan's thinking? The history of the New Haven colony shows how difficult it was, in spite of great care in the admission of inhabitants, to maintain the homogeneity of sentiment so marked among the first settlers.

After the consideration of the general foundations of church and state, the planters proceeded to select from their number certain persons to carry on the work of organization. The general meeting appointed twelve men for the "foundation work;" these selected seven "pillars" to organize a church. After they had completed this, and admitted others as church-members, the seven held a civil court at which those who were members of the new church or of some "approved" church were privileged to vote for civil officers.[1] At about the same time a "freeman's charge" or declaration of obedience to the government was composed.[2]

[1] *New Haven Col. Rec., 1638–1649,* 16–21; Atwater, *New Haven,* 101–102.

[2] *New Haven Col. Rec., 1638–1649,* 19.

"You shall neither plott, practise nor consent to any evill or hurt against this Jurisdiction, or any pte of it, or against the civill gouernment here established. And if you shall know any pson or psons wᶜʰ intend, plott, or conspire any thing wᶜʰ tends to the hurt or prejudice of the same, you shall timely discouer the same to lawfull authority here established and yow shall assist and bee helpfull in all the affaires of the

The method of initiating religious and civil government in Milford, Guilford, and perhaps in Southold, appears similar to that adopted in New Haven. Pillars of the church were chosen for beginning the "foundation work;" and after they had started the organization, others were admitted as church-members and as freemen of the respective towns.[1] At Guilford, however, an additional restriction was placed upon freemen. The agreement of the settlers of that town included the following clause:

> "We do now therefore, all and every of us agree, order and conclude that only such planters, as are also members of the church *here*, shall bee, and bee called freemen, and that such freemen only shall have power to elect magistrates, Deputies and all other officers of public trust or authority in matters of importance, concerning either the civill officers or government here, from amongst themselves and not elsewhere."[2]

Thus not church-membership in some "approved" church of New England, but, rather, membership of the local church was required in the Guilford settlement. They went one degree farther than New Haven. On the other hand, Milford appears to have been more lax in the admission of freemen than were her neighbors. Before her union with New Haven and Guilford, Milford admitted six non-church-members as freemen. But the action was esteemed so objectionable that it was thought worthy of a special place in the

Jurisdiction, and by all meanes shall promove the publique wellfare of the same, according to yo[r] place, ability, and opptunity, yow shall give due honno[r] to the lawful magistrats, and shall be obedient and subject to all the wholesome lawes and orderes, allready made, or w[ch] shall be hereafter made, by lawfull authority afforesaid. And that both in yo[r] pson and estate; and when yow shall be duely called to give yo[r] vote or suffrage in any election, or touching any other matter, w[ch] concerneth this common wealth, yow shall give it as in yo[r] conscience yow shall judg may conduce to the best good of the same."

[1] Atwater, *New Haven*, Chap. IX.
[2] Steiner, *Guilford*, 35–36.

agreements leading up to the union of 1643. Milford would not disfranchise her irregular freemen, but they were to be permitted to vote only for town officers and deputies, they and all non-church-members were excluded from holding office, and for the future " none shall be admitted freemen or free burgesses hereafter att Milforde, butt church members according to the practice of Newhaven." [1]

No change was made in the freeman principle nor in the qualifications of applicants by the fundamentals of 1643, which united the previously separate settlements of New Haven, Milford, and Guilford, except that non-freemen were specially guaranteed rights " to their inheritance & to comerce, according to such grants, orders and lawes as shall be made concerning the same." [2]   It was the aim of the New Haven government to keep the entire political control in the hands of the freemen.   In Connecticut and Massachusetts non-freemen could vote in some local elections, but not in those for the entire colony.   But no such distinction was made in New Haven; the freemen church-members alone could elect the colony officers, direct the affairs, and choose the officers of the towns,[3] and they only were privileged to select the militia officers,[4] a right almost universally granted to all soldiers.[5]   The newly organized government also required all persons admitted as inhabitants to take an oath of fidelity to the jurisdiction.[6]

Such was the simple basis of political organization in the " republic of New Haven."   All adult male inhabitants, who were members of some approved church in New England, were qualified electors of the commonwealth.   But in the

[1] *New Haven Col. Rec., 1638–1649*, 110; Atwater, *New Haven*, 158. It is interesting to note that of the fifty-four original planters of Milford, forty-four were at once admitted to church membership, a larger proportion of actual members than is seen among the early settlers of New Haven (Atwater, 157).

[2] *New Haven Col. Rec., 1638–1649*, 112.

[3] *Ibid.. 1653–1665.* 604.

[4] *Ibid.*, 361. 602.

[5] See subject of militia elections in other colonies.

[6] *New Haven Col. Rec., 1638–1649*, 130; *1653–1665*, 57, 98; Levermore, *The Republic of New Haven.* 101.

simplicity of the restriction there lay a danger which the state soon discovered. The church was the door to political power; but who should guard the entrance? " Who was to keep the keepers?" [1] Massachusetts had recognized the danger very soon after she laid the religious restriction upon freemen, and in 1635–6 had met the difficulty by forbidding the organization of any church without the consent of the magistrates of the colony and the elders of the approved churches.[2] The New Haven legal code of 1656 adopted the spirit of the earlier provision of Massachusetts, although changing somewhat the wording of the law. Full liberty was given to the " people of God within this jurisdiction, who are not in a church way, being orthodox in judgment, and not scandalous in life," [3] to gather themselves into a church organization according to the " rules of Christ, re-vealed in his Word." But no such company of persons join-ing in " any pretended way of church fellowship" should be recognized by the general court unless they had the approval of the magistrates and the elders of the churches.

> " Nor shall any person, being a member of any church which shall be gathered without such notice given and approbation had, or who is not a member of some church in New England approved by the magistrates and churches of this colony, be admitted to the freedom of this jurisdiction."

In this way the state protected itself against the deterioration of the political constituency by the acceptance of the members of irregular churches. The religious qualification for the suffrage implied a right upon the part of the political authorities to preserve the purity of the ecclesiastical spring whence flowed the freeman class. As in the colonies where freeholding was a prerequisite to political rights the legis-latures were compelled to define the term freehold, so in Massachusetts and New Haven the term church-member must be given a definite connotation.

Another feature of the fundamentals of the union of 1643

[1] Palfrey, *New England*, I, 436.
[2] *Mass. Col. Rec.*, I, 171.
[3] *New Haven Col. Rec., 1653–1665*, 588.

is the adoption of the proxy system. By the third fundamental it was provided that

> " for the ease of those free burgesses especially in the more
> remote plantations, they may by proxi vote in these elections,
> though absent, their votes being sealed vp in the prsence of
> the free burgesses themselves, thatt their severall libertyes
> may be preserved, and their votes directed according to their
> owne particular light." [1]

The constitution of 1643 did not state the manner in which
these proxy votes, or ballots, should be cast, but the code of
1656 permitted those freemen who could not conveniently
attend the election to " send their Votes, either written, or
in some other way sealed up." [2] The " other way" is illus-
trated by the corn-and-bean provision of the same code;
according to which the freeman might " send his Vote, as
he finds cause, either in the affirmative, by putting in an
Indian Corne, or in the Negative, by putting in a Beane, or
in such other manner, as the Generall Court shall judge
more convenient."

Despite, however, the early strictness with which the right
of election was limited to the freemen, there arose in practice certain exceptions to the principle, and popular clamor
demanded still greater compromises. In the militia elections
it was not always found possible to obtain efficient or willing
officers among the freemen, and although the electors appear
to have been freemen, yet on several occasions the officers
chosen were non-freemen. [3] In the town-meetings, Guilford, as early as 1645–6 permitted all planters to vote upon
a question of the division of the town lands. [4] It must be
remembered that non-freemen often were landowners and

[1] *New Haven Col. Rec., 1638–1649*, 113.

[2] *Ibid., 1653–1665*, 567.

[3] *New Haven Col. Rec., 1653–1665*, 97, 145, 407. In the last case the
general court permitted Southold to choose a non-freeman *drummer*
because of their " present necessity & his fitnes."

[4] Steiner, *Guilford*, 167. The attendance of non-freemen at the town-
meetings in Guilford was compulsory; the fines upon " planters" being
one-half those imposed upon freemen for lateness or absence (*ibid.*,
100).

proprietors in common lands, upon which matters they would have an ethical right to be heard when their property interests were at stake. But the boundary line between purely personal matters and political concerns was not easily determined, and some towns admitted non-freemen " to vote in things of weightie trust and concernment." The latter condition called forth an order from the general court requiring the fundamental orders to " be exactly attended and none suffered to vote but free-men." But the court itself was compelled in justice to add, " unless it be in some pticuler cases wherein the proprieties of the planters in generall are concerned and ought not to be disposed of w^thout their consent."[1]

As in local matters there was thus a slight lifting of the bars to the suffrage, so the restricted nature of the freemanship in general elections soon led to protests by the disfranchised against its narrowness. While restrictions were imposed upon the admission of inhabitants,[2] yet many who were not church-members acquired inhabitancy and lands in the towns.[3] It has not been possible to arrive at an estimate of the actual number or proportion of this disfranchised class, but it must have constituted a group of inhabitants almost, if not quite, as large as that of the freemen. As late as 1669, when the more lenient Connecticut laws were in force, the freemen of the town of New Haven did not include more than half the whole number of taxable males.[4] At an earlier time the proportion of freemen may have been even less than this.[5] A disfranchised class of this size was not likely to remain silent throughout the history of the colony.

During the war between the English Commonwealth and the Dutch the members of the New England federation discussed the expediency of an attack upon New Amsterdam. Through the opposition of Massachusetts the plan was not

---

[1] *New Haven Col. Rec., 1653–1665,* 177.

[2] *Ibid., 1638–1649,* 24, 40, 130; *1653–1665,* 610.

[3] Levermore, *Republic of New Haven,* 101–104.

[4] See *post;* and compare *Conn. Col. Rec., 1665–1677,* 290, with *ibid.,* 518–526.

[5] See Doyle, *The Puritan Colonies,* I, 198–199.

carried out, but the agitation of the subject led to great popular movements in Connecticut and New Haven, in the course of which two towns, Fairfield in Connecticut and Stamford in New Haven, even began to collect a force to attack the Dutch on their own account. The refusal of the authorities of both Connecticut and New Haven to sanction the proposed attack increased popular excitement in the towns, and led some of the inhabitants to attack the existing colonial governments; they declared themselves in favor of the " State of England," and were determined " to stand for their liberties, that they may all have their votes." [1]

Robert Bassett, of Stamford, appears to have been the most active man in the New Haven jurisdiction in favoring the popular movement. He was arrested, charged with being a " ringleader in these wayes of disturbance," and brought before the court at New Haven. The court believed he had wanted to " overthrow churches and comonwealthes;" and recorded how he had demanded, in a Stamford town-meeting, after being told that the meeting was held under English authority, " then let vs haue Englands lawes, for England doe not prohibbitt vs from our votes and liberties, and here wee are, and wee are cut of from all appeales to England." [2] He had also pointed to the more favorable suffrage laws of Connecticut. The court of New Haven proceeded to enlighten him with respect to the suffrage in England; and " hee was informed that many thousands in England, of great estates, and good repute in other respects, haue no vote in such elections." His own course, he was told, had been " full of pride & insolency, himselfe a leader to disturbe the peace both of churches and commonwealth, nay to ouerthrowe all foundations laid here for gouernment. wᶜʰ by oath he stands bound to maintayne and vphold, so he hath discovered a false and rotten spirit." [3] Another of the malcontents was charged with teaching the same doctrines, " wᶜʰ in him is worss then in another because hee is a freeman and

[1] Atwater, *New Haven*, 404–406; Trumbull, *Conn.* (ed. of 1898), I, 175.

[2] *New Haven Col. Rec., 1653–1665*, 52, 55, 59, 60.

[3] *Ibid.*, 60.

sometime hath bine a deputie in ye general court." [1]   Still
another was charged with " pleading for liberties in votes,
that all may chuse officers for publique trust, and chuse whom
they please; and because it is not granted, he growes surly
and discontented."   In the Stamford town-meeting he had
said the town deputies were really church deputies; " and
who must chuse them?" he asked.   " The free-men; then
said hee, wee are bond-men, and so will our chilldren bee,
therefore it is time for vs to looke to it."   So widespread
was the spirit of unrest in Stamford that the general court
was informed that " the generality of Stamford did desire
they might haue libertie in vots."

Southold, on Long Island, was the scene of a similar
popular movement.   The leaders claimed the government
was tyrannical; but the worst remark recorded against any
of them was the statement of John Youngs, that he was
" vnsatisfyed that he had not his vote in chusing millitary
officers." [2]   The general court had no compromise to offer
the discontented inhabitants.   They were fined in various
amounts, placed under heavy bonds, and required to make
confession of their error.   Steps were also taken to enforce
more rigidly the policy of tendering the oath of fidelity to
all inhabitants, and report was to be made to the general
court of those refusing to accept the oath. [3]   A few months
later, in May, 1654, all persons before being admitted as
inhabitants, were required to express approval of the fundamentals restricting the suffrage to church-members, and then
must take the oath of fidelity to the government established
in the jurisdiction.   This approval of the fundamental laws
is so unusual a provision that it may be quoted entire:

> " It is ordered that vpon the admittance of any man as a
> planter into any plantation in this jurisdiction, the funda-
> mentall lawes and orders concerning votes, &c., shall be read
> to them, and if approved, the oath of fidellitie shall be admin-

[1] *New Haven Col. Rec., 1653–1665*, 61
[2] *Ibid.*, 94. Where the right of election of military officers existed
in the colonies, it was almost uniformly vested in all the soldiers; so
Youngs' demand was a remarkably modest one.
[3] *Ibid.*, 57, 96.

istered to them, the plantation wch is to receive them being satisfyed in other respects by a satisfying certifycate from sufficient credible psons, of their good behaviour & conversation." [1]

In this way the new inhabitant was required to express approval of the fundamentals and swear to observe the rules by which he might be perpetually disfranchised.

Yet in spite of the firmness with which this popular movement was suppressed, only two years had passed when the general court was compelled to enter upon its records the fact " that in some of the plantations the fundamentall lawes of the jurisdiction haue not bine attended, but that others besides free-men haue had libertie to vote in things of weightie trust and concernment;" [2] and it was ordered that the fundamentals be " exactly attended, and none suffered to vote but free-men," except in cases where the land interests of proprietors were at stake.

Again, in 1661 the limited suffrage led to disorders in Guilford, where, however, there were other causes of discontent. [3] The appeal was made this time, not to the laws of England, but to the very fundamentals themselves, [4] the first of which, while limiting the suffrage to church-members, had closed with the guarantee that non-freeman planters should have rights " to their inherritance & to comerce." [5] Doubtless the non-freemen of Guilford, like disfranchised classes in almost all other communities, had discovered that the civil and economic rights granted in the fundamentals could not be fully protected without the political rights which the same fundamentals had denied. The general court declared [6] to all " godly and peaceable inhabitants" that they hoped there would be no cause to complain of withholding

---

[1] *New Haven Col. Rec., 1653–1665,* 98. The same express approval of the fundamentals was required of Oyster Bay when it applied for union with the colony (*ibid.*).

[2] *New Haven Col. Rec., 1653–1665,* 177.

[3] Steiner, *Guilford,* 100–103.

[4] *New Haven Col. Rec., 1653–1665,* 403.

[5] *Ibid., 1638–1649,* 112.

[6] *Ibid.,* 403–404.

just rights and liberties, but there must be no injury done to
the " cheife ends and interests, professed and pretended by
all at our coming, combineing and setling in New England;" and from which no " disturbers of their Israell" could
divert them to commit their " more weighty ciuill or military trusts into the hands of either a crafty Achitophell, or
a bloody Joab." With a bearing more conciliatory than
that of 1654, the court expressed the hope " that all planters
would make it their serious endeauour to come in by the
doore to enjoy all privilidges & beare all burdens equall wth
themselues, according to our foundation settlements & vni-
uersally professed ends, and yt there may be noe disorderly
or vncomely attempts to climbe vp another way."

But the malcontents were not to be left much longer in
their disfranchised state. A little over a year after the
trouble in Guilford the news was spread in the New Haven
towns of the terms of the new Connecticut charter, which
seemed to include all the New Haven lands within the territory granted to Connecticut. The possibility of enjoying
the wider political privileges of Connecticut was noticed at
once, and Southold, in which we have seen there was dissatisfaction with the suffrage, voted to send deputies to
Hartford, while individual planters in Guilford, Stamford,
and Greenwich were immediately admitted freemen of
Connecticut.[1] Thus the towns in which the agitation against
the restricted suffrage had existed for eight years were the
ones to first leave New Haven; and it is quite conceivable
that the terms later accorded to New Haven, although
favorable, might have been still more so if her population
had unitedly upheld the New Haven officers in their opposition to the claims of Connecticut.

Although the extension of the Connecticut jurisdiction
over New Haven territory by the charter of 1662 was
strongly opposed by the government of the latter colony,
evidence is not lacking that Winthrop, who secured the
charter in England, believed that the two colonies could be
harmoniously united.[2] But if such were the case his hopes

[1] Atwater, *New Haven*, 463–465; *Conn. Col. Rec., 1636–1665*, 386–391.
[2] See correspondence of Governors Winthrop and Leete, before the
departure of the former for England (Atwater, *New Haven*, 455–459).

were not immediately realized. A number of circumstances prevented the amicable union of the two colonies; among which may be mentioned the absence of Winthrop himself in England, the hasty action of Connecticut in accepting Southold and the inhabitants of the other towns, the natural reluctance of the New Haven authorities to yield their independence, and, as strong as any of the other reasons, the desire to maintain the New Haven religious restriction upon the suffrage. With the latter reason we are particularly concerned. The objection does not at first appear upon the surface of the New Haven Records, but in March, 1662-3 the Connecticut general court proposed to New Haven that there should be no interference with the church government of New Haven, that their magistrates might remain in office until the succeeding election, that representation in the Connecticut government be given to New Haven, and that all present freemen of New Haven be at once admitted into the Connecticut corporation.[1] No reference, however, was made to the future qualifications of freemen. New Haven rejected these overtures until more definite information could be obtained from England respecting the meaning of the charter.

In August, 1663, New Haven, on her part, suggested the making of a treaty between the two colonies.[2] She proposed that the " fundamentall lawes for governm^t, especially y^t touching the qualificacons of freemen shalbe the same wth Boston or our (i.e.) members of some one or oth^r of o^r churches;" that no infringement be made upon the church ordinances or the freedom of choosing ministers; that the present New Haven freemen be at once admitted upon an equality with those of Connecticut; that a new law book be drawn up; and that the *freemen* in each town should elect their town officers. Connecticut replied to the first question :

> " That the patterne or foundation from wch we cannot vary is o^r charter, nor dare we admit of any fundamt^{ls} varying from ye teno^r thereof, but w^t lawes may be concurring therewith and conduceable to ye publique weale of church and

[1] *New Haven Col. Rec., 1653-1665*, 475-477.
[2] *Ibid.*, 491.

state we are ready to grant yᵉ establishmᵗ thereof, & pticularly for quallification of freemen we are ready to grant that they shalbe men of a religious carriage visibly soe, hauing and possessing some competency of estate, and shal bring a certificate affirmatiue that they are thus quallified from yᵉ deacons of yᵉ church and two of yᵉ select men of yᵉ towne where they liue, and if there be noe deacons, then some other knowne & approued persons wᵗʰ yᵉ selectment as before." [1]

Connecticut agreed to respect the church ordinances and privileges and to accept as freemen of their colony all the present freemen of New Haven. She refused, however, to follow the plan, so unpopular even in New Haven, of limiting the town suffrage to freemen. Instead, the Connecticut committee proposed that all necessary town officers should be " yearly chosen by a maior vote of the approued inhabitants."

These propositions were the most liberal which Connecticut was willing at any time to offer, and, had they been accepted by New Haven, a modification of the Connecticut freemanship law might have resulted in the adoption of a rule as restrictive as that of Massachusetts after her apparent yielding in 1664 to the royal commissioners. But New Haven would not negotiate until the towns and persons lately accepted into the Connecticut colony should be restored to their old relationship. Connecticut refused to do this, and soon there appeared the greater danger of a union with the Catholic Duke of York's territory to the westward.[2] At last, in November, 1664, came the decision of the king's commissioners that New Haven was included within the charter limits of Connecticut, and there was no further opportunity for New Haven to make terms with her more fortunate neighbor. The towns of the New Haven colony were incorporated into Connecticut; those New Haven freemen who took the freeman's oath were to be admitted as freemen of the latter colony; [3] but New Haven, as a distinct political entity, was not permitted to enter into an agree-

---

[1] *New Haven Col. Rec., 1653–1665,* 493.

[2] Atwater, *New Haven,* 510.

[3] *Conn. Col. Rec., 1636–1665,* 437.

ment with Connecticut. In the light of the decision of the royal commissioners, Connecticut had no need to make compromises with the New Haven men. Her magnanimity in time of victory did not extend even to a modified recognition of the theocracy of New Haven; and the religious qualifications of New Haven, which a year earlier might have influenced the legislation of the united colony, now gave way before the more general economic and political qualifications of Connecticut.[1]

III. *Under the Charter of 1662.*

The Connecticut charter of 1662, secured through the exertions of Governor Winthrop, erected a civil corporation composed of nineteen named persons and " such others as now are or hereafter shall bee Admitted and made free of the Company and Society of our Collony of Conecticut."[2] Its affairs were to be directed by a governor, a deputy-governor, twelve assistants, and two meetings of an assembly in each year. The general assemblies were made up of the " freemen of the said Company, or such of them (not exceeding twoe Persons from each place, Towne or Citty) whoe shall be from tyme to tyme therevnto Elected or Deputed by the maior parte of the freemen of the respective Townes, Cittyes and Places." The governor, deputy-governor, and the assistants should be chosen annually on the second Thursday in May " by such greater part of the said Company for the tyme being then and there present." The future admission of freemen was vested in the general assemblies, to which full power was given " to Choose, Nominate and appoint such and soe many other Persons as they shall thinke fitt and shall bee willing to accept the same, to bee free of the said Company and Body Politique, and them into the same to Admitt and to Elect." Such other officers as the assembly " shall thinke fitt and requisite for the Ordering, mannageing and disposeing of the Affaires" of

---

[1] It is interesting to notice that the last meeting of the New Haven jurisdiction was made up not of freemen alone, but also of as many of the "inhabitants as pleased to come" (Atwater, 518).

[2] *Conn. Col. Rec., 1665–1677*, 4.

the company should be constituted by the general assembly. The territory included in the charter was not clearly defined, but as later interpreted by the king's commissioners it comprised not only the Connecticut jurisdiction, but the New Haven colony as well, with the exception of the Long Island dependencies of the two colonies, all of which were given by the king to the Duke of York.

It will be seen that the charter had the freemanship principle so strangely common to the English trading companies, to many of the English boroughs, and to the great political organizations of New England; a principle, too, which the colonists of Connecticut and New Haven had established for themselves in their autochthonous communities. Little change was made by the charter in the political organization of the Connecticut colony, but it did indirectly break down the religious qualifications of New Haven by bringing that colony under the rule of Connecticut. The two most noticeable changes in the Connecticut customs were the entire elimination of inhabitants from colonial elections and the apparent incompatibility of proxy voting with the terms of the charter.

Attention has been called to the two distinct classes of voters in early Connecticut; freemen only being permitted by the fundamentals of 1639 to vote for general officers, while properly admitted inhabitants of the towns, as well as freemen, could take part in the elections of deputies to the general courts. The old method in a sense made the deputies the direct officers of the towns; but the new charter, by limiting the suffrage for deputies as well as colonial officers to freemen, gave the representatives a colonial character. The deputies were no longer the representatives of the several towns, but of the freemen of the colony resident within the towns. Naturally, the elimination of inhabitants from such elections did not come without some opposition by the disfranchised and formal interpretation by the assembly. The general court, "understanding that trouble is like to ensue upon the apprehension of seuerall inhabitants amongst us respectinge the priuiledge of Freemen, and who are to make choyce of Deputyes and publiq' officers," felt compelled to order and declare that only those who were orderly admitted by the general assembly into the freemanship should have a share in such elections.[1] The democratic ballot, or " proxy" voting as it was called at the time, was also apparently forbidden by the charter. This had been permitted in both Connecticut and New Haven. It was now temporarily suspended, and an interpretation put upon the charter which is thus described: " The charter, then, required annual elections of Colony officers by popular vote, at a mass meeting of all the freemen in one place, and particularly specified as the electoral body the majority of the freemen present at the time of voting." [2]

In discussing the suffrage under the charter of 1662 we shall notice the facts both of colonial and of local elections. Under the former subject mention must be made (*a*) of the qualifications successively imposed upon voters down to the revolutionary period; (*b*) the re-adoption of the proxy system; (*c*) a few figures concerning the number of voters. Under the heading of local elections, the franchise for town, for church, and for militia elections must be summarized, and mention made of the voting in respect to proprietary claims to lands.

The charter of 1662 changed the basis for the suffrage in New Haven from a religious one to the good character and property qualifications of Connecticut, but it may be doubted whether this change would have resulted in an extension of the franchise if the Connecticut restriction of 1658-9 had been retained after the union. On the other hand, the charter, as has been noted, worked a limitation in Connecticut by barring non-freeman town inhabitants from the elections for deputies. Had the Connecticut freeman act of 1658-9 been retained after the enforcement of the charter a restriction of the suffrage in both colonies would have resulted. But the Connecticut politicians were too liberal— or too shrewd in the light of their impending struggle for the control of New Haven—to retain so high a property qualification. The meeting of the first general court after the proclamation of the charter, in October, 1662,—the meeting in which Southold and the inhabitants of other New Haven

---

[1] *Conn. Col. Rec., 1636-1665,* 417; March 10, 1663-4.
[2] *New Haven Hist. Soc. Papers,* V, 192.

towns were accepted into their government,—changed considerably the basis for the franchise. For the future, applicants for the freemanship must be twenty-one years of age; they must present " themselves with a certificate vnder ye hands of ye maior part of the Townesmen where they liue, that they are p^rsons of civill, peaceable, and honest conversation;" and they must be assessed for twenty pounds estate, besides their poll-tax, in the list of estate. Such persons were to be presented at the October general court or some adjourned court yearly, and might be admitted by the assembly in the following May after the election. Persons walking scandalously or being legally convicted of any scandalous offence were to be disfranchised by the courts.[1]

This act lowered the property qualification from the possession of twenty pounds personal property to the same amount of any form of taxable property; it required a definite certificate of the good character of the applicant, and it placed him upon a six months' probation.[2] In two and a half years before 1662 only three freemen had been admitted in Connecticut; but under the new law large numbers were admitted at once,[3] and many others propounded and admitted after the six months' probation,[4] while some were even admitted without their application and upon the condition that they accept the freemanship.[5] For eleven years after the passage of the law of 1662 it remained unchanged, and seems to have been administered with care. The records frequently show that the terms of the act were not mere formalities. In October, 1664, we read of seven persons accepted to be made free in the following May, " if nothing

---

[1] *Conn. Col. Rec., 1636–1665,* 389.

[2] The probation feature may have been taken from the similar feature in use in some of the New England churches (Atwater, *New Haven,* 254) ; or, more probably, it was copied from the Plymouth order of 1658, requiring freemen to stand propounded for one year.

[3] *Conn. Col. Rec., 1636–1665,* 386–389, 391, 406, 412, 425, 427–430. Many of the new freemen undoubtedly came from the New Haven towns, but a number were inhabitants of the original Connecticut jurisdiction.

[4] *Ibid.,* 413, 433.

[5] *Ibid.,* 429–430.

fall in as a just exception against either of them in the interrem;"[1] and at other times the applicants for freemanship are said " to stand for their freedom,"[2] or to be upon " tryall for freemen."[3]   In at least two cases the general court saw cause to defer giving the freeman's oath to certain probationers " until some farther opertunity."[4]

The few years following the grant of the new charter were a time of considerable interest in the suffrage question. The negotiations with New Haven were under way, bringing to the front the advisability of moral and religious qualifications; the new law of 1662 was being put in execution, while, on the other hand, the town inhabitants were trying to retain their right to vote for town deputies.   In the midst of these domestic difficulties came the royal commissioners to investigate the political and religious conditions of the New England colonies.   Colonel Nicholls and the other commissioners were directed to make known to Connecticut those terms of their instructions concerning Massachusetts which properly applied to Connecticut,[5] and the Connecticut authorities were compelled to respond to a list of requirements.[6]   They replied to the demand for all householders to take an oath of allegiance to the king that persons had been appointed to administer such oaths and that it had been taken by " seuerall persons allready."   To the demand " that all men of competent estates and of ciuill conuersation, though of different judgements, may be admitted to be freemen, and haue liberty to chuse or be chosen officers, both military and ciuill," the Connecticut general court replied, " our order for admission of freemen is consonant wth that proposition."   The requirement for liberty of conscience called forth the answer, " We know not of any one that hath bin troubled by us for attending his conscience, prouided he hath not disturbed the publique;" and the commissioners

---

[1] *Conn. Col. Rec., 1636–1665*, 433.

[2] *Ibid.*, 413.

[3] *Ibid., 1665–1677*, 66.

[4] *Ibid.*, 14, 118. In the latter case all were admitted " only except Annanias Turrener."

[5] *New York Col. Doc.*, III, 55–56.

[6] *Conn. Col. Rec., 1636–1665*, 439.

were also told that the court knew of no laws or expressions in laws derogatory to the king, but if any such be found they should consider it their duty to repeal them. How well these replies and those of Rhode Island contrasted with the attitude of Massachusetts has been told in the commissioners' own words.[1]

Interest in the franchise, however, did not cease with these replies. Three weeks later, in May, 1665, the general court re-enacted an earlier law by refusing to admit any freemen in the future unless they took the freeman's oath,[2] and at the same meeting the court adopted measures for the incorporation of New Haven freemen into the Connecticut company, with an implied extension of the suffrage in New Haven.[3] A year later the assembly was compelled to adopt the first law against " disorderly and corrupt practices in the election of the members of the Gen[ll] Assembly." [4] If the terms of such laws give any clue to the condition of elections,—and usually they are not passed until occasion demands it,— unqualified persons must have been voting, and some freemen had cast more than one vote. Both of these practices in the future were to be punishable with a fine of five pounds for each transgression. In 1669 an interesting entry in the records shows how several persons, who were unjustly " repulsed in the endeauoring to procure their freedome," brought in the assessment lists to show that they had sufficient property to qualify them for the freemanship.[5]   In

[1] *Rhode Island Col. Rec.*, II, 127.

[2] *Conn. Col. Rec., 1665–1677*, 15.

[3] *Ibid.*, 18. The Connecticut freeman's oath was to be administered to so many of the New Haven freemen as would accept it, and to such other persons who, by sufficient evidence, were shown to be qualified according to the Connecticut law.

[4] *Conn. Col. Rec., 1665–1677*, 37.

[5] *Ibid.*, 107. "In the list of Estates as foloweth,—John Tompson Jun[r], 47£. 15s. John Beardsley, 87£. 12s. 6d. John Wells, 71£. 5s. 0d. W[m] Robberts, 76£. Sam[ll] Fayrchild, 44£. Sam[ll] Mills, 39£. 10s. Theophilus Shearman, 44£. 10s. This Court orders that those aboue written or so many of them as haue unjustly been repulsed in the endeauoring to procure their freedome, they makeing it appeare that they haue been unjustly debarred of that priuiledg, and that they are qualified according

the same year the selectmen and constables of each plantation were required to make a list of the freemen in their several plantations and send it " fayrely written" to the general court, where the names were to be recorded by the secretary, " that soe when there may be any occasion or difficulty about that matter, whoe are freemen, it may be the easier determined." [1] In 1670 the democratic method of proxy voting was restored.

All these features show how large a place in the history of the colony was occupied by the subjects of elections and suffrage. In the eight years from 1662 to 1670 the possession of the freemanship was required for all electors in colonial elections; an oath was imposed upon all freemen; a new and more liberal property qualification was established, which resulted in large additions to the class of freemen; the religious qualifications were overthrown in New Haven and their place taken by the more worldly requirements of Connecticut; satisfactory answers were given to the inquiries of the English commissioners; and the first steps were taken towards perfecting the machinery of elections by laws against fraudulent voting, by the drawing up of lists of freemen, and by the introduction of the proxy system. The electoral system was, in these years, outlined in a form which was little changed during the colonial period.

Within the next five years two changes were introduced into the property qualifications,—one in 1673 raising the qualification and the other in 1675 reducing it somewhat. The printed code of 1673 changed the property requirement from the possession of twenty pounds of taxable property to twenty pounds value " in Housing or Land, beside their personal Estate in the common List." [2] But this amount seems to have been too high, for only two years later the

---

to lawe, to the sattisfaction of Mr. Gold & the Comrs of Fayrefeild and Stratford, they shall stand as nominated for their freedom at this court."

[1] *Conn. Col. Rec., 1665–1677,* 112.

[2] *The Book of the General Laws For the People within the Jurisdiction of Connecticut,* Cambridge, 1673, 26.

amount was diminished by one-half, and for the next four-teen years the property qualification stood at ten pounds value of taxable real estate.[1]   It is interesting to glance, in this connection, at the actual assessments made upon land. In 1676 the best "home-lots" were rated at forty shillings an acre, and the worst at twenty shillings; the most valu-able farm lands were listed at fifty shillings an acre, but by far the greater part were valued at from ten to twenty shil-lings an acre.[2]   At these valuations, a freeman, under the law of 1675, must be possessed of from five to ten acres of town lots, or from five to twenty acres of farm lands.   It is thus fairly easy, in this case, to transform the value in pounds into actual extent of freehold required for the voter.

Connecticut, with the rest of New England, passed under the government of Andros, and during the period of his administration popular elections were discontinued except for town officers, who, according to the laws of Andros, were to be annually elected by the inhabitants of the several towns.[3]   The Revolution of 1688 led Connecticut into political irregularities somewhat similar to those arising in many of the other colonies, and the same means were taken for the restoration of the charter government as were adopted in Rhode Island and Massachusetts.[4]   In May, 1689, the freemen met at Hartford and there three propo-sitions were made; one suggesting the reinstatement of the officers who were dispossessed by Andros, a second advising the retention of the officers appointed under Andros, and a third recommending the appointment of a committee of safety.[5]   By a somewhat irregular vote, the first measure, that of restoring the old officers who had not been permitted to serve out their terms, was adopted, and the officers installed as in Massachusetts.   All through this proceeding there was fear of offending England, and, in order that the terms of the charter

[1] *Conn. Col. Rec., 1665–1677,* 253.
[2] *Ibid.,* 294 ff.
[3] *Conn. Col. Rec., 1678–1689,* 427.
[4] *R. I. Col. Rec.,* III, 257–258.
[5] Bulkeley's *Will and Doom,* in *Conn. Hist. Soc. Coll.,* III, 153–160; *Conn. Col. Rec., 1678–1689,* 455–460.

might be the more fully observed, even proxy voting was forbidden.[1]

It may have been the desire to propitiate the English authorities, or, as Bulkeley states, perhaps only an effort to gain political advantage [2] that led the assembly in the fall of 1689 to adopt the exact provision of the English statute of 1430, and require for the future that all candidates for the freemanship should be " in possession of freehold estate to the value of forty shillings in country pay per annum." [3] The exact effect of this change from a taxable valuation to an income qualification is difficult to determine, but it was evidently in the direction of a more extended suffrage. Bulkeley believed the change was adopted by certain of the leaders in order that " their admission of freemen [be] enlarged, so to oblige more of the people to them and make them a greater party." [4] This may have been one reason for the change, but another must have been that desire to placate the English authorities by removing some of the freemanship restrictions, which is seen also in the propositions for a wider suffrage in Massachusetts at this time.[5] The act of 1689 also abolished the six months of probation which had been previously required, and provided for the admission of freemen by any assistant or commissioner,[6] to whom the certificate of age, good character, and property-holding was to be presented, and before whom the freeman's oath was to be taken. Thus the assembly delegated to colonial officers the power of admission of freemen, which it had up to this time, in accordance with the charter, kept in its own control.

With the dissipation of the fear of English intervention the colony reverted to its old method of a fixed valuation of property as prerequisite for the freemen. The code of 1702 established the suffrage qualifications in a form which combined the mediæval English requirement with a more liberal and practical American test. The forty-shilling freehold

[1] *Conn. Hist. Soc. Coll.*, III, 160.
[2] *Ibid.*, 159.
[3] *Conn. Col. Rec., 1689–1706*, 11.   [4] *Op. cit.*
[5] See *ante*, 335–336.
[6] Justice of the peace, by the act of 1702 and later years.

provision was, indeed, retained, and was to be kept during
the entire colonial period, but an alternative was now made
to it by which the applicant for the freemanship might enter
that class either by virtue of his freehold or by the holding
of *forty pounds personal estate.*[1]   In this dual form of personal property or real estate the suffrage restrictions continued without change during the remainder of the colonial
period.

The new personal property qualification evidently led to
election evils and carelessness in the admission of freemen.
In 1705 the assembly was compelled to refuse the freemanship to several persons to whom the freeman's oath had been
irregularly given;[2] and again in 1708 irregularly admitted
freemen were referred to the county court of New London.[3]
In 1709 the assembly ordered that the value of the personal
estate as well as of freehold should be taken from the tax-
lists of the year in which the applicant desired to be enrolled
a freeman.[4]   It is also remarkable, in the light of Rhode
Island's efforts to adapt the property qualification to the
changing value of the colonial paper money, that no such
attempt was made in Connecticut.   In 1710 the Connecticut
paper money was circulating at par; by 1724 it was worth
little more than one-half its face value in specie; by 1739
it had declined to one-third specie value, and in 1744 to one-
fourth.[5]   In spite of this depreciation in the value of money,
and consequent lowering of the standard of admission to the
freemanship, Connecticut made no changes in her qualifications.   Indeed, the forty-shilling freehold, translated later
into seven dollars income from land, was retained as one of
the alternative qualifications of the suffrage until the amend-
ment in 1845 of the constitution of 1818.[6]

[1] *Acts and Laws of His Majesties Colony of Connecticut in New-
England.   Printed in 1702 and now first reissued;* Acorn Club, 1901,
p. 40.

[2] *Conn. Col. Rec., 1689–1706,* 511.

[3] *Ibid., 1706–1716,* 70.   [4] *Ibid.,* 129.

[5] H. Bronson, *A Historical Account of Connecticut Currency, Con-
tinental Money, and the Finances of the Revolution,* New Haven Hist.
Soc. Papers, I, 50–52.

[6] *New Haven Hist. Soc. Papers,* V, 233.

Before 1662 admissions of freemen were sometimes made by the general court, and sometimes by specially appointed officers. Under the charter, with the exception of a few instances in connection with the admission of New Haven freemen, the assembly invariably acted upon the admission of each freeman until the year 1689. The election act of that year delegated to the assistants and local commissioners the duty of examining the certificates of age, good character, and property of applicants for the freemanship, and empowered these officers to administer the freeman's oath to those properly qualified. In 1729 this duty was made over to the " open Freemens-Meeting of the Town". [1] to which the applicant belonged; publicly before this meeting the oath of a freeman was to be administered, and the new freeman's name enrolled by the town clerk. No subsequent change was made in the colonial period.

Summarizing the restrictions upon the suffrage, we may say that there was no formal property qualification upon freemen either in New Haven, down to the union with Connecticut, nor in Connecticut until 1658–9. Up to this time the religious qualifications of New Haven may have been paralleled in practice in Connecticut; but after the passage of this law for almost two hundred years, or down to 1845, a property qualification was one of the alternative requirements of freemen. The amount was twenty pounds personal property in 1658–9; in 1662 it was changed to the same amount of taxable property; in 1673 it became that amount of housing or lands, and in 1675 it was changed again to ten pounds of real estate. From 1689 to 1702 the sole property qualification was forty shillings freehold; but in the latter year the alternative of forty pounds personal estate was established and retained until after the Revolution. From 1662 to 1689 a six months' probation was required; while from the earliest period to the latter date freemen were admitted by the general court. In 1689 admissions were made by certain officers, and in 1729 by the town clerks in open town-meetings of the freemen. The age of twenty-one years was first expressed in 1658–9,

---

[1] *Session Laws, 1729, 370*; Ch. XLVII.

although it is highly probable that it was in force from the beginning of the colony; the good-character clause appears first in 1657; both of these provisions were continued throughout the period. From 1640 down to the Revolution of 1776 every person admitted as a freeman was compelled to take some form of an oath.

Turning from the suffrage qualifications to the manner in which this franchise was exercised, mention must be made of the proxy system of Connecticut. Only a few words, however, can be said here concerning this interesting system of balloting, but the reader is referred to the papers of Judge Baldwin for a full exposition of the subject.[1]

The fundamental orders of 1639 provided for the election of colony officers by means of paper ballots;[2] and New Haven's constitution of 1643 permitted freemen to cast their votes by proxy if they did not find it convenient to attend the election in person.[3] The latter feature appears to have developed in Connecticut also; and, although there is no statutory provision for it, we read that in 1660 certain towns used " to send Proxies, at ye Election, by their Deputies." [4] This method of sending ballots up to the election, instead of personally attending, was temporarily suspended by the earlier interpretation of the charter of 1662; but in 1670 the system was restored, and this time elaborately outlined.[5]

> " This Court being sencible of the great charge, difficulty and expense of time the freemen of this colony are at by reason of their great numbers and remoatness from Hartford, the place of election, and considering the many inconveniences that otherwayes may arise upon the yearly day of election, and that the work of that day may be the more orderly, easily and speedily issued,—It is ordered by this Court and the Authority thereof, that henceforth all the freemen of this Jurisdiction, wthout any further summons, from yeare to yeare, shall or may upon the second Thursday in May yearly,

[1] *New Haven Hist. Soc. Papers*, V, 179–245; *Amer. Hist. Association Papers*, IV, 407–422.
[2] *Conn. Col. Rec., 1636–1665*, 22.
[3] *New Haven Col. Rec., 1638–1649*, 113.
[4] *Conn. Col. Rec., 1636–1665*, 346.
[5] *Ibid., 1665–1677*, 131–2.

either in person or in proxie, at Hartford attend and consum-
ate the election of Gouernour, Deputy Gouernour and Assist⁸,
and such other publique officers as his Mat_le hath appoynted
by oʳ Charter then to be yearly chosen."

The act directed the manner in which the election by proxies
should be managed, so "that there be no fraud or deceipt
used therein;" the constable was required to read to the
assembled freemen the freeman's oath and the law punishing
disorderly voting, and then to announce the names of those
persons who had previously been put in nomination for
office. From this list the freemen were to vote by ballot for
the several officers, and their ballots were to be sealed up
and sent up to the annual election at Hartford.

The records of the elections do not show the use of ballots
by non-attending freemen. One would not know, from a
perusal of these records, that many of the freemen never
attended the elections. We read such vague statements as,
" This day, being the day appointed by charter, and the laws
of this Colony, for the Election of the publick officers of
this corporation . . . the freemen of this corporation proceeded to give in their votes to persons chosen and appointed
. . . to receive and sort them . . . And the votes of the
freemen having now been brought in, sorted, and counted,"
certain persons were declared elected.[1] Better phraseology
to hide the existence of the proxy system and the absence of
a majority of the voters from the annual election could
hardly be conceived. The option between going personally
to the election or sending his vote was retained by the
freeman until 1750, when personal attendance was abolished
and the elections were conducted entirely by the counting of
ballots previously cast in the freemen's meetings of the
respective towns and carried up to Hartford by the deputies.[2]

Closely associated with the suffrage and the proxy system
was the Connecticut method of nominating candidates for
colonial officers by popular vote of the freemen in the towns.
The custom, without doubt, was drawn from the similar

[1] *Conn. Col. Rec., 1706–1716*, 309, and other volumes *passim.*
[2] *Acts and Laws Of His Majesty's English Colony of Connecticut*,
New London, 1750, p. 46.

feature of the Massachusetts code. In 1670 the nomination was made by the assembly;[1] in 1689 the power was given to the freemen in the towns to hand in the names of twenty persons fairly written on paper as nominees for the colonial offices;[2] and the twenty having the greatest number of votes for nomination were to be the number from which the freemen at the ensuing election should choose their officers. In 1692 the right of nomination was restored to the assembly;[3] but in 1697[4] the freemen regained the privilege and retained it throughout the period.[5]

One more feature respecting the colonial suffrage needs to be noted. The few facts which have been gathered concerning the number of voters can be stated briefly. The number of original freemen in the Connecticut valley is not accurately known; but the actual admission of freemen from 1639 to 1662 was only 229, and during this time it has been estimated that the population increased by about three thousand.[6] In other words, only one person in thirteen of the new population was admitted to the freemanship. On the other hand, some idea of the proportion of church-members, or freemen, to the entire population in New Haven may be gathered from the fact that only 99 men are mentioned as receiving seats in the church in 1646–7,[7] at a time when there may have been three hundred houses in the town.[8] If these 99 men were all heads of families[9] and householders, there would still remain the holders of twice that number of houses to be accounted for; so that it seems probable that only one-third of the householders were members of the church.

We know the exact number of freemen a few years after

---

[1] *Conn. Col. Rec., 1665–1677,* 133, 141.

[2] *Ibid., 1689–1706,* 11.

[3] *Ibid.,* 81.

[4] *Ibid.,* 223–4.

[5] For further details of the nomination system see Baldwin, *Amer. Hist. Assn. Papers,* IV, 407 ff.

[6] *New Haven Hist. Soc. Papers,* III, 313.

[7] Atwater, *New Haven,* 542.

[8] Doyle, *Puritan Colonies,* I, 198.

[9] Atwater, *op. cit.,* 251.

the securing of the charter, for in 1669 the general court ordered a list of all the freemen to be made.[1] These lists have been preserved, and they show a total of 777 freemen.[2] Comparing this with the figure 2050,—the whole number of men in the colony as given in the answers to the Committee of Trade and Plantations, in 1671,[3] it would appear that three out of every eight men in the population were freemen. In 1692 we have such general statements as " The greatest part of ye people are no freeman of theire Company;" [4] and " the other people of Connecticut (who yet were many times the greater number of the people) had nothing to do with it" [the election].[5] The same writer, the malcontent Bulkeley, says again, " The greatest part of the people of this colony (I believe five or six to one) never were made free of the company." [6] In the following year the legislature called for opinions from the freemen *and inhabitants* upon the propriety of addressing the English monarchs for the preservation of the charter privileges, and received an affirmative vote from 2182 persons; a far greater number than all the freemen in the colony.[7] Indeed, as late as 1723 the total poll in the annual election for magistrates was only 1618 freemen.[8]

The figures for two elections near to the Revolutionary period are extant, and they show an actual poll of one vote to fifty or sixty persons in the population. A contested election for treasurer in 1768 called forth only 3385 votes;[9] which, counting the population of the time at 155,000,[10]

[1] *Conn. Col. Rec., 1665-1677,* 112.
[2] *Ibid.,* 518-526.
[3] *Ibid., 1678-1689,* 298.
[4] *N. Y. Col. Doc.,* III, 853.
[5] *Conn. Hist. Soc. Coll.,* III, 146.
[6] *Ibid.,* 129.
[7] *Ibid.,* 75; *Conn. Col. Rec., 1689-1706,* 102.
[8] *Amer. Hist. Assn. Papers,* IV, 418.
[9] *Conn. Col. Rec., 1768-1772,* 4.
[10] *Ibid., 1757-1762,* 630. In 1762 the population was 146,590, an increase of 10.788 in the preceding six years. The same rate of increase would make 155,000 a conservative estimate for 1768 (see *Col. Rec., 1772-1775,* 492).

would make the voting class only one-fiftieth of the entire population. In 1775, at a poll of votes in October for nominees for the election in the following May, only 3477 voters took part.[1] In 1774 the total population of the colony was 197,856; of whom 40,797 were males over twenty years of age.[2] There was thus one voter in twelve of the male population over twenty years of age, and only one in fifty-seven of the entire population. The election for nominees may not have aroused the greatest interest; but yet the two elections of 1768 and 1775 show a similar proportion of voters to the population; and it is quite probable that the elections in the years preceding the Revolution did not call out more than two per cent. of the population.

In the local suffrage in Connecticut the class of voters differed more or less from the freemen of the colonial elections. There were four forms of local suffrage: town elections, church elections, militia elections, and proprietary meetings.

Attention has already been called to the difference in the town suffrage in Connecticut and in New Haven before the union of the two colonies. We have noted how Connecticut permitted non-freemen who were regularly admitted inhabitants of a town, to vote for deputies to the general court; and how the terms of admission were for a time left to the towns, but that in 1657 the assembly prescribed a general qualification for the class of admitted inhabitants. For military elections, the suffrage in Connecticut was still wider, the right being given to the soldiers alone to nominate their officers, and to the courts to accept and install them.[3] On the other hand, in New Haven an attempt was made to limit every election, except those concerning pro-

[1] See entire votes for 45 candidates in *Conn. Col. Rec., 1775–1776*, 173–174. Each voter under the law of 1697 voted for twenty candidates; and the number of votes in the text above is perhaps not accurate, as it has been gained by dividing the total ballots cast for all candidates by the number of candidates; some voters may not have voted for twenty persons.

[2] *Conn. Col. Rec., 1772–1775*, 491.

[3] Code of 1650, *Conn. Col. Rec., 1636–1665*, 543.

prietary rights in land, to the body of freemen. Elections
for colony officials, for town officers, and for military and
ecclesiastical leaders were all to be concentrated in the control of the adult male church-members. In the negotiations
for union, too, New Haven desired to retain this limitation
of entire political power to the freemen, but the Connecticut
authorities refused to yield the elective rights already
granted to inhabitants of their towns.[1]

After the union under the charter of 1662, the basis for
voting in the towns was fixed by the terms of the order of
May 17, 1660, which provided that no one should be received
as an inhabitant in any town unless he were known to be of
an honest conversation and admitted by the vote of the
majority of the town inhabitants.[2] The power thus vested
in the towns of receiving or rejecting applicants for inhabitancy was retained by them throughout the colonial
period, and the same authority is conferred upon the towns
by the first legal code of the state in 1784.[3] Such formal
admission to inhabitancy was, however, only required of
those who came from other towns; the sons of inhabitants,
after attaining their majority, appear to have been classed
as inhabitants without any formal vote of the town.[4] In
this respect the position of an inhabitant in a Connecticut
town was similar to that of a *freeman* in some English
boroughs or in the Rhode Island towns. Apparently, the
word inhabitant in Connecticut in the eighteenth century,
did not have its English legal meaning of a householder or
a landholder, but rather was applied to those who were
formally admitted into the town, or the descendants of such
persons.

This view seems to be borne out by the fact that the voters
of the towns are not co-extensive with the class of in-

---

[1] *New Haven Col. Rec., 1653–1665,* 494.

[2] *Conn. Col. Rec., 1636–1665,* 651.

[3] Code of 1784, 102. After 1750 the right to admit inhabitants might
be exercised by the town as a whole or by the selectmen, presumably
as the town should determine (code of 1750, 99).

[4] See the record of a contested election in Lyme in January, 1714–15,
and the decision of the Governor and Council respecting electors
therein (*Col. Rec., 1706–1716,* 486).

habitants.   The early laws concerning town elections vest
the right of suffrage in the " settled and approved Inhabitants" of the towns; [1] but these adjectives, implying acceptance by the town and land- or house-holding, were evidently
too loose a description of the class desired as voters.   As
early as 1679 we learn that " there are in most of the plantations a number of sojourners or inmates that doe take it
vpon them to deale, vote, or intermedle with the publique
occasions of the towne and places where they doe live, to the
dissatisfaction of their neighbours." [2]   To prevent such practices the assembly made the following restriction upon the
local suffrage :

> " This Court doe order that no person that is not an ad-
> mitted inhabitant, a householder, and a man of a sober con-
> versation, and have at least fifty shillings freehold in the com-
> mon list besides his person, shall adventure to vote in the
> choyce of towne or county officers or grant of rates or lands,
> vpon the penalty of the forfeiture of twenty shillings for the
> breach of this order;   provided that no freeman of the corpora-
> tion be hereby barred from voteing." [3]

It will be noticed that this act placed many restrictions upon
the town voter; he must be regularly admitted by the town
into its political and economic life; his character must be
good; he must be a householder in the town and also own a
specified amount of land in freehold.

Only three years after the passage of this law the assembly was compelled, by the actions of " sundry persons of an
ungoverned conversation" thrusting themselves into the
towns, to provide that no person should come to reside in
any town without the consent of the townsmen; and a fine
of twenty shillings for every week was imposed upon persons entertaining such sojourners without the consent of the
townsmen.[4]   In 1685 the assembly showed the same dis-

[1] Code of 1672, 65.
[2] *Conn. Col. Rec., 1678–1689*, 34.
[3] *Ibid.*
[4] Oct. 12, 1682 (*Col. Rec., 1678–1689*, 111).   The preamble of the
law is interesting: " Whereas sundry persons of an ungoverned conversation thrust themselves into oᵉ townships and by some underhand

position to guard carefully the town suffrage by reaffirming the provision of 1660, that before the owner of land in any town could dispose of his land to another individual, he must first offer it to the town. Only after the town's refusal to purchase could land be transferred to private persons.[1] Yet in spite of the care of the legislature, irregularities were frequent occurrences in the town elections. " Cunning contrivances and insinuations" were practised;[2] special mention is made of " young persons"[3] and those who were not freeholders or householders voting in such elections;[4] and a number of disputed elections took place.[5] In one of these cases the assembly made the decision that the towns possessed the power of judging the qualifications of inhabitants and voters.[6] A slight extension of the suffrage was made by the code of 1750, which gave an alternative to the fifty shillings of rateable freehold the possession of forty pounds value of rateable personal estate.[7]

The suffrage in church meetings and elections was not exactly like that in the towns. In 1667 a dispute in Windsor over the choice of minister was, by the general court, submitted to a vote of " all the freemen and householders" of the town;[8] but in another case the voters were merely described as inhabitants.[9] In 1699 a definite enactment gave to all the householders within any town or " allowed"

wayes, either by pretence of being hired servants or of hiring of land or houses, become inhabitants in our townships, whereby much inconveniency doth arise to such places, such persons often proveing vicious and burthensome and chargeable to the places where they come" . . .

[1] *Conn. Col. Rec.*, *1636–1665*, 351 ; *1678–1689*, 186.
[2] *J. H. Univ. Studies*, VII, 91.
[3] Code of 1715, 112–113.
[4] *Conn. Col. Rec.*, *1706–1716*, 483–485.
[5] *Ibid.*, 486; *1726–1735*, 85–86, 104; *1744–1750*, 368.
[6] *Ibid.*, *1726–1735*, 104.
[7] Code of 1750, 241.
[8] *Conn. Col. Rec.*, *1665–1677*, 73–74. The election return shows 138 voters in the town.
[9] *Ibid.*, *1678–1689*, 101.

church society the right to call a minister and enter into agreements with him.[1] This was a wider suffrage than that for town elections; but it was not long retained in this form. A new law, in 1708,[2] kept the broad householder or inhabitant franchise for those in full communion with the church, but required non-church-members who voted in church matters to possess the qualifications imposed by law upon voters in other town affairs.[3]

In 1728 the alternative of forty pounds personal estate to the fifty shilling freehold was introduced into the church elections, although not adopted in the town elections until much later. Under this act no one should " presume to vote in any society meeting for the choice of society officers, grants of rates, erecting of meeting-houses, regulating of schools, or any other thing proper to be voted in a society, unless such person or persons have a freehold in the same society rated at fifty shillings, or forty pounds in the common list, or that are persons that are in full communion with the church." [4]

Early in the eighteenth century the church suffrage was complicated by the privileges given to Episcopalians and Quakers, whereby members of these sects who regularly attended their worship, were exempted from the payment of taxes for the support of the established churches.[5] This led to an illogical position of such dissenters, who, in spite of their non-attendance upon " the ministry of the Presbyterian, Congregational or Consociated churches," had yet " adventured to vote" in meetings concerning the laying of taxes and selection of ministers of those churches.[6] In

---

[1] *Conn. Col. Rec., 1689–1706,* 316.

[2] *Ibid., 1706–1716,* 48.

[3] " The major part of the inhabitants of any town, plantation, or societie, qualified as the law directs to vote in all other town affairs, or are members in full communion with the church in the said town or societie, that shall be present at a town or societie meeting legally warned, shall have power by the major vote of them so met to call and settle a minister" . . .

[4] *Conn. Col. Rec., 1726–1735,* 211.

[5] In 1727 and 1729; *Conn. Col. Rec., 1726–1735,* 107, 237.

[6] *Ibid., 1744–1750,* 218.

1746, therefore, an act was passed excluding from participation in such meetings or elections all those who were exempt from the payment of taxes for the support of the regular churches.[1] After this time [2] the suffrage in religious societies, or in town meetings when religious subjects were discussed, was limited (1) to male persons, twenty-one years of age and in full communion with the church concerning which the suffrage was exercised; or (2) non-church-members, who paid taxes for the support of the established church, and who were possessed of a freehold rated at fifty shillings or a personal estate of forty pounds; but those who, by regular membership in and attendance upon certain legally determined churches dissenting from the Congregational form were freed from the payment of church taxes, were also excluded from the ecclesiastical elections of the regular churches.

The militia elections of Connecticut were based upon the reasonable and well-nigh universal custom of allowing all the soldiers to participate in the choice of their officers. In New Haven, indeed, it has been noticed that the suffrage in such cases was limited, as in all other forms, to the freemen of the colony; but that this method proved unpopular and sometimes even inconvenient has already been shown.[3] After the union of 1662, however, the militia elections of the entire colony were conducted according to the provision of the Connecticut code of 1650, which enacted " that the Souldgers shall onely make choyce of theire Millitary Officers and present them to the Perticular Courte; but such onely shall bee deemed officers as the Courte shall confirme." [4] The custom of nomination resulted almost always in the acceptance by the court of the persons chosen by the soldiers; [5] although the records do show that on infrequent

[1] *Conn. Col. Rec., 1744–1750*, 218. A similar act had been passed eighteen years earlier in Massachusetts.

[2] A slight change was made in 1750; see code of 1769, 165.

[3] See *ante.*

[4] *Conn. Col. Rec., 1636–1665*, 543.

[5] See records *passim; e.g., 1636–1665*, 187, 210, 237, 290, 336; *1665–1677*, 304.

occasions the court refused to confirm those who were presented to them.[1]   No change appears to have been made in
this liberal suffrage except one in words rather than in
spirit in the comprehensive military act of 1741.   This act
gave the right to vote for military officers to all those
" obliged by law to keep arms." [2]

The Connecticut and New Haven towns had an economic
organization of commoners similar to that in Massachusetts
and the other New England colonies.   Whatever may have
been the origin of the town, whether it was an indigenous
community or one erected by the colonial authorities, there
existed in either case an economic partnership in the
land; the settlers who obtained the land constituted a quasi-
corporation.[3]   The land belonged to the original settlers and
their legal successors; and the admission of an inhabitant
into a town did not necessarily entitle the new-comer to
rights in commonage and in the undivided lands.   In reality,
however, there was frequently no distinction made between
the town meeting of inhabitants and the corporation meeting of the proprietors of the town lands.[4]   In the early
history of many towns when the two classes were nearly
identical, land grants and distributions were made in the
open town meeting, and sometimes persons voted who had
no share in the common lands.   But changing conditions
gradually led to a separation of the two classes; many
persons came into the towns who could not purchase a
share in the town stock in lands, and to whom the town
refused to give such a share; the value of land rose after
the population increased, and soon the early liberality in
land distribution [5] gave place to a strong feeling of owner-

[1] *Conn. Col. Rec., 1678–1689,* 126; *1689–1706,* 45; *1706–1716,* 485.

[2] *Ibid., 1735–1743,* 379–387.

[3] Egleston, *Land System of the New England Colonies, J. H. Univ.
Stud.,* IV, 580.

[4] It is interesting to notice that the only cases in which New Haven
contemplated the extension of the suffrage to non-freemen were in
respect to the ownership of lands.

[5] New Haven, in her early distributions, gave so many acres for each
person, and so many for each share,—a combination of persons and
property very unusual (Levermore, *New Haven,* 83–85).

ship among the original proprietors or their successors. The process of integration of the class of proprietors in the face of opposition by the inhabitants led to differing development in the several towns. One writer says that in Wethersfield the town overshadowed the proprietors, in Windsor the proprietors overshadowed the town, while in Hartford the balance was about equally preserved.[1] As late as 1719 the entire town of Simsbury retained control of the lands and, much to the offence of the proprietors, made many land grants.[2] Even where the proprietors alone controlled land matters, the question of the suffrage was a burning one, for it was not clear at first whether voting in such meetings should be in proportion to the shares of the respective proprietors or whether each proprietor should have but one vote.[3]

For many years after the settlement of the colony there was no general statutory provision respecting the rights or duties of proprietors of the undivided lands,[4] and their position must have been determined by the local customs and circumstances of the respective towns. Although their lands became "an undoubted lawful estate of inheritance" to the proprietors and their successors, yet "the said proprietors did, for a considerable number of years in many of our towns, truly consent and agree that the said common lands might in whole or in part, be actually divided or disposed of by the major vote of the inhabitants of such towns in meeting assembled."[5] In 1701 was passed what is believed to be the first act distinctly separating the proprietors from the town; but even in this act, which only concerned the building of fences about common lands, the advice of the selectmen of the town was required upon such matters.[6] The code of 1702, however, went much farther in the erection of the proprietors as distinct corporations. Accord-

---

[1] Andrews, in *J. H. Univ. Stud.*, VII, 52.

[2] Egleston, *J. H. Univ. Stud.*, IV, 584.

[3] Andrews, *op. cit.*

[4] The code of 1672 makes no reference to proprietors of lands as possessing distinct communal rights or duties.

[5] *Conn. Col. Rec., 1717–1725*, 395.

[6] *Ibid., 1689–1706*, 346.

ing to the provisions therein, the " Proprietors in any Comon Field in this Colony, or so many of them as are residing in the Town or Plantation where such Common Field is Situate," were empowered to meet together for certain communal purposes, and choose committeemen to attend to the details of management of the fields.[1]   The question of suffrage was settled by allowing each person to vote in proportion to his holding, thus establishing an economic unit as a basis for voting in place of the earlier and more democratic personal suffrage.[2]

In spite of these requirements and of similar ones in an act of 1706,[3] the towns in some cases retained control of common lands.   But the contest for possession of these lands led at last to actual riots between claimants under the authority of the towns and those under the authority of the proprietors.[4]   In 1723 the assembly settled these differences by an act which acknowledged the property right of the proprietors; but it stated that the proprietors had, in many towns, voluntarily permitted the towns to legislate about their lands; and consequently that all land grants made in the past by towns under such circumstances should be valid.[5] For the future, however, no person by becoming an inhabitant of a town, or by any other means " against or without the consent of such proprietors," could gain any title or interest in the common lands.   The proprietors themselves or their legal representatives could hold meetings, and " by their major vote in such their meetings, (to be reckoned according to their interest in such common land,) to regulate, improve, manage and divide such common land in such manner and proportion as they shall see good."   Thus by this act the proprietors and town inhabitants were definitely distinguished; and the old political

---

[1] *Laws of Connecticut, 1702,* 16.

[2] All matters concerning common fields " shall be determined by the vote of the major part of the Proprietors, which major part shall be computed, not according to the number of Persons that are Proprietors, but according to their interest in such Field."

[3] *Conn. Col. Rec., 1689–1706,* 544.

[4] *Ibid., 1717–1725,* 332–348.

[5] *Ibid.,* 396.

idea of voting in the proprietary meetings was overthrown not only by making the suffrage proportional to the respective shares in land, but also by permitting the representation of the proprietors by means of their legal agents. These changes took away from the meetings what little political character they had possessed, and made them simply the gatherings of business co-partners.

CHAPTER XIV.

The Suffrage in Rhode Island.

I. *From the Time of Settlement to the Charter of 1663.*

The colony of Rhode Island owed its immediate existence to the religious intolerance of Massachusetts. Around the borders of the great Puritan Commonwealth there arose numerous small settlements founded by Massachusetts men. Sometimes lured by the fertility of the neighboring lands, the exile of these persons was voluntary; but in many cases the religious persecution of the Puritans drove their weaker opponents into new settlements where they hoped to live beyond the realm of Massachusetts interference. Some of the Connecticut, New Hampshire, and Maine settlements were founded for the first of these causes, and some on account of the second; but in the case of Rhode Island the religious motive was uppermost. Here to a greater degree than in Connecticut or New Hampshire we see a community of non-conformists; by no means a unit upon the points of difference with the Massachusetts religion, yet for one reason or another opposing the hierarchy, and out of the very multiplicity of their views compelled to tolerate one another's opinions. Williams had, of course, even in Massachusetts, spoken in favor of liberty of conscience; and under his influence the necessity for toleration arising from the multiplicity of beliefs became a conscious ideal of the new state.

And as their theory of religion was an original one, so Rhode Island's political organization was purely indigenous; there was no charter obtained from the king, no grant of land or town privileges from the General Court of Massachusetts, nor any delegation of authority from proprietor or chartered company. In defiance of the monarchical theories of the time, political organization proceeded not from above down to the people, but from the people up to their rulers. A small group of Englishmen found themselves in the

430

American wilderness, almost in a " state of nature," as the eighteenth century philosophers would say. Too poor and insignificant to expect formal incorporation by the English government, and under the impelling necessity of reaching a common rule of action among themselves, they were forced to adopt some form of association. The agreement might first be needed in order to get a joint stock to purchase lands from the Indians, it would be continued in order to provide for the distribution of the land so purchased, and be perpetuated by the necessity of adopting some rules for civil action, and the election of new members or of local officers. The association might be started with a written document, as when the settlers on Rhode Island, ignoring altogether English king or government, say with charming naïveté that we " incorporate ourselves into a Bodie Politick," and submit " our persons, lives and estates unto our Lord Jesus Christ, the King of Kings and Lord of Lords;" or it might be a personal arrangement, as that between Roger Williams and his five associates, or between Samuel Gorton and his friends at Warwick, of which to-day we have no written record. In any event a more or less formal agreement was voluntarily reached among these exiles, according to which they virtually erected themselves into a corporation, and proceeded to adopt such local laws and elect such officers as appeared to them necessary.

For a time these distinct town governments were the only form of political organization in the Narragansett region, but union among the towns came within a few years. First there was the voluntary federation in 1640 of Portsmouth and Newport, both situated on Rhode Island, and the latter an offshoot of the former. This was followed by the enforced union of all the towns under the charter of 1644. But a united colony was not so easily established, and the grant of a conflicting charter to the towns on Rhode Island led to great confusion. Another voluntary union of the towns under the charter of 1644 was made permanent by the grant of a royal charter in 1663. It is important for our study of the suffrage in Rhode Island to remember that the towns antedated the colony; there was a town freemanship, there were town meetings and town elections before any

colonial freemanship or elections existed.   And throughout
the whole period of our study we shall find that in each individual's case, as in the history of the colony, the town freemanship came before the colony freemanship; a person must
be admitted a freeman of some town before he could become a freeman of the colony.   We must, therefore, look at
the suffrage conditions in the towns before considering the
colonial franchise.

Before the granting of the first charter to the colony there
were three organized towns, Providence, Portsmouth and
Newport, and an unorganized settlement on the land later
called by the name of Warwick.   In Providence Roger Williams purchased a tract of land from the Indians; he admitted twelve others to an equal share in this land, and in
his " initial deed" he anticipated the association of " such
others as the major part of us shall admit into the same
fellowship of vote with us."[1]   A town organization was
early formed, but no record exists of a town agreement,
until a second party of thirteen heads of families was accepted and made " incorporate"[2] into the town.   The new-
comers signed the well-known agreement of obedience to the
town government in civil matters:

" We whose names are hereunder desirous to inhabitt in ye towne
of prouidence do promise to subiect ourselves in actiue or passiue
obedience to all such orders or agreements as shall be made for publick
good of oᵣ body in an orderly way by the maior consent of the present
Inhabitants maisters of families Incorporated together into a towne
fellowship and others whome they shall admitt unto them
only in ciuill things."[3]

In the case of Portsmouth and Newport the town life
began with a voluntary agreement among the intending
settlers before they arrived at the place of settlement.   Thus
nineteen persons intending to settle upon the Island of

[1] *Records of the Colony of Rhode Island and Providence Plantations,*
I, 19–24 (quoted hereafter as *R. I. Col. Rec.*) ; Arnold, *Hist. of R. I.*
(ed. of 1894), I, 100; Staples, *Annals of Providence,* 26–33.
[2] *R. I. Col. Rec.,* I, 20.
[3] *Providence Records,* I, 1 ; *R. I. Col. Rec.,* I, 14.

Aquedneck (Rhode Island), met at Providence on March 7, 1637-8, and incorporated themselves by the following agreement,

"We whose names are underwritten do here solemnly in the presence of Jehovah incorporate ourselves into a Bodie Politick and as he shall help, will submit our persons, lives and estates unto our Lord Jesus Christ, the King of Kings and Lord of Lords and to all those perfect and most absolute lawes of his given us in his holy word of truth, to be guided and judged thereby, Exod. 24, 3, 4. 2 Cron. 11, 3. 2 Kings 11, 17." [1]

The inhabitants who, in 1639, set out from the north of the island and founded Newport made a mutual promise to bear equal burdens according to their strength or property:

"It is agreed. By vs whose hands are underwritten, to propagate a Plantation in the midst of the Island or elsewhere; And doe engage ourselves to bear equall charges, answerable to our strength and estates in common; and that our determinations shall be by major voice of judge and elders; the Judge to have a double voice." [2]

The latter agreement shows a more compact organization than the earlier one, and a stronger political spirit, but it makes no mention of God. Another agreement entered into by those who remained behind after the officers and principal men had moved to the centre of the island, is the only one of the town agreements which makes reference to the English government.

"We, whose names are under written doe acknowledge ourselves the legall subjects of his Majestie King Charles, and in his name doe hereby binde ourzelves into a civill body politicke under his lawes according to matters of justice." [3]

In three of these agreements it will be noticed that the political organization is begun by the voluntary compact of the signers to the document, while in the Providence paper

[1] *R. I. Col. Rec.*, I, 52; Arnold, *History of Rhode Island* (edition of 1894), I, 124.
[2] *Ibid.*, I, 87.
[3] April 30, 1639; *R. I. Col. Rec.*, I, 70.

there is a joint agreement between a group of new-comers and the old proprietors. We have here democracy in the making; the fiat of the group of friends or neighbors that they will unite in a civil government based upon the principle of equality. This principle is here an outgrowth of two things; their entire isolation from any higher authority which might impose governors upon them, and the economic situation according to which they shared equally in the burden of purchasing land and enjoyed equally the right to lands so acquired. This was carried to such an extent that the widows of proprietors sometimes gave their consent to matters of a purely civil nature in a way which, if it cannot be called exercising the suffrage franchise, at least shows some participation in the political rights of land-holders.[1]

The original proprietors of the towns did not keep all their purchase, but they admitted others to their number under certain restrictions which differed somewhat in the several towns.[2] But since the original holders could admit new associates upon any terms they saw fit to impose, the suffrage qualifications in these towns are identical with the conditions imposed upon freemen at the time of their acceptance by the town.

In Providence, Roger Williams' first twelve associates together paid him thirty pounds, and the second group of thirteen persons gave him twenty pounds, for the privilege of associating with him on equal terms in the land and government.[3] In 1640 the town resolved that all present

[1] Among the signatures of persons accepting the report of the arbitrators in Providence in July, 1640, are those of two widows (*R. I. Col. Rec.*, I, 31).

[2] Persons so admitted were usually called freemen, following the Massachusetts custom with which the settlers must have been familiar; sometimes the word townsman is used, and occasionally they are called inhabitants; but generally the latter phrase is reserved for a class of persons who were permitted to live in the town, but to whom the political rights and land claims of the proprietors or freemen were not extended.

[3] *R. I. Col. Rec.*, I, 21, 23.

and future townsmen should pay thirty shillings.[1] But occasionally smaller payments were made, presumably for smaller land grants than those given to the early settlers.[2] On Rhode Island the general meeting on June 27, 1638, ordered that all persons, whether freemen or inhabitants, upon the island should pay two shillings for each acre of land occupied.[3] In one instance, in Providence, each one of a group of thirty-five settlers received a free grant of twenty-five acres; but they signed an agreement not to claim " any Righte, to the Purchasse of the Said plantation; Nor any privillidge of Vote, in Towne Affaires; untill we shall be received, as free-Men of the said Towne of Providence." [4] Besides the usual money payment, other conditions were imposed upon the new inhabitant. He must in all cases be acceptable to the town, and admitted by the vote of the town meeting [5] or of the town officers; [6] he might be required to fence his land,[7] or to build a house on his lot,[8] or not to be absent from his land longer than a specified time; [9] and on Rhode Island a purchaser who did not reside on the island lost his vote.[10] In practically all cases the new settlers were required to take some form of oath or " engagement" to the government of the town into which they were admitted. This is seen in the agreements made by later comers in Providence to abide by the laws and orders made by the major vote of the town; [11] and again on Rhode Island where

---

[1] *R. I. Col. Rec.*, I, 28. A list of the "names of Such as have paid all their purchase money and have quittances" is extant, showing the names of forty-two persons (*Providence Records*, II, 31).

[2] *R. I. Col. Rec.*, I, 15; *Providence Records*, I, 3.

[3] *Ibid.*, 56.

[4] *Providence Records*, II, 29. These were called quarter-right inhabitants, and they became entitled to one-quarter the share of a full proprietor in subsequent land divisions (Arnold, *History of Rhode Island*, I, 121).

[5] *R. I. Col. Rec.*, I, 53.

[6] *Ibid.*, I, 28, 84.

[7] *Providence Records*, II, 1.

[8] *R. I. Col. Rec.*, I, 72.

[9] *Providence Records*, II, 3.

[10] *R. I. Col. Rec.*, I, 125.

[11] *Providence Records*, I, 1; II, 29, 90.

the new settlers must submit themselves to the " government that is or shall be established according to the word of God." [1] In Warwick every inhabitant was compelled to sign the town compact and agree that he would not recognize any other jurisdiction than that of the colony; [2] while on Rhode Island an inhabitant or freeman endeavoring to bring in any other power was to be treated as a perjurer.[3]

Thus to become an inhabitant of one of the towns a person must first be accepted by the town; in most cases he must make a pecuniary payment; he was required to submit to the town government and promise to bring in no other authority; and he might be required to submit to various other conditions concerning the use of his land. Yet even admission as an inhabitant under all these restrictions did not necessarily make a man a freeman or voter of the town in which he was resident. The early records give abundant evidence of the existence of two distinct classes of inhabitants, composed of those who were admitted as freemen and those who had not yet received that privilege.[4] As time went on the tendency was to extend the freemanship and the suffrage to all freeholders, and in 1658 the town meeting of Providence ordered that " all those that injoy land in yᵉ jurisdiction of this Towne are freemen." [5] While thus extending the political rights of freemen, their economic rights in the town lands were restricted. In the early years we find the statement that the undisposed lands belong to the freemen,[6] but soon a distinction arose here, as in the other New England colonies, between the freemen and the proprietors of the town and common lands. Admission to the freemanship came to be considered merely as a grant of political power, while land matters were disposed of not in a general town meeting, but in meetings of those interested in the town lands, made up of the descendants and successors of the orig-

[1] *R. I. Col. Rec.,* I, 53, 91.
[2] Arnold, *History of Rhode Island,* I, 216.
[3] *R. I. Col. Rec.,* I, 118.
[4] *Providence Records,* II, 29, 96, 112;; *R. I. Col. Rec.,* I, 56, 58, 66, 118, 124.
[5] *Providence Records,* II, 112; see also *ibid.,* 96.
[6] *R. I. Col. Rec.,* I, 83.

inal proprietors.[1]   The homogeneous economic and social character of the early settlements gave place to those differences of wealth and occupation which led to the factional quarrels over the colonial paper currency.

The political activities in these towns must have been of a very narrow nature. The earliest form was the town meeting, or the " Bodye," upon which attendance was compulsory ;[2] but at a very early date, and in Portsmouth and Newport from the first, the practice arose of relieving the town meeting by giving details of administration to certain elective officers.[3] Portsmouth and Newport developed an administrative system earlier than did Providence, and before the settlers reached the island, a " judge" had been chosen ;[4] while within a few months three elders, a constable and a sergeant were elected by the town meeting.[5]   A similar organization was established at Newport when many of the Portsmouth (called Pocosset at that time) settlers moved to the southwestern side of the island.[6]   Providence and Warwick administered their affairs by irregularly appointed arbitrators[7] until 1640 in Providence, when five " disposers" were appointed by the town ; and until 1647 in Warwick, when a town organization was established.[8] The early elections in the towns may have been *viva voce,* but by 1639 the elders in Portsmouth, at least, were chosen by "votes" and by " Providence ;"[9] and at Newport a freeman who was unable to attend the elections could send a

[1] Arnold, *History of Rhode Island,* I, 256; *Providence Records, passim;* see *post,* 469.

[2] *R. I. Col. Rec.,* I, 13, 15, 57, 81.

[3] *Ibid.,* 15, 30, 55. The earliest officers were those appointed to dispose of the town lands.

[4] *Ibid.,* 52.

[5] *Ibid.,* 63, 64.

[6] *Ibid.,* 90, 93.

[7] *Ibid.,* 27; Arnold, *History of R. I.,* I, 176.

[8] *R. I. Col. Rec.,* I, 129, note.

[9] *Ibid.,* 64. We are not told what means were taken to ascertain the will of Providence, whether it were by lot or merely the principle *vox populi, vox dei.*

" sealed vote" to the judge.[1]   In all these elections the choice was made by the freemen in the town meeting.[2]

When the town isolation gave place to political union, the town suffrage mentioned above became the basis for the colonial freemanship.   The first step in this direction came in 1640 by the union of Portsmouth and Newport.   These towns were settled by the same persons, for many of the proprietors left the young town at the northern end of the island to plant a settlement at Newport, and their geographical situation could not but force some kind of political understanding upon the two towns.   After a short independent existence the island towns formed a union or confederation which provided for a freemanship of the island, in addition to that of the towns;[3] it established a general form of government for the whole island;[4] and it permitted each town to direct its local affairs by its own courts or town meetings.[5]

This government, with such remarkably modern political machinery, was not less radical in its theory of popular authority.   The general court of the island, on March 16, 1640–41, agreed unanimously

" that the Government which this Bodie Politick doth attend vnto in this Island, and the Jurisdiction thereof, in favour of our Prince is a Democracie, or Popular Government; that is to say, It is in the Powre of the Body of Freemen orderly assembled, or the major part

---

[1] *R. I. Col. Rec.*, I, 98.
[2] Only one form of broader suffrage has been noted. Newport set an example in her first year, which was adopted by the colony and became the custom for a number of years. In 1639 the town gave the militia, or " Traine Band," the privilege " to select and chuse such persons, one or more from among themselves, as they would have to be officers among them; to exercise and traine them;" but the officers so chosen must be presented to the magistrates for approval. As the soldiers included all males capable of bearing arms, later specified as between the ages of sixteen and sixty, it will be seen that this militia suffrage was considerably wider than the town freemanship (*R. I. Col. Rec.*, I, 93). This was probably drawn from Massachusetts custom.
[3] *R. I. Col. Rec.*, I, 100.
[4] *Ibid.*, 100, 101.
[5] *Ibid.*, 106.

of them, to make or constitute Just Lawes, by which they will be regulated, and to depute from among themselves such Ministers as shall see them faithfully executed between Man and Man." [1]

The short time during which this confederation on the island continued is no indication of its importance in the formation of the colonial government. When the organization under the first charter was completed, its makers drew largely from the forms of this first union. They adopted its general and local freemanship idea, its division of governmental powers, the names and functions of many of its officers, the proxy-elective system, and even the popular election of militia officers. Many of these features had, of course, been introduced into the island by the emigrants from Massachusetts, and then from Newport and Portsmouth the customs at last entered into the general colonial organization.

A second advance towards union came from England in the form of the charter granted on March 14, 1643–4, by the Commissioners of Plantations. The early town organization and the first union had been purely local in their origin, and had received no authority from the English government, although in some cases an allegiance to the king was recognized.[2] The charter of 1644 granted to the " Inhabitants of the Towns of Providence, Portsmouth, and Newport, a free and absolute Charter of Incorporation to be known by the Name of the Incorporation of Providence Plantations, in the Narraganset Bay, in New England." [3] It gave them " full Power and Authority to rule themselves, and such others as shall hereafter inhabit within any Part of the said Tract of land, by such a Form of Civil Government, as by voluntary consent of all, or the greater Part of them, they shall find most suitable to their Estate and Condition." They were impowered to make civil laws and constitutions, and choose or displace officers of justice; provided that such regulations for civil government should be conformable to

[1] *R. I. Col. Rec.,* I, 112. It is to be noted that this resolution antedated the commonwealth movement in England, and even contained a clause saving the authority of the king.

[2] *R. I. Col. Rec.,* I, 70, 112.

[3] *Ibid.,* 143–146.

the laws of England " so far as the nature and constitution of the place will admit."

Three years after the date of this charter, a general court of election was held at Portsmouth, at which a provincial organization was erected and a code of laws adopted. The new government, shared in by Warwick as well as by the three earlier towns, was partly representative and partly direct. The Rhode Island freemen, meeting May 19–21, 1647, agreed that their form of government was " DEMO-CRATICALL; that is to say, a Government held by yᵉ free and voluntarie consent of all, or the greater parte of the free Inhabitants." [1]   There was to be a general assembly of all the freemen held annually, not only for the election of officers, but also for the enactment of laws.[2]   In addition to this there were frequent meetings of a General Court composed of six committeemen appointed for each town; [3] and at least in one case other freemen, whose " helpe is desired," were permitted to tarry if they would.[4]   An inspection of certain of the acts of this assembly and the subsequent experience under them, down to 1663, may be of value to an understanding of the suffrage in the colony. These features fall into three classes; first, the admission of freemen, or the manner of granting the suffrage; second, the proxy system, or the manner in which the suffrage was exercised; third, the subjects upon which popular suffrage was exercised, including the election of general and town officers, the making of laws in general assembly, and the popular initiative and referendum of legislative topics.

The path to the provincial suffrage lay through the freemanship of the towns; he who had been accepted as an inhabitant of one of the towns and admitted as one of its freemen could hope, as a matter of course, to be granted the colonial freemanship. The charter of 1644, unlike that of 1663, did not use the word freemen, but simply incorporated the " inhabitants" of the three towns. Yet the practice was to require a formal vote and admission to the town and

[1] *R. I. Col. Rec.,* I, 156.
[2] *Ibid.,* 149, 150, 191.
[3] *Ibid.,* 149; also *passim* after p. 228.
[4] *Ibid.,* 209.

then a similar entrance into the colonial freemanship.[1] The acceptance of freemen during this period sometimes took place in the annual general assembly, or more often, in the representative court;[2] and it is noteworthy that no instance of refusal of the freemanship to those proposed for the franchise has been found for these nineteen years. Usually, the candidates were proposed and accepted by name; at other times there were wholesale admissions of freemen. Thus after the reunion of the four towns in 1654 following Coddington's abortive attempt to establish an independent government on the island, the commissioners of the four towns ordered " that all those inhabitants in this Collonie that have been received freemen to act in any Towne or Collonie since Mr. Coddington's commission was exhibited, shall be owned freemen of ye Collonie." [3] In 1656 the settlers at Patuxett were in a body to " be lovingly entertained as freemen of this Collony, to have theire free voates in makinge of lawes, choosinge of officers in Towne and Collony, with the enjoyment of all priviledges belonginge to freemen of this jurisdiction." [4] The interval between admission to the town franchise and the grant of the colonial freemanship might be very short. We have evidence of this in the case of Providence in 1658. On May 15th, the town meeting voted that all freeholders were to be accounted freemen of the town;[5] and on May 18th, twenty-nine freemen of Providence were proposed and admitted freemen of the colony,[6] who, it may be fairly supposed, were town freemen coming in under the new town regulation.

Aside from the prerequisite of town freemanship, few other qualifications appear to have been imposed upon the candidate for colonial freedom. We learn that in the first

[1] *R. I. Col. Rec.,* I, 263, 280, 299–302, 340, 387, 426. The records usually show that the candidate for the freemanship came from a particular town, and in only a few cases is the name of the town lacking (*ibid.*, 282, 303, 356).

[2] See above references.

[3] *R. I. Col. Rec.,* I, 280.

[4] *Ibid.,* 339, 340.

[5] *Providence Records,* II, 112.

[6] *R. I. Col. Rec.,* I, 387.

meeting in 1647 it was agreed that all should " set their hands to an engagement to the Charter;" [1] and it is probable that those subsequently admitted were required to subscribe to a similar agreement. During the Puritan Commonwealth period, the inhabitants of Rhode Island, as in the other colonies, were individually required to submit to the new " State of England" and render obedience to it, under the penalty of forfeiting the benefit accruing under any law of the colony,—which presumably meant disfranchisement.[2] Beyond these points, the towns enjoyed the right to fix the qualifications of town freemen, and consequently in an indirect manner, of the colonial freemen as well. Many years were to pass before any general law established their qualifications.

At the meeting in May, 1647, for the election of officers and enactment of laws under the charter of 1644, the freemen of the colony were present in person, the records stating that the " major parte of the Colonie was present." [3] Yet even this meeting lost its pure democratic character before the three days of its session had passed. It was agreed that if forty or more persons remained at the meeting, they should have the authority of the whole body; [4] and later it was ordered that " if any do depart, he shall leave his vote behind him, that his power remain, though his person be absent." [5] Thus in the first assembly, the principle of proxy voting was recognized; and by legislation it was permanently established. The assembly made provision for an annual election of officers in a general assembly of the freemen; but " forasmuch as many may be necessarily detained, that they cannot come to the General Court of Election, that then they shall send their votes sealed up unto the said Court, which shall be as effective as their personal appearance." [6] Nothing further was said concerning the method of returning the individual votes, but corruption inevitably crept into

[1] *R. I. Col. Rec.*, I, 147.
[2] *Ibid.*, 305.
[3] *Ibid.*, 147.
[4] *Ibid.*
[5] *Ibid.*, 151.
[6] *Ibid.*, 149.

such a lax system. Only two years later it was found necessary to appoint a special committee to examine some of the votes, and the assembly itself passed an order to prevent irregularities in the future by directing that " none shall bringe any voates but such as they receive from the voaters hands." [1] The proxy system here established was without doubt drawn from the custom of the town of Newport,[2] and, with some modifications it lasted throughout the colonial history of Rhode Island. The freeman was privileged either to attend the general court of elections in person, or to send his ballot in some prescribed manner to the meeting. Personal attendance was forbidden after 1760, but through the whole colonial period the written paper ballots were collected in the several towns and sent to the court of election to be examined and counted.[3] In a similar manner the voter's privilege to initiate legislation, or to pass upon that which had been adopted by the representative court of assistants, was exercised by means of individual ballots sent up to the general officers to be counted.

The Rhode Island freeman during the period 1647–1663 possessed a wider field in which to exercise his suffrage powers than did the voter of any other colony at that time. The freemen of the colony could attend in person or send their ballots to the annual election of colonial officers; the freemen of the respective towns could elect their town officers[4] and their commissioners to the colony courts;[5] while all the soldiers of the militia companies could vote in elections for military officers.[6] In the pure democratic legislative assembly the freeman had a voice in the passage

---

[1] *R. I. Col. Rec.*, I, 217.

[2] The colonial law of 1647 contains part of the language of an order of Newport of January 29, 1639–40, according to which the elections were to be held annually by the freemen, but " such as shall be necessarily detained to send in their votes, sealed up to the Judge" (*R. I. Col. Rec.*, I, 98).

[3] See *post*, 463–467.

[4] *R. I. Col. Rec.*, I, 150, 151, 215.

[5] *Ibid.*, 147, 209, 221, 228, 229, 236, 317.

[6] This feature, like the proxy voting, is also to be found in the early organization upon Rhode Island, *R. I. Col. Rec.*, I, 93, 115, 117, 120, 153.

of all laws; but this power did not last long, and the convenient representative assembly composed of six commissioners from each town was permitted to carry on the work of legislation, until in 1651, it was declared "the lawe makinge Assemblie" of the colony.[1] But although the freeman lost his right to attend the legislative body, he still possessed the power of initiating or disallowing legislation. One of the orders of the assembly of 1647 permitted the discussion of general matters in any town meeting, and provided that if any action was there determined upon, the town clerk should certify the matter to the other three towns. The subject was then to be "agitated" in the other towns, and voted upon; then the representative committeemen of the towns were to meet, and "finding the Major parte of the Colonie concurring in the case, it shall stand for a Law till the next Generall Assembly of all the people, then and there to be considered, whether any longer to stand yea or no."[2]

But more valuable than the initiative was the popular referendum which also dates from 1647. Another order of that year permitted (or perhaps compelled) the general court of committeemen to propose measures to the towns. The towns were then to discuss the subjects and "the votes shall be collected and sealed up," and sent to the general recorder; and "if major voice determine the case," the measure should become a law until the next meeting of the general assembly of the people.[3] The referendum became the subject of frequent legislation after 1647, evidently a result of attempts to put it into practice. In 1650[4] the representative assembly was required to submit all its laws

[1] *R. I. Col. Rec.*, I, 236. The members of these "general courts" were elected for each occasion, and not for a stated time; but by an order of 1655 they were to stand for a year unless the towns chose to send others (*ibid.*, 317). The frequent election and meeting of the commissioners seemed "to be some burden on the people," and in 1658 they were to meet but once a year unless specially called by the president and assistants (*ibid.*, 400).

[2] *R. I. Col. Rec.*, I, 149.

[3] *Ibid.*

[4] *Ibid.*, 229.

to the several towns within six days after its adjournment, and within the next three days the town was to be called together to consider the laws.

"And if any freeman mislike any law then made, they shall then send their votes with their names fixed thereto vnto the Generall Recorder within tenn dayes after the reading of thoss lawes and no longer. And if itt appeare that the major vote within that time prefixed shall come in and declare itt to be a nullity, then shall the Recorder signifie it to ye President, and the President shall forthwith signifie to ye Townes that such or such lawes is a null, and the silence to the rest shall be taken for approbation and confirmation of the lawes made."

In 1658 we are told that "it is conceived a wholesome liberty for the whole or major parte of the free inhabitants of this collony orderly to consider of the lawes made by the Commissioners' Courts, and upon findinge discommodity in any law made by the said court, then orderly to shew their dislike and soe to invalid such a law." [1]

No absolute evidence has been found in the records to show that the initiative and the referendum were ever exercised, and it is unlikely that the former was adopted. The frequent legislation upon the subject of the referendum, however, seems to point to considerable popular interest in the matter, if not to an actual fact of political organization; [2] and in Providence, at least, the records show that at this time, and for many years thereafter, the laws of each assembly were read in the town meeting.[3] There is no record of the popular veto of a legislative act. Yet the ideal, even if not carried into practice, shows a strength of democratic thought which is remarkable.

[1] *R. I. Col. Rec.,* I, 401. The determination of such invalidity was to be made by a majority of each town instead of a majority of the colony. But two years later, since the privileges of the people had not been "clearly evinced," it was enacted that the disallowance of laws should take place upon the vote of a majority of the free inhabitants of the colony, "although any one towne or other should be wholly silent therein" (*ibid.,* 429).

[2] A detailed study of the town records might throw some light upon this point, but the writer has not had opportunity to do this.

[3] *Providence Records,* III, 25, 37, etc.

II. *Under the Charter of 1663.*

After the restoration of the English monarchy, the Rhode Island assembly appointed an agent in England to see that their privileges, liberties and boundaries were preserved intact.[1] John Clarke, the agent, shortly afterwards presented a most humble and supplicatory letter to the king, praying for a confirmation of the charter privileges of the colony.[2] Accordingly, on July 8, 1663, a new charter was issued which erected a corporate political company, composed of freemen.[3] Twenty-seven named persons and " all such others as now are, or hereafter shall bee admitted and made ffree of the company and societie of our collonie of Providence Plantations in the Narragansett Bay, in New-England, shall bee, from tyme to tyme, and forever hereafter, a bodie corporate and politique, in ffact and name, by the name of the Governor and Company of the English Collonie of Rhode-Island and Providence Plantations, in New-England, in America." The general officers of the company were to be elected annually, although the first incumbents were named in the charter. An assembly composed of six deputies from Newport, four each from Providence, Portsmouth, and Warwick, and two for every other town, was to meet twice a year. Remarkably broad powers were given to this assembly, but we need note here only the clause for the admission of freemen. By it the assembly could " choose, nominate, and apoynt, such and soe manye other persons as they shall thinke ffitt, and shall be willing to accept the same, to bee ffree of the sayd Company and body politique." Officers should be chosen annually by the general court or assembly, " by such greater part of the sayd Company, for the tyme beinge, as shall bee then and there present."

The charter of 1663 stated in more definite terms than those of the charter of 1644 the form of incorporation of the colony, and it placed additional emphasis upon the freemanship idea ; but in practice it introduced very few changes into the constitution of the colony. Since the charter vested

---

[1] *R. I. Col. Rec.*, I, 433–435.
[2] *Ibid.*, 485–491.   [3] *Ibid.*, II, 3–21.

legislative power in the assembly, it was held that the power of the people to annul laws by vote in town meetings was inconsistent with the charter;[1] and some confusion was caused by the ambiguous terms of the charter in describing elections. It was uncertain whether the elections were to be by the representative assembly, or by an assembly of the freemen; and if the latter, there were doubts whether proxy votes could be received.[2] As the charter interrupted but slightly the customs and laws of the colony, we can proceed at once to consider the development of the suffrage during the next one hundred years under the charter. For this purpose, it will be best to treat, first, of the qualifications of electors in the colony elections; secondly, the proxy system or method of balloting and a few other facts concerning elections; and thirdly, other elections than those for colony officers.

Although the new charter gave over to the assembly the whole subject of admission of freemen, yet no change was made in the custom which had previously existed. The applicant for colonial freedom must first have been accepted as a freeman of some town before he was qualified for the higher duties. After gaining the town freedom, the freeman's name was usually proposed to the general assembly by the town clerk,[3] although sometimes the applicant himself petitioned for the colonial franchise.[4] There are very few instances in which the granting of freedom was refused or even postponed after the presentation of names to the assembly.[5] It was very unusual for the assembly to inquire into the returns from the towns; apparently, if a man was properly admitted into a town, he could, if he desired, obtain the colonial freedom as well. So strong was the custom in this particular that the assembly, when it came to impose qualifications upon the freemanship, found it necessary to

[1] *R. I. Col. Rec.,* II, 27.

[2] *Ibid.,* 28, 29, 39, 62.

[3] *Ibid.,* 147, 185.

[4] *Ibid.,* 110, 147.

[5] The only cases noticed in scores of references to the subject of admission of freemen will be found in *R. I. Col. Rec.,* II, 59, 185, 238, 337.

place the restrictions not simply upon the freemen of the colony, but also upon the town freemen.

Before 1663 there was practically no general qualification for the freemanship, since the towns admitted or refused to admit what persons they would. After the new charter, however, the admission of freemen in towns and colony became the subject of frequent legislation. The first general qualification was imposed as a result of the demands of the English government. The royal commissioners who made so much trouble for themselves and the colonists in Connecticut and Massachusetts also turned their investigations upon Rhode Island. Carr and Carter, two of the commissioners, made known the king's desires to Rhode Island. The requirements were the same as those discussed more fully under the other two colonies; all inhabiting householders were to take an oath of allegiance to the king; and " all men of competante estates and of civill conversation, who acknowledge and are obediante to the civill magistrate, though of differing judgements" should be admitted as freemen and have liberty to elect or be elected to office.[1] The assembly in complying with these requirements necessarily imposed new restrictions upon the suffrage. All present freemen, and all admitted in the future, were compelled to take an engagement of allegiance to the king and of obedience to the laws and charter of the colony,[2] and those refusing were to forfeit the suffrage franchise as well as all the other rights of freemen. The assembly accepted as readily the other proposed qualifications for the suffrage

[1] *R. I. Col. Rec.*, II, 110.
[2] *Ibid.*, 112. The oath is as follows: " You, A. B., sollemly and sincearly engage true and faithfull aleagiance vnto his Majestye Charles the Second, King of England, his heires and successors, to beare and due obediance vnto the laws established, from time to time in this jurisdiction to yeald vnto the vtmost of your power, according to the previlidge by his said Majesty granted, in religioues and civill concearnments to this Collony in the Charter; which said engagement you make vnder the perrill and penalty of perjury." The same oath was to be taken by all men over eighteen years of age (*ibid.*, 113). See also *Providence Records*, III, 64, 101, 199; IV, 55.

and embodied them in the following order,[1] that those persons who

"take the aforesaid engagement and are of competent estates, civill conversation, and obediant to the civill magistrate, shall be admitted freemen of this Collony vpon their represe desire therein declared to the General Assembly, either by themselves with sufficient testimony of their fittnes and qualificationes as shall by the Assembly be deemed satisfactory; or if by the chiefe officer of the towne or townes where they live, they be proposed and declared as aforesaid; and that none shall have admission to vote for publicke officers, or deputyes, or enjoy any priviledge of freemen till admitted by the Assembly as aforesaid, and their names recorded in the gennerall records of this Collony."

This full compliance of the Rhode Island authorities was very acceptable to the royal commissioners, who write to England in favorable terms concerning the colony, and relate how " they admitt all to be freemen who desire it." [2] The new qualification does not appear to have made the admission of freemen any easier, for during the next few years relatively few new freemen were admitted. On the contrary, it must temporarily have excluded many from voting, as some refused to take the form of allegiance required, and for several years there was a class of non-jurors in Providence who interfered in elections and caused heated contests.[3]

The close relationship between the freedom of the towns and that of the colony is clearly shown in an act of 1666.[4] This act impowered the town meetings " to make Such men freemen of their Towns as they Judge may be meet & may be seruiceable to serve in ye Towns in Town Offices." After admission by the towns, the names of all such persons were to be presented to the assembly, and if they " pass by vote to

[1] *R. I. Col. Rec.*, II, 113.

[2] *Ibid.*, 127.

[3] *Ibid.*, 141, 142, 200, 288–290, 292, 293; *Providence Records*, III, 105, 149, 150.

[4] *Laws and Acts of Her Majesties Colony of Rhode Island and Providence Plantations made from the First Settlement in 1636 to 1705*, S. S. and B. Rider, Providence, 1896, 35, 36. The phraseology but not the sense was somewhat changed in the code of 1730, *Acts and Laws of Rhode Island*, 1730, 16.

allow them freemen of yᵉ Colony then Shall they have their Vots of Electing Generˡˡ Officers." It thus came to be the custom for the town clerks to send lists of the new town freemen to the assembly at the time of the general election in May. As early as 1667 the assembly was compelled to order that no person should be admitted to the freedom of the corporation on election day,[1] and thereafter the admissions of freemen nearly always took place at an assembly session or preparatory meeting held the day before the election.[2]

Both the charter of 1663 and the assembly's order of 1665 in response to the English demands, had said that the freedom of the colony might be given to those who desire it, but they had not implied that the colony could compel persons to accept the honor. Yet in 1670 the assembly impowered the towns to admit such freemen as they " shall judge capable to doe publicke service in bearing office therein; although such person or persones desire not to be made a freeman or freemen." [3]   But in establishing compulsory freemanship Rhode Island was not acting without precedent. Massachusetts and Maryland had adopted somewhat similar orders, and throughout all of the colonies office-holding was compulsory; while frequently persons properly qualified to vote were fined if they did not perform that duty. Thus the compulsory freemanship of Rhode Island, although different in name, was practically equivalent to the compulsory voting and office-holding in other colonies.

From this time down to 1719 there were no further restrictions on the suffrage. During all this period the towns could choose any of their inhabitants as freemen who possessed " competent estates" and were of " civil conversation."

[1] *R. I. Col. Rec.,* II, 190.

[2] *Ibid.,* III, 311. In subsequent years this preparatory meeting was given up almost entirely to the acceptance of freemen and the appointment of committees to manage the election on the following day; and on one occasion it is called an " Assembly for making freemen."

[3] *Ibid.,* II, 357. This is similar to the order in Providence in 1656, that all inhabitants, although not freemen, should be liable to be chosen for town service (*Providence Records,* II, 96).

But in 1719 a religious qualification was established. In the code of laws drawn up in that year occur these words:

"and that all men professing Christianity and of competent estates and of civil conversation who acknowledge and are obedient to the civil magistrate though of different judgments in Religious Affairs (Roman Catholicks only excepted) shall be admitted Freemen and shall have liberty to choose and be chosen Officers in the Colony both military and civil."

The presence of the phrase, "Roman Catholicks only excepted," has been difficult to explain, but Mr. S. S. Rider, in his researches, has placed the matter beyond a doubt. It is now clear that this clause was inserted into the midst of an earlier law by some member of the revisory committee of 1719. Neither the clause nor the law is to be found in the early legislation, although a marginal note in the code of 1719 and the following ones attributes the law to the year 1663. Mr. Rider has shown that great carelessness existed in ascribing the dates to the laws in the digests; and more conclusively still, it is found that the clause excluding the Catholics does not appear in the manuscript digest of 1705. There can be no doubt that the clause in question was used for the first time in 1719 instead of 1663 as the digest states; and it seems probable that it was added by the committee in order to bring the colonial laws into supposed conformity to the English statutes.[1] The digest of 1719 was never accepted by the legislature, and hence the work of the committee has been held to have no more value than the work of any private persons. But in 1730 the assembly accepted as the law of the colony a new digest in which the clause against Catholics is retained; and from that time throughout the colonial period it was the law of the colony. The Rhode Island historians have succeeded in removing the responsibility for this religious qualification from the early

[1] The English statutes 7 and 8 Wm. 3, ch. 27 and 1 Geo. 1, Statute 2, ch. 13, while not excluding all Catholics as such from the suffrage, yet provided that no person could vote for members of Parliament who upon the request of any candidate refused to take the oaths or affirmations of allegiance, supremacy, and the abjuration. This would lead to a practical disfranchisement of many, if not all, Roman Catholics.

settlers of the colony, and placing it upon their successors, who, under English influence, introduced a political persecution quite foreign to the policy of the founders.[1]   It must be admitted, however, that there were very few Roman Catholics in the colony and the law was practically a dead letter, until in 1783, when the large number of French settlers remaining after the French occupation of Newport, caused its repeal.[2]

The law as stated in the digests excluded not only Roman Catholics, but all non-Christians as well, and would thus have barred out Hebrews.   There were some Jews in the colony as early as 1684,[3] and in 1763 they erected a synagogue in Newport.[4]   A number of Jews were naturalized, and despite the laws apparently admitted to the freemanship; but in 1762 the superior court refused that privilege to two Hebrews on the ground that " it appears that the free and quiet enjoyment of the Christian religion and a desire of propagating the same were the principal views with which this colony was settled, and by a law made and passed in the year 1663,[5] no person who does not profess the Christian religion can be admitted free of this colony." [6] The Rhode Island historian, Arnold, attributes this decision to the party strife then existing between the governor and the chief-justice; and if this be true, it is interesting to note that it was the same cause as that which led the New York assembly to disfranchise the Jews in 1738.

[1] For the proof of the opinions above stated, see S. S. Rider's introductions to his editions of the codes of 1705 and 1719; and *An Inquiry Concerning the Origin of the Clause in the Laws of Rhode Island (1719-1783) Disfranchising Roman Catholics*, by the same author, in *Rhode Island Historical Tracts*, Second Series, No. 1; also Walsh's *Appeal*, 427-435; Arnold, *History of Rhode Island*, II, 490-497.

[2] Arnold, *Hist. of R. I.*, II, 497.

[3] *Ibid.*, I, 478.   [4] *Ibid.*, II, 247.

[5] This reference by a court shows how the errors of the digest makers were accepted without question.

[6] Arnold, *Hist. of R. I.*, II, 494, note. The doctrine above stated ignores the broad toleration advocated by Roger Williams, who seems to have believed in religious liberty for " papists and protestants, Jews and Turks" (*Narragansett Club Publications*, VI, 278).

Turning from these religious restrictions which remained upon the law books from 1719 until 1783, we notice a great increase in the number of freemen, and an attempt thereafter to limit the franchise by imposing a definite property qualification. No early figures showing the proportion of freemen to population have been accessible to the writer; but in 1708 Governor Cranston, writing to the Board of Trade, gives the population of the colony as 7181, of whom 1015 were freemen in the towns.[1] This shows the remarkably high proportion of one freeman to every seven inhabitants, and a potential voting class of the same proportion. A few years after this, the number of the annual admissions to the freemanship increased largely. Taking the ten years preceding the passage of the restrictive act of February, 1723-4, a count of the names of admitted freemen shows the total to be 841; but the rapid increase is shown by the fact that in the five years, 1714–1718 inclusive, only 222 freemen were admitted; while from 1719 to February, 1724, the number is 619.[2] Almost three times as many persons were admitted during the last five years as were received during the first five years of this decade. Such a growth cannot be explained by mere increase in population;[3] other causes must have been at work. Since there was as yet no general property qualification, the towns could admit as freemen any persons that they thought possessed competent estates, were civil in conversation, and obedient to the civil government. That the towns were interested in keeping up their number of freemen is shown by the action of a town meeting in Providence. In June, 1720, a committee composed of persons taken from the different parts of the town was chosen to make lists " of all such as are Capable of being made free men and bring

---

[1] *R. I. Col. Rec.*, IV, 59.

[2] See the lists of admitted freemen in *R. I. Col. Rec.*, IV, *passim*. As has already been mentioned, the admissions were usually made on the day before the annual election, but occasionally they took place at the other sessions of the assembly, and infrequently even on election day (*R. I. Col. Rec.*, IV, 481, 496, 521).

[3] Arnold, *Hist. of R. I.*, II, 77.

there seueral Lists to the Townes next quarter meeting." [1]
The committee must have rendered efficient service, for in
the following October the general assembly admitted as
freemen, 143 inhabitants of Providence; [2] and in the three
and a half years from October, 1720, to the passage of the
freeman act in February, 1723–4, almost forty per cent. of
the freemen received were inhabitants of Providence.[3]

This industry of the towns in freeman-making, and the
low standard set by the towns for the freemanship, combined with the increasing population, led to the enactment
of the law of February, 1723–4,[4] " Directing the Admitting
Freemen in the several Towns of this Colony." After the
publication of this act

"no Person whatsoever shall be admitted a Freeman of any Town in
this Colony, unless the Person admitted be a Freeholder of Lands,
Tenaments, or Hereditraments, in such Town where he shall be admitted Free, of the Value of *One Hundred Pounds,* or to the value of
Forty Shillings per Annum, or the Eldest Son of such a Freeholder:
Any other Act, Custom or Usage, to the contrary hereof, notwithstanding."

Those already free were not to forfeit their freemanship
if they did not possess the property qualification. No condition, it will be noticed, was imposed by this act upon freemen of the colony, except by the indirect restrictions upon
the town freemen. The custom which had held from the
earliest period was not thrown aside here.

Other interesting features are to be seen in these first
suffrage qualifications. The English requirement of forty
shillings as an alternative to the one hundred pounds, again

[1] *Providence Records,* XIII, 38.

[2] *R. I. Col. Rec.,* IV, 289.

[3] See lists of freemen, *R. I. Col. Rec.,* IV, 289, 290, 293, 302, 309, 314,
325, 327.

[4] *Acts and Laws of His Majesty's Colony of Rhode-Island, and
Providence-Plantations* (Newport, 1730), 131. The act appears to
have brought about an immediate restriction of the suffrage; for while
618 freemen were admitted into the colony in the five years before
the passage of the act, only 319 were given the freemanship in the
five years following the act (see *Records, passim*).

shows how strong was the force of this precedent. In this case it may have been inserted with the desire of placating the English government, which was evincing considerable dissatisfaction with the administration of affairs in Rhode Island, and the Board of Trade had even suggested that Rhode Island and Connecticut be annexed to the royal province of New Hampshire.[1] English precedents can also be found for the admission to the freemanship of the eldest sons of freemen, when the sons did not possess the property requirements. It is believed that no American precedent can be found for this,[2] with the possible exception of the hereditary semi-commercial burgherrecht of the Dutch New Amsterdam, which is not likely to have influenced Rhode Island seventy years after the English conquest of New Netherland.

In England, however, we have an instance of the admission of the sons of freemen into a chartered company,— which, it will be remembered, was the legal status of the colony of Rhode Island. The Merchant Adventurers of England by an ordinance of their body provided that free-men could be admitted, among other ways, by " patri-mony." Under this ordinance, a freeman's son, born after his father had been made " an absolute ffree and sworn brother," was entitled to the freedom of the company with-out serving an apprenticeship or paying the heavy fee ordi-narily imposed.[3] The feature of hereditary freemanship is to be found also quite generally in the English municipal corporations. In some cases it was granted solely to the eldest son or heir of a freeman,[4] in others it was given to the youngest son;[5] occasionally to all the sons of free-

---

[1] Arnold, *History of R. I.*, II, 77.

[2] The somewhat similar feature in Pennsylvania was adopted in the constitution of 1776 (Poore, *Charters and Constitutions*, II, 1542), fifty years after the passage of the Rhode Island law.

[3] W. E. Lingelbach, *The Internal Organization of the Merchant Ad-venturers of England* (Philadelphia, 1903, 9, 12).

[4] In Retford (Oldfield, *English Boroughs*, II, 5) ; Exeter (Izacke, *Memorials of Exeter*, 38, 39, 74) ; Richmond (*Hist. of Richmond* [anon., 1814], 120) ; Hastings (Oldfield, II, 301–304) ; Rye (*ibid.*, 327–333), etc.

[5] In Durham (Oldfield, I, 244).

men,[1] and sometimes even to those marrying the daughters of freemen.[2] From some of these English precedents the authors of the act of 1723–4 must have drawn their hereditary suffrage provision, which, as a political anomaly, was to continue in the Rhode Island community until the middle of the nineteenth century.[3]

While there is thus abundant English precedent for the hereditary feature, the property qualification in the Rhode Island law led to a form of difficulty which England at this time was spared. The mother country was not afflicted with the paper money craze, while Rhode Island, in the generation following the passage of the election law of 1724, passed through all the day dreams and disillusions of a cheap money epoch. The first issue of paper money, made in May, 1710,[4] was speedily followed by other and larger issues. Depreciation came as a matter of course. By 1731 the paper was quoted at two-fifths of its value in 1710;[5] ten years later, in consequence of very large emissions in the interim, its sterling value was only one-fourth the nominal value.[6] In 1750, it was stated that £110,000 of the money was worth only £10,000 sterling,[7] and this ratio

[1] This sometimes included all sons, and sometimes only those born after the father's admission, as in London.

[2] As in Bristol (Evans, *Hist. of Bristol*, II, 40); Ludlow (Oldfield, II, 39); Dover (*ibid.*, II, 312), etc.

[3] The English town whose requirements for the suffrage apparently most closely approach those of Rhode Island is Nottingham. In that town the electors were all freemen, all freeholders of forty shillings income, the eldest sons of freemen by birth, and the youngest sons after having served a seven years' apprenticeship anywhere, and all other persons who had served a seven years' apprenticeship to freemen (*An Essay on the Elective Franchise*, Arthur Kelly, London, 1821, p. 63; Oldfield, II, 2). Cp. English franchise, *ante*, 13–15.

[4] *Acts and Laws of His Majesty's Colony in Rhode Island and Providence Plantations* (Newport, 1745), 42, and *passim* for later acts; *Some Account of the Bills of Credit or Paper Money of Rhode Island from the First Issue, in 1710, to the Final Issue, 1786*, by E. R. Potter and S. S. Rider (*R. I. Historical Tracts*, No. 8).

[5] *R. I. Col. Rec.*, IV, 459.

[6] *Ibid.*, V, 13.

[7] *Ibid.*, 284.

was accepted by the Rhode Island assembly and commented upon by the English House of Commons.[1] A " new tenor" of 1740 depreciated in the same manner. In 1756 provision was made for another new issue, called " lawful money," which was maintained at about the ratio of one and one-third to one pound sterling; and this money, or English and Spanish coins, remained the circulating medium until the Revolution.[2] In the mean time, by 1764, the old tenor paper was quoted at twenty-three and a third for one pound of lawful money.[3] These few figures concerning the fluctuations in value of the paper money render intelligible the frequent changes in the suffrage qualifications.

As the paper money declined in value the bars of the freemanship were lowered, and the assembly lagging years behind the depreciation, tried by legislation to maintain the standard fixed in 1724.[4] The first reform came in 1729–30, when the property qualification was changed from one hundred pounds value, or forty shillings income, to two hundred pounds value of freehold, or ten pounds annual income from land. Eldest sons of freeholders could still be admitted; but the provision was inserted that where the freedom of a town was obtained by " any fraudulent Means or Contrivance," such freemanship should be void.[5]

The acts of 1724 and 1730 merely required the freeman to possess the proper amount of freehold at the time of his admission to the freemanship, without inquiring into his qualification at each election. This naturally led to corruption and the defeat of the intention of the laws. By the preamble of a new act of 1742[6] it is charged that " many Persons have by Frauds and other indirect Means, procured

---

[1] Potter and Rider, *Some Account of the Bills of Credit*, 76, 84.

[2] *Ibid.*, 95, 97–99.

[3] *Ibid.*, 97.

[4] In only one other colony, South Carolina, has such a marked relationship between the suffrage and the currency been found to exist, although wherever the property qualification was expressed in pounds and not in acres there must have been such an influence of the one upon the other.

[5] *Acts and Laws of Rhode Island*, 1730, 209.

[6] *Ibid.*, 1745, 252.

themselves to be made Free of this Colony, who really are not possessed of such Estate," as by the former acts is required; and many persons formerly possessing the requisite estates " have afterwards disposed of such their Estates, and yet continue to act as Freemen in this Colony, from which many very ill Consequences have already arisen to the Colony, and many more will ensue, if not timely prevented." Acting under these impulses the legislature enacted that no person " shall be admitted to vote or act as a Freeman in any Town Meeting in this Colony, or at the General Election, but such only who, at the Time of such their voting, or acting as Freemen, are really and truly possessed of Lands, Tenements, or Hereditaments lying in this Colony of the full Value of Two Hundred Pounds or Ten Pounds per annum, being their own Freehold Estate, or the eldest Son of such Freeholder." [1] Under this act and all subsequent ones, the freeman's rights continued only so long as the freeman retained those qualities which were thought essential to the position. If his property were alienated, he lost as well the freeman's prerogatives. Thus the freemanship, formerly a grant for life, became conditioned upon the continuous holding of land; and in this respect approached more closely than ever before to the suffrage qualifications of the other colonies.[2]

Following the great depreciation of the currency during the decade beginning in 1740, the franchise prerequisite was still farther lowered. The assembly in the preamble to an act of 1746 [3] says that the " manner of admitting Freemen in this Colony is so lax and their qualifications as to their estates so very low that many Persons are admitted who are possessed with little or no property;" and that the admission of such " necessitous" persons has encouraged evil-minded persons to practice bribery and corruption in

[1] *Acts and Laws of Rhode Island,* 1745, 252. Suspected persons could be required to take oath that they were properly qualified.

[2] There was no saving of the rights of persons already admitted, as had been done by the acts of 1724 and 1730; but all, old freemen and newly admitted ones, must conform to the freehold requirements.

[3] *Acts and Laws of Rhode Island,* 1752, 13; *R. I. Historical Tracts,* No. 8, 59. 60.

elections, to the great scandal of the colony. To prevent these evils the assembly again doubled the nominal value of the freehold required of voters, now making it the apparently large amount of four hundred pounds, or an income of twenty pounds a year from rents. In reality, it may be doubted whether this amount represented as much purchasing power as the one hundred pounds required by the act of 1724.

Bribery and corruption were attacked by the same assembly. An act to prevent such practices, passed in 1746, is the most stringent known in colonial legislation. According to it,[1] not only every freeman thereafter admitted, but all freemen already admitted, were required to take the following oath or affirmation:

"You A. B. do solemnly swear [or affirm] That you have not, and will not, receive any Money, or other Reward, or other Thing, by which you may expect any Money or future Reward, at the Election of any Officer to be chosen in this Colony: And that you will not bargain or contract with any Person, directly or indirectly, contrary to the true Intent and Meaning of this Oath [or Affirmation]; but that you will use your Freedom for the Good of the Gov't only, without any other Motive: And this Declaration you make, without any Evasion, Equivocation, or mental Reservation whatsoever."

The town clerks were directed to send annually to the general assembly lists of all freemen taking the oath. To discourage candidates from "using any corrupt or unlawful Method" to obtain offices, it was enacted that if "One single Vote be unlawfully obtained by such Candidate's Procurement, Knowledge or Consent," the election should "be declared utterly null and void." Suspected persons refusing to purge themselves under oath were to be declared guilty. Any one convicted of bribery was to suffer the penalty of perjury and also "forever thereafter be excluded from being a Freeman, or voting, or bearing any public Office, whatsoever, in this Colony; And shall also forever be rendered incapable of giving Evidence in any Court of Justice."[2]

[1] *Acts and Laws of Rhode Island,* 1766, 24.
[2] *Ibid.* The act was repealed in 1767 (*Session Laws* of 1767, 11), and all persons having taken the oath were absolved therefrom as fully as though they had never taken it.

The assembly records show that the provisions of the act were carried out, no person being permitted to vote who had not taken the oath, and all new freemen were compelled to subscribe to it.[1] We cannot but imagine that the political corruption had reached a state alarming to the legislators when they felt compelled to administer such an oath to every voter in the colony.

By 1760, owing largely to the influence of the English government, the colonial currency was placed upon a rational basis, and thereafter sterling money circulated at the legal rate of 133 per cent.[2] Again the change in the money system demanded a restatement of the suffrage qualifications, for under the " lawful money" acts, the four hundred pounds requirement would be exorbitant. Accordingly, in 1760, the assembly enacted that for the future no person should

"vote and act as a freeman in any case, whatsoever, but such only, who at the time of voting, shall be truly and really possessed of land or real estate, to be valued and determined agreeably to the former laws, of the full value of £40, lawful money, or that will rent yearly for forty shillings, lawful money, or the eldest son of such a freeman."[3]

The same qualifications were embodied in the comprehensive election law of 1762,[4] and in the still more elaborate provisions of the Digest of 1767.[5]

We are told, in the preamble of the act of 1762,[6] that the charter right of the colony to elect their officers " is One of the noblest Privileges a People can enjoy;" and it " is of the greatest Importance" that the elections be impartial, and all precautions be taken to prevent collusive practices, particularly since some towns have admitted persons as freemen who were not qualified by the laws of the colony. The

[1] See *R. I. Col. Rec.*, V, 213, 487; VI, 43, 140, 201, 246.
[2] This " lawful money" of Rhode Island was equivalent to " proclamation money" in other colonies.
[3] *R. I. Col. Rec.*, VI, 257.
[4] *Session Laws* of 1762; *R. I. Col. Rec.*, VI, 322, 323, 343.
[5] *Acts and Laws of Rhode Island*, 1767, 78 ff.
[6] *Session Laws* of 1762.

new legislation impowered the towns to admit as freemen such of their inhabitants as were qualified according to the terms of the act,[1] and required the town clerk to certify the names of the freemen annually to the assembly. Those " so returned and admitted Freemen of the Colony shall be enrolled in the Colony's Book." The freehold qualification, now containing minor clauses to prevent fraud, is as follows:

"And be it further Enacted . . . That no person whosoever shall be permitted to vote, or act as a Freeman in any Town-Meeting in this Colony, but such only who are Inhabitants therein, & who, at the Time of such their voting & acting, are really & truly possessed, in their own proper Right, of a Real Estate, within this Colony, to the full Value of Forty Pounds or which shall rent for Forty Shillings *per Annum,* being an Estate of Fee-simple, Fee-tail, or an Estate in Reversion, which qualifies no other person to be a Freeman, or at least an Estate for a Person's own Life, or the eldest Son of such a Freeholder. And that no Estate of a less Quality shall entitle any Person to the Freedom of this Colony."[2]

A person who had previously obtained admission by virtue of his wife's dower, or by virtue of rented lands, or in other irregular ways, was to forfeit his freemanship at once. All persons, excepting the eldest sons of qualified freeholders, were to be propounded for three months before the respective towns, and the evidence of their qualification must be produced in open town meeting.[3] Suspected persons might be challenged in town meeting and compelled to take oath that they were properly qualified, and thereafter they could not vote until they had satisfied the town as to their qualifications. Persons convicted of executing or receiving any fraudulent deeds were " to be utterly incapable, forever, thereafter of sustaining any Office, or of voting for any Officer, in this Colony." The qualifications imposed by these acts were to be enforced upon all voters for town deputies in the assembly and for town officers, as well as for general officers. Inhabitants might be admitted as freemen and given a vote for general officers in the towns where they resided, if

[1] Digest of 1767, 78, 79.
[2] *Ibid.*
[3] *Ibid.*

they owned sufficient land in any part of the colony, and brought satisfactory proof of the same to the town clerk. Apparently a man voted where he resided, instead of where his land lay, as was the case in the central and southern colonies. The right of the eldest son to vote did not go to the second son upon the death of the first, unless the latter had died without issue.[1] A fine of twenty pounds was to be inflicted upon an unqualified person who voted unlawfully, or upon a freeman who voted more than once at the same election.[2]

With the repeal of the oath against bribery in 1767[3] the last change was made in the suffrage qualifications during the colonial period.   Beginning with complete control by the towns of the freeman qualifications, we have noticed first the influence of the English commissioners in securing the passage of the general provision for competent estates and civil conversation. About fifty years later came the insertion of clauses in the statute books which excluded Jews and Catholics from the freemanship. The policy of restricting the franchise to those owning a definite amount of real estate began in 1724 with the sum of £100, or forty shillings income; and this was subsequently raised to £200 and £400 as the value of money depreciated. The return of sound money compelled the restoration of a smaller qualification, which in 1760 was fixed at £40, or an income of forty shillings from land. In 1746, and for about twenty years thereafter, a most stringent oath against bribery was required from all freemen. Throughout the period the qualifications are said to be imposed upon town freemen; who, after satisfying the town meeting and being accepted thereby, were proposed to the assembly for admission to the colonial freedom. Only one instance has been noticed in the later years where the assembly refused to accept as freemen of the colony those proposed by the towns.[4] The later legislation

[1] Digest of 1767, 78, 79.

[2] In the latter case the offender was also to be disfranchised for three years. Such a punishment had first been adopted in 1736 (Digest of 1745, 193).

[3] *Session Laws* of 1767, 11.

[4] *R. I. Col. Rec.*, VI, 323.

is distinguished for as elaborate provisions concerning free-manship, the suffrage and elections as will be found in any other colony.

Turning now from the qualifications of voters to the man-ner in which the suffrage was exercised, we must glance at some of the features of the proxy system which was an in-tegral part of the Rhode Island election laws. In this sys-tem the observer always finds a valuable link between pure democracy and our modern representative and ballot meth-ods, and it has been deemed best, therefore, to collect the evidence respecting this Rhode Island custom.

Newport, apparently, pointed the way for such a system, when, as early as January, 1639-40, the town ordered that elections should be held annually by the " greater part of the Bodie of Freemen, then or ther present," and gave permis-sion to " such as shall be necessarily detained to send in their votes, sealed up to the Judge." [1] The assembly of 1647, the first to meet under the charter of 1644, and composed of all the freemen, permitted those who wished to do so to retire, but required them to leave their votes behind them.[2] The same assembly in almost the exact words of the Newport order of 1640 made the proxy system a permanent part of the colonial elections.[3]

In the face of the uncertainty as to whether the charter of 1663 required all freemen to attend personally or still per-mitted the use of proxies, or required all elections to be by the representative assembly, the first election under the char-ter was held in May, 1664, by the freemen " personally there present," [4] without the admission of proxy votes. But this assembly " seriously considered" the inconvenience of com-pelling the freemen of remote towns to come to Newport to vote, and referred the matter to the assembly meeting in October, 1664.[5] At the latter meeting[6] the following order was then adopted:

[1] *R. I. Col. Rec.*, I, 98.
[2] *Ibid.*, 151.
[3] *Ibid.*, 149.
[4] *Ibid.*, II, 29.   [5] *Ibid.*, 39.
[6] *Ibid.*, 62. They had the "helpfull presance" of John Clark, the agent who was instrumental in securing the charter.

"That the liberty and priviledge of electing and being elected vnto all publicke offices in this Collony, shall continue in the whole body or company of the freemen by ther parsonall and individuall votting; and whereas, it hath ben often vrged the difficulty . . . parsonall voting at Newport this presant Assembly ordaynes, that voting by proxces be enjoyed by all the freemen of this Collony, and that each freeman desiering to vote by proxces shall subscribe ther names on the outside, and deliver his votes sealed vp into the hands of a magistrate, in the face of a town meeting . . . ; and in case of sickness and nescecary absence from the sayd towne meetinge, vnto a magistrate, who shall deliver the sayd votes or cause them to be delivered into the hands of the Governor, or in his absence, of the deputy Governor, in the face of the Court of Election; . . . provided, that this order shall noe way prejudice or discorradge any who desier to be parsonally presant. . . . "[1]

By an order of 1666, it appears that not only the absentees but also those personally present at the election in Newport were to vote by means of "wrighten Votes."[2] The use of a written tablet was thereafter required of all voters in the colonial elections.

It is evident that from 1664[3] the proxy system of Rhode Island was nothing more than a method of collecting ballots in elections. The true proxy was a temporary grant of power by an absentee freeman to another who was attendant upon the assembly. Such forms of proxies are found in the assembly of 1647 and perhaps some of the later pure democratic meetings, but they disappear altogether after 1664. What the Rhode Island assembly called a proxy was simply a written ballot sent by a freeman who did not in person attend the general election. For over a century of the colony's history the freeman was privileged to attend the election in person and hand in an unsigned ballot, or he could give in his ballot, properly signed, at a town meeting before the general election, or, if detained by sickness, to some mag-

---

[1] *R. I. Col. Rec.*, II, 62.

[2] Rider's edition of MS. Code of 1705, 35, 36.

[3] There can be no doubt that voting by ballot at the general elections existed before 1666. As early as 1647 those whom the "major part of the General Assembly pitcheth upon by paper" were to be accounted elected (*R. I. Col. Rec.*, I, 191).

istrate; and the actual ballots thus received were " sealed up in a Packet," [1] sent to the officers of the colony and opened in their presence at the general election in Newport.[2]

By the year 1715 the inevitable election evils had crept into the ballot system. " Loose and fractious freemen" were found " putting or delivering into the hat sometimes two, three or more votes for one officer." [3] The assembly, " for the preventing said clandestine proceedings for the future," ordered that " every freeman admitted to vote, shall write his name at length on the back side of his vote, and all proxy votes shall have the same." [4] But the signing of ballots in this way did not prove popular. The next assembly found that it " hath given great dissatisfaction and uneasiness to many of the good people of this colony, who deem it a very great hardship to have their names exposed upon such occasions, to the creating of animosity and heart-burning of their particular friends, etc." [5] Accordingly, that part of the former act which required the voters present at the election to write their names upon their ballots was repealed. All proxy votes, however, were to be signed according to the former custom.[6] For a number of years after this, no material change appears in the method of balloting. Irregular proxies were sometimes thrown out by wholesale; [7] and in 1743–4 it was stated that " no Person Proxing at said Meet-

---

[1] *R. I. Col. Rec.,* IV, 208.

[2] We have abundant evidence to show that these two forms of voting were carried out. Thus on May 4, 1669, the day before the election, the assembly appointed two persons " to write the names of such as come to vote tomorrow, being the day of Election;" two others were " to receive the votes from such as vote and deliver them fayre [fair] into the hat on the table;" and two others " are to assist for the opening of the proxes" (*ibid.,* II, 242). In 1673 the proxies were divided into four parts and as many committees appointed " to open and putt in the votes as called for into the hat" (*ibid.,* II, 484).

[3] *Ibid.,* IV, 195.

[4] *Ibid.* A fine not exceeding five pounds, or corporal punishment not greater than twenty-one stripes on the bare back, were to be inflicted upon non-freemen who voted at general or town elections, and upon freemen who cast more than one vote for any officer.

[5] *Ibid.,* IV, 207.   [6] *Ibid.,* 208.

[7] *Ibid.,* 469, 507; Arnold, *History of R. I.,* II, 239.

ing shall have Liberty of withdrawing his Proxy at the General Election," [1] a right which may previously have been claimed.

In the meantime the custom of appearing personally at the elections at Newport had grown less popular. By 1760 we learn that the casting of proxy votes at the town meetings was "the ancient and laudable custom of most of the prudent freemen;" [2] and in that year the personal appearance of freemen at Newport for the purpose of casting their votes was prohibited to all except members of the assembly.[3] The reasons for abolishing this unique feature of the elections are given in the preamble to the act of August 18, 1760. The presence of the freemen at the election is said to have been "very injurious to the interest and public weal of the colony." It further occasioned "a very great loss of people's time, at a season of the year when their labor is abundantly necessary for preparing the ground and planting the seed, on which the produce of the whole summer must depend." The act directed that "every freeman, who is disposed to give his suffrage for the election of general officers," should do so by handing in a proxy vote at a town meeting on the third Wednesday of April preceding the election.[4]

Thus the picturesque gathering of the freemen at Newport, meeting perhaps in a kitchen [5] or in a Quaker meeting house,[6] and each man individually putting his ballot into the hat on the table, was discontinued. The custom had originated under the early charter, and was retained under that of 1663 because it was thought the charter required a general meeting of the freemen for elective purposes; [7] but by 1760 the assembly evidently thought they would incur no danger

[1] *Acts and Laws of Rhode Island*, 1745, 287.

[2] *R. I. Col. Rec.*, VI, 256.

[3] *Ibid.*, 256, 257.   [4] *Ibid.*

[5] *Ibid.*, II, 541.   [6] *Ibid.*, IV, 569.

[7] Bellomont, writing to England in 1699 concerning irregularities in Rhode Island, said, "Their Election of Generall Officers is partly made by proxies, and allowed of by an Act of the government, contrary to the rules of their Charter in that respect; which prescribes that the Elections be made by such greater part of the Company as shall be present at the Generall Assembly" (*R. I. Col. Rec.*, III, 386).

of forfeiting the charter by adopting a more convenient method of holding elections. On the other hand, the method of sending the actual ballots (proxies) from the several towns to Newport to be counted, was still continued.[1]

We must now notice what other forms of the suffrage existed than that for the general colonial officers. There were several types of elections in which the suffrage included persons who were not freemen of the colony. The most important of such elections were those held in the towns for deputies and for town officers. There are also meetings and elections among the groups of land proprietors which existed in almost all the towns; and finally, the militia franchise was considerably wider than that of the town or colony.

The suffrage in the towns was vested in those inhabitants who had been admitted by the town meeting as freemen. Some comment has been made concerning the early restrictions imposed by the towns; and the legislation by the assembly upon the subject has been reviewed at length. The several property qualifications were in each case placed by the assembly upon those admitted to the town freemanship, and not directly upon the freemen of the colony. Hence the qualifications already mentioned are those required of town freemen, varying as we have seen from one hundred to four hundred pounds and back again to forty. In addition to these compulsory qualifications, the towns in the early period had wide liberty in the admission and rejection of inhabitants, and by this means could impose other qualifications.[2]

---

[1] By the act of 1762 (*Session Laws*) and the Digest of 1767 (83, 84), the freemen were required to hand their proxies "one by one, in their own proper Persons" to the moderator of the town meeting, and the clerk must keep a record of all persons voting and send the list to the assembly.

[2] In 1682 town councils were authorized to require a bond from newcomers (*R. I. Col. Rec.*, III, 117). In 1728, because persons of a "flexible Disposition" might tender bonds for "profligate Persons," the town councils were empowered to accept such bond or not as they saw fit; and if they refused to accept it, the person in question was to be conveyed out of the town (*Acts and Laws of R. I.*, 1730, 150, act of Feb., 1727-8). See *Providence Records*, VI, 151, for instance of refusal to admit an inhabitant.

But by 1766 and perhaps before that time, the town could not refuse to recognize as an inhabitant any one (*a*) who had resided in the town for one year and had not been warned to depart: (*b*) who had purchased a freehold of the value of forty pounds in the town; or (*c*) who was an apprentice and had served out his time in the town.[1] By these provisions the town must accept as an inhabitant any one who had purchased land sufficient to qualify him for the freemanship. Whether they could refuse to accept him as a town freeman and thus prevent his gaining the colony freedom as well, does not appear on the face of the records or the laws. By this date, however, it is believed that there was little discretion exercised by the towns.[2]

The only difference, then, between the town suffrage and that of the colony was in the action taken by the general assembly upon the name of the town freeman. After the admission of a freeman to the town, the town clerk was required by law to send the new freeman's name to the general assembly, to be acted upon by them for the colonial freemanship; and the latter was granted, so far as the records show, as a matter of course. Thus the man would be a freeman of a town only a few months or at most a year before he would obtain the colonial franchise. For our purposes the two classes may be taken as identical.[3]

[1] *Acts and Laws of Rhode Island*, 1767, 228 ff.

[2] This is supported by the word "shall" in the Digest of 1767 (p. 78): "Be it Enacted . . . That the Freemen of each respective Town in this Colony, at their Town Meeting Days, *shall,* and they hereby have full Power granted them to admit so many Persons, Inhabitants of their respective Towns, Freemen of their Towns, as shall be qualified according to this Act."

[3] That they were not absolutely so in practice is shown by the express statement that town deputies to the assembly were to be elected by the freemen of the towns, and not merely by freemen of the colony (*R. I. Col. Rec.*, IV, 338). But this provision was probably made in order that newly elected freemen of the towns might have a voice in the election of assemblymen. The same care is shown in the permission that new town freemen may vote for all general officers, and if the general assembly admit them as colony freemen the votes were to be counted; if not admitted, the votes were declared void (*Acts and Laws of R. I.*, 1767, 78–87).

Within the towns there soon arose a more exclusive group than that made up of the freemen. We have noticed how in the early days a person accepted by a town as a freeman was usually entitled to share in the town lands upon an equal plane with the first proprietors.[1] But ouher inhabitants or small freeholders entered the settlement, and might purchase or receive grants of land without any interest in the undivided portions of the town. Thus about the early "purchasers" or "proprietors" there grew up a large class who did not share their rights.

The town records of Providence show admirably the gradual separation of these two classes. In the earliest period land matters were discussed in the general town meeting;[2] but about 1661 the majority of the "purchasers" ordered that requests to the town for lands should be referred to the purchasers for acceptance or refusal.[3] Thereafter frequent references are made to "purchasers meetings."[4] The records of their meetings are still kept in the town book, their meetings and elections are held on the same days as the town meetings and elections,[5] but care is taken that the acts be recorded as performed by the purchasers. After 1706 no further records of the purchasers are included in the town books, and by 1715 the town and the purchasers form two distinct bodies which are compelled to appoint committees to settle differences with one another.[6] The rights of purchasers could be alienated and devised or inherited.[7] A final land division among the Providence "purchasers" took place in 1719, in which one hundred and one persons participated.[8]

[1] See *ante*, 434–436.

[2] *Providence Records*, I, II, *passim*.

[3] *Ibid.*, III, 10. The record is badly mutilated and lacks date, but follows an item dated 1661.

[4] *Ibid.*, III, 11; IV, 36; IX, 9, 12, 18, etc.

[5] *Ibid.*, IX, 18, 19, 23, 34, 49, 90, 91, 102–108.

[6] *Ibid.*, XI, 178.

[7] *Ibid.*, III, 157; VIII, 69. In Providence there was also a group of purchasers who received only twenty-five acres, who may have been entitled to only one-fourth of a vote in proprietors' meetings (*ibid.*, II, 74, 125, 127; IV, 36; VIII, 154). See Chapter VII for similar case on Long Island.

[8] Arnold, *History of R. I.*, I, 121.

Far broader than any other form of suffrage in the colony was that granted for the militia elections, which for many years was vested in all the soldiers of the "train bands." The custom was evidently brought from Massachusetts by the Newport settlers, who, as early as 1639, directed the train band to choose their own officers.[1] In the code of 1647 under the charter of 1644 the militia officers were to be chosen by the "inhabitants" of the several towns from among themselves.[2] The same method was retained under the new charter of 1663.[3]

When the office of major was erected in 1677, that officer was to be elected as follows: "every soldier listed and appearinge in armes on the traininge day in March, appointed by law in his or their respective towne or place in the Collony, shall have free liberty to vote in writinge for one person to be Major for the ensuinge year."[4] Under this law, as under the early laws of other colonies, the right of suffrage for military officers and the duty of serving in the militia went together. If a person were compelled to serve in the band, although only a boy of sixteen or an indentured servant, he had a right to vote for the military officers.

Such popular elections[5] did not fail to meet the disapproval of Bellomont in 1699, when seeking grounds of complaint against the colony; and he called the attention of the English government to the fact that the commissioned officers were elected by the soldiers, instead of being appointed by the assembly or the governor and assistants as the charter enjoined.[6] Perhaps it was this report which led the assem-

---

[1] *R. I. Col. Rec.*, I, 93.

[2] *Ibid.*, I, 153.   [3] *Ibid.*, II, 52, 568.

[4] *Ibid.*, II, 587. The actual ballots were to be delivered to the general assembly as in the case of proxies for general officers. The listed soldiers included all male persons between the ages of sixteen and sixty years, including servants, and excluding some few persons holding important political or economic positions.

[5] *Ibid.*, 386.

[6] Later it was seen that these orders excluded old men—"ancient freemen"—who, being over sixty years of age, were exempt from military training; and consequently the elections of major for the future were ordered to be by the freemen and the train bands (*R. I. Col. Rec.*, III, 9, 118).

bly, by 1705, to perceive " the great inconveniences and dishonor it brings to the Collony in admitting the listed soldiery" to a vote in the choice of officers, and to realize that the votes of " transient persons and many youth of small consideration" led to the choice of officers who were " not honorable to her Majesty nor capable of serving" in the offices to which they were elected.[1]   At any rate the suffrage in such elections was thereafter to be limited to the freemen of the towns or colony.   Only a year afterwards, however, the old elections by all the soldiers were restored.[2]

But in 1713 Bellomont's interpretation of their charter was accepted and provision was made for the annual election of militia officers by the assembly.[3]   Again, in 1726, the elections were ordered to be held by the soldiers and freemen of the towns.[4]   In fifteen years this policy had been found to be " vastly prejudicial" to the colony, and in 1740–1 the selection of the military officers was permanently vested in the assembly, the governor retaining his right to commission the officers.[5]

We may conclude this section by summing up what few facts have been found concerning the size of the freeman class in Rhode Island.   In the early years the freemen corresponded closely in number to the free male inhabitants, although almost from the first there were some inhabitants not enjoying freemen's rights.   Yet we are told that in 1677 the inhabitants were " generally freemen." [6]   The comparatively high proportion of one freeman to every seven of the population in 1708 has already been noted; [7]   but in 1713 the assembly thought the non-freeman inhabitants so numerous that the militia elections should be taken from them.[8]   The

[1] Rider, MS. Code of 1705, 116; *R. I. Col. Rec.*, III, 534.
[2] *Ibid.*, III, 563.
[3] *Ibid.*, IV, 155; *Acts and Laws of R. I.*, 1730, 90–99.
[4] *R. I. Col. Rec.*, IV, 377.
[5] *Ibid.*, V, 1.
[6] *Ibid.*, IV, 155
[7] *Ibid.*, 59.
[8] *Ibid.*, 155.

applied to voters in other colonies; and the word *freeman*
applied to electors in many colonies would exclude women.

2. *Age.* The adoption of the legal age of twenty-one
years was almost as universal as was male suffrage. In
only two colonies, New Jersey and Maryland, is it lacking
from the election laws, and there is no doubt that it was enforced in those colonies. There were, however, several
instances in which the age of voters differed from the common English requirement. Massachusetts as early as 1647
required non-freemen who were chosen to participate in local
government to have attained the age of twenty-four years;
between 1664 and 1686 the same age was required of non-
church-members who were admitted to the freedom of the
colony; and the twenty-four years' provision was incorporated into the short-lived Cutt code of New Hampshire as
a requirement for all voters. In the New England militia
elections, on the other hand, the voting age was less than
twenty-one years, for usually all the soldiers or all those required to equip themselves with arms were permitted to share
in the choice of militia officers; and as the trained bands
included nearly all males over sixteen years of age, it is
probable that some under twenty-one years voted in these
elections. Plymouth, late in her history, set a new age requirement of twenty years for voters in militia elections.
Aside from these few exceptions, it is believed that elections
were never legally open to persons under the age of twenty-
one years.

3. *Race and Nationality.* A racial distinction arose naturally in the colonies possessing a large negro slave population. Apparently the first law upon the subject is that of
North Carolina of 1715 which excluded negroes, mulattoes
and Indians from the franchise. In 1716 South Carolina
inserted the word "white" into her election law; while
Virginia adopted the phraseology of North Carolina in
1723, and Georgia followed with the word "white" in
1761. The North Carolina statute was repealed in 1734-5
and the racial restriction does not again appear during the
colonial period.

At English common law no foreigner could exercise political rights in England, and this general principle was ex-

tended to the colonies, where the only noteworthy infringement upon it is to be found in the position of the Huguenots
in South Carolina before 1696-7. Foreigners, when they
received a citizen's rights, obtained it either by treaty right,[1]
by special act of a colonial legislature,[2] or under the terms of
general laws passed for that purpose. After the year 1740 an
act of parliament forbade the naturalization of any Catholic
aliens in the colonies, a policy which New York and Massachusetts had anticipated by twenty-five and ten years respectively. In a few cases,[3] there was an explicit exclusion of
aliens from elections or office-holding; but this was unusual,
and the force of English precedent was generally the only bar
between the foreigner and the franchise.

4. *Religion and Good Character.* Religious qualifications,
as is well known, were more exclusive and more rigidly enforced in New England than in any of the other colonies.
Massachusetts from 1631 until 1664 required all freemen to
be church-members, and after that date, while membership
in the church was not required of persons who possessed certain other qualifications, yet even the few freemen who were
admitted under the terms of the law of 1664 were compelled
to bring certificates from the ministers of their towns that
they were orthodox in religious belief. The New Haven
freemen must be members of some approved church in New
England; Plymouth disfranchised those who set up churches
without the approbation of the authorities; and even Connecticut in practice, if not in law, appears to have enforced
religious conformity.

Besides this general exclusion in New England of those
who did not belong to the established churches, there were
particular sects upon whom were visited, not in New England
alone, the pains of disfranchisement. In the middle of the
seventeenth century the Quakers were outlawed in all the
colonies from Virginia to Massachusetts with the exception
of Rhode Island, and Baptists had but little more leniency

[1] As the Dutch and Swedes within the Duke of York's patent.

[2] As early as 1666 in Maryland, *Archives, Acts, 1666–76*, 144, 205, 270–
272, 330, 400, 460.

[3] North Carolina, 1715; Pennsylvania, 1694; Delaware, 1734; New
Hampshire, 1680.

shown to them. But the sect which received the most liberal share of political persecution was the Roman Catholic. The colonial attitude, outside of New England, where it was always hostile, varied with the changes in English politics. The English commonwealth movement led to the disfranchisement of Catholics in Maryland, and a similar but short-lived result appeared in Maryland and New York after the Revolution of 1688. In New Hampshire in 1680 the franchise was distinctly limited to Protestants, but this was in force only two years. In 1699 Virginia permanently disfranchised " recusant convicts," and two years later New York excluded Catholics from elections. In 1718 Maryland, and in 1719 Rhode Island took similar action, while not until 1759 did South Carolina limit her voters to those professing the Protestant faith.

Jews were disfranchised almost as frequently as Catholics. In 1682 the first Pennsylvania assembly restricted political privileges to those who believed in " Jesus Christ the Son of God and Saviour of the World"; between 1716 and 1759 South Carolina required voters to be Christians, and Protestants after the latter date. New York in 1737, by resolution of the assembly, disfranchised Jews, and Rhode Island in 1719 limited the suffrage to Protestant Christians.

Good character qualifications, like the religious requirement, were most common in New England. Connecticut, in 1657, 1659 and 1662 required candidates for the freemanship to be of " peaceable and honest conversation;" Massachusetts, in 1664, required non-church-members applying for the freemanship to be " not vicious in life; " Plymouth, in 1658, disfranchised lyers, drunkards, swearers and those refusing to take the oath of fidelity to the government. Rhode Island's " civil conversation" and " obedience to the civil magistrate" were taken from the instructions to the king's commissioners of 1664, and, in turn, were adopted in part by Plymouth in 1669; while New Hampshire, in 1680, copied the good character clause of the Massachusetts law. A somewhat similar feature is to be found in the Rhode Island compulsory oath administered to all freemen between 1746 and 1767, that they would use no bribery or dishonest methods in elections. Outside of New England the good character provisions are unusual. We may note the clause in Penn's Laws Made in England which excluded persons convicted of ill-fame or of unsober and dishonest conversation; and the Virginia act of 1762 which excluded from the colonial franchise freeholders who were convicts during the time for which they were transported.

5. *Residence.* In New England, owing to the close life of the towns and to the early and numerous restrictions upon the reception of inhabitants into the towns, there is rarely any formal term of residence required for freemen. Practically no one could gain a residence without the consent of the town; and in some cases, as in Plymouth particularly and in Massachusetts, the consent of the colonial authorities was also required before one could settle in a town. To the southward of New England, where the personal sifting process of the New England town life did not exist, it was more necessary that a term of residence for voters be established by law. And yet this did not come very early and in some cases it was never adopted. Thus in Maryland, in 1642, we learn that neither the holding of land nor the possession of a definite place of residence was required, and the same tolerant spirit is seen in the Carolinas and Virginia. After this early laxity residence restrictions were gradually adopted. In Virginia and the Carolinas there is an effort to limit the suffrage to housekeepers, but this soon gives place to other qualifications, such as freeholding or tax-paying, which imply a residence in the colony or an evident interest in its concerns. By the Revolutionary days a residence within the county was required of those voting in Maryland under the personal property qualification; in North Carolina the voter must have resided six months in the province; in South Carolina, after an early requirement of only three months' residence, the term was permanently fixed, in 1721, at one year, and Georgia followed North Carolina with a six months' provision. Pennsylvania and Delaware compelled the voter to reside two years in the province; New Jersey required a year's residence in the county, city or town where the elector voted; while New York was content with a simple requirement that a freeholder must have held his land three months before the election at which he offered to vote. Virginia,

New York and New Hampshire, apparently, had no definite residence qualifications.

6. *Property Qualifications.* During the seventeenth century some property qualification upon voters was implied in the laws and customs of many of the colonies, and in the eighteenth century such a requirement was universal. Property qualifications, for our purposes, may be divided into (*a*) those which do not state the form of property required; (*b*) those which limit the necessary property to freehold alone; (*c*) those which give an alternative between a real and a personal property minimum, and (*d*) those establishing a tax-paying requisite for voters. Instances of each of these can be found during the colonial period.

A. Of the indefinite property qualifications, perhaps the most general was that in force in Rhode Island between 1665 and 1723, which, adopting the language of the king's letter to the New England colonies, required all freemen to be persons of " competent estates." More specific, but still vague, are the South Carolina laws of 1692 and 1716 requiring the voter " to be worth" ten pounds or thirty pounds respectively; and of a similar nature is the thirty pounds estate in Connecticut in 1657. More definiteness was gained by the requirement that the property be taxable; as in the twenty pounds of rateable estate in Plymouth in 1669 and in New Hampshire in 1680, and the Connecticut twenty pounds assessment of 1662.

B. Where freeholdership was a requisite for the suffrage, there might be no minimum size or value of the freehold, as in Virginia from 1676 to 1736, in West Jersey after 1682, or New Hampshire from 1682 to 1699. But this early extension of the franchise to all freeholders without respect to the size or value of the real estate soon gave place to a less liberal policy. The minimum freehold was measured in one of three ways; either by the English custom of requiring a definite income from land, or by fixing a certain value of freehold, or a certain size in acres or town lots. The first of these tests, in the form of a forty-shilling income from freehold estate, was in force in New York from 1683 to 1699; in New Hampshire from 1699 to 1727; in Massachusetts after 1691, and Connecticut after 1689, but in the last two cases some other alternative was permissible; and it was part of the qualifications of Rhode Island between 1723 and 1730, and after 1760. Thus all the New England colonies possessed the English standard of freehold, and in two of them, the forty shillings, translated into dollars, was maintained well into the nineteenth century.

In other cases the freehold possessed by the voter must be of a certain value. This was true in New York after 1699, where the freehold must be of the value of forty pounds, and of New Hampshire after 1728, where it was ten pounds greater than in New York. In Rhode Island in 1723 the freehold must be of the value of one hundred pounds or yield an income of forty shillings; in 1730, owing to the depreciation in the paper currency, this was changed to two hundred pounds, or ten pounds income, and again in 1746 both of these figures were doubled. After 1760 the amount was expressed as forty pounds value in lawful money, or a forty-shilling income. South Carolina after 1745 permitted freeholders in towns to vote if they possessed sixty pounds value of taxable land or houses in towns.

All the colonies to the southward of New York expressed the freehold in acres or lots rather than in value or income, as was the case in New England and New York. In New Jersey after 1702 the minimum amount where no personal property was held, was one hundred acres; in Pennsylvania, after some slight changes, it was fixed at fifty acres, twelve of which must be cleared, and Delaware had an identical provision; while Maryland after 1670 also required fifty acres. Virginia up to 1736 had expressed no legal size for the freehold, but after that year the voter could qualify by virtue of one hundred acres of unsettled land, or twenty-five acres with a house and settled plantation, or a house or lot in some legally established town. In 1762 this was changed to fifty acres of unsettled land, and the house either on plantation or in town must be at least twelve feet square. North Carolina after 1735 possessed the fifty acres qualification, and Georgia had the same provision imposed upon her by royal instructions in 1754. South Carolina from at least 1704 had the fifty acres provision in connection with other qualifications. In 1745 this was elaborated into a settled plantation, or three hundred acres of unsettled land, or sixty pounds value in taxable houses and lands in towns; but in 1759 the three hundred acres were reduced to one hundred.   Thus, immediately before the Revolution, from New Jersey to Georgia the freehold, with one exception in South Carolina, was expressed in acres of land; in six colonies the size was fixed at fifty acres, with other options in Virginia; while in New Jersey and South Carolina, one of the requirements was one hundred acres of freehold.   In Georgia and North Carolina the fifty acres freehold was the sole property qualification for the suffrage at the close of the colonial period; in all the other colonies the acres of freehold were linked with other alternatives, such as different forms of freehold, as in Virginia and South Carolina, or personal property requirements, as in New Jersey, Pennsylvania, Delaware and Maryland, or the payment of taxes, as in South Carolina.

C. At the close of the colonial period a freehold of some size or value was required of voters in seven colonies: New Hampshire, Rhode Island,[1] New York, New Jersey, Virginia, North Carolina and Georgia.   In the six other colonies there were alternatives to the real estate qualification in the form of the holding of personal property or the payment of taxes.   The forty-shilling income from freehold was, in Massachusetts and Connecticut, paralleled by a personal property requirement of forty pounds;[2] and the same amount of personal property was placed upon a parity with fifty acres of land in Delaware and Maryland.   Pennsylvania made fifty acres of land and fifty pounds value of personal estate equivalent terms.   New Jersey after 1705 and New Hampshire between 1699 and 1728 possessed an unusual qualification, which permitted freeholders to vote if they did not possess the requisite freehold, but instead owned fifty pounds value of personal estate, together with any amount, however small, of freehold land.   South Carolina, also, from 1704 to 1721, had a personal property qualification at first of

[1] With the exception of the eldest sons of freeholders, who could vote, although not themselves possessing real estate.

[2] I have taken here the colonial interpretation of the Massachusetts charter of 1691.

ten, and later of fifty pounds, as equivalent to the fifty acres of land.

D. At the time of the Revolution only one colony,—South Carolina,—retained the tax-paying feature of the suffrage requirements. In that colony by the law of 1721 persons paying twenty shillings in taxes were permitted to vote. This was discontinued in 1745, but in 1759 the principle was again adopted, and the amount of taxes necessary to qualify the voter was reduced from twenty to ten shillings. A similar practice of conditioning political privileges upon the payment of taxes is found at one time or another in other colonies. As early as 1656 in Virginia the principle is affirmed; from 1715 to 1735 it is the sole basis for the suffrage in North Carolina; and in 1664 tax-paying in an excessive amount was required of non-church-members who desired to be admitted as freemen in Massachusetts.

7. *Freemanship in Corporations.* The manner in which the English theory of corporations received a wide political interpretation in America has been seen already in the studies of the charter colonies; and in the summary just made, the qualifications required of freemen in those colonies have been grouped, where possible, under similar headings with the qualifications of voters in other colonies. But in addition to the requirements already given, the corporation colonies had practices in the admission of their freemen which virtually amounted to further qualifications upon the suffrage. One of the most general of such features is the taking of an oath, a " charge," or an " engagement" of fidelity to the government. This custom was practically universal in the New England corporations, and in Rhode Island and New Haven, even existed in the separate towns before they were incorporated into larger unions. Another frequent, but not universal, custom was that requiring the candidate for the franchise to pass a period of probation after his name had been proposed and before he was formally accepted as a freeman. Plymouth originated this custom at least as early as 1636 by requiring those proposed at one court to " stand propounded" until the next court; and in 1658 this was changed to a whole year's probation. Connecticut after 1662 required a six months' probation, and Rhode Island, after 1762 had the

shorter term of three months.   Massachusetts never adopted
the probation plan except from 1673 to 1683 for applicants
who were not church-members.

Still another restriction upon freemen was the requirement
in Connecticut and Massachusetts that the candidates present
certificates from the civil or ecclesiastical authorities of the
town that they possessed the desired moral or property qualifications.   But more interesting than this, was the Plymouth
rule of 1656 that applicants for the provincial freedom must
first have been approved for that honor by the freemen of the
town in which they dwelt, and later proposed by the town
deputies to the court.   This virtually left the control of the
freemanship with the body of existing freemen in each town.
Similar perhaps in theory, but different in practice, was the
Rhode Island distinction between town freemen and colony
freemen.   In this colony, after a period of town control of
the subject, the legislature imposed various qualifications
upon the freemen of the towns, and having fulfilled these requirements for the town freedom, a man could gain the colonial franchise as a matter of form.   The most remarkable of
all the colonial suffrage qualifications is also to be found in'
Rhode Island, where, after 1723, the political power of the
freeman-freeholder included not only himself, but his eldest
son as well if the latter were of legal age.   The latter could
be admitted to the town and colonial franchise by virtue of
his birth, in a manner similar to that in which the freedom of
certain English municipalities could be gained.

8. *Qualifications Similar to the English Borough Franchise.*   The details of suffrage qualifications heretofore mentioned may all be held to correspond to the county franchise
in England.   It is true that the New England colonies were
political corporations differing but little in their origin from
the various municipal political corporations of England; but
the manner in which the franchise was exercised in these
colonies conforms closely to the county suffrage in England.
It must be remembered, too, that a distinct town franchise
was not greatly needed in those colonies which possessed a
personal property alternative to the freehold requirement;
or, where, in Virginia or South Carolina, the size or value of
freehold was so stated that it would admit to the franchise

many of the inhabitants of the towns. But in addition to such general provisions, there are some cases of the formal adoption of the English borough franchise.

In North Carolina, to a greater degree than in any other colony, was the distinction between the county and the town franchise elaborated, and in that colony also the variety of suffrage provisions gave an opportunity for partisan electioneering in the boroughs. The voters' qualifications in the nine towns varied among the towns and at different times in the same town. In one case all who happened to be present at the election, without respect to residence or ownership of property, had the right to vote. While, in most cases, the town suffrage was extended to those who occupied a house of lawful size in the town, or who were owners of unoccupied houses, yet there are instances of the limitation of the borough franchise to freeholders alone. Thus the qualifications varied from mere residence in the town, to the tenancy of a house, or to the possession of a freehold within the town limits. In the main, however, the qualifications of voters in these towns conformed to those of the inhabitant-householder boroughs of England.

The same statement is true of the towns of Perth Amboy, Burlington and Salem in New Jersey, of Williamsburg and Norfolk in Virginia, and of Annapolis in Maryland; in all of which the voter must be a freeholder or an inhabiting householder of the town. St. Mary's, in Maryland, on the other hand, possessed the narrow corporation franchise, in which the officers were as open to corruption as they were in the similar towns of England. The English freeman-borough franchise also finds its exact counterpart in the elections by freemen of the corporations of the cities of New York and Albany. In these places the freemanship was acquired by apprenticeship or purchase, and was linked to a residence requirement of three months after securing the freedom in New York City, and of six weeks in Albany. Thus in the borough suffrage, as in the county franchise, the force of English precedent is everywhere apparent. The English freeman borough, the householder-inhabitant borough, the corporation borough, all have their counterparts in America.

9. *The University Franchise.* Only one instance has been

found of the extension to America of the principle which gave political representation to institutions of learning. This is the case of the College of William and Mary in Virginia, where the president and six masters possessed the right of choosing a member of the house of burgesses. New England, with all her respect for education, never put political power within the control of her colleges.

The preceding summary makes it apparent that English customs and precedents exercised a determining influence upon the qualifications of voters in the colonies. Local conditions sometimes suggested or compelled variations from the English customs, but such divergences were rarely so vital as to impair the true nature of the suffrage as an English practice. In two ways these English customs came into colonial elections; first by the natural and perhaps unconscious adherence of the colonists to the forms already familiar to them; and, secondly, by the determined effort of the English authorities to place the colonial suffrage upon a basis similar to that in England. Thus, consciously or unconsciously, the elective system was brought into conformity to English ideas. Of the old world qualifications, those of age and sex seem to have been adopted most readily in the colonies; while those of property were changed in many ways to adapt them to the new conditions.

At the outset the suffrage in most of the colonies conformed to the voters' qualifications in the English towns rather than to the freehold requisite of the English county. Thus in New England,—where the feeling of community membership was strengthened by the church system, by the town life and by the precedent of the charter of the Massachusetts Bay Company,—the freeman principle of the English boroughs became the basis of the suffrage. In the southern colonies, on the other hand, while the word freeman was occasionally used in a sense referring to membership in the colony, the term soon lost the intensely exclusive meaning which made it so valuable to the New England Puritan. It came to be identified with the word inhabitant, and thus the early suffrage in Virginia, Maryland and the Carolinas is similar to the franchise in those English towns where all adult male housekeepers participated in elections. In the middle colonies this early phase is not apparent. But in the south and in New England the holding of land came to be the sole qualification, or an alternative one with the ownership of personal property. And in this process the borough basis of freemanship or inhabitancy gave place to the ownership of property; that is, a qualification akin to the county franchise in England.

It has been held [1] that this movement toward higher qualifications and a restricted suffrage came upon the demand of the English government; and, indeed, as we shall see, the weight of English authority was almost uniformly in favor of a property qualification. But before commenting upon the efforts of the home government in this direction, it should be noted that there are indications of a similar spirit among the colonists themselves. Thus Connecticut in 1657 and 1659 imposed a property qualification upon freemen and voting inhabitants; in 1658 Massachusetts required non-freemen voting in town meetings to possess twenty pounds value of taxable property; Maryland, as early as 1666, shows evidence of a tendency toward government by freeholders; and Virginia in 1670 adopted a restrictive clause. Thus with the growth of population and the removal of the frontier from the coast plains, property-holding and non-property-holding classes became distinct; vested interests arose; and these in turn demanded a political interpretation of their favored position. It is probable, under the prevailing seventeenth and eighteenth century political ideals, that a restricted suffrage would have been adopted throughout the colonies even if the English government had not endeavored to obtain the same end. But that the restriction took the frequent form of a freehold qualification, especially in the forty-shilling provision, is due in very large degree to the influence of the English government.

This influence is seen first of all in the royal charters to proprietors, in which, with the exception of that to the Duke of York, distinct provision is made for representative assem-

---

[1] Bishop, *History of Elections in American Colonies,* 72.

blies. The Maryland, the Carolina and the Pennsylvania charters mention assemblies elected by the freemen or by the freeholders, and thus, although no distinction is made between them, two of the features of the English franchise are imposed upon these colonies. But a more definite control of the franchise is obtained in the royal provinces, where the authority of the English government is almost uniformly used to limit the suffrage to freeholders. The earliest instance noticed of this policy is found in the instructions of 1676 to Governor Berkeley of Virginia, which directed him to "take care that the members of the assembly be elected only by ffreeholders, as being more agreeable to the custome of England." After that date, the same policy, often in the same words, was copied in the instructions of the governors of Virginia and other colonies. So general was the insertion of this clause after 1689 that it may be called universal. It appears in New Hampshire in 1682 after the remarkable suffrage acts of the Cutt assembly; in New York it is found in 1689 in the instructions to Governor Slaughter; and in New Jersey, the Carolinas and Georgia it appears in all the royal instructions or commissions from the beginning of the royal government in each case. The policy thus laid down was not weakly administered; and it is to be noted that in all the seven royal governments, with the exception of a subordinate clause enfranchising certain tax-payers in South Carolina, the suffrage was strictly limited to freeholders. The personal property alternatives are to be found either in boroughs in these royal provinces, or in the general provisions of the three proprietary provinces and the charter colonies of Massachusetts and Connecticut.

In addition to this continuous policy of the English government, there were occasions upon which more particular attention was paid to the suffrage in certain colonies. An instance of this is seen in the instructions to the parliamentary commissioners sent to reduce the Chesapeake Bay settlements during the Commonwealth period, directing them to exclude from the suffrage those who would not swear to support the new English administration. But a much more noted case is that of the Stuart commissioners to New England in 1664. The account of their duties and acts has already been given.

As a result of their labors the Massachusetts law of 1664 admitting non-church-members was passed; Rhode Island adopted the very words of the commissioners in its suffrage law; and the influence of the commission was felt in Connecticut and Plymouth. Similar instances of English interference with the suffrage franchise have been noticed in New Jersey, in North Carolina and in Georgia; and the policy is summed up in 1767 in a circular instruction to the governors of all the royal provinces directing them to give assent to no law altering the number of members of the legislature of their colonies, or the time of continuance of the assembly, or *changing the qualifications of electors or elected.*[1] It is evident that throughout the colonial period the English authorities took a deep interest in the question of the colonial suffrage, and uniformly used their influence in favor of the freehold qualification.

In closing, reference may be made to the figures obtained showing the size of the voting class. In Virginia in several elections between 1744 and 1772 there appeared to be about nine per cent. of the white population actually participating as electors. In New York City, in the elections of 1735, 1761 and 1769 the actual voters numbered about eight per cent. of the population. In Pennsylvania the tax-list figures give only potential voters, but they show about eight per cent. of the rural population qualified for the suffrage, and only two per cent. in the city of Philadelphia, a condition quite in contrast to that of New York City. In New England the actual voters appear to be less proportionately than in the middle and southern colonies. Massachusetts, for instance, shows only one person in fifty as taking part in elections, and Connecticut, in elections immediately preceding the Revolution, had about the same proportion. In Rhode Island the freemen or potential voters numbered only nine per cent. of the population. These figures are entirely too few, and too scattered in time and territory, to justify any accurate generalization from them. The potential voters seem to vary from one-sixth to one-fiftieth of the population, and the actual

[1] *N. J. Archives,* IX, 637 (July 24, 1767).

voters show almost an equal variation; Massachusetts and Connecticut showing at times only two per cent. of actual voters among a population where perhaps sixteen per cent. were qualified electors; and New York City and Virginia showing the far larger proportion of eight per cent. of the population as actual voters. At best, however, the colonial elections called forth both relatively and absolutely only a small fraction of the present percentage of voters. Property qualifications, poor means of communication, large election districts and the absence of party organization combined to make the most sharply contested elections feeble in their effects upon the community as compared with the widespread suffrage of the twentieth century.

INDEX

Abjuration, oath of, in Del., 270.

Acadians, presence of, probable cause of disfranchisement of Catholics in S. C., 158.

Acrelius, account of elections in Pa., 285.

Actual voters, number of, in Mass., 356–357.

Admission, of inhabitants to towns on Long Island, 192; in N. Y. under Duke's Laws, 203–204; of partners in Plymouth, 303 note; of freemen in Mass., 302–304; terms of, 308; in distant towns, 309; of freemen, 328–329; into Plymouth partnership, 340; into freemanship, 341; of inhabitants, 342–343; of inhabitants to towns in Mass., 363; to towns in N. H., 378; to towns in Conn., 383–385; refusal to grant, 385; of freemen, by local officers, 413; of inhabitants, 421.

Agamenticus, Maine, city government in, 350.

Age, as qualification of electors, in England, 2; origin of legal age, 2 note; twenty-one years in Va., 35; twenty-one years in N. C., 92, 111; twenty-one years in S. C., 140, 146, 153, 155, 157; twenty-one years in Ga., 172; in N. Y., twenty-one years, 212; in Del., twenty-one years, 270; in Pa., twenty-one years, 275, 279, 282; in Mass., twenty-one years, 310; in Mass., twenty-four years in case of certain town electors, 318; under law of 1664, twenty-four years, 324; town elections, twenty-four years, 362; in Plymouth militia elections, twenty years, 366; in N. H., in 1680, twenty-four years, 374; in 1682, twenty-one years, 375; in Conn., twenty-one years, 386, 388, 408; in colonies generally, 474.

Albany, N. Y., suffrage in, 222–223.

Aliens, as electors in S. C., 132, 135, 137, 138, 141; excluded from assembly, 141.

Alms, persons receiving such disfranchised in England, 11; but may vote in some towns, 15.

Altona, Del., 267.

Amsterdam, obtains settlement on Delaware, 263; inducements to settlers, 264; all Delaware lands ceded to, 265; government of colony, 267.

Andros, Sir Edmund, as governor of N. Y., claims authority in N. J., 237; in Mass., 334; arrest of, 335; in N. H., 375, 377; in Conn., 412.

Anglican party in S. C., influence elections, 136.

Annapolis, Md., elections in, 72.

Annuities, as freeholds in England, 9.

Antinomians in Mass., 307.

Apprentices, as electors in S. C., 147; excluded, 148; in Mass., to be admitted as town inhabitants, 363 note 2; copied by N. H., in 1718 and 1719, 378; as town inhabitants in R. I., 468.

Aquedneck, R. I., settlement of, 433; agreements among inhabitants, ibid.

Archdale, John, governor of N. C., 90; of S. C., 134.

Aristocracy, in Mass., 304.

Artisan class in S. C., 156; as electors in Pa. under laws made in England, 275; disfranchised in Pa., 292.

Assembly, first representative in America, 19–21; first in Carolina, 84, 85; biennial, in N. C., 88, 97, 98; a grievance in N. C., 99; at Hemptead, L. I., called by Col. Nicholls, 198; suffrage for, ibid.; promulgates Duke's

489

franchise, 13; restricted corporation franchise, 15; university franchise, 16; as interpreted by New Haven, 399.

English government, influence in favor of suffrage qualifications, 484-487.

Englishmen, petition in S. C. that suffrage be limited to, 134; on Long Island, peculiarly favored by Dutch authorities, 185, 190, 193; as electors, in Mass. town elections, 362; as electors, in N. H., 374.

Englishmen, rights of, interpreted by East Jersey assembly in 1680, 237; demanded in Mass. in 1646, 315.

Exeter, borough suffrage in, 14.

Exeter, N. H., settlement of, 370; compact of settlers, *ibid.*; number of voters in, 373 *note* 4.

Faggot voters, in England, 9.

Fairfield, Conn., popular movement in, 399.

Families, Heads of. See Heads.

Fendall, Governor, in Md., 59-60.

Fenwick, John, in West Jersey, 244, 245.

Fletcher, Governor, of Pa., attitude towards suffrage, 278.

Flushing, L. I., charter of, 190, 191; suffrage in, 206.

Fort Beversrede, Dutch settlement on Schuylkill, 260.

Fort Casimir, Dutch settlement near Newcastle, Del., 260; 262; name changed to New Amstel, 263.

Fort Christina, Swedish settlement on the Delaware, 260.

Fort Nassau, Dutch settlement in N. J., 260.

Forty-shilling freehold, as qualification of electors, in England, 1, 5, 6, 9; origin of, in English statute of 1430, 5-6; adopted in N. Y. in 1683, 200; the legal qualification in N. Y. in 1691, 210; compared with Mass. qualification of 1690, 336 *note;* in Mass. charter of 1691, 354; adopted in N. H. in 1699, 376; in Conn. in 1689, 413; in R. I., 454, 460.

Fractional voting, in Va., 40, 41; in Southampton, L. I., 207 *note;* on Long Island, 225.

Frame of government, in Pa., in 1682, 274.

Free, qualification of electors in N. C., 92; in S. C. in 1719, 151; in 1721, 153; in 1745, 155; in 1759, 157; in Ga., 172.

Free men as electors, in England at early period, 5; in Va., 21, 29, 33; in Md., 53 *note*, 55.

Free Society of Traders, incorporated by Penn, and given manorial powers, 294.

Freedom, of English towns, how obtained, 14; of New York City, how obtained, 220-222; of Albany, N. Y., how obtained, 222.

Freehold, definition of, in Va., 34, 36; in N. C., 102; in N. Y., in 1683, 200, 213; in N. J., difficulty of determining, 231, 232; fixed by proprietors, 234; in R. I., 461.

Freehold, extension of meaning of in England leads to extended suffrage, 9.

Freehold, qualification of electors in Va., 31; in 1676, 34; in 1684, 34; of 100 acres unsettled land, or 25 acres with house and plantation, in Va., 1736, 38; lowered to 50 acres unsettled land in 1762, 40; in Md., 62, 71; in Md., in governor's instructions, 70; in S. C., fifty acres, 148, 153; three hundred acres, or settled plantation, or sixty pounds value in town lots, 155; reduced to one hundred acres in 1759, 157; in Ga., fifty acres, 170; opposed by assembly, 172; established by law, 172; in N. Y., 198, 199, 200, 201, 205-207; in 1691, 210; in 1699, changed to forty pounds value, 212; in county elections, 219, 220; in town elections, 223; in N. J. in 1665, 230; in 1668, 232; in East Jersey fundamentals of 1683, fifty acres, ten cultivated, or house and three acres in borough, 239; in West Jersey, 247, 248; in N. J. in 1702, one hundred acres, 249; opposition to,

THE END.

Printed in the United States
102422LV00002B/27/A

9 780548 573549